THE
AWKWARD
YEARS

THE
AWKWARD
YEARS

American Foreign Relations
Under Garfield and Arthur

DAVID M. PLETCHER

University of Missouri Press • Columbia

Winner of a McKnight Foundation Humanities Award for 1961

Publication of The Awkward Years has been made
possible by a grant from the Ford Foundation

University of Missouri Press, Columbia, Missouri 65201
Printed and bound in the United States of America
Library of Congress Catalog Number 62-15589
ISBN 0-8262-0143-1

Price $10.00

For Charlie and Marilyn
John, David, and Michael

Acknowledgments

I AM heartily grateful to the McKnight Foundation of St. Paul, Minnesota, which selected the manuscript of this book as the winner of a McKnight Foundation Humanities Award for 1961. I am also much indebted to President Paul H. Giddens of Hamline University for several summer grants which facilitated my research.

A number of persons and institutions have assisted me with advice and information. My good friends, Dr. and Mrs. Walter V. Scholes, were on hand throughout my work to offer encouraging or deflating suggestions, as circumstances seemed to warrant. Others who have read parts of the manuscript and helped me in various ways include Mrs. Shirley A. Bill, John L. Gignilliat, William T. Hutchinson, Miss Lillian Kibler, and Benjamin M. Lewis.

I am indebted to the staff of my home library, that of Hamline University, for obtaining books for me on interlibrary loan and for many other courtesies. The librarians of the University of Minnesota and the Minnesota Historical Society also very kindly extended me the full facilities of their institutions. Like all scholars who use the documents of the State Department, I owe sincere gratitude to Mrs. Julia Carroll and the efficient staff of the Foreign Affairs Section of the National Archives. Without their help I might still be fumbling around among instructions and dispatches. I acknowledge a similar debt to the Manuscripts Division of the Library of Congress.

Many other libraries and organizations have generously furnished material for this project: the Thomas Scott Buckham Memorial Library (Faribault, Minnesota), the Chicago Historical Society, the Illinois Historical Society, the Library of Congress (Divisions of Newspapers and Books), the National Archives (Legislative Sec-

tion), the New Hampshire Historical Society, the New York Public Library, the Public Record Office (London), the Wisconsin Historical Society, and the libraries of George Washington University, Harvard University, Johns Hopkins University, the University of Pittsburgh, the University of Rochester, the University of South Carolina (South Caroliniana Library), the University of Virginia, the University of Washington, and the University of Wisconsin.

I am grateful indeed to the Ford Foundation for the grant which made possible the publication of this book.

D. M. P.

Hamline University
February, 1962

Contents

Introduction

AMERICAN foreign relations of the 1880's have seldom received from historians the attention which they deserve. The first Venezuelan crisis of 1895, the Spanish-American War, and the gaudy diplomacy of Theodore Roosevelt tend to blind our eyes to the less dramatic events of the earlier decade until we run the risk of assuming that American imperialism of the 1890's "resurged" suddenly, without apparent warning, out of a coma.

An important source of this misunderstanding is the record of bickerings, reversals, and failures which made up most of our foreign relations during the presidential term shared by James A. Garfield and Chester A. Arthur, from March, 1881, to March, 1885. We argued with Britain over the rights of Irish-American agitators and with France and Germany over the trichinae in American pork. We undertook to help Chile, Peru, and Bolivia put an end to the War of the Pacific and only succeeded in making all three nations resent our interference. We invited Latin America to a peace congress but withdrew the invitations a few weeks later. In apparent violation of the Clayton-Bulwer Treaty we agreed to dig an isthmian canal across Nicaragua and then changed our minds. We signed reciprocity treaties with Mexico, Spain, and the Dominican Republic but decided not to carry them out. Finally we joined the European Powers in a conference to determine the future status of the Congo Valley in central Africa, a place as remote as the moon from the ordinary concerns of all Americans but missionaries, geographers, and Henry M. Stanley.

This is a superficial view of the foreign relations of the Garfield and Arthur administrations. The real importance of the 1880's, in diplomacy as in the history of American business, labor, and agriculture, is that the decade formed a bridge between the problems of the Civil War and Reconstruction and those of the tempestuous

fin de siècle. In the field of foreign affairs the "manifest destiny" spirit of the 1850's, which Seward and Grant had kept alive after the war, was now combined with new forces, reshaping public opinion and subjecting officials to irresistible pressures. After the quiet administration of President Rutherford B. Hayes—the "dead center" in the history of foreign relations between 1865 and 1898—the State Department and Congress became more and more active in adapting American foreign policy to changing conditions (by trial and error) and thereby prepared the country in some measure for the imperialism and internationalism of Theodore Roosevelt.

One of the forces which helped to alter policy was an increased concern for American prestige. Americans had never been known for their bashfulness, and, encouraged by the outcome of the Civil War and the great economic growth which followed it, many now demanded vociferously that their country play a role in international affairs commensurate with its real power. National prestige meant different things to different Americans: the right to be consulted on international questions, increased markets, or the spread of republican forms and popular rule. Many were willing to limit direct American influence to the Western Hemisphere, but all wished American power and glory to be respected in the capitals of Europe.

Although prestige included some economic considerations, during the early 1880's the productive capacity of the United States became almost an independent factor in American foreign policy. Artificially stimulated by the Civil War and only temporarily checked by the depression of the 1870's, American output of manufactures and farm products had leaped upward, decade by decade, until it seemed that the Great Republic might die of a surfeit, smothered in its own yield. Could Malthus be wrong? Surely the means of production must outstrip even the fertile American population. Where could the surplus go but abroad? More and more people demanded that the United States government help its tooactive producers to find new customers overseas.

The desire to play a larger role in international affairs and to dispose of the mounting surplus was reinforced by alarm, as Europe entered upon the most intense rivalry for trade and colonies in over a century. Experienced European salesmen elbowed Americans out

of one market after another, and between 1880 and 1885 Egypt, Tunis, Indo-China, New Guinea, and large portions of tropical Africa lost most of what independence they had possessed. As this imperialism got under way, it seemed to threaten the New World as well, for European manufacturers sold their wares all over Latin America. Also, in 1879 and 1880 Ferdinand de Lesseps, full of prestige from the success of his Suez Canal, called for capital and formed a company to dig its counterpart across the Isthmus of Panama. At the same time Britain seemed to be meddling in the War of the Pacific, a boundary feud between Chile, Peru, and Bolivia.

Without distinguishing very carefully between trade competition and political domination, American nationalists warned their countrymen that the Monroe Doctrine was in deadly peril, and the press of the 1880's indulged in much ill-defined talk about national security. Today we recognize (as many did then) that during the 1880's the Western Hemisphere did not face the least danger of European military intervention and only slight danger of political colonialism. When publicists talked or wrote of obtaining security, what they really meant was leveling obstacles to the free growth of American economic or ideological influence abroad—above all in Latin America. Although security was sometimes regarded then as a distinct goal of foreign policy, it might be more accurate to treat it as the defensive aspect of the campaign for increased prestige and markets.

We shall use the term *expansionism* to designate the pursuit of these overlapping goals—prestige, markets, and security—beyond the nation's borders. The vigor of the pursuit varied from place to place, being relatively great in the Caribbean and Central America and much less so in the Old World (although American interest in Korea and central Africa might be cited as exceptions). The consistency and the future prospects of expansionism suffered from the determined attacks of its opponents: isolationists who wanted to keep American trade, capital, and troops at home; nationalists who opposed any sort of tariff concessions to foreigners; and economizers who feared that foreign commitments meant higher taxes. Repeatedly the criticism of these groups in Congress and in the press broke up expansionists' plans and forced them on the defensive, but so powerful were the outward-pushing forces

that before long the expansionists would try again.

The period covered by this study is clearly defined at both ends. It begins with two abrupt changes in the national climate: the restoration of prosperity in 1879 and the substitution of the aggressive James G. Blaine for easy-going William M. Evarts as secretary of state in 1881. The end comes four years later with the overthrow of Republican rule in the election of 1884 and the inauguration of Grover Cleveland. During the intervening time the Republican party, shopworn and schismatic, made ineffectual efforts to clean house and find new excuses for continuing in power. It would not be accurate to say that foreign relations contributed heavily to the Republican defeat in 1884, but the plight of the party undoubtedly affected the foreign policy of the Garfield and Arthur administrations, so that their diplomacy and their domestic politics cannot be separated from each other.

On two occasions between 1880 and 1885 American political catastrophies interrupted the slow unfolding of expansionist measures and forced the administration in power to overplay its hand in a vain effort to hurry the process. During the summer of 1881 the exaggerated partisanship of the Garfield administration, for which Blaine bore considerable responsibility, led to the assassination of Garfield. Unwilling to continue in office under Arthur, Blaine then tried to carry out his long-range plans for the State Department in the short space of three weeks by a series of abrupt dispatches and policy decisions during November and December, 1881, only to see the most important of these repudiated by his successor, Frederick T. Frelinghuysen.

During the next two years Arthur and Frelinghuysen, more cautious than Blaine and hampered by lack of experience and by intraparty splits, gradually drew up an expansionist program as persuasive as that of Blaine, if somewhat less melodramatic. The first accomplishment of this new program was a reciprocity treaty with Mexico whereby its creators hoped to foster trade and investment in that country as a model for American influence in the rest of Latin America. Had Arthur won a second term, he would probably have continued along this line at a deliberate pace, but after he failed to secure renomination at the Republican convention of 1884, he and Frelinghuysen realized that time was running out.

Like Blaine in 1881, they tried to force through every possible measure while they still had the power: other reciprocity treaties, a canal treaty with Nicaragua, and finally, American participation in the Berlin Congo Conference. Like Blaine they attempted too much and ended in repudiation, for the "lame duck" Congress of 1884-1885 preferred to await the judgment of the new president, and Cleveland rejected the hastily proffered measures.

While the administrations of Garfield and Arthur followed roughly the same pattern of slow beginning and precipitate ending, their policies were not absolutely identical. The goal of Garfield and Blaine was primarily that of prestige. By intervening in the international affairs of Latin America and even of Hawaii, they sought to make the United States the arbiter of hemispheric differences and to restrict the role of Britain and France. Expanded American influence would mean larger markets for American producers, but markets were not always the principal or the immediate goal of the Garfield administration. On the other hand, after 1882 the Arthur administration never lost sight of the problem of the surplus, and Arthur's principal undertakings in the field of foreign policy—the Nicaragua canal, the Caribbean reciprocity treaties, and the Berlin Congo Congress—were directly based on hopes for trade. Blaine's emphasis on prestige may have been due in part to his own personal magnetism and ambitions, while Arthur's increasing interest in trade and exports possibly reflected his own earlier connection with the New York customs and, even more likely, the fading of national prosperity from 1882 to 1884.

Despite this shift of emphasis, however, the fully unfolded policies of the two administrations contained more similarities than differences. Neither Blaine nor Frelinghuysen favored territorial annexations or war. Both believed in furthering American interests by active but peaceful means, although Blaine was not above resorting to warlike bluff. As a result of this bravado and his penchant for blunt language, most of the praise or blame for this expansionism has stuck to his reputation, and Frelinghuysen's efforts have been almost forgotten.

The principal purpose of this book is to trace the unfolding of expansionism under Garfield and Arthur, to relate it with political and economic developments inside the United States, and, as far

as possible, to explain the reasons why their policies failed. It will be necessary to follow the story through the diplomatic dispatches of the two secretaries of state and their ministers abroad, their communications with Congress, the debates of the two houses, and the reactions of the press, where alone one can gain some inkling of the rudimentary, ill-focused American public opinion. From these incomplete sources emerges the spectacle of four awkward years in American diplomatic history, when two successive administrations tried to take a shortcut into the next decade.

Blaine, the Expansionist

CHAPTER 1

1881: The State of the Nation

The Christmas sun rises in America upon a peculiarly prosperous and happy people. We are at peace with all the world and with ourselves. The great industries thrive. Labor is well paid. Enterprise is rewarded, and there are no signs of social, moral, or political decadence.
Harper's Weekly, XXI (January 8, 1881), 18

DURING the week of New Year's Day, 1881, the editor of *Harper's Weekly* recorded his complete satisfaction with the condition of his country. He was not alone in his contentment. At about the same time the Treasury Department of the outgoing president, Rutherford B. Hayes, was drawing up a paean of thanks at America's recovery from one of the worst depressions which she had ever known, and a writer in the *Atlantic Monthly* was listing the national economic blessings in more condensed form: public credit established through the resumption of specie payments, a succession of large harvests, railroad building resumed, factories busy, unemployment and business failures decreasing.[1] The good Republicans who wrote these articles did not mention an additional auspicious circumstance. After the narrowest of victories over the Democrats in 1876 and four years of President Hayes's unpopularity, the Republican party had pulled itself together and won an undoubted decision in the autumn election of 1880. As 1881 began, God was in His heaven, James A. Garfield would soon be in the White House, and all seemed right with the world.

Nevertheless, under the fair surface disrupting forces were at work, and at the end of 1881 the Christmas sun shone on an America that was less prosperous, less peaceful, and less united

[1] Unidentified statement, February, 1881, apparently issued by the Treasury Department, Rutherford B. Hayes Papers (Rutherford B. Hayes Library, Fremont, Ohio). Henry Hall, "The Future of American Shipping," *Atlantic Monthly*, XLVII (February 1881), 166.

than a year earlier. Few persons then realized that the fat years from 1879 to 1881 only punctuated but did not finally end the hard times of the 1870's, for the temporary prosperity was largely due to a lucky combination of circumstances impossible to prolong or repeat.

As late as July, 1878, five years after the onset of the depression, over half of the nation's iron and steel furnaces were idle; in the following May the American Iron and Steel Association reported that prices were lower than at any time since colonial days.[2] Suddenly a series of European disasters rescued the American economy. During the spring and early summer of 1879 snow, frost, and heavy rains ruined nearly all grain from England east to India, while American farmers reaped the largest crops in the memory of man, and the new "Granger" railroads of the Middle West prepared to funnel wheat and corn into the world market from lands which had never before produced for export. American shipments of wheat rose from forty million bushels in 1877 to over one hundred fifty million bushels in 1880.[3]

Where the American farmer led, the American factory-owner was quick to follow, for the influx of gold from Europe to pay for the grain inflated the whole American money market. The price of Number One anthracite pig iron, the standard for the iron and steel industry, rose from a low of $16.50 per ton in September, 1878, to the extraordinary figure of $43 in January, 1880, and production of all pig iron increased by about one-quarter during the same period. After a slight break early in 1880, prices recovered and held firm for over a year—partly because of the 7,174 miles of new railroads laid in 1880. The American Iron and Steel Association declared flatly that 1881 was the most prosperous year which the industry had ever known. Every other economic index confirmed their report: the rate of business failures reduced from 158 per thousand concerns in 1878 to 63 per thousand in 1880, new records set in railroad traffic and exports from the principal Eastern ports, and millions of dollars of gold imported each week during the first

[2]David A. Wells, *Recent Economic Changes and their Effect on the Production and Distribution of Wealth and the Well-Being of Society* (New York, 1889), pp. 6-8, 12.
[3]*Ibid.*, pp. 6-7. Alexander Dana Noyes, *Forty Years of American Finance* (New York, 1909), pp. 53-57.

months of 1881, to raise prices further and fatten the government's gold reserve.[4]

Some hardheaded American observers, however, mistrusted the increased speculation which accompanied the boom, and the economist, David A. Wells, privately warned President Garfield in March that, judging from the overextended condition of American railroads, the country was in for a financial crisis. In July the shooting of the President caused the first break. Prices fell off sharply, rose again, and then for weeks "fluctuated more upon the reported state of the President's pulse, temperature and respiration than they did upon the actual or speculative values of the properties themselves."[5] In September, when Garfield died, even grimmer news had begun to reach the money markets, for a drought had wiped out all hope of normal crops, and only similar bad weather in Europe could prevent a disastrous fall of prices and returns. By the end of the year grain, cotton, and other commodity exports had fallen far behind imports, and businessmen could scarcely disguise their fear that the 1870's were repeating themselves.

Just as during the earlier depression, officials and laymen argued over the causes of the hard times: the depreciation of silver, protective tariffs, crop failures, bad loans, or speculation. Among these rationalizations one argument had risen to prominence since the mid-seventies—that America was shifting too fast from the production of raw materials to a manufacturing economy, and that she would soon have no market for the goods that poured from her factories. After the dramatic price rise of 1879 the argument lost strength for a time, but in the autumn of 1881, when the

[4]*Ibid.*, pp. 57-65. U. S., Bureau of the Census, *Historical Statistics of the United States, Colonial Times to 1957* (Washington, 1960), p. 540. American Iron and Steel Association, *Statistics of the American and Foreign Iron Trade in 1880. Annual Report of the Secretary of the American Iron and Steel Association* [etc.] (Philadelphia, 1881), pp. 11-14 *et passim*. The financial columns of the *New York Tribune* contain good brief summaries of economic conditions. See especially February 7, 1880, p. 5.

[5]*New York Herald*, July 24, 1881, p. 15. David A. Wells to James A. Garfield, Norwich, Connecticut, March 10, 1881, James A. Garfield Papers, CXXXIV, Pt. 1, No. 4 (Library of Congress). For the immediate effects of the shooting see *New York Herald*, July 3, p. 18, and *Bradstreet's* (New York), IV (July 9, 1881), 17.

bottom fell out of the export trade, fears of a surplus once again appeared.[6]

Most writers on overproduction between 1878 and 1881 urged American producers to export their surplus, suggesting as potential markets nearly every part of the world except the polar icecaps. Two days after Garfield's inauguration, for example, the *Boston Sunday Herald* called South America "the great market for our surplus manufactures . . . [which] lies at our door neglected." A little earlier another critic declared that considering American and European exports to Brazil, "we have indeed to blush at our backwardness."[7] Other publicists predicted that under favorable circumstances "China and Japan would soon offer us one of the largest outlets that we may ever be able to secure for our products of all kinds." In the Near East and Balkans, reported the minister to Austria, America had opened a "flattering field" for trade, and even the European market itself did not seem too formidable to penetrate.[8]

Unfortunately for the optimists, European merchants, especially the British, still controlled most of the desirable markets. During 1881 Britain sold perhaps thirteen times as many yards of cotton goods in Latin America as the United States, and the proportions were not much different in the Far East. Even while the American smelters were enjoying the most prosperous year in their history, British iron and steel exports exceeded those from the United States by at least a hundred to one.[9] Only in foodstuffs, raw ma-

[6]Wells, *Recent Economic Changes*, pp. 17, 20-26. For a good sample of the overproduction argument see *New York Tribune*, January 5, 1880, p. 2.

[7]*Boston Sunday Herald*, March 6, 1881. *New York Tribune*, January 5, 1880, p. 2. See also *Atlantic Monthly*, XLIV (July 1879), 81-96.

[8]*The American Protectionist*, I (February 5, 1881), 37-38. William Walter Phelps to Frederick T. Frelinghuysen, Vienna, April 20, 1882, No. 63, U.S., *Papers Relating to the Foreign Relations of the United States* (Washington, 1861-   ), 1882, pp. 5-6. Hereafter cited as U.S., *Foreign Relations*. See also U.S., Department of State, *Commercial Relations of the United States with Foreign Countries* (Washington, 1856-1914), 1879, I, 11-12, 86, 110-13, 132-33, 172-74. Hereafter cited as U.S., *Commercial Relations*. *Harper's New Monthly Magazine*, LV (September 1877), 601-4.

[9]Jacob Schoenhof, *The Destructive Effect of the Tariff upon Manufacture and Commerce and the Figures and Facts Relating Thereto* (2d ed.; New York, 1884), pp. 8 ff. *Westminster Review*, CXII (July 1879), 15. British and American iron exports for 1880 were about $134,000,000 and $1,000,000, respectively. U.S., *Historical Statistics*, p. 546.

terials, and a few manufactures such as petroleum products did the Americans excel. No spot seemed too close to the United States for the British monopoly, for in 1881 the American minister to Haiti wrote to the *New York Tribune*:

> The trade . . . is nearly all in the hands of the English, I regret to say. They bring coffee from Hayti [*sic*] to New York and ship it to Europe. They of course favor English manufactures. . . . The people have come to know that American goods are better, yet half of the time they can't get them. English goods are forced upon them.[10]

By itself, the European economic rivalry would not have greatly alarmed many Americans, for they had long been accustomed to buying European goods. Many protectionists belittled foreign customers, confident that high tariffs would preserve their monopoly of the American market. European control of trade in most of Latin America, however, became a cause for serious concern in 1879 and 1880, when it seemed that France and Britain were about to expand their political power there at the expense of the Monroe Doctrine. All Americans remembered the Mexican adventures of Napoleon III and what had appeared to be British dalliance with the Confederate cause during the 1860's. Many were acquainted with the new imperialism of Disraeli during the 1870's and impressed with the new power of Germany following the Franco-Prussian War. It was not surprising that some professed to see a gigantic conspiracy in the activities of European merchants, promoters, and diplomats, and that motives of trade and security became badly mixed in the public mind.

The most dramatic new challenge to American influence in Latin America was the French canal project in Panama. In 1879 Ferdinand de Lesseps, fresh from his engineering and promotional triumphs at Suez, announced plans for an even more ambitious canal at sea level across the Isthmus of Panama. Unable to obtain sufficient funds in France and England after a whirlwind publicity campaign, the tireless old man crossed to New York, entertained

[10]*New York Tribune*, September 4, 1881, p. 2. See also U.S., *Commercial Relations*, 1879, I, 49.

a list of celebrities at well-publicized banquets, and opened his subscription books.[11]

The Hayes administration was taken aback by De Lesseps' boldness. At the beginning of his term Hayes had favored an internationalized canal, but in 1878, on his instructions, the American minister to Central America had started desultory negotiations with Nicaragua looking toward the construction of a canal under the "protective auspices" of the United States. When De Lesseps arrived in New York, Hayes wrote indignantly in his diary that the time had come for the American government to take a stand on the isthmian question; and in March, 1880, he sent a special message to Congress declaring an interoceanic canal to be "virtually a part of the coast line of the United States."[12]

Before De Lesseps' visit the Colombian minister to the United States had told American newspapers that the canal concession was an entirely private affair, and the French minister assured the State Department that French diplomats in Colombia would not lift a finger to support the canal project. Nevertheless, congressmen introduced resolutions of disapproval, while American newspapers predicted that in wartime the French navy would prey upon American coasts, and that even in peace European merchant ships, aided by the canal, could "seize a large part of the American coastwise commerce by the throat." The *New York Tribune* warned De Lesseps: "The Frenchmen may go ahead and dig the canal, but we give them notice, in the language of book publishers, that 'all rights are reserved'."[13]

[11]For accounts of the De Lesseps project see Gerstle Mack, *The Land Divided, a History of the Panama Canal and Other Isthmian Projects* (New York, 1944), Pt. III; Chester L. Barrows, *William M. Evarts* (Chapel Hill, North Carolina, 1941), pp. 362-68, and L. M. Keasbey, *The Nicaragua Canal and the Monroe Doctrine* (New York, 1896), pp. 362-64, 370-77.

[12]James D. Richardson (ed.), *A Compilation of the Messages and Papers of the Presidents, 1789-1897* (10 vols.; Washington, 1898), VII, 585-86. Charles R. Williams (ed.), *Diary and Letters of Rutherford Birchard Hayes* (5 vols.; Columbus, Ohio, 1922-1926), III, 586 *et passim*. Sidney T. Mathews, "The Nicaragua Canal Controversy: the Struggle for an American-Constructed and -Controlled Transitway" (Ph.D. dissertation, Johns Hopkins University, 1947), pp. 27-30. Hayes's secretary of the navy, Richard W. Thompson, resigned from the Cabinet to become De Lesseps' legal counsel.

[13]*New York Tribune*, March 11, 1881, p. 4. See also *ibid.*, March 2, 1880, pp. 1-2; February 2, 1881, p. 1; February 10, p. 4; December 16, p. 4; January 1, 1881, p. 1; January 23, pp. 1 ff., and January 6, p. 4.

Somewhat less easily dramatized than the French menace at Panama but in the end almost as important to American foreign policy was the rising British influence on the west coast of South America. An American resident of Valparaiso wrote that it made his heart sick to see "one industry after another monopolized by the English, especially as most of these industries were originally developed by Americans." In 1879 Chile attacked Peru and Bolivia in the War of the Pacific for control of the nitrate fields which lay along the border of the three countries. Although Britain had trade and investments in all three, her shipbuilders had recently renovated the Chilean navy, and as the conquering Chilean forces pressed northward, the American consul at Callao wrote: "The British Lion dominates this coast and to a great extent forges Chile's thunderbolts."[14] Prematurely and on slender evidence, Americans assumed that a Chilean victory in the War of the Pacific would create a British protectorate in western South America. As will be seen, this fear motivated an important part of Garfield's Latin-American policy.

Even outside Latin America, concern for trade or prestige caused an occasional pang of fear or envy as Americans watched the new imperialism in Asia and Africa. During 1880, for example, it appeared briefly that King Kalakaua of Hawaii had come under the influence of an unscrupulous adventurer who might be trying to sell that influence to Germany. The adventurer soon fell from grace, but not before Secretary of State William M. Evarts had directed the American minister at Berlin to inquire privately about German intentions in Hawaii. Samoa and Liberia were also among the areas which aroused American concern at the end of the Hayes administration.[15]

*   *   *

The outward pressure from America for new markets and the apparent European threats to American influence in Latin America

[14]Quoted in Herbert Millington, *American Diplomacy and the War of the Pacific* (New York, 1948), pp. 42-43. See also *New York Tribune*, March 14, 1882, p. 2.

[15]William M. Evarts to Andrew D. White, October 16, 1880, No. 145, Instructions to the United States Legation, Berlin, XVII, Records of the Department of State (National Archives, Record Group 59). Hereafter such documents will be cited as, for example, U.S., Instructions, Germany. For memoranda on Samoa and Liberia, see U.S., Reports of the Diplomatic Bureau, IV, *ibid*.

and elsewhere stimulated an expansionist impulse in the United States which had never entirely disappeared since the days of "manifest destiny" during the 1850's. The domestic problems of Western expansion, civil war, and reconstruction might divert American attention for a time, but the imperialism of William H. Seward and Ulysses S. Grant, though only partly successful, revived old memories, and the debates over Alaska, the Danish West Indies, and Santo Domingo furnished politicians of the 1880's with patterns and arguments.

Some of the new expansionists thought of peaceful economic activity as the most effective way of reaching their goal. Their methods are epitomized by the advice of Consul E. L. Baker in Buenos Aires, eager to encourage flagging American trade with the Plata Basin:

> Our interests in the political prosperity of the South American Republics, nearly all of whose foreign business associations are now monarchical instead of democratic, should prompt us, if possible, to bind our own to the Republics of the River Plate [sic] by the strong bonds of a mutual reciprocal trade. Commerce is the great civilizer and political missionary of the world. . . . In no other way could we better spread and propagate the principles and ideals which have built us up as a great nation than by the secret, silent influences of a closer and more intimate [commercial] intercourse.[16]

Others were more impatient. As the passive Hayes administration drew to a close, John A. Kasson, then American minister to Austria, called on his government to reassert the Monroe Doctrine with force, strengthen the Navy, and annex any valuable Pacific islands which might be useful to American trade and power. "American statesmen must contemplate a change in our extraterritorial policy . . ." Kasson declared. "It is to our discredit that the first century of our Statesmanship has developed but one formula of Foreign Policy, and that the plagiarism of the 'Monroe Doctrine'."[17]

[16]Statement of Consul E. L. Baker, Buenos Aires, quoted in Charles de Montferrand and Francisco P. Suárez to Evarts, Washington, February 1, 1881, William M. Evarts Papers, XXIX (Library of Congress).

[17]John A. Kasson to Evarts, Vienna, March 18, April 30, 1880, Nos. 300, 319, quoted in Edward L. Younger, *John A. Kasson: Politics and Diplomacy from Lincoln to McKinley* (Iowa City, Iowa, 1955), pp. 293-94.

The inauguration of Garfield raised expansionist hopes for a new policy which would extend American trade, safeguard American coasts, and raise American prestige. Proadministration newspapers, led by the *New York Tribune*, called for a return to the prewar days when American diplomacy "was in the main directed toward enhancing the power and dignity of the United States in the family of nations" and based on the assumption that "as the only great Power in America, we have an interest in the affairs of the continent which is paramount to that of any European Power." The times were ripe, continued the editorialist:

> Now that we are rid of the virus of slavery, our public sentiment is healthful and just in its workings. It would not tolerate any oppressive interference with the rights of weaker communities. . . . [However,] it would keep the Danish West Indies out of the hands of any great maritime Power; it would checkmate any project for a French protectorate over the Isthmus of Panama; it would foster and extend our foreign commerce, and it would place the United States in the front rank of the great directing forces of human freedom and progress.[18]

This ambitious policy of expanding American trade and influence raised many objections among both Republicans and Democrats, for, as usual in American history, a large part of the people believed firmly that freedom and progress, like charity, ought to begin at home. A California correspondent of the *Tribune* warned the editor that widespread naval bases would make us, "like England, an unwilling participant in every war that may happen to occur in any quarter of the earth." "We have no outlying empires to protect;" added the *New York Herald*, "we have no vast standing army to employ; we have no navy to guard our coasts, because they can take care of themselves. . . . Our foreign policy is a domestic policy." Other writers opposed the application of the Monroe Doctrine to the isthmian question. At the end of 1881 *Harper's Weekly* declared that "there was never less occasion for 'serving notice upon all mankind' that America is for Americans."[19]

[18]*New York Tribune*, July 16, 1881, p. 4.
[19]*Harper's Weekly*, XXVI (January 7, 1882), 2. See also *New York Tribune*, June 6, 1881, p. 5; *New York Herald*, December 19, p. 6; *Washington Post*, August 20, p. 2, and *Catholic World*, XXXI (April 1880), 132.

In the midst of these contrary admonitions, James A. Garfield assumed the presidency. Intelligent and well-educated, with experience as minister, professor, and college president, Garfield was for years one of the genuine intellectuals in the House of Representatives but managed to escape condemnation for this distinction by his brilliant oratory, his open and friendly manner, and a certain well-cultivated manliness. He could be sanctimonious and self-righteous on occasion, and he changed his mind so often that his political rival, Roscoe Conkling, unkindly called him an angleworm. When he entered politics, he made public finance his special concern, embracing the cause of sound money. He had little interest in foreign affairs, except that during the 1870's he mastered the arguments in favor of a protective tariff.

Garfield's hopes for a successful administration were blighted from the outset by the division of the Republican party into two quarreling factions: the "Stalwart" followers of former President Grant, dominated by Roscoe Conkling, and the "Half-Breeds," led by James G. Blaine. In June, 1880, after a long deadlock between Grant and Blaine, the exhausted Republican convention tried to compromise by nominating Garfield, a less controversial Half-Breed, with Chester A. Arthur, one of Conkling's New York henchmen, as vice-presidential candidate. Conkling and most of the Stalwarts refused to join the campaign until October, when Garfield seemed in danger of losing, but Blaine and his Half-Breeds contributed heavily from the beginning. Both factions assumed that Garfield would accept their advice in matters of patronage. For his own part, he tried to consider himself the candidate of all Republicans and made pathetic efforts to avoid antagonizing anyone, but he could not hold the party together. The only result of his caution was a sterile, negative campaign.[20]

[20]The standard accounts of these events are contained in Ellis Paxson Oberholtzer, *A History of the United States Since the Civil War* (5 vols.; New York, 1917-1937), IV, chap. xxvi; David Saville Muzzey, *James G. Blaine, a Political Idol of Other Days* (New York, 1934), chap. viii; Robert Granville Caldwell, *James A. Garfield, Party Chieftain* (New York, 1931), chap. xiv, and Theodore Clark Smith, *The Life and Letters of James Abram Garfield* (2 vols.; New Haven, Connecticut, 1925), II, chaps. xxv-xxvi.

The election won, Garfield tried to pay his political debts. Usually, however, both Stalwarts and Half-Breeds wanted the same offices, and nearly four months passed after the election before he had even chosen his cabinet. When he finally let it be known that Blaine would be his secretary of state, many assumed that the appointment was forced on him, but examination of his papers and diary suggests that he made a relatively free choice. However, he exacted of Blaine the unusual pledge that he would not be a presidential candidate in 1884 under any circumstances. Conkling and the Stalwarts cynically assumed that Blaine accepted the office for the express purpose of breaking this pledge or at least of dominating a weak president. In later years Blaine and his followers declared that he entered the Cabinet in order to carry out a well-matured foreign policy, but it is significant that in his correspondence with Garfield between election and inauguration he wrote much about politics and little about diplomacy. It would be safe to assume that prestige, power, and patronage dominated his thinking.[21]

The opposition to Blaine's appointment was remarkably intense, even considering his controversial record and the hot-blooded political hatreds of the time. Stalwarts raised cries of "Prime minister!" and Garfield's followers warned him against accepting too much of Blaine's advice on matters outside the State Department. Perhaps most disturbing of all was the reaction of respectable persons who professed to disdain political squabbles. The old patrician, Hamilton Fish, for example, called Blaine "valiant & irrepressible when in *assured* position & power, reckless in a crisis, but vacillating & timid in emergencies of which the issue is uncertain." Ex-President Hayes later wrote in his diary that Blaine, while able, was "a scheming demagogue, selfish and reckless," and the British minister, Sir Edward Thornton, described him to the Foreign Office as an "ambitious, arbitrary and even imperious" man with a thin skin and a short temper, who would

[21]Blaine may also have been glad to get out of Maine politics, where he was facing increased rivalry. Muzzey, *Blaine*, pp. 184-86.

"lay hold of any plausible excuse to get up a quarrel with a foreign Power with a view to making political Capital for himself."[22]

The subject of these unvarnished opinions appeared to his followers as the brightest light in a generation of American politicians: brilliant (although less intellectual than Garfield), witty, a magnetic orator and conversationalist, a thoughtful, courteous man, and a crafty parliamentarian who had dominated the unruly House of Representatives for years through the force of his personality. His enemies pointed out, however, that not a single piece of important legislation was associated with his name, and reformers were revolted by the faint odor of corruption which hung over his actions after the episode of the Mulligan letters during 1876.

As a congressman, Blaine, like Garfield, had seldom paid much attention to foreign affairs, but on receiving his appointment he determined to conduct a "spirited" foreign policy which would raise American prestige among nations and his own prestige among Republican politicians. After he left office he laid great emphasis on his desire to extend American trade and, in general, "seek the conquests of peace," but his writings of 1880 and early 1881 contain few references to economics except protectionist arguments.[23] In any case, he brought to the State Department a strong, almost instinctive Anglophobia and brooded over the slighting remarks made about the United States in Parliament and the British press. However, both Thornton and his successor later admitted that Blaine made every effort to be agreeable.[24]

[22]Sir Edward Thornton to Viscount Granville, Washington, June 14, 1881, Paul Knaplund and Carolyn M. Clewes (eds.), "Private Letters from the British Embassy in Washington to the Foreign Secretary Lord Granville, 1880-1885," *Annual Report of the American Historical Association for the year 1941* (3 vols.; Washington, 1942), I, 136. See also Hamilton Fish to J. C. Bancroft Davis, Glenclyffe, New York, July 29, J. C. Bancroft Davis Papers, XXIX (Library of Congress). Williams, *Diary and Letters of Hayes,* IV, 152. However, some cooler heads recognized that Western interests would probably restrain Blaine from serious quarrels with Britain. New York *Daily Commercial Bulletin,* March 9, 1881, p. 2.

[23]The principal evidence of Blaine's later attitude toward his foreign policies is contained in his article, "The Foreign Policy of the Garfield Administration," in James G. Blaine, *Political Discussions: Legislative, Diplomatic, and Popular, 1856-1886* (Norwich, Connecticut, 1887), pp. 411-19.

[24]Thornton to Granville, Washington, April 5, 1881; Victor Drummond to Granville, October 24, Knaplund and Clewes, "British Embassy Letters," pp. 125, 149.

In foreign affairs Garfield allowed his secretary of state free rein, and although the Cabinet discussed most important actions taken during the spring of 1881, the President apparently made few suggestions.[25] In matters of patronage and domestic affairs Garfield heeded the advice of other friends and tried to restrict Blaine's influence, but he found it difficult to hold an even balance between the two principal Republican factions, and a third group of reformists got short rations indeed. In May, after both Stalwarts and Half-Breeds had won concessions, Blaine persuaded the pliable President to turn over the richest reward in Conkling's own state, the collectorship of the Port of New York, to Judge William H. Robertson, one of Conkling's worst enemies. The incumbent collector, a reform appointee of Hayes, was unceremoniously dumped into the Foreign Service as consul general in London, and this appointment necessitated a series of ill-advised shifts among Stalwarts in the service, which produced general hard feelings.[26]

The wholly unnecessary challenge to the Stalwarts completed the split in the Republican party and, in a sense, sealed Garfield's fate. After weeks of wrangling the Senate confirmed Robertson's appointment, whereupon Conkling and a colleague resigned in a huff, but the victory was an expensive one, for Congressional business had slowed almost to a halt, and party discipline was crumbling. Worst of all, a frustrated officeseeker named Charles Guiteau, who had been bombarding Garfield with applications for the post of consul general in Paris, convinced himself that the President was the enemy of all good Stalwart Republicans. On July 2, after stalking Garfield for days, he managed to get close to him in a crowd, fired a bullet into his back, and cried triumphantly that now the Stalwart, Arthur, would be President. A shocked nation prayed for Garfield's recovery, while public busi-

[25]On the relations between Garfield and Blaine see Muzzey, *Blaine*, pp. 174, 92-93, and Caldwell, *Garfield*, pp. 332-33. Garfield's diary for the months of his presidency contains few references to foreign affairs. The diplomatic topic bulking largest was the Paris monetary conference of 1881, which fell within his special interest, public finance. The Diaries of James A. Garfield, *passim* (Library of Congress).

[26]Two of former President Grant's friends had to be shifted, and Hamilton Fish's son, Nicholas, lost his post as minister to Switzerland. Grant was indignant about several of Garfield's appointments. See his letter reprinted in *New York Herald*, May 20, 1881, p. 2.

ness virtually stopped, and newspapers, stock market, and even foreign observers reacted to every bulletin from the bedside, but the inadequate medical knowledge of the day could neither locate the bullet nor cure the infection which it caused, and on September 19 the President finally died.

Garfield's long illness created an unprecedented problem for his government, since he was too weak to discuss public affairs, although undoubtedly in his right mind. He begged the attending physician to call Blaine to his bedside soon after the shooting, but the Secretary saw him only once during the first ten days and seldom thereafter. From time to time the Cabinet held private meetings, apparently under Blaine's leadership, carried on necessary business, and considered whether to summon Vice-President Arthur and make him a participating member of the government. At the same time Grant, Conkling, and other Stalwarts met at Arthur's home to determine their own policies, but the two groups could never manage to get together until forced by the imminence of the President's death.[27] Inspection of State Department documents during the summer of 1881 shows that Blaine postponed nearly all important decisions, confining himself to routine matters. Fortunately no new crises developed during Garfield's illness, but, as will be seen, Blaine's forced inactivity complicated the handling of several existing and highly delicate questions.

By the time of Garfield's death both of the principal Republican factions had lost face before the American people. During the President's illness, Blaine and the Half-Breeds had carefully avoided any appearance of usurping power, but few expected them to take kindly to the leadership of Arthur and Conkling. As for the Stalwarts, Guiteau's exultant cry had made them seem indirectly responsible for the killing. Although Arthur dissociated himself from Conkling and avoided a general purge of Half-Breed officeholders, the Stalwarts never entirely recovered their reputation, and in the next years the cause of civil service reform prospered as never before. By the end of 1881 the most popular leader of the Republican

[27]Mrs. James G. Blaine to William E. Chandler, Washington, July 12, 22, August 6, 25, 1881, William E. Chandler Papers (New Hampshire Historical Society, Concord, New Hampshire). *Washington Post*, July 31, p. 1; August 20, p. 1; August 27, p. 1; September 10, p. 1; September 11, p. 2.

party was dead, the most able was out of office, and it did not seem likely that the titular leader in the White House could ever unite all dissident elements behind him.

* * *

If the United States had possessed a well-trained, semipermanent staff of Foreign Service officers during the 1880's, the intraparty strife of the Garfield administration need not have materially affected the nation's foreign affairs. Unfortunately, few American diplomats had either training or tenure, so that as they dealt (or fumbled) with their many problems during 1881, they were constantly casting nervous glances over their shoulders at Washington.

The organization of the department was simple enough. Under the secretary of state were three assistant secretaries, a chief clerk, and eight bureaus (diplomatic, consular, and six others), each with a chief and several clerks. The first assistant secretary, like the secretary himself, was supposed to have political experience and contacts and to act with the full confidence of the administration in his superior's absence. To fill this important position Blaine invited J. C. Bancroft Davis, who had been an effective assistant secretary under Grant and Hamilton Fish, but Davis declined, and Blaine had to settle for Robert R. Hitt, an undistinguished minor Republican politician.

Although the secretary and his first assistant often conducted business with foreign diplomats in Washington (if the language barrier was not too great), the permanent staff of the department assumed most of the daily burden of correspondence with American diplomats abroad and the preparation of memoranda for Congress. Foremost among the permanent officials was the second assistant secretary, William Hunter, full of experience with precedents and protocol (he had served continuously for over fifty-five years), but now suffering from high blood pressure and old age. The man who eventually succeeded Hunter as *doyen* of the permanent staff, Alvey A. Adee, was chief of the diplomatic bureau in 1880 and later became third assistant secretary. Well-educated, keen-witted, and tireless, Adee quickly learned the forms and customs of diplomacy and furnished his superiors many

a long, minutely documented memorandum, usually leaning in the direction of more active diplomacy.

Although Hunter and Adee brought some sense of professionalism into the department, it remained stunted and amateurish in comparison with the major foreign offices of Europe. Despite the American democratic theory of popular responsibility for government, the State Department worked virtually in secret, and no one was directly accountable to Congress. Although the permanent officials took rigorous care to preserve the departmental archives from the public eye, a politician-secretary such as Blaine sometimes embarrassed his own diplomats by prematurely publishing correspondence for its effect on Congress or the public. Also, the department was occasionally careless: for example, a valuable book of records, missing for weeks, was finally found under a pillow on the seat of Hunter's chair, which had been too low for him![28] A critic declared that the department ought to require its clerks to know French and ought to employ a single officer to supervise forms and protocol, important to European monarchies however repugnant it might be to democrats. Indeed, he added, it was fortunate that the nation sent and received no ambassadors, for no one in the State Department would know how to do it properly.[29]

In 1880 the diplomatic representatives of the United States abroad consisted of thirteen ministers plenipotentiary, twelve ministers resident, and five chargés d'affaires. Some of these doubled as consuls general. In addition the State Department maintained just under three hundred consulates and a great many commercial agencies, mostly manned by merchants or natives. Most ministers were selected for past political services, if not for even more

[28]U.S., Congress, House, 47th Cong., 1st Sess., 1882, H. Rept. 1790, p. 19. Except where indicated, this description of the organization of the State Department is summarized from Eugene Schuyler, *American Diplomacy and the Furtherance of Commerce* (New York, 1886), and U.S., *Register of the Department of State* (Washington, 1869-   ), *1880, passim*. In 1880 the secretary of state received a salary of $8,000, the assistant secretaries $3,500, the chief clerk $2,500, and the bureau chiefs $2,100.

[29]Schuyler, *American Diplomacy*, pp. 12-15. In 1881 the British government proposed that ambassadors be exchanged, and the question was discussed for several years in Washington. On instructions from Frelinghuysen, Adee drew up a memorandum (dated June 10, 1885, No. 6) which set forth all objections. U.S., Reports of the Diplomatic Bureau, VII.

casual reasons—Garfield promoted General Lew Wallace from Paraguay to Turkey because he had greatly enjoyed *Ben Hur* and wanted Wallace to gather local color for a sequel.[30] A few, such as James Russell Lowell (Britain) and Andrew D. White (Germany), enhanced American prestige in important posts by their scholarly reputations and genuine ability. Haphazardly selected, American ministers were badly paid, housed, and equipped, so that John Hay deemed the Foreign Service "like the Catholic Church, calculated only for celibates," and the lucky appointees had to possess independent incomes or go into debt to serve their country.[31]

All too often the American minister took an inferior position behind the ambassadors of less wealthy countries and did his business in some cramped third-floor suite which American visitors could scarcely find. The American legation in London had no guard at night, and there was a tradition among the staff that once, in moving from one building to another, all files and books had spent a night out on the street, packed in carts and covered with tarpaulins. Conditions in the lesser legations can be imagined. In Blaine's time only twelve legations even had secretaries to take charge of papers and business if anything happened to the minister —a circumstance which seriously imperiled American interests during the War of the Pacific after our ministers to both Peru and Chile died. Before leaving office, Blaine drafted a memorandum to the President on this subject, but nothing was done.[32]

Whatever might be said about the appointment and treatment of American ministers would apply in double measure to American consuls. After each election the president and the secretary of state were besieged with applications; the witty Secretary Evarts

[30]Entries for April 17, 19, 1881, Garfield Diaries.

[31]John Hay to William L. Stone, March 8 [1881], John Hay Papers (Library of Congress). That wealthy Americans could become successful diplomats was shown by the experiences of Levi P. Morton, a New York banker who became minister to France and soon made his stylish *soirées* a magnet for influential Frenchmen. Robert McElroy, *Levi Parsons Morton* (New York, 1930), pp. 133-34.

[32]James G. Blaine to Chester A. Arthur, December 1881, No. 64. Draft in U.S., Reports of the Diplomatic Bureau, V. See also W. J. Hoppin to Frederick T. Frelinghuysen, London, November 10, 1883, private, U.S., Despatches from the United States Legation, London, CXLVIII, Records of the Department of State (National Archives, Record Group 59). Hereafter cited as U.S., Despatches, England.

proposed to carve above his door "Come ye disconsulate." Yet
when the new appointee arrived at his post, he was often disillusioned to learn that he must spend hours each day at routine
paper work in a dull commercial town, and that on his meager
salary he was expected to circulate respectably among local merchants and bankers in the interests of American trade. At Matamoros, for example, the consul (earning $2,000 plus $400 for
office rent) was expected to prevent smuggling over the border,
supervise bonded imports, and watch the movements of Indians,
in addition to his other tasks. At Shanghai, the American consul
general supervised all other American consulates in China, helped
to govern the large foreign settlement in the city, tried cases in
which Americans were defendants, operated a jail and courts of
divorce, probate, and equity, and served as postmaster to all
Americans in the area. By 1885 salaried consuls earned from $1,500
to $6,000 a year, but many others depended largely on fees and
were allowed to trade on the side.[33]

The chronic mismanagement of the United States Foreign Service reflected the prevalent American sentiment that foreign affairs
were not really important enough to bother about. The New York
Sun, never friendly to diplomats, expressed this feeling exactly:

> The chief end of an American Consul is to write home for
> supplies. . . . Duties of secondary importance are to ship
> consignments of beetles to Commissioner Le Duc, to provide
> for distressed seamen, and to send to the Department of State
> occasional reports on the . . . country he is in. . . . This
> momentous intelligence . . . is published by the State Depart-
> ment at the public expense. Some day the people will under-
> stand that it is not worth their while to go on paying for the
> collection and circulation of such unmitigated trash.[34]

Each year during the debates on the diplomatic and consular appropriation bill, isolationist congressmen wove variations on these
themes, until the administration counted itself lucky to keep the
officers it had, at their existing salaries. Even the *Nation,* while

[33]Barrows, *Evarts,* p. 344. Schuyler, *American Diplomacy,* pp. 66-68, 86. For a
vivid description of consular disillusionment see *New York Tribune,* March 16,
1881, p. 4.
[34]New York *Sun,* December 25, 1880.

deploring the poor quality of ministers and consuls, compared them to the Swiss Guard at the Vatican: "They may be armed, and tall, and brave, and well drilled; but everybody knows, and they know, that they will never have to attack anybody or defend anybody."[35]

For many years after 1881 this continued to be the most common popular attitude toward the State Department and the Foreign Service. At the time of Garfield's inauguration, however, the economic isolation of the United States was rapidly disappearing under the outward pressure of goods seeking markets. Soon American investments would follow, and then political connections and entanglements. In a period of shifting orientation like the 1880's, mistakes and blundering were probably inevitable. They would be all the more numerous and serious if American policymakers persisted in treating foreign affairs as a football in the game of party politics, and if the American people sneered at their diplomats as useless ornamentation.

[35]*Nation*, XXVI (May 28, 1878), 209-10.

CHAPTER 2

Blaine and the Isthmian Question

WHEN Blaine entered the State Department in March, 1881, prepared to undertake a more aggressive, "spirited" foreign policy, he enjoyed the advantages of a free rein from President Garfield and considerable support by the Half-Breed press. At the same time he was to labor under heavy liabilities: the bitter quarrel over patronage which had already begun in Washington and was soon to cost Garfield his life; the possibility of united opposition in Congress by Stalwarts and Democrats; and the inefficiency of a spoils-ridden Foreign Service, which his own partisan appointments and his shallow background in foreign affairs tended to aggravate. His foreign policy developed by fits and starts, and his naturally impetuous temperament and language sometimes pushed him, almost unawares, into exposed diplomatic positions which a little more training and caution would have enabled him to avoid. The aims and shortcomings of his foreign policy are well illustrated in his handling of the isthmian canal question—the most dramatic and best publicized threat to American interests which confronted him on his entry into office.

*   *   *

Before considering Blaine's isthmian diplomacy it is necessary to review the canal projects of Ferdinand de Lesseps and certain American rivals. By 1881 De Lesseps had secured enough capital to reconnoiter the jungles of Panama and begin his immense excavations. From the outset most of the operations were largely experimental, for the French promoter and his engineers found that they had to unlearn their experience with the sands and marshes of Suez and substitute mountains of rock, landslides, and the torrential Chagres River, which was apt to overflow with little warning. In addition, they found labor more expensive than at Suez, and malaria and yellow fever made the diggings a virtual pesthole. Fights

broke out repeatedly between native laborers and those imported from the West Indies, and from time to time organized strikes halted operations and created friction between the company, the local government, and the British and American consuls at the ports. As a result of these difficulties excavation work at Panama lagged behind schedule almost from the outset.[1]

Of course it was impossible to keep these shortcomings entirely secret, although De Lesseps and the French press did their best. Eventually reporters from American newspapers visited Panama, described the operations, and predicted the early collapse of the enterprise. Several observers sent out by the United States Navy agreed with the journalists that the French would probably fail.[2] In 1881 knowledge of De Lesseps' activities was somewhat more indefinite than later, but rumors of his difficulties undoubtedly stimulated American promoters in their efforts to outdo the foreigners.

For decades before De Lesseps arrived on the scene, engineers and promoters in the United States had dreamed of an interoceanic canal. In 1872 President Grant appointed an Interoceanic Canal Commission to examine isthmian data already collected by the Navy and to conduct further explorations. The leading voice on this commission was that of Rear Admiral Daniel Ammen, an old personal friend of the President who had become a canal enthusiast during the 1850's. In February, 1876, the commission declared itself in favor of an alternate canal route across Nicaragua, and Secretary Hamilton Fish proceeded to draw up a draft treaty. Fish's terms, however, did not satisfy Nicaragua, and the project was dropped for the time being.

Rumors of De Lesseps' plans revived the drowsing American

[1]Mack, *Land Divided*, pp. 317-23. Keasbey, *Nicaragua Canal*, pp. 429-30. On strikes and riots see *New York Tribune*, January 25, 1882, p. 1; Robert W. Turpin to William Hunter, Panama, April 4, 1883, No. 182, and Thomas Adamson to Hunter, Panama, May 17, No. 10, U. S., Consular Despatches, Panama, XVI. On the purchase of the Panama Railway see *New York Tribune*, June 4, 1881, p. 5. For samples of public confidence by French officials see *ibid.*, January 5, 1883, p. 5; April 11, p. 5.

[2]Keasbey, *Nicaragua Canal*, p. 433. José Carlos Rodrígues, *The Panama Canal, its History, its Political Aspects, and Financial Difficulties* (New York, 1885), pp. 136-47, 151-57 *et passim*. U.S., Congress, Senate, 48th Cong., 1st Sess., 1884, Senate Executive Doc. 123, pp. 1-4.

ambitions, and late in 1879 Admiral Ammen, Captain Seth L. Phelps, U.S.N., General George B. McClellan, Levi P. Morton, and other dignitaries organized the Provisional Interoceanic Canal Society and obtained a concession from Nicaragua. With Grant's public support, Ammen and Phelps then reorganized this company on a permanent basis as the Maritime Canal Company of Nicaragua and published plans for a canal slightly over fifty miles long which would follow the route of the San Juan River along the southeastern edge of Nicaragua, cross Lake Nicaragua, and pierce through a narrow but steep range of mountains along the Pacific coast, using about a dozen locks. Ammen and Phelps estimated the maximum total cost of a Nicaragua canal as about $93,000,000 compared with $300,000,000 for De Lesseps' sea-level canal at Panama, and they denounced the French promoter for misrepresenting conditions in Panama and the amount of his American support.[3]

De Lesseps did not need to reply in detail to the charges of Ammen and Phelps, for a second group of American promoters had set out to divert public support to their own project, a ship-railway across Tehuantepec. This isthmus, in southern Mexico, was wider than either Nicaragua or Panama, although it contained lower mountain passes, and during the preceding forty years it had become a veritable graveyard of railroad and canal concessions. The current project seemed more bizarre than any of these: a many-track railway and especially designed "cradle cars," large and solid enough to carry loaded ships from the Gulf of Mexico to the Pacific Ocean. Bizarre it might seem, but the project bore the cachet of James B. Eads, a great engineer-promoter who had already matched De Lesseps' reputation for doing the impossible by his construction of jetties at the mouth of the Mississippi River. Knowing the American weakness for "gadgets," Eads and his assistants built a portable working model of the ship-railway, exhibited it around the country, and flooded the public with pamphlets advertising his project. Thus threatened from the rear, Ammen and

[3]Ulysses S. Grant, "The Nicaragua Canal," *North American Review*, CXXXII (February 1881), 107-16. Keasbey, *Nicaragua Canal*, p. 365, note. U.S., Congress, Senate, 47th Cong., 1st Sess., 1882, Senate Rept. 368, as reprinted in 56th Cong., 2d Sess., Senate Executive Doc. 231, Part 5, pp. 112-25. *New York Tribune*, December 28, 1880, p. 1; October 8, 1882, p. 3; January 26, 1884, p. 7.

Phelps replied with pamphlets of their own, and the battle was on.[4]

Although the rival propaganda of the two groups was directed in part at American investors, its principal target was Congress, for at the outset both groups of promoters had asked the government to guarantee profits during the first years of operation. Originally, Ammen and Phelps requested a guarantee of 3 per cent for twenty years on a maximum capital stock of $100,000,000, while Eads wanted a guarantee of 6 per cent for fifteen years on a stock of $50,000,000, after he had demonstrated the workability of his ship-railway over ten miles of track. The Nicaragua group also offered to allow the American government to appoint a representative to the company's board of directors and to take possession of the canal temporarily in an emergency.[5] Thus its proposals more closely resembled the eventual American isthmian protectorate.

It is unnecessary to give in any detail the arguments used by the rival promoters. Both fired an occasional shot at De Lesseps but saved most of their ammunition for each other. Both agreed that an isthmian transit route would benefit America as the Suez Canal had benefited Europe by opening the trade of the Golden Orient to the East Coast and the Gulf states. At many other points, however, they disagreed: the relative cost of their projects, the time required for ships to make the passage, the healthfulness of the climate, and even the prevalence of earthquakes and hurricanes. Eads held an advantage in the political stability of Mexico, but Ammen and Phelps forced him on the defensive by attacking the ship-railway as unproved and dangerous.[6]

[4] The best short description of the Eads project is Mack, *Land Divided*, pp. 232-34. The standard biography of Eads is Florence Dorsey, *Road to the Sea: the Story of James B. Eads and the Mississippi River* (New York, 1947).

[5] *New York Tribune*, December 16, 1881, p. 1. James B. Eads, "The Isthmian Ship-Railway," *North American Review*, CXXXII (March 1881), pp. 235-36.

[6] Among the many pamphlets and articles which both sides put out, the following are typical: [Seth L. Phelps], *Review of the Proposed Tehuantepec Ship-railway. June 1, 1881* [Washington, 1881]; Daniel Ammen, *The Certainty of the Nicaragua Canal Contrasted with the Uncertainties of the Eads Ship-railway* (Washington [1886]); Elmer L. Corthell, *An Exposition of the Errors and Fallacies in Rear-admiral Ammen's Pamphlet Entitled, "The Certainty of the Nicaragua Canal* [etc.]" (Washington, 1886); James B. Eads, "Review of Captain Phelps' Pamphlet Entitled 'Transportation of Ships on Railways,'" in Estill McHenry (ed.), *Addresses and Papers of James B. Eads, Together with a Biographical Sketch* (St. Louis, 1884).

Before long the opponents had fallen into mudslinging. Ammen denounced Eads's earlier inventions as frauds, while partisans of Eads declared that Ammen was "cooking" his expense estimates and shamelessly exploiting his friendship with Grant. As for the former President, he helped to raise capital for the Nicaragua project and for a time allowed his name to be used in company pamphlets, but he tried to remain friendly with both sides.[7]

*   *   *

During the last months of the Hayes administration the American public and Congress began to take increased interest in the canal question. Considerable support for the projects came from the West Coast and the South, areas which stood to benefit from the proposed new trade route. The San Francisco Board of Trade, for example, declared that California languished for want of cheap transportation to market and petitioned Congress to support the Nicaragua project. Residents of the Mississippi Valley, especially in New Orleans and Missouri, enthusiastically pushed the Eads ship-railway, both because Tehuantepec lay much closer to the Mississippi than did Nicaragua, and because they identified Eads with the Mississippi jetties and other measures to develop the valley.[8] Many other Southerners, however, saw in a Nicaragua canal the chief hope for their section's economic recovery. The leader of this group came to be Senator John T. Morgan of Alabama, a gruff, aggressive ex-brigadier general of the Confederate Army, who was elected to Congress by the Bourbon "Redeemers" of his state, became the most influential Democrat on the Senate Foreign Relations Committee, and often thereafter cooperated with the Garfield and Arthur administrations in behalf of an expansionist foreign policy. To Morgan the principal goal of this policy was to open Latin-American markets to southern textiles and other American products.[9]

[7]Ammen, *Certainty of the Nicaragua Canal*, pp. 15-20. *New York Tribune*, February 12, 1881, p. 2. Corthell, *Exposition of the Errors*, pp. 27-30, 41-50. *New York Herald*, February 13, 1883, p. 5.

[8]San Francisco Board of Trade, *Report of Special Committee* (San Francisco, 1880), *passim*. Dorsey, *Road to the Sea*, chaps. xv-xvii, *passim*. Southern Democrats complained because Northern Democrats voted against the Eads bill. *Washington Post*, January 31, 1881, p. 4.

[9]*Dictionary of American Biography* (New York, 1928-1944), XIII, 180-81. August Carl Radke, "John Tyler Morgan, an Expansionist Senator, 1877-1907"

At the same time, opposition to an American transit project began to appear. Spokesmen for the Union Pacific and other transcontinental railroads kept very quiet at this time but undoubtedly worked behind the scenes to discourage the opening of a rival trade route. Others saw in a canal project the dangerously attractive gateway to unlimited expenditures and commitments abroad. How could the United States make any profitable use of an interoceanic canal with her small merchant marine? How could she defend it with a weak navy and a standing army of 25,000? Far better, they thought, to reserve the trade of the Pacific to California ports and concentrate on internal development than to set out on "a questionable enterprise in a foreign land."[10]

Until the end of 1880 Congress confined itself largely to belligerent resolutions, but shortly before its last regular session began in December, both Eads and the Ammen-Phelps group applied for governmental guarantees. A special House Committee on Interoceanic Canals heard testimony from both groups of promoters and, for good measure, from Ferdinand de Lesseps, then visiting the United States. Apparently for a time supporters of Eads felt confident of passing their bill, for a majority of the committee reported favorably on the ship-railway. The minority, however, managed to put the House on its guard against granting a subsidy to an untried experiment, and the bill was tabled. The Senate ignored the two isthmian groups, but during its special session of 1881 Senator Morgan revived one of the old defiant resolutions denouncing foreign-sponsored canals and prevailed upon the Foreign Relations Committee to endorse it emphatically.[11]

The debates in Congress, accompanied by approving newspaper editorials, struck an aggressive note on the isthmian question without committing the United States to any definite plan of action or settling the rivalry between Tehuantepec and Nicaragua. Leaving the question of routes and charters of incorporation strictly to

(Ph.D. dissertation, University of Washington, 1953), pp. 202-5 *et passim.* For a sample of Morgan's thinking on cotton textile markets see U.S., *Congressional Record,* 47th Cong., 1st Sess., 1882, XIII, 2105-17.

[10]*Washington Post,* February 7, 1881, p. 1. John Lawrence Smith, *Interoceanic Canal, Practicability of the Different Routes, and Questionable Nature of the Interest of the United States in a Canal* (Louisville, Kentucky, 1880), pp. 15-18.

[11]Sarah Georgia Walton, "The Frelinghuysen-Zavala Treaty, 1884-1885," (M.A. thesis, University of Virginia, 1953), pp. 27-31. Mack, *Land Divided,* p. 235. *Wash-*

Congress, Blaine set out to translate into executive policy the defiant if vague resolutions of Morgan and his nationalist colleagues. He would advance American prestige in Latin America and secure the American coastline by isolating De Lesseps from support by either France or any other European Power.

*   *   *

Any sort of isthmian policy, active or inactive, had to begin with the republic of Colombia, which tried to rule Panama from its remote national capital of Bogotá, deep in the mountains and fully twenty days' journey away. (Americans could reach Panama in less than four days from New Orleans.) In 1846, realizing how precarious was her hold, Colombia signed a mutual assistance treaty with the United States, by which she guaranteed free transit across the isthmus in return for an American guarantee of Colombian sovereignty and isthmian neutrality. As it turned out, the government at Bogotá was not always able to keep open the transit route, but when revolutions occurred, American marines would restore order and then return the province to the proper authorities. Both sides grew tired of this indeterminate arrangement, but they could not agree on a better one, and the United States dared not withdraw, lest Colombia transfer the guarantee to Britain or France.[12]

When Colombia granted a canal concession to French interests identified with De Lesseps, the usually passive Hayes and Evarts felt compelled to take some action to defend American interests under the treaty of 1846. In January, 1880, invoking an old, unused American concession, Hayes sent two warships to establish a coaling station at Chiriquí Lagoon, in northwestern Panama. Two former senators, William M. Gwin of California and Samuel C. Pomeroy of Kansas, who had bought up the old concession, announced plans for a railroad across the isthmus at this point and prevailed on Congress to appropriate $200,000 for permanent coaling stations at the termini of the railroad. The Colombian government protested

ington Post, January 8, 1881, p. 2. Chicago Tribune, February 14, p. 2. U.S., Congress, House, 46th Cong., 3d Sess., 1881, House Miscellaneous Doc. 13; H. Rept. 322, passim. U.S., Congressional Record, 47th Cong., Special Sess., 409, and U.S., Congress, Senate, Senate Rept. 1, as reprinted in 56th Cong., 2d Sess., Senate Executive Doc. 231, Part 5, pp. 105-7.

[12]E. Taylor Parks, Colombia and the United States, 1765-1934 (Durham, North Carolina, 1935), chaps. xii-xv.

dress restated Hayes's policy of American "supervision and au·
thority over any interoceanic canal," he touched off a furious
debate in the Colombian Senate. At this point an unfortunate cool-
ness developed between the Colombian foreign office and the
American minister, Ernest Dichman, who was trying to persuade
the government to reopen negotiations. The foreign minister told
Blaine that Dichman had been heard "upon a festive occasion"
threatening that if Colombia did not see reason, the United States
would negotiate with the province of Panama. Dichman denied
the indiscretion, but Blaine had to recall him, and he departed in a
temper, leaving behind more ill feeling than ever.[15]

So far, Blaine was not responsible for the friction between Colombia and the United States, but he soon did his part to prolong
it by interfering with Colombian efforts to settle other foreign disputes. On December 27, 1880, Colombia had signed a treaty with
Costa Rica for the arbitration of a long-standing isthmian boundary
dispute between the two countries. As arbiters the treaty named
the King of Belgium, the King of Spain, and the President of Argentina, in that order. When Blaine learned of this treaty, shortly
after taking office, he chose to regard it as an affront to the United
States, for European arbitration might injure the rights of the
United States under the treaty of 1846. He declared that the American government would not consider itself bound by any judgment
given under the new arrangement and intimated to the Belgian
and Spanish governments that the United States would prefer them
not to become involved in the delicate question. The King of Belgium at once declined to serve as arbiter, and the Spanish government replied that whatever happened, American interests would
not suffer.[16] Colombians and Costa Ricans both fulminated against

[15]Parks, *Colombia and the United States*, pp. 368-69. Ernest Dichman to James
G. Blaine, Bogotá, April 29, May 6, 11, 19, June 7, 19, July 17, August 15, 23, 27,
1881, Nos. 268, 271, 277, 282, 284, 297, 304, 305, 306; William L. Scruggs to Frederick T. Frelinghuysen, Bogotá, August 23, 1882, No. 18, U.S., Despatches, Colombia, XXXV, XXXVI.

[16]Alice Felt Tyler, *The Foreign Policy of James G. Blaine* (Minneapolis, Minnesota, 1927), pp. 64-71. This account is based on correspondence in U.S., *Foreign
Relations, 1881, passim*. The King of Spain did not decline to serve as arbiter,
but he died in 1885, and the matter was dropped. Gordon Ireland, *Boundaries,
Possessions, and Conflicts in Central and South America and the Caribbean* (Cambridge, Massachusetts, 1941), pp. 30-31. In contrast to this policy, about two years
later Frelinghuysen declared that he would not object if a boundary quarrel

"a policy, troublesome, radically egotistical, that would sacrifice the sacred principles of justice to the spirit of *mercantilism*."[17]

Another action of the Colombian government alarmed Blaine even more than this proposal for European arbitration. On May 9, 1881, shortly before his recall, Dichman reported that the Colombian foreign office had sent copies of the Trescot-Santodomingo protocol to its representatives in Europe with instructions to invite Britain, France, Germany, Spain, and Italy to join in a treaty guaranteeing Colombian sovereignty over a neutral isthmus.[18] Dichman was not sure that the Colombian diplomats would obey these instructions, but the mere rumor of such an invitation touched a sensitive American nerve. De Lesseps' presence at Panama as a private promoter was bad enough, but under no circumstances could the United States allow European governments to meddle in the political aspects of the isthmian question.

Accordingly, in early June Blaine prepared a full and explicit statement of American policy toward the projected joint guarantee of the neutrality of Panama. After presenting the note to the Cabinet, the Secretary sent it out on June 24 to each of the American legations in Europe.[19] He began by reminding the Powers of the provisions of the 1846 treaty with Colombia and intimated that the American government would consider any effort toward a supplementary guarantee as "an uncalled-for intrusion into a field where the local and general interests of the United States of America must be considered before those of any other power save those of the United States of Colombia alone." He defended this bluntly exclusive assertion primarily on grounds of American security, adding that the Pacific states, "imperial in extent and of

between Colombia and Venezuela were submitted to Spanish arbitration. Frederick T. Frelinghuysen to Dwight T. Reed, January 4, 1883, No. 123, U.S., Instructions, Spain, XIX, 254-57.

[17] *El mensajero* (San José, Costa Rica), August 4, 1881, quoted in U.S., *Foreign Relations, 1881*, pp. 112-13.

[18] Dichman to Blaine, Bogotá, May 9, 1881, No. 269, U.S., Despatches, Colombia, XXXV.

[19] The Cabinet had earlier had a long discussion of the 1846 treaty. Entries for May 6, June 14, Garfield Diaries. It is interesting to compare the final note with a preliminary draft in Volume II of the James G. Blaine Papers (Library of Congress). The note as sent preserves the wording of the original draft but adds many sentences which tend to dilute and soften the exceedingly blunt effect of the earlier draft.

extraordinary growth," would surely supply most of the traffic through an interoceanic canal.

Blaine was careful to point out that the American government sought no special economic privileges at Panama and did not oppose European investment in an isthmian canal, any more than it opposed European investment in American transcontinental railroads. However, the United States would draw the line at any sort of political dominance or naval use of the canal in wartime, just as it would refuse to allow European Powers to transport their troops on American railroads. He conceded that if the canal had been located in or near the Old World, it would be subject to European controls commensurate with European interests, and he reminded the Powers that his government had never interfered with purely European guarantees of neutrality, as in the case of Belgium. Without mentioning the Monroe Doctrine by name, Blaine implicitly applied it to the problem at hand.[20]

The note of June 24 was not published in the American press until October, but at that time most newspapers praised it and agreed that a joint guarantee would imperil American interests. The Colombian government called in the American minister for an explanation but accepted his defense of the policy. Santodomingo Vila, passing through the United States, told reporters that his government fully approved of the Monroe Doctrine.[21] Nevertheless, in the light of later events, Blaine's critics rightly concluded that his actions rested on a strained and unreasonable interpretation of the 1846 treaty. The treaty guaranteed only the isthmian transit route, not the whole province of Panama. It gave the United States no rights over an isthmian canal comparable to sovereignty over its own transcontinental railroads. Also it might be argued that in any case of guarantors, the more the better, and that covetous Europeans were more apt to respect each other's strength than to defer to the ramshackle United States Navy. Lastly, the note ignored the Clayton-Bulwer Treaty of 1850, an American

[20]Blaine to James Russell Lowell, June 24, 1881, No. 187, U.S., *Foreign Relations, 1881*, pp. 537-40.

[21]*New York Tribune*, October 26, 1881, p. 4; October 29, p. 4. *New York Herald*, December 17, p. 3. New York *World*, October 25. George Maney to Frelinghuysen, Bogotá, January 2, 1882, No. 7, U.S., Despatches, Colombia, XXXVI. Interview with Santodomingo Vila in *New York Tribune*, October 27, 1881, p. 1.

commitment to Britain which no one in his right mind could expect London to overlook.[22] As Blaine must have anticipated, he eventually heard from the British Foreign Office on the subject, but not until November, when Garfield was dead, and he himself was about to leave office.

* * *

While Blaine was warning the European Powers away from the isthmian question, he set out to expand American influence in Central America by helping the small nations of that region to preserve peace and attain stability. The two objects proved incompatible, for real stability seemed to require the union of Central America under the leadership of its most powerful nation, Guatemala, but some of the other Central American states would not yield such leadership to Guatemala without war. Furthermore, Guatemala had ambitions in other directions, even less congenial to American interests. As a result, Blaine's well-meant intervention produced still more Latin-American resentment against the United States.

In 1881 Guatemala had been governed for a decade by one of her most able dictators, Justo Rufino Barrios, who had determined to use American capital and influence to make his backward country prosperous. Under his rule Americans and other foreigners introduced railroads, telegraphs, telephones, modern farm implements, and many other improvements into the country. Barrios not only gave the best concessions to Americans but offered to sell strategic islands in the Bay of Fonseca to the Hayes administration, even though these belonged to his ally, Honduras. In February, 1880, he told the American minister, Cornelius A. Logan, that he intended to proclaim a confederation of Guatemala, Honduras, and El Salvador and conquer Nicaragua by force. He intimated that he would then be ready to talk business with the United States about a canal concession across Nicaragua.[23]

[22] [Edward H. Strobel], *Blaine and his Foreign Policy* (Boston, 1884), pp. 7-20. See also Ira D. Travis, *History of the Clayton-Bulwer Treaty* (Ann Arbor, Michigan [1899]), pp. 215-17.

[23] J. Fred Rippy, "Relations of the United States and Guatemala during the Epoch of Justo Rufino Barrios," *Hispanic American Historical Review*, XXII (1942), 596-605. J. Fred Rippy, "Justo Rufino Barrios and the Nicaraguan Canal," *ibid.*, XX (1940), 190-92. Chester Lloyd Jones, *Guatemala, Past and Present* (Min-

The Hayes administration did not accept the offer of the Bay Islands, but Logan took care not to antagonize Barrios, who, he thought, held in his hand the future of American influence in Central America. On February 1, 1881, Logan sent home a long, confidential dispatch in which he declared that both Britain and Germany were trying to displace American trade in Central America, not only so that their own salesmen might find new markets, but also in order to control the eventual isthmian canal and protect their interests on the Pacific coast. Since the Central American nations could not unite of their own free will, Logan felt that an American protectorate was the only solution.[24]

Between Central America and the United States stretched another nation in which Americans had even larger actual and potential interests—Mexico. In spite of serious border troubles along the Rio Grande, American capital had entered Mexico more freely than Central America, until by 1880 American investments totaled several million dollars. During that year the administrations of Hayes and Porfirio Díaz settled the border question amicably, and in September Díaz confirmed two long American railroad concessions, extending from the Rio Grande to Mexico City, which would inevitably furnish avenues to further investment from the north. Thus the future of American capital in Mexico seemed assured by the spring of 1881, but suspicions and anti-Americanism still lingered south of the border, and Mexican nationalists watched every American move eagerly for signs of aggression or trickery.[25]

Under the circumstances it might have suited the United States to place an impassable mountain range between two such unstable neighbors as Mexico and Guatemala, but instead, the border ran

neapolis, Minnesota, 1940), chap. v and especially p. 61. Cornelius A. Logan to Blaine, Guatemala City, June 15, 1881, No. 189, U.S., Despatches, Central America, XVII.

[24]Logan to Evarts, Guatemala City, February 1, 1881, No. 147; Logan to Blaine, June 2, July 3, Nos. 187, 201, *ibid*.

[25]On the introduction of American capital into Mexico see David M. Pletcher, "México, campo de inversiones norteamericanos, 1867-1880," *Historia mexicana*, II (April-June 1953), 564-74; and "Mexico Opens the Door to American Capital, 1877-1880," *The Americas*, XVI (July 1959), 1-14. On the border controversy see Robert D. Gregg, *The Influence of Border Troubles on Relations between the United States and Mexico, 1867-1910*, The Johns Hopkins Studies in Historical and Political Science, Series LV, No. 3 (Baltimore, 1937); and Daniel Cosío Villegas, *Estados Unidos contra Porfirio Díaz* (México, 1956).

through a flat jungle, and both countries claimed that jungle. In colonial times the disputed province, Chiapas, had formed part of the captaincy general of Guatemala. Historians could not agree whether the two nations had revolted from Spain separately or under Mexican leadership, whether Chiapas had remained with Mexico willingly or by compulsion, and whether Chiapas included a smaller disputed area, Soconusco, which had asserted its independence from 1825 to 1842. In 1877 the two countries had agreed to appoint a mixed boundary commission, but Mexico, which held the disputed territory, arrested the Guatemalan surveyors for alleged violations of the agreement. The work of the commission broke down, and Guatemala professed to fear aggression from the stronger Mexican army.[26]

When Blaine entered office, he made no immediate public announcement of Central American policy, although he told the Nicaraguan minister that he favored a canal through Nicaragua and a strong unified government in Central America. On May 7, 1881, he instructed Logan at length to do all he could to further such union and to ward off European intervention as being contrary to the Monroe Doctrine. Even before this, Barrios had suggested to Logan that Guatemala cede Soconusco (which she did not possess) to the United States for a naval base. At the same time the Guatemalan minister to the United States, A. Ubico, appealed to Blaine to restrain Mexico, as "the natural protector of the integrity of the Central American territory."[27]

There is no evidence that the Secretary paid any attention to the offer of cession, since territorial gains rarely figured in his

[26]A convenient summary of the Mexican case is Ignacio Mariscal to Philip H. Morgan, Mexico City, July 25, 1881, in U.S., *Foreign Relations, 1881*, pp. 785-91. A convenient summary of the Guatemalan case is Lorenzo Montúfar to Blaine, Washington, November 2, 1881, *ibid.*, pp. 604-9. The most detailed modern account is Daniel Cosío Villegas, *Historia moderna de México* (México, 1955-   ), V, chaps. i-ii (*El Porfiriato: La vida política exterior, Parte primera*).

[27]Macismo Jérez to Dr. Adolfo Zuñiga, Washington, May 17, 1881 (translation) enclosed with Logan to Blaine, Guatemala City, June 24, No. 195, U.S., Despatches, Central America, XVII; Logan to Blaine, May 2, 24, 27, Nos. 177, 179, 183, *ibid.*; Blaine to Logan, May 7, No. 145, U.S., *Foreign Relations, 1881*, pp. 102-4; A. Ubico to Blaine, Washington, June 15, *ibid.*, p. 598. Matías Romero believed that Simón Camacho, a member of the Venezuelan legation, was influential in arousing Blaine's interest in Central American unification. Matías Romero, "Mr. Blaine and the Boundary Question between Mexico and Guatemala," *Journal of the American Geographical Society*, XXIX (1897), 295-96.

plans. However, he could not resist the appeal as protector, and he agreed to tender American good offices. On June 16 he instructed the American minister to Mexico, Philip H. Morgan, to place this offer before the Mexican government—as he disarmingly put it, in the spirit of friendship and not as "self-constituted arbitrator of the destinies of either country."[28]

Soon after sending this note, he received reports that Mexican troops were marching on Guatemala; five days later he sent another and stronger note in which he declared that aggression against Guatemala would be deemed an unfriendly act against the best interests of America. He preceded this statement with a remarkable justification of intervention: "The now established policy of the Government of the United States to refrain from territorial acquisition gives it the right to use its friendly offices in discouragement of any movement on the part of neighboring states which may tend to disturb the balance of power between them." As the disinterested friend of Latin America, the United States had a moral obligation to prevent aggression and filibusters. Blaine ended by announcing that the United States intended to "hold up the republics of Central America in their old strength" and by asking for Mexican cooperation as a matter of her own self-interest. In a confidential note he added that he was concerned lest Guatemala cede her rights in Chiapas or Soconusco to a European Power.[29]

Having asserted American rights in such strong language, Blaine sent no further instructions to Morgan during the period of Garfield's illness but left him to work out his own method of persuading the Mexican government to accept American mediation in the boundary question. The Mexican foreign minister, Ignacio Mariscal, declared that there was nothing for an outsider to arbitrate, since the authority of the joint commission had expired, and since Mexico could not permit examination of her title to the provinces. Courteously he presented Morgan with several thick tomes setting forth the Mexican claim to Chiapas and Soconusco.

[28]Blaine to Morgan, June 16, 1881, No. 138, U.S., *Foreign Relations, 1881* pp. 766-68.
[29]Blaine to Morgan, June 21, 1881, Nos. 142, 143, *ibid.*, pp. 768-70. Blaine did not instruct Morgan to read his long note to Mariscal but informed him that he might do so if circumstances made it necessary.

Morgan began his campaign by explaining to Mariscal cautiously and at great length that the United States, having opposed the French intervention of 1861-1867 in Mexico, would also look with disfavor on a Mexican intervention in Guatemala, which might easily result if the two countries stationed troops near each other. After a few weeks he began to tighten the screws by telling the foreign minister that if his government continued to resist the friendly actions of the United States, it would make further American investment in the country difficult. He asked Mariscal "how it was possible that the expenditure of, I might say, hundreds of millions of dollars of American money in Mexico, giving, as it did, employment to many thousands of its citizens, could be any detriment to the country."[30]

At one point in the conversations, in response to an inquiry by Mariscal, Morgan outlined a procedure which he thought that the State Department would approve, although it went beyond the letter of his instructions. If Mexico and Guatemala would admit the existence of differences between them and submit them to the President of the United States for arbitration, the President would agree to hear the rival cases, much as if Guatemala were the plaintiff and Mexico the defendant in a suit at law. If Mexican title to Chiapas were as solid as Mariscal insisted, the President would undoubtedly rule it beyond arbitration, and the three countries would then name a three-man commission to draw the exact boundary. Mariscal replied that the proposal had merits, provided that the Mexican title to Chiapas were never subject to doubt. The Guatemalan minister to Mexico, Manuel Herrera, thought that his government would accept the loss of Chiapas at the hands of the United States, but he did not make it clear (as Mexico wished) that Guatemala would recognize this in advance of arbitration.

Throughout the conversations rumors circulated that the Mexican government was actually much offended at the Guatemalan appeal for American mediation and would make Guatemala pay for her

---

[30]Morgan's account of his negotiations with Mariscal appears in his dispatches to Blaine of July 12, 19, August 5, 11, 24, 25, September 1, 22, 1881, Nos. 232, 240, 247, 253, 258, 259, 268, 273, U.S., *Foreign Relations, 1881*, pp. 773-78, 784, 794-803, 805, 806-9. Portions of the dispatches of July 12 and August 25 were omitted from *Foreign Relations* and appear in U.S., Despatches, Mexico, LXXIII. The passage quoted appears in U.S., *Foreign Relations, 1881*, p. 807.

that the concession had expired, and the governor of Panama ordered the American warships away from his shores. The two countries ironed out this misunderstanding before Blaine entered office, but on May 12, 1881, Rear Admiral R. H. Wyman, who had inspected the lagoon for the Navy, reported that it was too isolated and the most leeward point in the whole Caribbean: "No place on the isthmus could . . . be less desirable as a coaling station." Little more was heard about Chiriquí.[13]

Shortly before the end of the Hayes administration Secretary Evarts also decided that the time had come to clarify the American-Colombian treaty of 1846 and to strengthen the guarantee. Under his instructions William H. Trescot began negotiations with the Colombian minister, Rafael Santodomingo Vila, in January, 1881. Trescot asked that Colombia give the United States power to approve any future canal concessions or, indeed, any construction work under the existing De Lesseps concession. He also asked for permission for the United States to construct permanent fortifications on Panama and keep a permanent garrison there. Since these terms amounted to an American protectorate over Panama, it is not surprising that Santodomingo Vila refused point-blank and prepared to leave for home. Trescot, however, hurried after him with a revised protocol which said nothing about American approval of canal projects and divided the responsibility for fortifying the isthmus between the two nations. Santodomingo Vila accepted this change and signed the protocol on February 17.[14]

To Evarts half a loaf would have been better than none, but the Colombian government repudiated the protocol, and the Colombian Senate asked the President to abrogate the treaty of 1846. Evarts' diplomacy had misfired, and Colombian opinion had become so anti-American that when Garfield in his inaugural ad-

[13]Mack, *Land Divided*, chap. xxiii. *New York Herald*, January 12, 1882, p. 8; December 6, 1884, p. 3. Unsigned memorandum, July 14, 1886, No. 15, U.S., Reports of the Diplomatic Bureau, VII. Rear Admiral R. H. Wyman to Secretary of the Navy, Hampton Roads, Virginia, May 12, 1881, in U.S., Congress, House, 47th Cong., 1st Sess., 1882, House Executive Doc. 46, pp. 5-6.

[14]Parks, *Colombia and the United States*, pp. 364-68. Drafts and counterdrafts of the protocol, together with Trescot's reports, appear in U.S., *Foreign Relations, 1881*, pp. 361-87. Colombia actually granted the French concession to Lucien N. B. Wyse, who transferred it to the De Lesseps company, but I have called it "the De Lesseps concession" for simplicity.

boldness. In his annual address to the Mexican Congress on September 16, President Manuel González announced that he had sent more troops to the Guatemalan border. This set the whole foreign community in Mexico City to buzzing, and Morgan mildly reproved Mariscal for the "Napoleonic" tone of the message. On September 22 he wrote to Blaine that his conversations with the foreign minister had left him

> . . . more than ever convinced that nothing would prevent a war between the two countries unless a positive position is taken by the United States, and I venture to suggest that unless the government is prepared to announce to the Mexican Government that it will actively, if necessary, preserve the peace, it would be the part of wisdom on our side to leave the matter where it is.

Mere negotiations would not benefit Guatemala, he concluded, and those of the last three months had only injured Mexican-American friendship.[31]

Morgan's advice was sound. If the United States were to assume "the right to use its friendly offices" in Latin-American disputes, as Blaine had announced in his instructions of June 21, it would need more than moral force in reserve. Since Blaine and Garfield had shown no disposition to build up army or navy or to marshal the feeble resources which they possessed, it was apparent that Blaine's pretensions rested solely upon persuasion—or bluff. If he was bluffing, he was unlucky that Garfield's illness and death weakened him at a critical point. If persuasion was his real intention, he began at the wrong end by asserting as fact what he was actually trying to prove.

Meanwhile, Guatemala was making further efforts to obtain American protection. On June 23 President Barrios asked American Minister Logan if the United States would lend Guatemala $2,000,-000 with which to buy a warship and equip troops to cow the nationalists in Nicaragua and Costa Rica. (He did not mention Mexico.)

At the same time, in Washington Guatemalan Minister Ubico presented to Blaine the effusive thanks of his government for the

American offer of mediation and a memorandum proposing American aid in forming a Central American union and an alliance with the resulting united nation. In September the Guatemalan foreign minister, Lorenzo Montúfar, made a special trip to Washington, ostensibly to express Guatemalan hopes for Garfield's recovery but actually to present the Guatemalan case in the border controversy with Mexico. After a series of unrecorded conversations and several long, flattering letters Montúfar ended his campaign on November 21 with a final note in which he predicted that Central America would support Guatemala against Mexican aggression and appealed for American intervention to prevent war.[32]

Montúfar's implication was clear. If the United States wished to see Central America united, she must protect the natural leader of Central America from attack. Blaine now seemed to be in a position where he must choose between Mexico and Guatemala.

[32]Logan to Blaine, Guatemala City, June 15, 24, 1881, Nos. 189, 195, U.S., Despatches, Central America, XVII. Ubico to Blaine, Washington, June 17, 22, 23, October 31, 1881, Notes from Foreign Legations, Guatemala and Salvador, VI, Records of the Department of State (National Archives, Record Group 59). Hereafter such documents will be cited as U.S., Notes from Foreign Legations. Blaine to Ubico, June 21, U.S., Instructions, Guatemala and Salvador, II, 67-68; Lorenzo Montúfar to Blaine, Washington, November 21, U.S., Congress, Senate, 47th Cong., 1st Sess., 1882, Senate Executive Doc. 156, pp. 20-21.

CHAPTER 3

Blaine and the War of the Pacific

A T THE same time that Garfield's energetic secretary of state was developing the American role of patron and protector of Central America, he was extending a similar policy to the west coast of South America, where Chile, Peru, and Bolivia were fighting over another disputed boundary. The War of the Pacific, which began in 1879 and dragged out a tedious existence for four years, did not directly affect American interests, but it seemed to offer the United States an opportunity to enhance its prestige and set a precedent of hemispheric leadership by helping the combatants to restore peace. Blaine undertook what he thought was judicious intervention, but, hampered by incompetent agents and by his own lack of attention to details, he bungled the delicate operation and brought down on himself a storm of criticism in Latin America, Europe, and at home.

*   *   *

The causes of the War of the Pacific went back to the early national history of South America. When the new republics of Chile, Peru, and Bolivia drew their boundaries through the great desert between the Andes and the Pacific coast, everyone thought this desert worthless. It proved, however, to contain immense deposits of guano and nitrates for which farmers, industrialists, and promoters would pay well. Peru, receiving the first big windfall from guano and controlling extensive and accessible nitrate deposits in her province of Tarapacá, could have used her new revenue to increase her military and economic strength; but she wasted her opportunity, while Chile, originally the weaker of the two, managed to develop a stable government and a tight, expanding economy. (Bolivia, dictator-ridden and backward, changed but little and played a minor role at all times.) The immediate causes of the war were a "secret" alliance between Peru

and Bolivia and a quarrel over concessions and taxes in the border provinces. Chile declared war and attacked first but explained that she was acting defensively to forestall a plot by the allies.

Since the centers of population in the three countries were cut off from each other by deserts and mountains, and since both Chile and Peru possessed small but modern navies, it was apparent from the start that the first decisive battles would be fought on the sea. Few, however, even in Chile, expected the action to be so one-sided. Chile's crack small navy set out methodically to blockade and shell the principal ports of southern Peru. Just over six weeks after the beginning of the war one of Peru's two ironclads stuck on a rock and was captured. A few months later the other surrendered after a terrific battle. Chile lost no time in occupying the disputed coastline, and, after a vigorous assault on south-central Peru, her army captured Lima on January 16, 1881. When Garfield and Blaine entered office, it seemed that the War of the Pacific was over except for the mopping-up.

From the beginning Europe took a lively interest in the war, since bankers and promoters of several nations had played a large part in developing the guano and nitrate industries and had floated government loans, especially for Peru. At the same time British merchants and steamship lines did an ever-increasing business in Valparaiso and Santiago, and British shipyards built new warships for the Chilean navy. When the war began, many British investors tended to support the Chilean cause, but British merchants deplored the fighting, and there is no evidence that the Foreign Office contemplated any sort of active intervention.[1] Nevertheless, Anglophobes in the United States saw the war as one more example of British imperialism. One of these was Blaine, who declared after leaving office:

[1] V. G. Kiernan, "Foreign Interests in the War of the Pacific," *Hispanic American Historical Review*, XXXV (1955), 15-19. This is also the conclusion reached in William Freer Beck, "A Comparison of British and United States Relations with Chile, 1879-1883; a Study in Diplomatic History" (Ph.D. dissertation, University of Pittsburgh, 1942), p. 141 *et passim*. On European economic relations with Peru and Chile see Emilio Romero, *Historia económica del Perú* (Buenos Aires, 1950), pp. 407-9; and William H. Wynne, *State Insolvency and Foreign Bondholders* (2 vols.; New Haven, Connecticut, 1951), II, 135-40.

It is a perfect mistake to speak of this as a Chilian war on Peru.
It is an English war on Peru, with Chili [*sic*] as the instrument,
and I take the responsibility of that assertion. Chili would never
have gone into this war one inch but for her backing by English capital. . . .[2]

Before the war had been long under way, both Europe and the
United States were weighing the possibilities of mediation. Twice
during 1879 and 1880 Britain offered to mediate, and on other
occasions Britain and other Powers put out tentative peace feelers
without success. Peru would not accept mediation, and Evarts
discouraged European interference.[3] Meanwhile, the State Department was feeling pressure on all sides to intervene and end
the war, for some Americans were shipping munitions to Peru,
and American residents there had suffered much property damage
from the fighting. Business interests at home, no matter where
their sympathies, concluded that the American government must
"take the initiative in the matter, in the cause of humanity, civilization and trade . . . [and] in view of its protestations concerning the Monroe Doctrine."[4]

American efforts at mediation suffered from two inherent weaknesses of amateur diplomacy: lack of objectivity and lack of
discipline. Most of the ministers whom Hayes, Garfield, and
Arthur sent to the warring states were politicians rather than
professional diplomats; each of them sided with the government
to which he was accredited; and each tended to regard himself
as the chief mediator. Hayes's minister to Peru, Isaac P. Christiancy, was an elderly ex-judge from Michigan, who described
Peru as a capital field for American development but felt somewhat less regard for the country's inhabitants.[5] His colleague in
Chile, Thomas A. Osborn, who was younger and more resilient, ad-

[2]Blaine made this statement in the midst of a heated investigation and may have
oversimplified his earlier feelings while secretary. U.S., Congress, House, 47th
Cong., 1st Sess., 1882, H. Rept. 1790, p. 217. Hereafter cited as U.S., "Chile-Peruvian
Investigation."

[3]See, for example, a statement of his quoted in Millington, *American Diplomacy
and the War of the Pacific*, p. 55.

[4]*Bradstreet's*, II (September 15, 1880), 4. See also *New York Herald*, June 12,
1879. On neutral rights problems see Millington, *American Diplomacy and the
War of the Pacific*, chap. ii.

[5]*Dictionary of American Biography*, IV, 96-97. Isaac P. Christiancy to William
M. Evarts, Lima, January 22, 1881, No. 230; Christiancy to James G. Blaine, May 4,

mired the Chilean war effort and tried to work out some means of making American mediation palatable to the government. Osborn's hopes for American mediation were perhaps not unreasonable, since during 1881 he and the American minister to Argentina, Thomas O. Osborn, succeeded in bringing Chile and Argentina to a peaceful settlement of the Patagonian boundary question.[6]

As the war progressed, however, the likelihood of easy mediation decreased, for the Chilean victories stimulated imperialism in Santiago, and the Peruvian defeats weakened the government in Lima. During October, 1880, Osborn and Christiancy finally managed to bring together six representatives of the belligerents on board the U.S.S. "Lackawanna" in the Bay of Arica to discuss terms. The Chileans demanded the cession of two nitrate provinces, Atacama (Bolivia) and Tarapacá (Peru), temporary occupation of three more Peruvian provinces, and an indemnity of $20,000,000. The Peruvian delegates refused point-blank, and a deadlock developed. Peru and Bolivia then proposed American arbitration, but Osborn cautiously avoided a direct answer, and the conference broke up, a failure.[7]

Evarts was disappointed at the breakdown of negotiations and reproved Osborn for his caution, but the vagueness of the American position was largely due to fundamental disagreements between Osborn and Christiancy. Osborn now believed that the cession of Atacama and Tarapacá was an absolute prerequisite of peace, while Christiancy predicted that territorial cessions would only lead to the partition of Peru among her neighbors.[8] As long

U.S., Congress, Senate, 47th Cong., 1st Sess., 1882, Senate Executive Doc. 79, pp. 434-35, 485-90. Hereafter cited as U.S., "War in South America." A long anti-clerical diatribe, omitted from the second dispatch, may be found in U.S., Despatches, Peru, XXXVI.

[6]*Dictionary of American Biography*, XIV, 70-72. Thomas A. Osborn to Evarts, Santiago, September 9, 1880, No. 164, U.S., "War in South America," pp. 125-26. Since the two Osborns did almost all their negotiating by telegraph, one of them proposed to call the resulting agreement "the wire treaty." Thomas O. Osborn to Evarts, Buenos Aires, April 4, 1881, No. 317, U.S., Despatches, Argentina, XXIII.

[7]Millington, *American Diplomacy and the War of the Pacific*, pp. 70-78. W. R. Sherman, *The Diplomatic and Commercial Relations of the United States and Chile, 1820-1914* (Boston, 1926), pp. 126-27. Barrows, *Evarts*, pp. 373-74.

[8]Evarts to Thomas A. Osborn, December 27, 1880, No. 115; Thomas A. Osborn to Evarts, Santiago, February 24, 1881, No. 195; Christiancy to Evarts, Lima, February 16, No. 242, U.S., "War in South America," pp. 147-48, 151-53, 447-49.

as these two disagreed, it was unlikely that American mediation could succeed.

At the time of Garfield's inauguration the power of the Peruvian dictator, General Nicolás Piérola, was rapidly crumbling as a result of the Chilean capture of Lima, and on March 12, 1881, Francisco García Calderón, a wealthy Peruvian lawyer who enjoyed some Chilean support, proclaimed a new government in central Peru. Blaine's first problem would be to determine whether to recognize this new government. Evarts' minister, Christiancy had little confidence in García Calderón's ability to pull the country together, and on May 4 he even suggested to Blaine that the nation's only hope lay in an American protectorate or in outright annexation to the United States.[9]

Before Blaine received Christiancy's advice, he had already made up his mind to recognize the government of García Calderón. Early in May he informally received García Calderón's minister J. F. Elmore, who smoothly assured him that the new government would re-establish law and order, negotiate a peace treaty, and look to the United States for advice and support. Blaine then told Christiancy that he might recognize García Calderón if he found the government "supported by the character and intelligence of Peru." Puzzled by Blaine's vague language and realizing that the Pierolistas still controlled northern Peru, Christiancy went so far as to call in the rest of the diplomatic corps for advice. (They advised against *de facto* recognition.) Learning, however, that Blaine had received Elmore, Christiancy soon swallowed his doubt and recognized García Calderón, placing the responsibility on his chief.[10]

[9]Christiancy to Blaine, Lima, May 4, 1881, *ibid.*, pp. 485-90. See also Christiancy to Blaine, March 21, No. 262, U.S., Despatches, Peru, XXXV.

[10]J. F. Elmore to Blaine, Washington, May 4, 1881; Blaine to Christiancy, May 9, No. 143, U.S., "War in South America," pp. 482-84, 495. Christiancy to Blaine, Lima, June 16, 21, 28, Nos. 319, 320, 322, *ibid.*, pp. 501-5. The Chilean minister to the United States, Marcial Martínez, an eminent lawyer without diplomatic experience, did not even know of Elmore's arrival until after the recognition. He reported that Blaine seemed to have little real interest in Peru. Francisco A. Encina, *Historia de Chile desde la prehistoria hasta 1891* (20 vols.; Santiago de Chile, 1948-1956), XVII, 400-401. Gonzalo Bulnes, *Historia de la guerra del Pacífico* (3 vols; Santiago de Chile, 1955), III, 46-47.

During May, Blaine decided to remove Osborn and Christiancy, but in their place he appointed two others who were inferior in almost every way. At Garfield's request Blaine sent to Santiago General Hugh J. Kilpatrick, a spirited cavalry leader who had already served three years as minister to Chile during the 1860's. He shared Osborn's Chilean sympathies without his discrimination, and his wife, acquired during his previous ministership, was the niece of the Archbishop of Santiago. Also, Kilpatrick soon contracted Bright's disease and became too ill to attend to his duties. Since his legation had no secretary, he had to depend on his wife and her Chilean friends for help in writing his official correspondence, so that the Chilean government was probably informed of everything that he did or said.[11]

The new minister to Peru, Stephen J. Hurlbut, had been, like Kilpatrick, a flashy general in the Civil War. During his command of occupation forces in Louisiana after the war he had made a reputation for drunkenness, had handled the local government roughly, and had been convicted for taking a bribe. He became first commander of the Grand Army of the Republic, then a hack Republican politician in Illinois, and finally in 1880, managed Blaine's campaign for nomination in the Middle West. Along the way he served as minister to Colombia for three years, which was enough time to give him the reputation, if not the training, of an expert in Latin-American politics. Shortly after Garfield's inauguration Hurlbut predicted to a Chicago reporter that Blaine would abandon "the higgle-haggling that so distinguished Mr. Evarts, whose namby-pambyism and inexcusable want of vim and manliness have lost to the United States numberless opportunities." The War of the Pacific, Hurlbut added, gave the American government "a magnificent opportunity" to intervene "in such a way as to compel an honorable peace, thus securing lasting National prestige and commercial superiority for us."[12]

[11]*Dictionary of American Biography*, X, 374-75. *New York Tribune*, May 19, 1881, p. 2. In recognition of his ability, Osborn was transferred to the Brazilian legation. Beck, "British and United States Relations with Chile," p. 48.

[12]The interview was originally reported by the Chicago correspondent of the Louisville *Courier-Journal*. Unidentified newspaper clipping, Garfield Collection, CXXXV, Pt. 2. See also *Dictionary of American Biography*, IX, 425-26, and *New York Tribune*, May 19, 1881, p. 2.

Blaine's written instructions to his new appointees were mild enough. To Kilpatrick he pointed out that since American "friendly intervention" would probably not be acceptable to Chile, there was no point in suffering the embarrassment of a refusal, but that the United States would always be ready to extend its good offices. On the subject of territorial annexations he chose his words carefully:

> While the United States does not pretend to express an opinion whether or not such an annexation of territory is a necessary consequence of this war, it believes that it would be more honorable to the Chilian Government, more conducive to the security of a permanent peace, and more in consonance with those principles which are professed by all the republics of America, that such territorial changes should be avoided as far as possible; that they should never be the result of mere force, but, if necessary, should be decided and tempered by full and equal discussion between all the powers whose people and whose national interests are involved.

He would be "exceedingly gratified" if Kilpatrick could influence Chile to restore constitutional government in Peru and postpone territorial settlements.[13]

Blaine's instructions to Hurlbut were quite consistent with these sentiments. He hoped that Hurlbut could impress on any Chilean officials he might meet that a liberal, considerate policy would probably be more permanent, but he did not authorize him to stand out against territorial annexations:

> The United States cannot refuse to recognize the rights which the Chilian Government has acquired by the successes of the war, and it may be that a cession of territory will be the necessary price to be paid for peace. It would seem to be injudicious for Peru to declare that under no circumstances could the loss of territory be accepted as the result of negotiation. . . . As far as the influence of the United States will go in Chili, it will be exerted to induce the Chilian Government to consent that the question of the cession of territory should be the subject of negotiation and not the condition precedent upon which alone negotiation shall commence. If you can aid the Govern-

[13]Blaine to Hugh J. Kilpatrick, June 15, 1881, No. 2, U.S., "War in South America," pp. 157-59.

ment of Peru in securing such a result, you will have rendered the service which seems most pressing.[14]

lvey A. Adee later summed up the instructions tersely. The dispatch, he said, "distinctly admits Chile's right, as victor, to insist n the cession of territory, but deprecates such a course."[15]

It would have been difficult for Hurlbut to justify an aggressive olicy with these cautious words alone. From the beginning his riends whispered that Blaine had added much bolder oral instructions to make clear to Chile that the United States would not tolerte any cessions, and that she must end the war if Peru offered a cash demnity. At the Congressional investigation in the following pring Hurlbut's half-brother, William Henry Hurlbert, testified hat the Minister had told him

> . . . that substantially he was to have elastic powers to carry out and give effect to the policy . . . of bringing about peace on the west coast by the exercise, in all legitimate and effectual ways, of American influence, . . . to induce the republics to cease fighting and to prevent the spoliation of Peruvian territory and the dismemberment of Peru.

laine was also rumored to have written, "Go it, Steve!" on the argin of one of his dispatches, but he flatly denied that he had one this, or that he had given his minister any verbal instructions.[16] n any case, a hothead like Hurlbut would not have needed more han a few unguarded words to convince him that the written hrases were only for show. It is clear that when he left the United tates he was determined to prevent the cession of the nitrate rovinces if he could.[17]

Hurlbut sailed from New York on July 2, the day Garfield was hot. When he arrived in Lima, he found the Peruvian coast and he disputed provinces entirely in the hands of the Chileans, but e established cordial relations with García Calderón, whom he eclared to be supported by all people of quality. The Peruvians

[14]Blaine to Stephen J. Hurlbut, June 15, 1881, No. 2, *ibid.*, pp. 500-501.
[15]Memorandum by Alvey A. Adee, December 29, 1881, No. 74, U.S., Reports of he Diplomatic Bureau, V.
[16]*Cincinnati Daily Gazette*, December 19, 1881, p. 1. U.S., "Chile-Peruvian vestigation," pp. 133-34, 178, 181, 197, 230.
[17]Hurlbut to Blaine, New York, June 30, 1881, U.S., Despatches, Peru, XXXVI. ee also U.S., "War in South America," pp. 507-8.

would not hear of territorial cessions, and since, according to
Hurlbut, Peru could and would pay a money indemnity, he felt
that the United States ought not to permit forcible annexation
He wrote to Blaine that he would not interfere with the peace
negotiations then going on "unless it shall be apparent that the
purpose is to crush out the national life of Peru. In that case
shall calmly and strongly protest against such a course, and in
dicate in distinct terms that such action does not at all conform
to the wishes of the United States." He then urged Blaine to tele
graph approval or disapproval of his views and added that he would
stall the negotiations as long as possible, in order to give the State
Department time for deliberation.[18]

Long before this dispatch could have reached Washington, Hurl
but decided to enter his calm and strong protest. On August 2,
he paid a courtesy visit to the Chilean admiral in command
Patricio Lynch, and conversed with him amicably about American
policy toward the war. Next day he summarized the conversation
in a stern memorandum. While the United States recognized the
laws of war, declared Hurlbut, it did not approve of "territoria
aggrandizement" or of "the violent dismemberment of a nation'
except in extreme cases. Peru ought to have an opportunity to
pay a cash indemnity; the transfer of territory as a *sine qua non*
of peace "would meet with decided disfavor on the part of th
United States"; and the seizure of the nitrate provinces "would
justly be regarded, by other nations, as evidence that Chile had
entered upon the path of aggression and conquest."[19] Except in
language and tone, Hurlbut's sentiments were roughly the senti
ments of his instructions, but in diplomacy language and tone ar
as important as substance. Furthermore, neither his instruction
nor ordinary diplomatic procedure authorized him to exchang
official written communications of this sort with the Chilea
authorities.

During the next month Hurlbut added to his indiscretions. O

[18]Hurlbut to Blaine, Lima, August 10, 17, 24, 1881, Nos. 2, 5, 6, *ibid.*, pp. 510-1
[19]Hurlbut to Blaine, Lima, August 27, 1881, No. 8, *ibid.*, pp. 515-17. Accordin
to Lynch, Hurlbut assured him verbally that the United States recognized th
Chilean right of annexation. Chile, *Memoria que el Contra-almirante D. Patric
Lynch, jeneral en jefe del ejército de operaciones en el Norte del Perú presen
al Supremo Gobierno de Chile* (Lima, 1882), pp. 104-7.

receiving a letter from Piérola's foreign minister, who urged him to abandon García Calderón and support the "constitutionally proclaimed" president, he replied bluntly that Piérola's seizure of power had been "a crime against liberty," his method of rule "simple tyranny, autocratic and despotic," and his decrees against García Calderón's supporters "inhuman and barbarous." He ended with an appeal to all Peruvians to unite and save their country from ruin. Soon after this Hurlbut composed and privately circulated a memorial to the "notables of Lima," assuring them that the United States favored peace and opposed "all dismemberment of Peru, except with the free and full consent of the nation."[20] To cap the climax, on September 20 he went entirely beyond the most strained interpretation of his written instructions and negotiated an agreement with García Calderón under which Peru would grant to the United States a coaling station on the Bay of Chimbote. Hurlbut himself was to receive a partly built railroad to the interior which he might transfer to American promoters.[21] Chile must not dismember Peru, but an American sphere of influence was quite another matter!

At the prospect of outside aid, the followers of García Calderón took heart, and some of the rival *caudillos* joined his forces, while European diplomats in Lima aggravated the effect of Hurlbut's pronouncements with even more exaggerated rumors of American designs.[22] In Santiago the British minister to Chile at first assumed that Hurlbut had exceeded his instructions, but the minister soon reported to London that large financial interests in New York were probably influencing American policy. Naturally, the news

[20]Hurlbut to Blaine, Lima, September 13, 1881, No. 11, U.S., *Foreign Relations, 1881*, pp. 928-31. Since Hurlbut did not report his memorial to the "notables," some disagreement has arisen as to its date. Millington places its composition in late November, but two Chilean historians show it to have been circulated two months earlier in an effort to counteract European influence in Lima and strengthen García Calderón. Millington, *American Diplomacy and the War of the Pacific*, p. 93. Encina, *Historia de Chile*, XVIII, 12-13. Bulnes, *Guerra del Pacífico*, III, 70-72.

[21]Hurlbut to Blaine, Lima, October 5, 1881, No. 19, U.S., *Foreign Relations, 1881*, pp. 938-39.

[22]The British minister, Sir Spencer St. John, circulated the false text of a treaty between Peru and the United States providing for the outright cession of Chimbote Bay and much adjacent territory. Hurlbut forced him to admit that he had done it as a practical joke. Hurlbut to Blaine, Lima, December 7, 11, Nos. 32, 33, U.S., "War in South America," pp. 579-83.

of Hurlbut's actions wrecked Kilpatrick's efforts toward friendship with the Chilean government. After several preliminary conversations the secretary of state had given him a reluctant but fairly binding promise that Chile would support the government of García Calderón and would give Peru time to offer a cash indemnity before demanding territorial cession. Whether the Chilean government would have carried out this promise in any case, Hurlbut's actions gave its members a welcome excuse to suspect Kilpatrick's sincerity, and Chile began to prepare for war.

On September 11 the government at Santiago received the alarming news that Hurlbut had asked the Argentine government to send an accredited minister to Peru. Considering the precarious state of Argentine-Chilean relations, the request could only foreshadow further defiance. Pressed by the Chilean foreign minister for information, the unhappy Kilpatrick, already fatally ill, explained away Hurlbut's statements as unofficial and cited Blaine's promise of good offices. "The Government of the United States," he declared, "has not at any time interfered officiously [i.e., informally] in the public affairs of other countries."[23]

Before Kilpatrick could deliver these dubious reassurances, Chile had acted. During the last week of September Admiral Lynch seized García Calderón's treasury and ordered him to surrender authority over that part of Peru occupied by Chilean troops. Hurlbut, outraged at the Chilean presumption, hinted that the British and French ministers were responsible and suggested to Blaine that the time had come for the United States to assert its hemispheric leadership and order Chile to accept American arbitration and a cash indemnity. When Lynch went one step further on November 6 and sent García Calderón and his foreign minister to Santiago under arrest, Hurlbut chose to regard this as a deliberate affront to the United States. He told the State Department that he would recognize the temporary authority of Vice-President Isidro Montero, then in the interior.[24]

[23]Beck, "British and United States Relations with Chile," p. 97. Kilpatrick to Blaine, Santiago, August 15, 1881, No. 3; Kilpatrick to José M. Balmaceda, October 8, enclosed with Kilpatrick to Blaine, October 14, No. 8; Marcial Martínez to Blaine, Washington, October 24, 27, 28, U.S., "War in South America," pp. 160-67.
[24]Hurlbut to Blaine, Lima, October 4, 13, 26, 31, November 9, 1881, Nos. 16, 20, 23, 24, 26, ibid., pp. 526-30, 532-33, 537-39, 545-47, 560-61.

Thus by the autumn of 1881 Hurlbut had practically committed the United States to defying Chilean plans to annex Tarapacá, but without the strength to enforce this defiance. Although American warships were on hand at Callao to observe events, it was doubtful that their wooden hulls and smooth-bored guns could match the modern Chilean ironclads. If Blaine wished to withdraw to a more moderate diplomatic position he would have to act fast. In such a withdrawal he knew that he would face renewed danger of European interference, for on August 10 President Jules Grévy of France had proposed joint mediation by France, England, and the United States to end the war, recognizing the principle that Chile was entitled to some sort of indemnity. Blaine was quick to reply that joint intervention would be against the best interests of the United States. Grévy subsided for the moment, but the French suggestion undoubtedly heightened the urgency of the Chile-Peruvian question.[25]

* * *

As the United States learned of Hurlbut's brash diplomacy, there began to appear disquieting rumors that his defense of Peruvian territorial integrity rested on more than sympathy and the desire to advance American leadership in the hemisphere. The disputed provinces contained guano and nitrates worth perhaps hundreds of millions of dollars. All three governments, but especially Peru, had borrowed heavily in the past from foreign banking houses. Might this not mean claims, lawsuits, and financial deals? The idea would occur readily to a generation which remembered "Black Friday," the Crédit Mobilier investigation, and the attempt to annex Santo Domingo. During the first two years of the war several groups of claimants did, indeed, hire influential Americans to urge their cases upon the United States government in the hope of diplomatic support.

One such claimant was a French organization, the Société Générale de Crédit Industriel et Commercial, usually called the Crédit Industriel. This company represented holders of Peruvian government bonds in Europe and a few in the United States, and it

[25]Levi P. Morton to Blaine, Paris, August 11, 1881, No. 6; Blaine to Morton, September 5, No. 30, U. S., *Foreign Relations, 1881*, pp. 420-21, 426-27.

proposed to market guano and nitrates in Europe to pay off the bonds and furnish an income to Peru. Early in 1881 two European agents of the company and Robert E. Randall, a brother of the speaker of the House of Representatives, presented a plan to Evarts. The Crédit Industriel would market enough guano and nitrates to pay an indemnity of £550,000 a year to Chile, an income of £550,000 a year to Peru, and £1,200,000 a year to the bond-holders. All that it needed was an American protectorate to prevent Chile from keeping the nitrate provinces. Evarts apparently approved of the financial aspects of the plan, but he did no more than send a copy of it to Christiancy for his information.[26]

Meanwhile, Randall obtained the services of a New York banking house, Morton, Bliss and Company, which became agent for the sale of guano and nitrates at a generous commission of 5 per cent. Levi P. Morton, a partner of the firm, was one of the leading Republican Stalwarts. Before the contract was completed, Garfield named him minister to France, a post where he could be of considerable service to the Crédit Industriel. Morton denied that there was any connection between the appointment and the contract, or that he used his official position in any way for the company. His denials were probably genuine, but the firm should have refused the agency in view of his new assignment.[27]

There are two completely contradictory accounts of Blaine's

[26]Charles de Montferrand and Francisco P. Suárez to Evarts, Washington, February 1, 1881, William M. Evarts Papers, XXIX (Library of Congress). U. S., "Chile-Peruvian Investigation," pp. 322, 386-87. Evarts to Christiancy, February 17, 1881, No. 129, U. S., "War in South America," pp. 449-52. Millington, *American Diplomacy and the War of the Pacific*, pp. 98-99. M. H. Guillaume to Frederick T. Frelinghuysen, Paris, June 30, 1882, Miscellaneous Letters, Records of the Department of State (National Archives, Record Group 59). Hereafter cited as U. S., Miscellaneous Letters. Cited in Beck, "British and United States Relations with Chile," pp. 92-96.

[27]U. S., "Chile-Peruvian Investigation," pp. 304-21. Levi P. Morton to Frederick T. Frelinghuysen, Paris, March 14, 1882 (telegram), U. S., Despatches, France, XC. Before being appointed minister to France, Morton was offered the Navy Department in Garfield's cabinet but declined it at the urging of Roscoe Conkling. Morton's partner was unhappy at his being sent to France, as he thought that the Navy would have given Morton more prestige and better served the firm's interests. George Bliss to Morton, New York, March 3, 1881, Levi P. Morton Papers (New York Public Library). See also Frelinghuysen to C. G. Williams (Chairman of House Foreign Affairs Committee), March 15, 1882, Report Book, XIV, 407-10, Records of the Department of State (National Archives, Record Group 59). Hereafter cited as U. S., Report Book.

relations with the Crédit Industriel. Randall declared that he and his colleagues had placed the company's old offer before Blaine: if the United States would assume a protectorate over Peru and thereby guarantee the security of the company's interests, the Crédit Industriel would make it possible for Peru to pay a cash indemnity and avoid both bankruptcy and territorial cessions. Blaine, he said, thought the idea perfectly feasible. Randall and the Peruvian minister, J. F. Elmore, told of a conversation with Blaine and Hurlbut on June 27, five days before Hurlbut sailed for his post, at which they agreed on a policy of "preserving to Peru her *old boundaries*' (Mr. Blaine's own words), through the political action of the United States of America, aided by the financial action of the Crédit Industriel of France."[28]

For his part, Blaine denied that he had ever expressed the slightest approval of this plan. Later, when the House of Representatives investigated the Peruvian imbroglio, he admitted that Elmore and Randall might have conversed with him before Hurlbut's departure, but he insisted that he had never considered American intervention on behalf of the Crédit Industriel.[29] Whatever the group may have said in informal conversation about the company's plan and the Peruvian debt, Blaine's written instructions to Hurlbut on foreign claims were once again perfectly proper. On June 15 he informed him as follows:

> As you are aware, more than one proposition has been submitted to the consideration of this government looking to a friendly intervention by which Peru might be enabled to meet the conditions which would probably be imposed. Circumstances do not seem at present opportune for such action; but if, upon full knowledge of the condition of Peru, you can inform this government that Peru can devise and carry into practical effect a plan by which all the reasonable conditions of Chili can be met without sacrificing the integrity of Peruvian territory, the Government of the United States would be willing to offer its good offices towards the execution of such a project.[30]

[28]U. S., "Chile-Peruvian Investigation," pp. 326-27, 374-75.
[29]*Ibid.,* pp. 227, 336, 347, 352, 380-82.
[30]Blaine to Hurlbut, June 15, 1881, No. 2, U. S., "War in South America," p. 501. In testifying before the House Committee, William H. Trescot admitted that he had written much of the dispatch and with the Crédit Industriel project in mind. U. S., "Chile-Peruvian Investigation," pp. 359-61.

As far as the written records indicate, Hurlbut received no further instructions about the Crédit Industriel during the summer of 1881.

The phrase "more than one proposition" in Blaine's note of June 15 undoubtedly referred as well to the claim of the Landreau brothers for a share of $400,000,000 worth of guano which they alleged to have discovered some twenty years before under contract with the Peruvian government. One of the brothers, J. C. Landreau, who said that he was a naturalized American citizen, had appealed to the Grant administration for aid; after rather casual inspection of his claim, the State Department and the House of Representatives had pronounced it valid. Blaine felt bound by these actions, and on August 4 he told Hurlbut to call the attention of the Peruvian government to the Landreau claim so that Peru might place it before an impartial tribunal and protect Landreau's rights in case his guano deposits were ceded to Chile.[31] Blaine thus went beyond his predecessors in supporting the Landreau claim and committed himself to a dubious interpretation of Peruvian law.

The project which eventually embarrassed Blaine most of all in his dealings with Peru and Chile was more fantastic than either of these. It was based on the claim of Alexandre Cochet, a Frenchman who had conducted scientific tests about 1840 to prove the fertilizing value of guano. Appealing to a Peruvian law which promised to anyone discovering concealed government property one-third of the amount discovered, Cochet had vainly insisted that he was entitled to one-third of the nation's guano. Early in 1881 an American organization, calling itself the "Peruvian Company," issued a prospectus declaring that it had acquired this claim from Cochet's illegitimate son and that it would ask damages of Peru totaling $900,000,000. Whether it collected this amount, it proposed to open up to American enterprise "by far the richest country on the globe, now almost a waste."[32]

Grandiose speculations like this were part of America's growing pains through much of its history. However, the president of

[31]*Ibid.*, pp. v-vi, x-xiii, 185, 186, 291. Blaine to Hurlbut, August 4, 1881, No. 7, U. S., "War in South America," pp. 508-9, 632-33.

[32]A prospectus of the Peruvian Company, dated May 20, 1881, appears *ibid.*, pp. 634-78. Another, dated December 1, appears in U. S., "Chile-Peruvian Investigation," pp. 166-76. On the origins of the Cochet claim see *ibid.*, pp. iv-v. The Peruvian law in question was intended to refer to suppressed convents.

the Peruvian Company displayed such an unusual amount of shrewdness and "cheek" that he involved the whole Garfield administration in a mass of rumors and contradictions which no one has ever untangled. This man, Jacob R. Shipherd, was a true denizen of the Gilded Age—a minister turned shady promoter. Shipherd was a nephew of the founder of Oberlin College, which graduated him in the Class of 1862. At the end of the Civil War he became a missionary among the freed Negroes of the South, then pastor of Plymouth Congregational Church in Chicago and publisher of *The Advocate*. From the ministry he went into the real estate business and was admitted to the New York bar in 1878. Short, stout, with auburn hair and a full beard, Shipherd was alert, talkative, and very sure of himself.[33] In his later appearances before a House investigating committee he never lost his temper or dropped his courteous manner, while he cheerfully led his questioners into a maze of inconsistencies.

At that time Shipherd said that the Cochet claim had come to his attention during March, 1881, in the ordinary course of business. When he realized its potentialities, he began to collect prominent men, mostly Stalwarts, who could help him to attract money. Among these were George S. Boutwell, formerly secretary of the treasury under Grant, who became legal counsel for the company, ex-Senator William W. Eaton, and William H. Robertson, the newly-appointed collector of the New York Customs. Shipherd said that the members of the company had considered asking Grant himself to be president but decided against it after Grant began to quarrel with the Garfield administration over patronage. However, he added, Grant approved the project and did various little favors for the company.[34]

If one believes Shipherd's testimony at the House investigation (a difficult task, since other witnesses contradicted him at nearly every point), he established similarly close connections with Blaine.

[33]Robert Samuel Fletcher, *A History of Oberlin College from its Foundation through the Civil War* (2 vols.; Oberlin, Ohio, 1943), II, 910-12, 914. *Washington Post*, March 23, 1882, p. 1. *New York Tribune*, March 16, p. 1.
[34]U. S., "Chile-Peruvian Investigation," pp. 39-41, 45, 46, 52, 68, 69, 102-4, 107, 126-28. Shipherd listed over three dozen names of individuals and firms with whom he was or intended to be "in confidential negotiation." Many of these at once denied any connection.

"Shipherd," he had Blaine say on one occasion, "you can trade with those fellows in 24 hours. You have got exactly what they have not got and what they absolutely need—an American basis on which you have a right to ask for the interference of the American Government." Later, when Shipherd became restive at Chile's resistance, Blaine reassured him, "Now, if you will just be patient, Shipherd, in a little while Martínez [the Chilean minister] will drop into your lap like a ripe apple. See if he doesn't." The promoter admitted that Blaine never indicated that he expected to profit personally from the venture, but until mid-November, insisted Shipherd, he never wavered in his support.[35]

Although Shipherd always referred to Blaine courteously, he made it clear throughout his testimony that he considered Hurlbut "most emphatically" purchasable: "I dealt with him as I would with a man who was a recognized criminal." Having lived in Hurlbut's home state for years, he knew the politician's unsavory reputation. As soon as he learned of Hurlbut's appointment in May, he had a "satisfactory" conference with him, and on June 2 he wrote to offer him $250,000 of company stock, to be paid for at his convenience. "I . . . never intended to seek to influence him to do anything for us officially," Shipherd explained to the committee, "but only to prevent him from doing something against us."[36]

As in the case of the Crédit Industriel, Blaine contradicted virtually everything which Shipherd said about his relations with the State Department. He declared that he had never heard of Shipherd before July 25. On that day the two had a brief interview, and Shipherd described his company and the Cochet claim. After that Blaine did not hear of him again until October. Blaine's opinion of Shipherd was simple: "I do not consider the man responsible. Falsehood with him is an employment and perjury is a pastime."[37]

Hurlbut, too, denied any improper connections with Shipherd,

[35]*Ibid.*, pp. 32-33, 67, 85-86, 88-89, 94-95, 123-24, 132-33.

[36]*Ibid.*, pp. 30-31, 40, 64, 83, 100-101. For the note offering Hurlbut the stock and the House committee's interpretation thereof see *ibid.*, p. ix.

[37]*Ibid.*, pp. 188, 189, 200. Some of Blaine's testimony was supported by letters from Henry W. Blair, Boutwell, and other men whom Shipherd had named as supporters of the project. *Ibid.*, pp. 194-98.

whom he called "a curious mixture of the knave and the fool, with a decided preponderance of the former," but he neglected to inform the State Department of Shipherd's letter of June 2, offering him company stock, until he realized late in October that it might cause trouble. He also made one false move which may be traced to his association with Shipherd. During August Shipherd prevailed upon the Venezuelan minister to the United States, Simón Camacho, to write a letter to a Peruvian friend close to President García Calderón, advising him to recognize the Cochet and Landreau claims and rely on the powerful protection of the United States:

> I am able to tell you, on the highest authority, that the Department of State has long ago notified Chili in the plainest words that she will not be permitted to take any territory from Peru or Bolivia, except it be found that there is no other possible way of securing her war indemnity . . . [and] that no cession of territory or property by Peru will be permitted until the Cochet and Landreau claims have first been provided for.[38]

Hurlbut delivered this letter (although not the supporting documents) and thereby placed an implicit seal of endorsement on the rumors which it contained. Even without any official status the letter could only have stimulated Peruvian hopes and Chilean suspicions, coming as it did at the time of Hurlbut's other indiscretions.

In his covering letter with the Camacho note Shipherd made further grandiose statements about his intentions and associates which apparently aroused Hurlbut's suspicions, for on September 14 he sent Blaine an enclosure from this letter and added: "As at present I have no faith whatsoever in the 'Peruvian Company,' not much in Mr. J. R. Shipherd, and am wholly in the dark as to the honesty or value and extent of the Cochet claim. If half of his statement is true, and the United States assumes charge of the claim, we should own Peru by a mortgage which can never

[38]Simón Camacho to Manuel Arizola, New York, August 20, 1881, U. S., Congress, House, 47th Cong., 1st Sess., 1882, House Executive Doc. 68, pp. 19-23. See also U. S., "Chile-Peruvian Investigation," p. 273.

be paid."[39] Not long after this, however, he negotiated the agreement for a naval base at Chimbote Bay. Presumably if the United States were to own Peru, he might as well make preparations.

By late September, when Garfield died, American diplomacy in the War of the Pacific was getting out of control. The contradictory advice which Hurlbut and Kilpatrick had given at Lima and Santiago, respectively, had encouraged Peruvian resistance and Chilean intransigence, rather than promoting a settlement. In particular, Hurlbut's indiscreet pronouncements had aroused general bewilderment and suspicion as to American intentions. At one side representatives of the Crédit Industriel and the Peruvian Company waited to see what morsels they could rescue from the melee, but their influence cannot be precisely determined, for, although Hurlbut's relations with Shipherd have a dubious smell, the promoter's evidence against Blaine is totally unsupported.

The presumption that Blaine was innocent of collusion, however, does not absolve him from considerable responsibility for the failure of American diplomacy in the War of the Pacific. In Hurlbut he had chosen a minister completely unsuitable for the delicate assignment of persuasion and consolation. Hurlbut's character was so well known that, no matter what were Blaine's written instructions, one might well suspect the Secretary of having chosen Hurlbut deliberately to bluff Chile away from territorial annexations. Having appointed such an erratic minister, Blaine should have watched him carefully, but he seems to have paid little heed to dispatches from Peru during most of August and September. To be sure, he was following a similar laissez-faire policy toward Minister Philip H. Morgan in the Mexico-Guatemalan question, but if he thought Hurlbut as reliable as Morgan, he was a poor judge of men indeed.

[39] Jacob R. Shipherd to Hurlbut, August 19, 1881, U.S., Congress, House, 47th Cong., 1st Sess., 1882, House Executive Doc. 68, pp. 17-19. Hurlbut to Blaine, Lima, September 14, No. 12, with enclosure, U.S., "War in South America," p. 522.

Chapter 4

The Repudiation of Blaine

Since James G. Blaine had spent nearly half a lifetime in politics, weighing and maneuvering members of both parties, it is unlikely that misjudgment of Hurlbut explains his inattention to Peruvian affairs during the late summer of 1881. Throughout August and September the decline and death of President Garfield overshadowed all diplomatic developments. Equally uncertain about the future and about the constitutional authority of a leaderless government, all Cabinet officers confined themselves as much as they could to routine business while the President lay ill. As a result, when Arthur entered the White House and Blaine came to consider his imminent retirement from the State Department, American foreign policy was a mass of loose ends and unanswered questions. Blaine's efforts to tie up these loose ends and redirect that foreign policy during his last weeks in office form the first climax in the history of the new Republican expansionism of the early 1880's.

* * *

At Garfield's death reformers and moderates looked forward unhappily to an orgy of spoils politics under "Chet" Arthur, who was known primarily for his administration of the nation's largest "pork barrel," the New York Customs. Arthur, however, was no grimy ward heeler: handsome and portly, over six feet tall, with wavy hair and long sideburns, he cut an elegant and dignified figure, somewhat given to procrastination. Senator Thomas C. Platt once wrote of him: "Though 'one of the boys' when with 'the boys' he never lost his poise. He possessed the rare faculty of adapting himself to conditions, that made him a good 'mixer'. . . . He would have proved a most excellent Secretary of State or Ambassador to the Court of St. James['s]." His past connection with the New York Customs caused some observers to expect that he would pay more attention to American shipping interests than

his predecessors, and some even suspected him to be a free trader.[1]

Many friends and enemies also assumed that former President Grant, the patron saint of the Stalwarts, would wield strong influence over patronage and possibly foreign affairs. During Hayes's administration Grant had taken a leisurely trip around the world, refurbishing his reputation with foreign applause and broadening his horizons. In particular, the Far East had impressed him as an area in which American influence ought to be expanded. After his defeat in the Republican nominating convention of 1880 he had founded the banking firm of Grant and Ward and allowed himself to become connected with several business ventures having a flavor of American economic imperialism—among them the Nicaragua canal and a railroad in southern Mexico. "Grant is now in the financial vortex," wrote a journalist in August, 1881. "He haunts Wall-street, although not as a general speculator, talks stock and Mexican railroad prospects continually, has become brusque in manner, more dashing in dress and more talkative than ever before."[2]

Despite general expectations, the new President did not immediately surround himself with his friends or with followers of Grant but kept Garfield's cabinet intact for two months. As soon as Arthur had taken the oath of office on September 22, he held a full meeting of the Cabinet and asked each member to remain in office until after the opening of Congress in December. On October 13, Blaine offered to step down, but Arthur repeated his request, and there are some indications that he would have been happy to keep Blaine in the State Department indefinitely for the sake of party unity.[3] However, it was becoming clear to the

---

[1]Thomas C. Platt, *The Autobiography of Thomas Collier Platt* (New York, 1910), pp. 182-83. *The American Protectionist*, I (October 15, 1881), 461. *Washington Post*, October 11, p. 2.

[2]*Ibid.*, August 23, 1881, p. 2. William B. Hesseltine, *Ulysses S. Grant, Politician* (New York, 1935), pp. 430 ff. Adam Badeau, *Grant in Peace: From Appomattox to Mount MacGregor* (Hartford, Connecticut, 1887), pp. 320-21.

[3]*New York Tribune*, December 29, 1881, p. 1. James G. Blaine to Chester A. Arthur, Washington, October 13, 1881 (draft), Blaine Papers (Library of Congress). *The American*, II (October 1, 1881), 389. New York *World*, November 14, 1881. Blaine and Arthur were more friendly than most Half-Breeds and Stalwarts, partly because Blaine had defended Arthur in the Senate when he was under attack over scandals in the New York Customs. Muzzey, *Blaine*, p. 265.

ambitious Secretary that the longer he remained, the less were his chances of resuming leadership. His faithful lieutenant, Whitelaw Reid, wrote to him, calling him "the residuary legatee" of Garfield's popularity and advising him to retire to Maine, take care of his health, and mend his political fences.[4]

Arthur's eventual choice for secretary of state was thoroughly orthodox by the standards of the day but undistinguished—a Republican "party-liner" who had contacts with Congress, few enemies, and no experience in foreign affairs. Frederick T. Frelinghuysen, the scion of a distinguished New Jersey family of ministers, teachers, and lawyers, had entered Republican politics at the beginning of the Civil War and sat in the Senate through most of the Reconstruction period, serving his party dependably on the joint committee which decided the disputed election of 1876. Surprisingly, he had declined the post of minister to Britain in 1870—according to report, because he felt that his background in diplomacy was unequal to the complexities of Anglo-American relations. At first Arthur thought of him for the position of attorney general, but in the last week of October he offered him the State Department. Frelinghuysen hesitated for a time because of ill health, but in mid-November he accepted the appointment.[5]

After the vagaries of Blaine the appointment brought a great sigh of relief from Stalwarts, moderates, and respectable Republicans in general. "Purest character . . . conceded ability . . . experience . . . conservative temperament . . . urbane manners . . ." burbled *Harper's Weekly*. However, some sarcasm greeted the new secretary, who was "understood to hold that the American Eagle should not strain his naturally fine voice by shrill and prolonged screaming on small occasions." Unlike Blaine, he would be a "safe" secretary, if only because he would put up with dull routine when nothing more was offered. The *Washington Post* summarized the left-handed compliments:

[4]Whitelaw Reid to Blaine, London, October 28, 1881, quoted in Royal Cortissoz, *The Life of Whitelaw Reid* (2 vols.; New York, 1921), II, 77.

[5]*New York Tribune*, December 13, 1881, p. 1. *New York Herald*, May 21, 1885, p. 3. Frederick T. Frelinghuysen to Arthur, Newark, New Jersey, October 26 (telegram), November 1, 19, 24, 1881, Chester A. Arthur Papers (Library of Congress).

That [Frelinghuysen] is a statesman will not be claimed by
his intimate friends. . . . That there is any comparison between
his natural or acquired ability and that of his predecessor, Mr.
Blaine, is not even a matter for discussion. As an incumbent
of the office, he will be dignified, and perhaps heavy, as be-
cometh a man of his wealth, family and social position. A com-
monplace and routine management of the State Department,
during his continuance in office, is all that the public will expect, and nobody is likely to meet with either agreeable or unhappy disappointments.[6]

Arthur's decision to appoint Frelinghuysen to the State Department precipitated at least two delicate problems in relation to
Blaine. Frelinghuysen chose as his assistant secretary John Chandler
Bancroft Davis, an experienced lawyer and diplomat who had
held the post under Hamilton Fish in the Grant administration,
but Davis had declined a similar offer from Blaine in March and
had to strain his diplomacy to the utmost to explain his change of
mind.[7] More embarrassing yet—after offering his resignation in
October, Blaine was now unwilling to leave the State Department.
Frelinghuysen accepted office no later than November 22, but
Arthur did not announce the appointment until December 12,
when he sent Frelinghuysen's name to the Senate. (It was approved
at once.) Blaine remained at his desk and attended Cabinet meetings for another week, amid much newspaper speculation. When
he finally bowed out on December 19, Arthur expressed his regret publicly, and the Blaines held a brilliant reception for the
Frelinghuysens.[8]

"Why don't [Frelinghuysen] take possession and stop the fili-
busterin'?" Hamilton Fish wrote to Bancroft Davis shortly before
the transfer. "I fear that the few days *grace* allowed him [Blaine]

[6]*Washington Post*, December 13, 1881, p. 2. *Harper's Weekly*, XXV (December
24), 866. *Springfield* (Massachusetts) *Republican*, December 12, as quoted in
Muzzey, *Blaine*, p. 222. *Nation*, XXXIII (December 15), 461. See also *New York
Herald*, December 13, p. 6. Whitelaw Reid called Frelinghuysen "an abject wor-
shipper of Grant, [with] a timid flunkey's distrust of everybody on the other side."
Reid to D. D. Lloyd, December 20, Letterbook, pp. 942-48, Whitelaw Reid Papers
(Library of Congress).

[7]Bancroft Davis to Fish, Washington, March 10, 1881, Hamilton Fish Papers,
CXXX (Library of Congress). Frelinghuysen to Arthur, Newark, November 24,
1881, Arthur Papers. *New York Tribune*, December 16, p. 1.

[8]*Washington Post*, December 10, 1881, p. 1; December 13, p. 1; December 14,
pp. 1, 4; December 16, p. 4; December 17, p. 1; December 20, pp. 1, 4.

will develop some mischievous work." Frelinghuysen, too, was uneasy about the delay,[9] and not without reason, for, as the State Department records were to show, Blaine used his last weeks to commit the Arthur administration to a series of bold new departures in foreign policy, tying up the loose ends of American diplomacy in hard knots awkward to untie. The extent to which Arthur understood or approved Blaine's actions cannot be determined, but it is impossible to believe that the policies of November, 1881, did not originate with Blaine.[10] Whether from friendship or inertia, with or without full understanding, the President left the initiative with his secretary of state at a time when that secretary's successor had already accepted office.

Although Arthur's motivations and reasoning defy analysis, it is clear why Blaine acted as he did. On leaving office, he intended to launch a campaign to regain his former influence in the party and possibly also the presidential nomination in 1884. Hampered by Garfield's illness, his tour of duty in the State Department had produced disappointingly little glory for either the nation or himself. Hostile newspapers had begun to criticize Hurlbut's bungling in Peru, and when they learned more about the Crédit Industriel and Jacob Shipherd, they would surely raise the old cries of corruption against him. Partly to gratify Half-Breed hopes and partly to blunt and divert Stalwart jibes, Blaine set out at the eleventh hour to complete his "spirited" foreign policy.

*   *   *

It is now necessary to discuss each of Blaine's new departures in some detail. His first major diplomatic statement, dated November 19, 1881, was directed at Great Britain and concerned the application of the Clayton-Bulwer Treaty to the question of the interoceanic canal. At the beginning of the summer he had protested against a joint European guarantee of the canal on the grounds that such a guarantee would threaten the prior interests and rights

[9]Fish to Bancroft Davis, New York, December 16, 1881, Bancroft Davis Papers, XXX (Library of Congress). Frelinghuysen to Arthur, Newark, December 2, 12, Arthur Papers.

[10]Mrs. Blaine declared, doubtless on evidence from her husband, that Arthur understood and approved Blaine's actions fully. Mrs. James G. Blaine to M., New York, January 28, 1882, Harriet S. Beale (ed.), Letters of Mrs. James G. Blaine (2 vols.; New York, 1908), I, 293-94.

of the United States. On November 10 the British foreign minister Lord Granville, replied that the relationship of Britain to the canal was already determined by the Clayton-Bulwer Treaty. Although Blaine had not yet received this reply nine days later, he must have guessed its contents, for his note anticipated the British line of argument.

The Clayton-Bulwer Treaty had floated for decades across the sea lanes of Anglo-American relations like a great iceberg, largely submerged and often hidden by fog. At the time of its signature in 1850 and for some years thereafter, the treaty had prevented open conflict between the two countries over Central America but only through a compromise of interests which no one really approved and a vagueness of language which no one really understood. Its terms seemed clear enough on the subject of canals: neither signatory might build or operate a canal without the participation of the other. What it left undefined was the degree of influence which Britain might continue to exercise in her semi-protectorates over the Indian tribes of Nicaragua and the Bay Islands. It would appear that the British did their best to expand this influence, but the United States lost an opportunity to press its interpretation of the treaty while Britain was embarrassed by the Crimean War, and in 1860 President Buchanan even declared that the Clayton-Bulwer Treaty had "resulted in a final settlement entirely satisfactory to this government."[11]

To the dismay of imperialistic Americans, Buchanan's statement restored the battered treaty to its original authority at the very time that its restrictions were beginning to chafe and bind. The rapid growth of American settlements on the Pacific Coast seemed to require additional protection to ports and trade. The frequent disturbances on the Isthmus of Panama seemed to invite European intervention. The completion of the Suez Canal revived canal projects in Central America. Britain and Nicaragua engaged in a dispute over jurisdiction, arbitrated in 1880 by the Emperor of Austria. Throughout the administrations of Grant and Hayes

[11] Mary W. Williams, *Anglo-American Isthmian Diplomacy, 1815-1915* (Baltimore, 1916), chaps. iii-viii. On the vagueness of the treaty's wording see also Keasbey, *Nicaragua Canal*, pp. 211-16, and John B. Henderson, Jr., *American Diplomatic Questions* (New York, 1900), pp. 120-23. On Anglo-American arguments during the 1850's see also Keasbey, *Nicaragua Canal*, pp. 254-63.

American grumbling against the Clayton-Bulwer Treaty had grown, so that if Garfield had lived, Blaine would probably have started negotiations with Britain to change or remove it.[12]

In his note of November 19 he attempted to compress these negotiations into six pages of print. The treaty, he complained, forbade the United States to use a single regiment of troops to defend its interests in Central America, while leaving the British Navy free to move at will. During the intervening decades Britain had protected her great stake in India by fortifying Gibraltar, Malta, Cyprus, and Aden, by securing control over the Suez Canal, and by making the Red Sea a *mare clausum*. American economic interests in the Pacific coast states would soon be as great as British interests in India, and the ties of blood were already far closer. In order that the United States might provide "impartial justice and independence" on the isthmus, Blaine asked that the treaty be amended to allow the United States to fortify and control a Nicaragua canal; that joint control over other routes be given up as obsolete; and that the approaches to the canal be neutralized. He concluded by saying that the United States could never submit the neutrality of a canal to Europe for its assent, for "it is the fixed purpose of the United States to confine it strictly and solely as an American question, to be dealt with and decided by the American governments."[13]

A week after sending this dispatch to London, Blaine received the brief reply of the British foreign secretary, Lord Granville, to his note of June 24. Instead of awaiting British reactions to his recent requests, Blaine set out to demolish the Clayton-Bulwer Treaty by a debater's tactics. On November 29, after combing the archives for several days, he rushed off another note. In this one his argument leaped nimbly across a series of quotations from the 1850's to show that both nations had repeatedly considered modifying or abrogating the treaty. (However, he made no reference to Buchanan's unfortunate statement of 1860.) Blaine also sug-

[12]Travis, *Clayton-Bulwer Treaty*, pp. 207-11. Keasbey, *Nicaragua Canal*, pp. 331-37, 390-91, 397-98. For examples of American opinion in 1880 see U. S., Congress, House, 46th Cong., 2d Sess., 1880, H. Rept. 1121, *passim*, and *New York Tribune*, April 28, 1880, p. 4.

[13]Blaine to James Russell Lowell, November 19, 1881, No. 270, U. S., *Foreign Relations, 1881*, pp. 554-59.

gested that the promise of joint participation in canal-building referred only to Nicaragua and not to Panama or Tehuantepec, and that in the case of Panama nothing in the treaty could be construed to limit American rights under the earlier treaty of 1846 with Colombia.[14]

Nearly a month after Blaine left office, Granville replied to these notes, demolishing Blaine's arguments and concluding that amendments to the Clayton-Bulwer Treaty were not justified by circumstances and would actually threaten the interests of third parties. He found Blaine's general principles "novel in international law" but confined himself to facts and practical considerations. Britain had not fortified Cyprus or made any effort to restrict the use of the Suez Canal. The United States might control California, but Britain had possessions in the Pacific too. Granville could not believe that other commercial nations would welcome a fortified canal, defended as part of the United States coastline. He answered Blaine's historical quotations with even longer ones in which Buchanan's statement of satisfaction was given full prominence, and he concluded with a thoroughly unacceptable solution: that, inasmuch as the Clayton-Bulwer Treaty could not be undone, it ought to be broadened to include all Europe in a joint guarantee.[15]

Since Blaine could hardly have expected any other sort of answer from Granville, it seems clear that his two notes were designed "for the record" and in the hope that, if Frelinghuysen chose to follow them up, much of the credit would go to Blaine. Whitelaw Reid privately deplored the inaccuracies which had crept into Blaine's arguments, but his *New York Tribune* loyally declared the United States entitled to the same rights at Panama as the British had at Suez. Other newspapers, however, criticized Blaine's methods, either because he sought to amend instead of abrogating the treaty or because he had chosen to demand rather than to negotiate. The *Nation* also counseled caution, since there seemed no immediate likelihood of a completed canal: "Quarrelling over its [the treaty's] provisions is very

[14]Earl Granville to W. J. Hoppin (American chargé d'affaires at London), November 10, 1881; Blaine to Lowell, November 29, No. 281, *ibid.*, pp. 549, 563-69.
[15]Granville to Lionel Sackville West (British minister at Washington), January 7, 14, 1882, U. S., *Foreign Relations, 1882*, pp. 302-14.

like litigation over the bequest of a testator who has left no assets.
It was worth Mr. Blaine's while to write about it, because he
needed the despatch for home use, but nobody else can get any
good out of the question."[16]

Observers abroad were generally irritated at the Secretary's
pretensions. De Lesseps denied any designs on the Monroe Doctrine but added that Blaine's views would not have the slightest
effect on his project: "A diplomatist is like a lawyer: he may
draw up the marriage contract, but he cannot perform the ceremony or produce the children." In Canada Prime Minister Sir
John Macdonald briefly considered making a formal protest on
the grounds that Canada had as great an interest in an isthmian
canal as the United States. The British press, disdaining Blaine's
arguments but amused at his predicament, took the attitude that
the American government would have to make the best of a bad
bargain until it could offer a reasonable inducement for the abrogation of the treaty. Perhaps the most judicious and farsighted comment was that of the *Times*:

> Blaine's position is stronger in some ways than he ventures to
> make it. The United States are indisputably the chief Power
> in the New World. The time must arrive when the weaker
> States in their neighbourhood will be absorbed by them. The
> United States coast line may come by and by to extend in
> reality to the full limits which Mr. Blaine fancifully or pro-
> phetically assigns to it. Manifest destiny is on one side. The
> Clayton-Bulwer treaty is on the other.[17]

In other words, it seemed clear to at least one shrewd observer
that although the United States had lost a battle, in time it would
probably win the war.

[16]*Nation*, XXXIV (February 16, 1882), 131. See also [Reid] to [William Walter
Phelps], February 10 [1882], Letterbook, XXXIX, 422-33, Reid Papers. *New York
Tribune*, December 21, 1881, p. 4. *New York Herald*, December 17, p. 6; January
16, 1882, p. 6. *Harper's Weekly*, XXV (December 31, 1881), 890-91.
[17]*Times* (London), December 17, 1881, p. 9. See also *ibid.*, October 26; *Daily
News* (London), October 27; *Pall Mall Gazette*, October 29. (Clippings enclosed
with Hoppin to Blaine, London, October 28, 29, Nos. 211, 212, U.S., Despatches,
Britain, CXLIII.) *St. James's Gazette*, n.d., reprinted in *Washington Post*, January 2, 1882, p. 2. *Saturday Review*, LII (1881), 528-29, 688, 778-79; LIII (1882),
720-21. De Lesseps' statement appears in *New York Tribune*, May 21, 1882, p. 2.
On the Canadian reaction see Donald Creighton, *John A. Macdonald, the Old
Chieftain* (Boston, 1956), p. 327.

While he proposed sweeping changes in the Clayton-Bulwer Treaty, Blaine was drawing up other notes which set forth in even more peremptory language a special American relationship with the Hawaiian Islands. The idea of this relationship was not exactly new, for in 1842 Secretary of State Daniel Webster had declared that American interest in the islands was paramount among foreign nations and warned Europe not to seek political control or commercial monopoly. As the American population of the islands grew, trade relations and a movement for political annexation kept them well within the American sphere of influence, and in 1875 the Grant administration negotiated a reciprocity treaty which guaranteed Hawaiian sugar a market in the United States. In 1877 American Minister Henry Peirce boasted that the islands were "an American colony in all their material and political interests."[18]

However, during the next two years native nationalists, reinforced by declining sugar prices, caused a clouding over of American hopes, so that when Garfield and Blaine entered office, American relations with Hawaii seemed to need close attention. The immediate focus of American worry was a world tour by the King of Hawaii. Fat and easygoing like most of his family, King Kalakaua admired both American and European institutions and hated to start trouble by excluding either. When he set forth on his travels in February, 1881, the American settlers in his government sent some of their countrymen with the royal party to indoctrinate the King with liberal American principles during the tedious intervals between sight-seeing visits and drinking bouts.[1]

Partly because Kalakaua postponed visiting the United States until the end of his tour, Blaine and Garfield were suspicious from the outset, and in April Blaine told the British minister, Sir Edward Thornton, that "he believed the King to be a false and intriguing man, and that the principal object of his journey was to endeavour

[18]S. K. Stevens, *American Expansion in Hawaii, 1842-1898* (Harrisburg, Pennsylvania, 1945), pp. 148-50 *et passim*. Jean I. Brookes, *International Rivalry in the Pacific Islands, 1800-1875* (Berkeley, California, 1941), pp. 276-79, 344-45. W. D. Alexander, *History of the Later Years of the Hawaiian Monarchy and the Revolution of 1893* (Honolulu, 1896), pp. 3-4.

[19]William N. Armstrong, *Around the World with a King* (New York, 1904), pp. 23-25 *et passim*.

o sell his kingdom to some European Power." Blaine added that he United States would not permit such a transfer. A few days ater he sent a circular note to the American ministers in London, Paris, and Berlin, repeating the warning in more diplomatic but no less forceful language: "The position of the Hawaiian Islands n the vicinity of our Pacific Coast, and their intimate commercial and political relations with us, lead this Government to . . . regard unfavorably any movement, negotiation or discussion, aiming to transfer them in any eventuality whatever to another power." He concluded by warning European citizens not to take any sort of financial lien on Hawaiian territory.[20]

As Kalakaua's world tour drew to an uneventful end, another question arose to disturb the American secretary. The increased sugar production since 1875 had caused an acute labor shortage on the islands for which immigration seemed the only remedy. By 1880 Chinese labor had proved unsatisfactory; Portuguese immigrants were too expensive, and contract labor from the South Seas would have aroused opposition from the missionaries. During his world tour Kalakaua had expressed interest in Japanese immigration. None of these solutions actively displeased the American government, but during the summer and autumn Blaine was horrified to read in dispatches from Honolulu that British representatives in Hawaii were pressing Kalakaua's regent to introduce coolies from British colonies in the Far East. The American minister expected that if this took place, Britain would ask Hawaii for permission to establish special consular courts to protect the interests of these British coolies and thus offset the influence of the American reciprocity treaty. In October he reported that the Princess Regent was corresponding directly with the British commissioner and bypassing her cabinet, with its American members.[21]

Accordingly, Blaine added Hawaii to his agenda of unfinished business. On November 19 he wrote to the American minister

[20]Sir Edward Thornton to Granville, Washington, April 12, 1881, in Knaplund and Clewes, "British Embassy Letters," p. 128. Blaine to Lowell, April 23, No. B150 (circular note), U.S., Instructions, Britain, XXVI, 112-15. The Hawaiian question is almost the only diplomatic matter in which Garfield's diary expresses an independent opinion. Entry for June 7, 1881, Garfield Diaries.

[21]James M. Comly to Blaine, Honolulu, July 4, 1881, No. 178, U.S., Despatches, Hawaii, XX. Comly to Blaine, August 29, October 24, Nos. 189, 194, U.S., Foreign Relations, 1881, pp. 627-29, 630.

at Honolulu that the United States would allow no subterfuge
to substitute foreign for native control over the people. The scheme
to transplant "a large mass of British subjects, forming in time
not improbably the majority of its population" would violate
American treaty rights. Several weeks later he instructed Lowell
that, should Granville initiate a discussion on Hawaii, he must
be guided by this principle:

> The United States regards the Hawaiian group as essentially
> a part of the American system of states, and the key to the
> North Pacific trade, and . . . , while favorably inclined toward
> the continuance of native rule on a basis of political inde-
> pendence and commercial assimilation with the United States,
> we could not regard the intrusion of any non-American in-
> terest in Hawaii as consistent with our relations thereto.[22]

On December 1, ten days before sending the above note, Blaine
set down for the benefit of the American minister to Hawaii
exactly what he meant by calling Hawaii "essentially a part of
the American system of states." It was the most explicit statement
of a protectorate policy to leave his pen. He began by recalling
his note of June 24 to the principal European Powers, in which
he opposed a joint guarantee of an isthmian canal, "a purely American waterway to be treated as part of our own coast line." Now
he declared trade channels in the Pacific to be "no less vitally
important" to American development. In the last thirty years
the United States had "acquired a legitimately dominant influence
in the North Pacific, which it can never consent to see decreased."
Geography had brought the question of the possession of Hawaii
"within the range of questions of purely American policy. . . .
The reciprocity treaty of 1875 . . . gives to our manufacturers
therein the same freedom as in California and Oregon."

Having proved (to his own satisfaction) the American claim to
dominance in Hawaii on grounds of history, geography, and economic interest, Blaine then explained that his country meant no
immediate threat to Hawaiian independence, but that, as in the
case of Cuba, it would preserve the status quo as far as possible.
However, the American government could not permit the lessen-

[22]Blaine to Comly, November 19, 1881, No. 111, *ibid.*, pp. 633-35. Blaine to Lowell,
December 10, No. 286, *ibid.*, pp. 569-70.

ing of its ties by any expedient such as the introduction of alien coolies. In a separate, confidential dispatch Blaine proposed another solution to the Hawaiian labor shortage—American colonists, under a kind of "Hawaiian homestead act," supplemented by voluntary emigration schemes in the United States.[23]

Blaine's Hawaiian notes were more sweeping than those on the Clayton-Bulwer Treaty, but the occasion for them was probably less compelling, since later investigation reveals no British plan of annexation in the 1880's. A recent critic also points out that they were essentially a restatement of Webster's warning of 1842, however emphatic.[24] What seems more important than the necessity or the originality of Blaine's Hawaiian notes is their close integration with the rest of his continental policy. In his last weeks as secretary of state, when he flung out the American mantle over Latin America, he managed to save a few folds for Hawaii too.[25]

* * *

While warning Europe away from the Western Hemisphere, broadly defined, Blaine attempted to prove that the United States was perfectly capable of leading Latin-American nations to settlement of their two most serious international disputes: the War of the Pacific and the Mexico-Guatemalan boundary controversy. Hitherto the State Department had achieved remarkably little success in these questions, and Blaine was determined to commit the new secretary to bolder policies than before.

The more urgent of the two problems was the War of the Pacific, because it was a war instead of a mere controversy, because it aroused more danger of European intervention, and above all because it would furnish more ammunition to Blaine's enemies in the United States. When news of Hurlbut's indiscretions began to appear in American newspapers, some editors admitted that he probably reflected the general American opposition to territorial conquest, but others warned Americans "how near they are to being brought to one of those little wars which so frequently annoy

[23]Blaine to Comly, December 1, 1881, No. 114, U.S., Instructions, Hawaii, II, 429-33. See also Blaine to Comly, December 1, No. 113, U.S., *Foreign Relations, 1881*, pp. 635-39.

[24]Stevens, *American Expansion in Hawaii*, p. 158.

[25]In this connection see Tyler, *Foreign Policy of Blaine*, pp. 191-200.

Great Britain" and declared that if we supported his contentions we would be entering on a policy of "aggression and interference for our own aggrandizement." Later, after Blaine had published his instructions to Hurlbut and Kilpatrick, the *New York Tribune* praised them as "clear, explicit, and consistent" but by the same token had to condemn the two ministers severely for factionalism.[26]

More damaging than Hurlbut's ineptness were rumors of his corruption. On October 8 the *Washington Post* printed a vague story about a guano "ring" working through Hurlbut to persuade the American government to assume Peru's debts. Further details were not forthcoming, but two weeks later the same newspaper denounced Hurlbut as a "busy-body" and "attorney of a guano company, that proposes to get possession of a monopoly in the business."[27] Well aware of Hurlbut's past, Blaine must have experienced several uncomfortable days as he imagined what might have happened in Peru and how this could be interpreted at home.

Accordingly, on October 27 Blaine telegraphed to Hurlbut: "Influence of your position must not be used in aid of Crédit Industriel, or any other financial or speculative association." Hurlbut replied, "It has not been; it will not be." Then he gathered together the letters which he had received from Shipherd and sent them to the State Department, adding that he knew nothing of the recent activities of the Crédit Industriel. In longer dispatches of November 17 and 19 Blaine then commended Hurlbut's "prudent and discreet course" in reference to the Cochet and Landreau claims and warned him to have nothing to do with Shipherd.[28]

So far, the Secretary had said nothing about Hurlbut's political activities during August and September, although news of them had begun to arrive in Washington as early as September 27. On November 22, after many newspapers had raked Hurlbut over the coals, Blaine wrote him that his acts were not to be interpreted as "a policy of active intervention . . . beyond the scope of

[26]*New York Times*, October 21, 1881. *New York Herald*, October 21, p. 5; October 31, p. 6. *Nation*, XXXIII (November 17), 390-91. *New York Tribune*, November 18, p. 4.

[27]*Washington Post*, October 8, 1881, p. 1; October 22, p. 2.

[28]Blaine to Hurlbut, October 27, 1881 (telegram); Hurlbut to Blaine, Lima, November 2, No. 25; Blaine to Hurlbut, November 17, No. 17, U.S., "War in South America," pp. 545, 547-62, 564.

your instructions." Since the State Department kept an accredited minister in Chile, Hurlbut had no business discussing policy with Admiral Lynch. Blaine added, "While the United States would unquestionably 'regard with disfavor' the imperious annexation of Peruvian territory as the right of conquest, you were distinctly informed that this government could not refuse to recognize that such annexation might become a necessary condition in a final treaty of peace." Similarly, he saw no justification for Hurlbut's rough language to Piérola's foreign minister, especially since the language might unduly arouse Peruvian hopes of American aid. As for the naval station on Chimbote Bay, Blaine thought it possibly desirable at some future time, when the United States might not seem to be forcing the arrangement upon a helpless Peru.[29]

At the same time the Secretary of State sent a somewhat shorter reprimand to Kilpatrick in Santiago, saying that he should not have taken upon himself to discuss Hurlbut's memorandum to Lynch with the Chilean foreign minister, and adding that he could not understand why Chile had arrested García Calderón. Anticipating confusion in the State Department, Kilpatrick had rallied suffi-ciently from his illness on December 2 to dictate a feeble explanation of the arrest, but he never saw Blaine's reprimand, for a few hours after signing this dispatch, he collapsed and died.[30] As for Shipherd, Blaine saved him for the last, and on December 3 sent him a rigid note which would have shriveled a more sensitive soul. At the end he suggested contemptuously that Shipherd must be insane: "I am inclined to believe that you . . . are not morally responsible for the improper proposals you have made."[31]

From this point Hurlbut played only a minor role in the Ameri-can diplomacy, for Blaine had decided to wipe the slate clean and send two envoys to the belligerent governments. In charge of this delicate mission he placed the State Department's ablest "trouble shooter," William Henry Trescot, a South Carolinian whose diplo-matic experience extended back to the 1850's. Within the preceding

[29]Blaine to Hurlbut, November 22, 1881, No. 19, *ibid.*, pp. 565-67.

[30]Blaine to Kilpatrick, November 22, 1881, No. 13; Kilpatrick to Blaine, Santiago, December 2, No. 9, *ibid.*, pp. 168-69, 179-80. Lucius Foote to Blaine, Valparaiso, December 3, No. 81, U.S., Consular Despatches, Valparaiso, X.

[31]Blaine to Jacob R. Shipherd, December 3, 1881, U.S., "War in South America," pp. 683-84.

five years Trescot had served on the Fisheries Commission, had gone to China to help negotiate an immigration treaty, and had signed the unratified Trescot-Santodomingo protocol with Colombia, fixing American rights and obligations on the Isthmus of Panama. Since his return from China Trescot had served as unofficial adviser on Latin-American affairs.[32] With Trescot the Secretary sent his son, Walker Blaine, then third assistant secretary of state, in case negotiations should have to be conducted simultaneously in two capitals.

Blaine's instructions to Trescot (December 2) epitomized his attitude toward the War of the Pacific. He had apparently accepted Hurlbut's suggestion that Chile might have arrested García Calderón as a deliberate insult to the United States. Trescot was to determine if this were true. If so, continued Blaine, "you will say to the Chilian government that the President considers such a proceeding as an intentional and unwarranted offense . . . an act of such unfriendly import as to require the immediate suspension of all diplomatic intercourse." Should Chile explain the arrest as the result of Hurlbut's conduct, Trescot might accept any statement which did not require him to disavow Hurlbut. As for the peace settlement, if Chile insisted on setting up a Peruvian government which would agree to territorial cessions before a peace conference, Trescot must express American "disappointment and dissatisfaction," for the United States still maintained that Peru was entitled to an opportunity to pay or guarantee a cash indemnity instead. If Chile received this suggestion in a friendly spirit, Blaine suggested that Trescot might find it convenient to draw up a temporary convention. However,—and this was the crucial point:

> If our good offices are rejected, and this policy of the absorption of an independent state be persisted in, this government will consider itself discharged from any further obligation to be influenced in its action by the position which Chili has assumed, and will hold itself free to appeal to the other republics of this continent to join it in an effort to avert consequences which cannot be confined to Chili and Peru, but which threaten

[32]Muzzey, *Blaine*, p. 213. Walker Blaine to James G. Blaine, Washington, October 3, 1881, in Gail Hamilton, *Life of Blaine* (Norwich, Connecticut, 1895), p. 545.

with extremest danger the political institutions, the peaceful progress, and the liberal civilization of all America.[33]

On the following day Blaine told Trescot that he must be prepared to visit the governments of Argentina and Brazil on his way home.[34]

As David S. Muzzey has pointed out, these instructions were "dangerously near to the language of an ultimatum," particularly since Chile would undoubtedly regard the reference to other Latin-American nations as a threat of force. As early as December 5, before the text of Trescot's instructions had been made public, the New York *Daily Commercial Bulletin* warned its readers against "crafty, underhanded diplomacy which permits a nation, in spite of itself, as it were, to *drift* into war all the time that diplomacy is professedly striving to avoid it." At Blaine's request, Trescot later declared the suggestion that Blaine intended war "too absurd for serious discussion," but the *Nation* replied that he had missed the point: "While talking about peace [Blaine] kept exasperating the Chileans, so that it was obvious that sooner or later they must be forced into war."[35]

* * *

Blaine's disposition of the boundary controversy between Mexico and Guatemala was much less drastic than his intervention in western South America. It will be remembered that in September, after two months of conversations with the Mexican foreign office, American Minister Philip H. Morgan came to the conclusion that only positive action by the United States would prevent war. At the same time the Guatemalan foreign minister, Lorenzo Montúfar, made a special visit to the United States to seek American support, both in the boundary controversy and in President Barrios' plan to unify Central America. Blaine's problem was to end the controversy without mortally offending either side, so that if Barrios succeeded in creating a strong Central American nation, he would

[33]Blaine to William Henry Trescot, December 1, 1881, No. 2, U.S., "War in South America," pp. 174-79. In the original the suggestion of a convention follows the paragraph quoted.
[34]Blaine to Trescot, December 2, 1881, No. 3, *ibid.*, p. 181.
[35]*Nation*, XXXV (July 27, 1882), 62-63. See also Muzzey, *Blaine*, pp. 248-49. New York *Daily Commercial Bulletin*, December 5, 1881, p. 2. Trescot to Blaine, York, Maine, July 17, 1882, in *New York Tribune*, July 25, p. 1.

acquiesce in future American control of the Nicaraguan canal route.

On November 28, a week after receiving Montúfar's last wheedling note, the Secretary sent Morgan a major policy statement on the boundary question—his first since the preceding June. In order to prevent war between Mexico and Guatemala, he instructed Morgan to press the earlier American views on Mexico once more and to suggest a limited arbitration of the disputed boundary, recognizing the Mexican title to Chiapas. Blaine rejected Foreign Minister Mariscal's suspicious view of Barrios and declared that Central American union was one of the fondest American hopes. He conceded that Mexico would be within her rights to refuse arbitration by the United States, but he warned the Mexican government that he would construe a hostile demonstration against Guatemala as "not in harmony with the friendly relations between us, and injurious to the best interests of all the republics of this continent." This was strong language, but Blaine softened it at two points with the suggestion that the two countries, acting together, could exert great influence in favor of general arbitration:

> Mexico and the United States, acting in cordial harmony, can induce all the other independent governments of North and South America to aid in fixing this policy of peace for all future disputes between the nations of the western hemisphere. . . . [But, he concluded,] this country will continue its policy of peace even if it cannot have the great aid which the co-operation of Mexico would assure; and it will hope, at no distant day, to see such concord and co-operation between all nations of America as will render war impossible.[36]

*   *   *

If the last sentence seemed obscure to Morgan and the Mexican government, they were soon enlightened, for on the following day Blaine disclosed the idea which was to be the crown of his new policy and which has since formed the principal basis of his diplomatic reputation: a great inter-American peace congress to tighten the bonds of friendship in the Western Hemisphere and make future wars difficult or impossible. On November 29 he sent out invitations

[36]Blaine to Philip H. Morgan, November 28, 1881, No. 198, U.S., *Foreign Relations, 1881*, pp. 814-17.

to most of the Latin-American governments, and two or three days later he instructed Trescot verbally that he was to convey similar invitations to Chile, Peru, and Bolivia and deliver them to these governments at a suitable moment.

Blaine based his invitations to the peace congress on the "well-known" desire of the United States to avoid war "through pacific counsels or the advocacy of impartial arbitration." Its good offices, he said, "are not and have not at any time been tendered with a show of dictation or compulsion, but only as exhibiting the solicitous good-will of a common friend." Since, unhappily, Latin-American nations insisted on resorting to the sword despite "the just and impartial counsel of the President," he had concluded that the time was ripe for a general conference which would seek ways of avoiding foreign and civil war. Perhaps in the hope of reassuring Chile and Mexico, Blaine hastened to explain that the congress would not deal with existing controversies. "Its mission is higher." For that reason he had scheduled it for November 24, 1882, in the hope that by then the War of the Pacific would be over.[37]

Contemporary observers and later historians have variously explained Blaine's sudden decision to call an inter-American peace congress at a moment when he was about to retire from office. His personal enemies accused him of simply trying to make trouble for his successor, while his friends took at face value his expressed desire for hemispheric peace. Nearly a year after leaving office Blaine himself remarked that the foreign policy of the Garfield administration had had two principal objects: "first, to bring about peace, and prevent future wars in North and South America; second, to cultivate such friendly commercial relations with all American countries as would lead to a large increase in the export trade of the United States."[38] Some historians have gone even further and asserted that the commercial motive was actually first in

[37]For the text of the invitations see Blaine to Thomas O. Osborn, November 29, 1881, No. 156, *ibid.*, pp. 13-15. On the verbal instructions to Trescot see Russell H. Bastert, "A New Approach to the Origins of Blaine's Pan-American Policy," *Hispanic American Historical Review*, XXXIX (August 1959), 404, note 78.

[38]"The Foreign Policy of the Garfield Administration," in Blaine, *Political Discussions*, pp. 411-419, and especially 411. For contemporary criticism see Fish to Bancroft Davis, December 16, 1881, Davis Papers, XXX. A sample of Blaine's earlier attention to economic considerations is Blaine to Morgan, June 16, 1881, A.G. No. 137, U.S., Instructions, Mexico, XX, 283-96.

Blaine's mind, even though the text of his invitations to the congress contains no reference whatever to trade.[39]

A recent student of Blaine's diplomacy, while conceding that economic considerations may have played a part in his thinking, accepts at face value his primary concern for peace but declares that his reasoning was far more subtle and complex than would appear from the invitations. Warned by the polite inquiry of France during the preceding August whether the time had not arrived for joint mediation in the War of the Pacific, Blaine realized that the United States must bring peace to Chile and Peru before Europe could use their troubles as an excuse for intervention. Anxious to retain the friendship of both Mexico and Guatemala, he sought to create a type of arbitration which Mexico could not reject. Alarmed by the criticism of Hurlbut in the opposition press, he hoped to close his record as secretary of state with a brilliant stroke which would obliterate his past reverses and the blunders of his agents.[40]

As in the case of his correspondence on the Clayton-Bulwer Treaty, Blaine was attempting too much, too quickly. It was unrealistic to suggest a sober discussion of the rules of war and peace while Peru and Chile were still fighting, in the hope that the prospect of such discussion would induce them to lay down their arms. It was unfair to burden his successor with a half-developed policy, requiring much finesse to mature, without consulting him on any point in that policy. Blaine's invitations, though brilliant in conception and far-reaching in effect, were wretchedly timed. Considering the difficulties of the First Pan-American Conference, held eight years later under much more auspicious circumstances,

[39]Examples of primarily economic emphasis are Muzzey, *Blaine*, p. 207, and A. C. Wilgus, "James G. Blaine and the Pan-American Movement," *Hispanic American Historical Review*, V (1922), 667. A degree of balance between trade and peace may be found in Tyler, *Foreign Policy of Blaine*, p. 165, and Joseph B. Lockey, "James G. Blaine," in Samuel F. Bemis (ed.), *American Secretaries of State and their Diplomacy* (10 vols.; New York, 1927-1929), VII, 275.

[40]Bastert, "Origins of Blaine's Pan-American Policy," pp. 375-412, and especially pp. 387-90, 403-4, 411-12. Blaine sent other dispatches worthy of note during this period: a series of protests against French decrees prohibiting the importation of American pork and a warning to Switzerland to stop deporting criminals to the United States. See U.S., *Foreign Relations, 1881*, pp. 434, 436, 437, 1172-73. Space does not permit discussion of the Swiss note, but the French pork prohibition will be traced in Chapter 9.

was probably just as well the proposed congress of 1882 never took place.

* * *

While Blaine completed his business in the State Department, Frelinghuysen was standing nervously in the wings, waiting for his cue to enter and take charge, while Bancroft Davis, already appointed first assistant secretary, worried with him over the unexpected delay. Further in the background stood Davis' patron, Hamilton Fish, who was always suspicious of Blaine. Fish warned Davis that when he finally got into office, he must examine carefully all that had been done. While the three waited, Blaine published his original instructions to Hurlbut and Kilpatrick, confirming the rumors of claims ventures. Newspaper speculation increased, and Senator George F. Edmunds of Vermont, the "self-appointed keeper of the congressional conscience regarding contracts," called on the President to submit to Congress all diplomatic correspondence pertaining to the War of the Pacific.[41]

On December 20, about a month after Frelinghuysen had accepted his appointment to the State Department, he and Davis took possession. On the twenty-third, Frelinghuysen, never an energetic soul, left for the Christmas holidays, but Davis stayed on to "burrow into the Peruvian correspondence," which he found badly disorganized. By New Year's he had convinced himself that Fish's suspicions were well founded, and that "we were on the highway to war for the benefit of about as nasty a set of people as ever gathered about a Washington Dept." When Frelinghuysen returned to Washington, Davis met him at the railroad station with the evidence in his hands. Frelinghuysen agreed on immediate action and consulted Senator Edmunds. Then the three of them held a council and decided that the whole mass of papers, both public and private correspondence, should go to Congress.[42]

First of all, however, something had to be done about Trescot and Walker Blaine, who had started for South America on December 3. Between January 3 and January 9 Frelinghuysen sent

[41]Fish to Davis, New York, December 16, 1881, Davis Papers, XXX. Russell H. Bastert, "Diplomatic Reversal: Frelinghuysen's Opposition to Blaine's Pan-American Policy in 1882," *Mississippi Valley Historical Review*, XLII (March 1956), 656.

[42]Davis to Fish, Washington, January 1, February 1, 1882, Hamilton Fish Papers, CXXXIV.

Trescot two telegrams and a longer instruction, in which he reversed Blaine's defiant policy of the preceding month. To begin with, he made it clear that the United States had no desire to "dictate or make any authoritative utterance to either Peru o Chili as to the merits of the controversy existing between those republics" or any part of the settlement. Then he specifically revoked that section of Blaine's instructions which had threatened a rupture of relations with Chile, told Trescot that he must no visit Buenos Aires on his way home, and informed him that the President had decided to reconsider the advisability of holding a peace congress for the Western Hemisphere. At the same time Frelinghuysen came to a friendly understanding with the Chilean minister, Martínez, accepting his assurance that Chile had no intended the arrest of García Calderón as an insult to the United States.[43]

Having changed the whole character of the Trescot mission and cast doubt on the holding of Blaine's peace congress, Freling-huysen then released his communications to Congress and to the newspapers without waiting to hear from his envoys. The State Department also published nearly every Peruvian and Chilean dis-patch in the archives as fast as Davis and his helpers could sort them out. A Democratic member of the House of Representatives Perry Belmont of New York, obtained a copy of the Morton Bliss guano contract from the Peruvian minister, along with rumors about the Crédit Industriel, which he turned over to the *New York Herald* and the New York *Sun*.[44] Before long the press was regaling the public with all the juicy details (and many exaggera-tions) of the preceding year's secret diplomacy.

The newspapers soon had personal interviews to add to the documents. When Blaine left the State Department, he had sensibly determined to maintain "the dignity of perfect silence," but he and his wife became convinced that his enemies had captured Arthur and were attempting genteel character-assassination. In

[43]Frelinghuysen to Trescot, January 9, 1882, No. 6; Marcial Martínez to Freling-huysen, Washington, December 28, 1881; Frelinghuysen to Martínez, January 7 1882, U.S., "War in South America," pp. 185-87.

[44]Bastert, "Diplomatic Reversal," p. 661. Davis to Fish, Washington, February 8 1882, Fish Papers, CXXXIV. Perry Belmont, *An American Democrat; the Recol-lections of Perry Belmont* (New York, 1940), p. 220.

one interview he complained testily that Frelinghuysen had sent Trescot on a "fool's errand," and a little later he wrote to the *New York Tribune* that Arthur, not he, had issued the invitations to the peace congress, and that if we abandoned it out of fear of offending Europe, we would humiliate ourselves and antagonize Latin America. Hamilton Fish warned Bancroft Davis that Blaine was trying to divert attention from his mistakes again. Frelinghuysen thought it necessary to deny the charge of truckling to Europe, but Arthur said nothing, having already taken both sides of the question.[45]

Members of Congress were unable to resist the call to action and discharged volleys of badly aimed shots at both Arthur and Blaine. Senator Wilkinson Call of Florida proposed a special conference of hemispheric nations to end the War of the Pacific and delivered a long, florid speech about Peruvian resources and markets, but not a single colleague supported him. Representative W. C. Whitthorne of Tennessee gave mild praise of Blaine's vigorous policy, whereupon a Stalwart, John A. Kasson of Iowa, accused him of trying to divide the Republicans. So it went. In April Arthur even asked Congress for advice on the peace congress, but after more weeks of intermittent debate neither house could make up its mind.[46]

From March to June, while Senate and House discussed the peace congress, the House Committee on Foreign Affairs held hearings ostensibly to determine whether certain papers missing from the State Department had been lost or stolen, and whether American ministers in South America "were either personally interested or improperly connected with business transactions in which the intervention of this government was requested or expected." Actually the subject under discussion was Blaine's honesty as secretary of state. The committee never found the missing papers (which were probably of little value), but Shipherd, William

[45]Bastert, "Diplomatic Reversal," pp. 662-63. Mrs. Blaine to M., New York, February 2, 1882, in Beale, *Letters of Mrs. James G. Blaine*, I, 295-96. *New York Tribune*, February 4, 1882, p. 1. Fish to Davis, New York, February 7, 1882, Davis Papers, XXXI.
[46]Bastert, "Diplomatic Reversal," pp. 664-69. Wilgus, "Blaine and the Pan-American Movement," pp. 677-78. For the text of Arthur's request for Congressional advice see U.S., *Congressional Record*, 47th Cong., 1st Sess., 1882, XIII, 2993.

Henry Hurlbert, Robert E. Randall, and Blaine himself spent days in the witness stand contradicting each other's stories. Many questions could only have been answered by Minister Hurlbut, but he had died suddenly in Lima on the eve of coming home to testify—more of Blaine's luck, grumbled Fish. The hearings undoubtedly damaged Blaine's reputation further, especially when he lost his temper under Perry Belmont's goading. In the end the committee censured Shipherd and declared that it could see no official malfeasance, while Belmont insisted on adding minor criticism of Blaine's policies.[47]

Throughout the winter and spring of 1881-1882 the newspapers greeted each new disclosure with jeers or explanations, depending on their party affiliations. With Blaine's encouragement Whitelaw Reid published scathing letters and editorials in the *New York Tribune*, attacking Arthur's indecision about the peace congress: "Much bloodshed might have been saved, great prosperity might have been promoted, civilizing and christianizing influences might have been carried where they are sadly needed." The New York *World*, even more extreme, declared that only "the unacknowledged protectorate of the United States" had preserved Colombian independence and the neutrality of Panama and added: "It is difficult to see why a force to which the whole world pays practical homage should not be formally defined and admitted as a permanent and intelligible factor in human affairs."[48] However, others pointed out that such claims would only offend Latin America and asked why Canada had been left out. One declared that "to submit any really important question to the decision of Peru, Costa Rica, and other such states, would be . . . an act of sheer folly."[49]

In a similar manner the sudden shift of policy toward Peru and Chile inspired a variety of comments. Blaine predicted that under the new dispensation, "Peru is to be despoiled and destroyed, and

[47]U.S., "Chile-Peruvian Investigation," *passim*, but especially pp. i-xxvii. For Fish's comment on Hurlbut's death see Fish to Davis, April 3, 1882, Letterbooks, Fish Papers.

[48]*New York Tribune*, May 15, 1882, p. 2; May 26, p. 4. New York *World*, January 7, p. 4.

[49]*New York Herald*, February 1, 1882, p. 6. *Harper's Weekly*, XXVI (February 18), 98. *Nation*, XXXIV (February 9), 114-15.

. . . the profits of spoliation are to be divided between Chili and the English bondholders and speculators who furnished her the money and the guns and the iron-clads that destroyed Peru." The Half-Breed press declared that the State Department had exceeded all precedents in "reckless abandonment of the interests of our people."[50] But Blaine intended war, answered the *New York Herald*—"war in a bad cause, unnecessary and to us disgraceful." This was the only possible explanation of his "disgraceful attitude of bullying Chile on the pretense of a friendly mediation." His actions were "not diplomacy . . . [but] simply a vulgar intrigue."[51]

Hurlbut's letters from Shipherd and the revelation of nitrate claims aroused more suspicion. The *Herald* asked: "Did the character of a Minister Plenipotentiary become so confounded with that of a lobby agent and nitrate speculator that the government did not dare venture to discipline this gentleman in one character lest he should retort in the other?" The *Nation* called Shipherd an "adventurer of the lowest order," attacked Morton for his alleged connection with the Crédit Industriel, and praised Belmont for his impertinent baiting of Blaine at the House investigation. On the other hand, the *Tribune* insinuated that Shipherd's references to Grant would bear investigation—sauce for the gander, it might have added—and proclaimed that the hearings had completely exonerated Blaine: "His enemies . . . started into this investigation with an interrogation point, and they came out with an interrogation point, and nothing besides."[52]

Outside the United States Blaine's "brilliant foreign policy" aroused much indignation and little sympathy or support. The Toronto *Globe* called it "a stock-jobbing intrigue for the acquirement of guano beds" and declared that the peace congress "amounted to nothing at all if it was not meant to pave the way for the assumption by the United States of a protectorate over all the smaller republics of the continent." In London the *Times* supported a reasonable, magnanimous peace between Chile and

[50]*New York Tribune*, January 30, 1882, p. 1; March 7, p. 4; March 24, p. 5; June 16, p. 4. *Washington Post*, March 25, p. 2.

[51]*New York Herald*, January 20, 1882, p. 6; January 27.

[52]*New York Tribune*, February 22, 1882, p. 4; May 10, p. 1. See also *New York Herald*, December 23, 1881, p. 6; and *Nation*, XXXIV (February 23, 1882), 160-61 (March 2), 175; (March 23), 239; (May 4), 374.

Peru but bridled at Blaine's accusations of British plots: "[Britain] seeks no political favour for her trade in South America or elsewhere. . . . If anything, she is more inclined to be careless of the future than to prepare warily for remote contingencies." Other British publications agreed that the United States sought to guarantee the Latin-American nations against an imaginary threat and advised them respectfully to decline the invitations to the peace congress.[53]

The Latin-American reaction to Blaine's invitations was complicated by the existence of a rival proposal for a purely Latin-American conference. Late in 1880, at the suggestion of Chile, Colombia had proposed a meeting at Panama to consider the arbitration of disputes, apparently without intent to slight the United States. In accepting the invitation of Colombia, the Argentine government proposed to discuss the War of the Pacific, whereupon Chile turned against her own creation and persuaded the rest of South America not to send representatives. Mexico also declined, not wishing to bind herself to arbitrate future disputes. When the conference opened on December 1, 1881, the only delegates on hand were those from Colombia, Costa Rica, El Salvador, and Guatemala; after a brief, futile discussion the meeting adjourned. Making one final effort, the Colombian government sent a special envoy to Guatemala in January with a draft treaty of arbitration. Although the envoy tried to reassure the suspicious American minister, Cornelius A. Logan, that Colombia would gladly consider the President of the United States as a possible arbiter, Logan opposed the treaty, feeling that it would conflict with Blaine's peace congress. At his suggestion President Barrios quietly smothered the draft treaty in committee.[54]

[53]Toronto *Globe*, February 6, 1882, p. 4. *Times* (London), January 31, p. 9; February 1, p. 9. *Saturday Review*, LII (December 3, 17, 1881), 688, 745; LIII (January 14, 1882), 38.

[54]Bernardo Irigoyen to Eustaquio Santa María, Buenos Aires, December 30, 1880 U.S., *Foreign Relations, 1881*, pp. 3-6. José C. Valadés, *El porfirismo, historia de un regimén; El nacimiento (1876-1884)* (México, 1941), p. 336. Cornelius A. Logan to Frelinghuysen, Guatemala City, January 29, February 1, 20, 1882, Nos. 254, 255, 267, U.S., *Despatches, Central America*, XVIII. The Argentine government was also somewhat nettled because the American action upset its own plan for mediation in the War of the Pacific. Thomas O. Osborn to Blaine, Buenos Aires, October 20, 1881, No. 337, *ibid.*, Argentina, XXIV. Richard Gibbs to Frelinghuysen, La Paz, October 25, 1883, No. 13, *ibid.*, Bolivia, IX.

Fortunately, few Latin Americans knew of Logan's action. Some nations, such as Guatemala, Venezuela, and Brazil, welcomed Blaine's invitations, although the Mexican government postponed action as long as it could, and the president of Chile regarded the congress as a trap. A New York journalist who attended the abortive Panama congress discussed Blaine's proposal with the Colombian delegate, who felt that his own country and nine others would almost certainly take part and that the congress would greatly extend American influence in Latin America. It is possible, however, that the judgment of Gustave Koerner, Lincoln's minister to Spain, was more to the point:

> Don't People in Congress know, that there is . . . no people on earth, that dislikes & fears the United States more, than Mexico, & all the Central & South American Republics? . . . They will send delegates to the Blain [sic] Kasson Whitthorne Congress, and instruct them to do nothing. But they will make very nice speeches. . . . The Yankees they hate instinctively, as they hold them to be smarter than they themselves are, and fully intend to cheat them upon other points at another time.[55]

*   *   *

Whatever the real feelings of Latin Americans toward Blaine's peace congress, they were given slight opportunity to show them, for in August, 1882, Arthur and Frelinghuysen quietly withdrew the invitations. Arthur said nothing further on the subject, other than a bland reference in his annual message, but Frelinghuysen explained to Senator William Windom, Chairman of the Foreign Relations Committee, that the disturbed condition of Latin America did not augur well for a peace congress at that time, and that he objected to submitting international policy to a body in which the United States would have only one vote. However, he felt

[55]Gustave Koerner to William Morrison, Belleville, Illinois, March 13, 1882, William Morrison Papers (Illinois State Historical Society, Springfield, Illinois). For reactions of Latin-American governments see Montúfar to Frelinghuysen, New York, June 5, 1882, U.S., Notes from Foreign Legations, Guatemala and Salvador, VI. Rafael Seijas to Simón Camacho, Caracas, September 16, U.S., Notes from Foreign Legations, Venezuela, IV. Enclosure with Thomas A. Osborn to Frelinghuysen, Rio de Janeiro, March 23, No. 21, U.S., Foreign Relations, 1882, pp. 23-25. Encina, Historia de Chile, XVIII, 35. The government of Haiti was deeply offended at being omitted from the list. Rayford W. Logan, The Diplomatic Relations of the United States with Haiti, 1776-1891 (Chapel Hill, North Carolina, 1941), pp. 365-67.

that the proposal for a congress had served an important purpose in promoting discussion on Latin-American affairs, and he would be willing to consider the project again at some future time after proper preparation.[56]

Although Blaine soon published a widely reprinted article explaining and justifying the policies of the Garfield administration (which had actually blossomed under Arthur), it changed nothing. The withdrawal of the invitations to the peace congress completed his repudiation by the Arthur administration. The nervousness of Frelinghuysen and Bancroft Davis, coupled with the exultant denunciations by Blaine's enemies in Congress and the press, had been too much for the President. Whether he had only partly understood what Blaine was up to or had not particularly cared what happened in South America, he abandoned that part of Blaine's "spirited" policy pertaining to Chile, Peru, and the peace congress and allowed Frelinghuysen and Davis to throw the diplomatic machine into reverse. Their impetuous actions offended Blaine, but he was in no position to complain of anyone's impetuosity.

As Frelinghuysen recognized, Blaine's actions of November, 1881, had a long-range effect on American foreign policy. In defending or attacking them, statesmen and journalists re-examined the Monroe Doctrine, the Clayton-Bulwer Treaty, the Hawaiian reciprocity treaty, and other old stand-bys of American foreign policy. They discussed arbitration, trade with Latin America, hemispheric cooperation, and other ideas which bore increasing significance for the future.[57] Blaine's bold, ill-considered proposals were rejected but not forgotten, and when Arthur and Frelinghuysen eventually developed their ambitious system of hemispheric reciprocity treaties, it bore more resemblance to Blaine's Latin-American dreams than they were willing to admit.

[56]Frelinghuysen to William Windom, July 24, 1882, U.S., Report Book, XIV, 648-50.

[57]For examples see John A. Kasson, "The Monroe Doctrine in 1881," *North American Review*, CXXXIII (December 1881), 523-33; and a speech of Representative W. C. Whitthorne in the House, March 2, 1882, U.S., *Congressional Record*, 47th Cong., 1st Sess., 1882, XIII, 1553-56.

The Search for a New Policy

CHAPTER 5

Mopping Up the War of the Pacific

A LTHOUGH Frelinghuysen and Bancroft Davis acted quickly in January, 1882, to reverse some of Blaine's precipitate decisions, many months passed before the Arthur administration could be said to have a consistent, deliberate foreign policy of its own. The President and his secretary of state, both of them courtly, dignified, and prudent, would have moved slowly in any case. Facing a Congress in which the Democrats looked forward hopefully to the by-elections of 1882 and would do anything to widen the Republican split, Arthur carefully divided his cabinet between Stalwarts and Half-Breeds, kept the controversial Half-Breed, Judge William H. Robertson, in the New York Customs Office, and otherwise indicated a strong desire to bury the hatchet. The storm which raged over Blaine's foreign policies throughout the winter and spring of 1882 meant that even the most routine actions of the State Department would be subjected to merciless scrutiny by the Half-Breed press. Consequently, the new administration devoted itself as far as possible to domestic issues, such as civil service reform and the investigation of the "Star Route" scandals in the Post Office Department.

Another factor delaying the formulation of a systematic foreign policy was that of confusion and friction within the State Department. The two preceding secretaries of state, Evarts and Blaine, had not been careful administrators, and Bancroft Davis found correspondence considerably disorganized. Also it was soon apparent that he and his new chief were not suited to each other, for the capable but blunt Davis regarded the easygoing Frelinghuysen with impatience and some contempt, and Frelinghuysen, sensing this, offended Davis by going to others to confirm his advice. In June, 1882, Davis decided to resign, softening the effect of his departure by undertaking a confidential mission to Britain to discuss the Irish-American problem. (See Chapter 13.)

Frelinghuysen replaced him with John Davis, a young man who was both Bancroft Davis' nephew and Frelinghuysen's own son-in-law. The younger Davis had had considerable experience in the field of foreign claims, and he was highly praised for his work in the State Department, but, being less forceful than his uncle, he seems to have had less effect on the determination of policy. Bancroft Davis remained on good terms with Frelinghuysen and was occasionally called in for consultation.[1]

As a result of the division in the Republican party, the pressure of domestic business, and uneasiness in the State Department, therefore, Arthur and Frelinghuysen experimented cautiously during their first year of power, reversing some of Blaine's policies and improvising solutions for the most pressing diplomatic problems. One problem which they could not avoid was the War of the Pacific. If the United States did not propose to insist that Chile return to Peru the conquered province of Tarapacá, did this mean absolute nonintervention? Also, if the American government withdrew from the argument, how could it prevent Europeans from moving in to fill the vacuum thus created?

*   *   *

Nothing illustrates the new administration's lack of orientation or finesse better than its handling of the Trescot mission. Having received their instructions from Secretary Blaine during the first week of December, 1881, Trescot and Walker Blaine pressed southward, unaware of the storm rising at home. When they arrived in Lima, they were somewhat dismayed at the tumultuous welcome given them by the Peruvian people, who clearly regarded them as *dei ex machina* who would obtain García Calderón's release, order Chile to withdraw, and save the nitrate provinces. Trescot remarked wryly that his mission was so little calculated to realize these fantasies that the State Department would have to send a warship to rescue him at the end.[2]

In Santiago, where the envoys arrived on January 7, they found

[1]J. C. Bancroft Davis to Hamilton Fish, Washington, January 1, February 8, June 4, 24, July 9, 1882; Sevellon A. Brown (Chief Clerk of the State Department) to Fish, Washington, October 3, 1883, Fish Papers, CXXXIV, CXLI. *Washington Post*, December 14, 1881, p. 1. *New York Tribune*, July 4, 1882, p. 1.

[2]*Ibid.*, January 25, 1882, p. 1.

American diplomatic business in confusion, as Kilpatrick's death a month earlier had left no one but the American consul at Valparaiso to take over the legation. Since then one rumor had followed another concerning American intentions. The Chilean government had given Kilpatrick one of the most lavish funerals in the history of the country to demonstrate its appreciation of his sympathetic policy, while at the same time the army and navy continued to prepare for war with the United States. Nevertheless, under the surface Chile was much worried by Blaine's sternness. As the shrewd Trescot analyzed the situation, he saw elements which, properly exploited, might enable the United States to bring about a reasonable negotiated peace. The Chilean troops in Peru were tired and sick, the treasury strained by the expenses of the occupation. Unfortunately, in seizing García Calderón, the Chileans had compromised the only Peruvian government with which they could treat for peace. If Trescot could undo that blunder without applying too much pressure, negotiations might proceed quickly.[3]

Accordingly he and Walker Blaine presented their credentials on January 9 and began cautious, informal conversations with Foreign Minister José M. Balmaceda, guided only by their original instructions and one brief telegram from Frelinghuysen, urging them to avoid a rupture. Trescot obtained a list of Chile's preliminary terms, very similar to her demands at the "Lackawanna" conference more than a year before, and wired these to Washington, hoping to receive instructions for further discussions with Balmaceda. No instructions arrived, but on January 26 the mail brought a bundle of American newspapers, full of State Department documents and outraged editorials about Blaine's Peruvian policy which the Chilean newspapers avidly reprinted.[4]

A day or so later the envoys learned that Hurlbut in Lima, without consulting anyone, had invited the provisional government of Peru to the peace congress. Hoping to act before the news from

[3]Lucius Foote to James G. Blaine, Valparaiso, November 26, December 3, 7, 1881, Nos. 80, 81, 82, U.S., Consular Despatches, Valparaiso, X. *New York Tribune*, January 20, 1882, p. 5. William H. Trescot to Bancroft Davis, Viña del Mar, January 27, 1882; Valparaiso, March 16, Davis Papers, XXXI. Trescot to Frederick T. Frelinghuysen, Viña del Mar, January 27, No. 5, U.S., *Foreign Relations, 1882*, pp. 61-63.
[4]Trescot to Davis, Viña del Mar, January 27, 1882, Davis Papers, XXXI; Trescot to Frelinghuysen, January 13, 23 (telegram), U.S., *Foreign Relations, 1882*, pp. 58-61.

Lima was made public, Trescot and young Blaine went to the Chilean foreign office on January 31 to issue a similar invitation. Foreign Minister Balmaceda read the invitation, looked up, and remarked with evident satisfaction: "It is useless. Your government has withdrawn the invitation." He added that Trescot's original and revised instructions had been published, that news of them had reached Chile by wire from Paris, and that it would soon be announced in the newspapers.

Humiliated and powerless to act, the Americans managed to break off the conversation politely and returned to their quarters to await word from Washington. Trescot, the professional diplomat, had suffered for the inexperience of his amateur chief, complicated by poor communications and downright bad luck. He and Walker Blaine had arrived in Chile just after Frelinghuysen and Davis decided to reverse the Blaine policies. Even at that time the State Department could have instructed the envoys—and did, indeed, place in their hands a brief, uninformative telegram of January 3—but the vital longer dispatch was sent by ordinary mail from Panama and arrived too late. A secretary of state with more sense of diplomatic propriety would have withheld from publication all the correspondence with Trescot at least until the end of the mission, no matter what rumors circulated at home; but, like Blaine, Frelinghuysen was still more politician than diplomat.[5]

On February 4 the State Department finally telegraphed briefly that Trescot might act to further negotiations between the belligerents unless Chile insisted on the cession of Tarapacá and an indemnity. Trescot ignored the restriction as unrealistic, and a week later, at Balmaceda's request, he agreed to summarize their earlier informal conversations in a protocol. In this statement Chile expressed her willingness to negotiate a peace treaty if it provided for the cession of Tarapacá and the occupation for ten years of Tacna, Arica, and the Lobos Islands, pending the payment of

[5]Bastert, "Origins of Blaine's Pan-American Policy," p. 408. Walker Blaine to Frelinghuysen, Viña del Mar, February 3, 1882, No. 7; Trescot to Frelinghuysen, February 3, U.S., *Foreign Relations, 1882*, pp. 65-69. Walker Blaine to James G. Blaine, February 4, in Hamilton, *Blaine*, pp. 554-55. Trescot to Davis, Viña del Mar, February 24, Davis Papers, XXXI.

twenty million pesos by Peru.[6] These terms were quite unacceptable to the State Department and, of course, to Peru as well, but the protocol at least cleared away enough mist to reveal the extent of the disagreement between Chile and the United States.

Then followed several weeks of futile and often heated discussion between Trescot and Balmaceda, who rejected every alternative to occupation of the desired provinces. By mid-March Trescot had given up all hopes of success, for the Chilean newspapers had whipped up new frenzies of anti-Americanism by quoting attacks on Blaine's policies from the American press, and the State Department had further undermined the envoys' position in Santiago by publishing all their progress reports. Trescot finally poured out his feelings in a long, angry letter to Bancroft Davis, upbraiding him for his poor support and violations of confidence and declaring that the State Department had thrown away all chances of saving Tacna and Arica for Peru. "Get me home at the earliest practicable moment," he concluded. "I can't stand this much longer."[7]

On March 22 Trescot sailed again for Peru, hoping to confer with Hurlbut, but when he arrived in Lima he learned that the blustering minister was dead, felled by a sudden heart attack. Trescot then reported a confidential conversation with Balmaceda before his departure in which the Chilean had indicated that he might consider milder terms for Tacna and Arica, if offered by Peru. Hoping against hope, Trescot set off into the mountains of southern Peru on pack mule to see if Acting President Isidro Montero would offer such terms. Instead, Montero asked that Chile recognize his government first and enable him to call a provisional congress. This proposal only irritated the Chilean officials at Lima, who had expected Trescot to be more persuasive.

[6]Frelinghuysen to Trescot, February 4, 21, 1882 (telegrams), February 24, No. 7; Trescot to Frelinghuysen, Viña del Mar, March 4, No. 13, U.S., *Foreign Relations, 1882*, pp. 73-76, 79-85.

[7]Bulnes, *Guerra del Pacífico*, III, 117-20. Trescot to Davis, Valparaiso, March 16, 1882, Davis Papers, XXXI. Apparently Martínez, the Chilean minister in Washington, failed to make clear the change in American policy under Frelinghuysen, so that both governments suffered from poor communications. Encina, *Historia de Chile*, XVIII, 34-36, 43.

They refused to promise recognition.[8] At the same time Walker Blaine visited La Paz, where he found the isolated Bolivians bewildered and unhappy at the news of the Trescot-Balmaceda protocol. Fearing that they might conclude a separate peace with Chile, young Blaine exhorted them to cooperate with Peru, but he could say little more, since he did not know Frelinghuysen's intentions.[9]

On May 13 Trescot and Walker Blaine left Peru for home. Upon their arrival Trescot summed up the results of his futile mission. He felt that Montero's requests were not excessive, but, he added, "the reason which induces the hesitation of Chili is that she believes that, so long as the Peruvians are convinced that the United States will finally intervene, they never will negotiate in earnest." The moral was clear: If the United States hoped for peace, she must convince Peru that Tarapacá, at least, must be given up. On the other hand, if the United States withdrew completely, Peru would apply to Europe for intervention.[10] To such an impasse three years of backing and filling had brought the United States.

*   *   *

While Trescot was still in Chile, Frelinghuysen had chosen two seasoned diplomats to replace Kilpatrick and Hurlbut. Cornelius A. Logan, who became minister to Chile, was then minister to Central America and had already represented the United States in Chile before Osborn's appointment. He was a physician turned politician and a cousin of John A. Logan, a Stalwart senator from Illinois. The new minister to Peru, James R. Partridge, was a Maryland lawyer of some distinction who had served as minister in Central America, Venezuela, and Brazil. Unfortunately he was in poor health. George Maney, who was appointed to Bolivia, had been minister to Colombia.[11]

[8]Trescot to Frelinghuysen, Lima, April 5, 12, 1882 (telegram), May 3, Nos. 19, 24, U.S., *Foreign Relations, 1882*, pp. 89-95. M. Álvarez to J. F. Elmore, Huaraz, April 28, copy in U.S., Notes from Foreign Legations, Peru, VII.

[9]W. Blaine to Trescot, Arequipa, March 24, 1882; Lima, May 8, Nos. 1, 4, U.S., *Foreign Relations, 1882*, pp. 96-101.

[10]Trescot to Frelinghuysen, Washington, June 5, 1882, No. 26, *ibid.*, pp. 103-5.

[11]*Dictionary of American Biography*, XI, 357-58; XIV, 282-83. *New York Tribune*, March 3, 1882, p. 1. Millington, *American Diplomacy and the War of the Pacific*, pp. 128-29.

Recognizing at last that Santiago and not Lima controlled the outcome of the War of the Pacific, Frelinghuysen explicitly placed Dr. Logan in charge of negotiations. In his instructions to Logan, the Secretary assumed that Chile was "entitled to the reasonable and natural fruits of victory," including an indemnity and security against future attack, but he did not presume to define these terms precisely. In the hope of preventing injustice Logan ought to save as much territory for Peru as possible through judicious advice, but without attempting to dictate to either government. At the same time Frelinghuysen informed Partridge that the United States could do nothing to help Peru unless she resigned herself to losing some territory. He and Maney were told to cooperate with Logan, and Maney was further warned to take no steps at all unless requested.[12]

Possibly feeling resentful at his subordinate position, Partridge soon began to question and criticize Frelinghuysen's instructions. Either because he expected Acting President Montero's government to collapse at any time, or because he felt too weak for the rigorous trip, he made no effort to present himself at Montero's headquarters in Arequipa but remained in Lima. Here at first he complied with his instructions by assuring the Peruvians that the United States had no intention of coming to their aid. Gradually, however, he convinced himself that Chile's territorial demands were outrageous, that no conceivable Peruvian government would grant them, and that the continued deadlock would lead inevitably to European intervention.[13]

Arriving in Santiago, Logan found García Calderón "imprisoned" in a de luxe hotel and set out to persuade him to accept the latest Chilean terms: recognition of himself as president of Peru, cession of Tarapacá and the cities of Tacna and Arica (but not their hinterland), and a cash payment to Peru. Chile was now asking for more territory than at the time of Trescot's mission

[12]Frelinghuysen to Cornelius A. Logan, March 18, 1882, No. 2, U.S., Instructions, Chile, XVII, 6-8. Same, June 26, No. 12, U.S., *Foreign Relations, 1883*, pp. 74-77. Frelinghuysen to James R. Partridge, June 26, No. 5, *ibid.*, pp. 707-8. Frelinghuysen to George Maney, June 26, No. 2, U.S., Instructions, Bolivia, I, 354-55.

[13]Partridge to Frelinghuysen, Lima, June 21, September 5, October 25, November 22, 1882, Nos. 5, 32, 55, 64, U.S., Despatches, Peru, XXXVII, XXXVIII. Logan to Frelinghuysen, Lima, August 15, No. 5, U.S., Despatches, Chile, XXXII.

but was willing to pay for it. Logan felt that Peru could obtain no better terms in the predictable future.[14]

García Calderón and other Peruvian officials detained in Chile agreed that Tarapacá was beyond saving, but the other Peruvians refused to assume any responsibility for the cession of Tacna and Arica. For a few days Logan and the Chileans assumed that this noncommittal attitude removed all obstacles, but García Calderón decided that he could not give up the cities on his own authority alone. Logan proposed other expedients, but either the Chileans or García Calderón opposed each one, and the Chileans began to suspect that the Peruvian president was merely stalling for time. Finally García Calderón demanded that Chile recognize all Peruvian debts based upon a mortgage of deposits in Tarapacá and make arrangements to pay the creditors. He also asked to be released under a truce so that he could secure the approval of a special Peruvian congress.[15]

Logan now saw little hope of success, for neither party would trust the other. Furthermore, he suspected that Partridge was encouraging Peru to hold out, just as Hurlbut had done before him. In this extremity Logan stretched his instructions and wrote an unofficial letter of advice to Acting President Montero of Peru bypassing Partridge because of the latter's prejudice. The letter dated November 13, reported the breakdown of negotiations and asked whether it would not be better for Peru to cede the disputed territory and use the purchase money for much-needed reconstruction. Mexico had sold California and New Mexico to the United States for $15,000,000; Peru would do very well indeed, he said to get $10,000,000 for Tacna and Arica. He urged Montero to empower García Calderón to accept the proffered terms.[16]

Logan's letter was a risky gamble, for it was not worded to spare Peruvian feelings, and it endangered the secrecy of his negotiations. Montero delayed his reply until December 21 and

[14]Logan to Frelinghuysen, Santiago, September 8, 22, 1882, Nos. 6, 7, *ibid.*

[15]Logan to Frelinghuysen, Santiago, September 22, 26, October 5, 17, 1882, Nos. 7-10, *ibid.* For a Chilean account of the negotiations see Bulnes, *Guerra del Pacífico* III, 177-85.

[16]Logan to Frelinghuysen, Santiago, October 26, November 6, Nos. 15, 19, U.S., Despatches, Chile, XXXII. Logan to Isidro Montero, November 13, U.S., *Foreign Relations, 1883*, pp. 86-87.

then wrote simply that if Chile released García Calderón, he could secure his own authorization from the Peruvian congress. Meanwhile the text of the letter leaked out through one of Logan's servants, and the Panama *Star and Herald*, a newspaper which circulated down the whole Pacific coast, printed it *in toto*. The letter naturally aroused a storm of protest in Peru and Bolivia, and one editor declared that "not even the most super-Chilean would dare to make such a suggestion to the head of the Peruvian Government. . . . [Logan's] protestations of *impartiality* belong in a madhouse."[17] Partridge burst into exasperated complaints; García Calderón denied that he had ever approved the letter; and Frelinghuysen telegraphed from Washington that henceforth Logan had better refrain from making such positive suggestions to either side.[18]

Logan received these suggestions with bad grace, for, as he replied to Frelinghuysen, he had understood from his instructions that he was to give advice to both sides; no one else, not even Partridge, was in a position to see the whole question at once. He suggested that the United States ought to set forth reasonable terms to both belligerents, and if these were refused, withdraw its good offices.[19] Logan's ill humor is understandable, but by that time the American government had indeed taken one step toward a firmer policy. In his annual message to Congress on December 4, Arthur had deplored Chile's terms as too rigorous, but he had said flatly that United States intervention would be "utterly at odds with our past policy, injurious to our present interests, and full of embarrassments for the future." As Logan himself admitted,

[17]*La Nación* (Guayaquil), enclosed with Partridge to Frelinghuysen, January 22, 1883. For the text of the letter as printed in the *Star and Herald* see Partridge's dispatch of January 3, No. 75, U.S., Despatches, Peru, XXXVIII. See also Montero to Logan, Arequipa, December 21, 1882, U.S., *Foreign Relations, 1883*, pp. 89-90. Logan to Francisco García Calderón, Santiago, January 16, in [Francisco García Calderón], *Mediación de los Estados Unidos en la guerra del Pacífico. El Señor Doctor Don Cornelius A. Logan y el Dr. D. Francisco García Calderón* (Buenos Aires, 1884), pp. 115-17.

[18]Partridge to Frelinghuysen, Lima, January 3, 1883, No. 75, U.S., Despatches, Peru, XXXVIII. Logan to Frelinghuysen, Santiago, January 22, No. 56, U. S., Despatches, Chile, XXXII. García Calderón's account, which is not altogether convincing, appears in [García Calderón], *Mediación de los Estados Unidos, passim.*

[19]Logan to Frelinghuysen, Santiago, January 8, 12, 1883, Nos. 52, 53, U.S., Despatches, Chile, XXXII.

this firm statement stifled the last lingering Peruvian hopes of American aid and improved the prospects for a peace treaty.[20]

Meanwhile in Lima Partridge was making a final effort on behalf of nitrates, granted by Peru in 1877, which Grace had bought up. his own with García Calderón in Santiago. Partridge's idea of a settlement was to cede Tarapacá to Chile and either transfer Tacna and Arica to Bolivia or neutralize them under the guarantee of all three nations, thereby assuring the future security of Chile. Since Chile would recognize no Peruvian government with which to discuss such a settlement, Partridge resorted to a measure which even Hurlbut would not have considered. On January 16 and 22, 1883, he met the diplomatic representatives of Britain, France, and Italy at his house, and the four of them drew up a memorandum suggesting that their governments cooperate in urging negotiations on Chile. Partridge thus profaned the one principle which Evarts, Blaine, and Frelinghuysen had managed to keep inviolate: that the United States must settle the Chile-Peruvian question alone, without European "aid." As soon as Frelinghuysen heard of the memorandum, he disavowed Partridge's action and recalled him.[21]

In Santiago Logan continued to discuss terms occasionally with the Chilean foreign minister, but during February and March he discovered what he should probably have guessed before: that García Calderón was double dealing. Not only had he corresponded secretly with Partridge, but even while he professed that only his congress could authorize the transfer of territory, Montero had gone off to La Paz and offered to cede Tacna and Arica to Bolivia. Finally Logan learned the reason for the Peruvian president's concern for his country's debt and creditors: García Calderón was president of a nitrate company owning a large concession in Tarapacá. Suspicion or knowledge of this connection probably also explained Chilean resistance to his offers.[22]

[20]Richardson, *Messages and Papers*, VIII, 130. Logan to Frelinghuysen, Santiago January 20, February 1, 1883, U.S., Despatches, Chile, XXXII.

[21]Logan to Frelinghuysen, October 19, 1882, No. 12, *ibid*. Partridge to Frelinghuysen, Lima, November 2, 1882; January 23, 1883, Nos. 58, 83, U.S., Despatches Peru, XXXVIII. Frelinghuysen to James Russell Lowell, February 19, 1883 (telegram), U.S., Instructions, Britain, XXVI, 594. Frelinghuysen to Partridge, March 7 No. 34, U.S., Instructions, Peru, XVI, 565-67.

[22]Logan to Frelinghuysen, Santiago, December 26, 27, 1882; February 28, March 8, 1883, Nos. 41, 42, 66, 70, U.S., Despatches, Chile, XXXII.

From this point on, American diplomats played only a minor role in the negotiations. Logan made no further effort to mediate between the Chilean government and its slippery prisoner, while in Peru General Miguel Iglesias took advantage of the prevailing spirit of disillusionment to revolt against both García Calderón and Montero. Seth L. Phelps, who replaced Partridge at Lima during the summer of 1883, advised Frelinghuysen to recognize Iglesias as president, since it was obvious that he already had European approval. Logan agreed, but Frelinghuysen preferred not to interfere in Peruvian domestic affairs. On October 20, without aid or hindrance from the American ministers, Iglesias signed the Treaty of Ancón with Chile, ceding Tarapacá outright and allowing Chile to occupy the provinces of Tacna and Arica for ten years. After that time the question of ownership would be submitted to the inhabitants in a plebiscite. On April 24, 1884, the United States finally recognized the Iglesias government.[23]

Just as Frelinghuysen avoided all appearance of coercing Chile or Peru, so also he shunned the influence of claimants. Francisco Suárez of the Crédit Industriel wrote to him in October, 1882, urging him to enforce American mediation or leave Peru free to appeal elsewhere, but there is no evidence that Suárez got any satisfaction. Earlier in the year W. R. Grace and Company, an undeniably American firm with many commercial connections on the Pacific coast of South America, submitted to the State Department a claim against Chile on the basis of a contract for the sale of nitrates, granted by Peru in 1877, which Grace had bought up. The Department recognized that Chile had some sort of obligation, but it declared that since the original concessionaire was an operating company domiciled in Peru, the American government could do nothing.[24]

Although Frelinghuysen avoided any hint of scandal, both the

---

[23]Logan to Frelinghuysen, Santiago, May 29, 1883, No. 100, *ibid.*, XXXIII. Millington, *American Diplomacy and the War of the Pacific*, pp. 138-40, 156-59.

[24]Francisco P. Suárez to Frelinghuysen, Paris, October 9, 1882, U.S., Miscellaneous Letters. John Davis to W. R. Grace and Co., August 17, U.S., Domestic Letters, CXLIII, 358-59. Memorandum by F. N. Edwards, October 9, 1884, U.S., Reports of the Diplomatic Bureau, VI. In contrast to Frelinghuysen's caution, the British government vigorously pushed all its claims and in 1883 induced Chile to sign a general claims convention. Beck, "British and United States Relations with Chile," pp. 231-33.

pro-Blaine and the anti-Blaine press were convinced by now that the State Department had thoroughly mismanaged its diplomacy in Peru and Chile. As the *New York Herald* put it, the American eagle had flown into "the South American *mêlée*" twice, once as a game bird and once as a dove of peace. Each time he had only lost feathers. Needless to say, the *Tribune* attacked Frelinghuysen' nerveless inaction in order to praise Blaine's boldness. Some felt that both men had lost ground to Europe: "The gamecock policy of Mr. Blaine, followed by the hymn book policy of Mr. Freling huysen, together with the miserable impotence to which our navy is reduced, have sunk the influence of the United States in that quarter of the world to a lower level than it ever touched before. Others, however, declared that Chile, fearing European interven tion had executed a "master stroke" by "stimulating us to such vigorous assertion of the Monroe doctrine that neither England nor France thought it best to interfere; and having accomplished this she . . . snapped her fingers in our face, and went forward to the complete despoiling of Peru according to the plan she had originally proposed to herself."[25]

The American government was not the dupe of either Europe or Chile, but it certainly had little to boast about in its treatment of the War of the Pacific. From the beginning it had the choice of three alternative policies regarding the peace settlement. One of these was to stay out of the argument altogether and risk some sort of European intervention. The idea of British or French mili tary attack was absurd, but the fear of European economic ad vancement was so compelling that no secretary of state adopted this policy until everything else had been tried. If the United States had to intervene, it could either rush to Peru's defense and save the nitrate provinces or accept Chilean supremacy and pro mote a quick settlement. Evarts and Frelinghuysen realized that American public opinion would oppose active intervention on the side of Peru. Blaine, prompted by his desire to establish an American beachhead against British influence, wanted to interven for Peru without *seeming* to intervene—one of the most difficul

<hr>

[25]*Atlantic Monthly*, LIV (July 1884), 115. See also *New York Herald*, October 6, 1883, p. 4; October 8, p. 4; March 27, 1884, p. 6. *New York Tribune*, March 1883, p. 4; March 24, p. 4.

of diplomatic tricks, requiring a far steadier hand than his. In the end events proved that the most sensible role of the United States would have been that of a catalyst, to speed peace-making while war damage was still moderate, and Chile was still content with Tarapacá.

Common sense might require the unsentimental stifling of Peruvian hopes, but no one could bear to do this until it was too late. If Blaine, on coming to office, had sent the realistic Trescot as sole envoy to both countries, he might have ended the war with credit to the United States and himself. If Frelinghuysen had given Trescot adequate support during the winter of 1882, much could still have been saved. Instead, American sympathies, applied first with rashness, then with diffidence, and usually entrusted to unworthy agents, dragged down to defeat the best interests of both the United States and Peru.

Chapter 6

Impasse in Central America

IN KEEPING with his cautious reversal of Blaine's South American policies, Frelinghuysen might well have preferred to put off further action on the isthmian question, at least until De Lesseps had shown more signs of progress. However, many persons, even in Frelinghuysen's own wing of the Republican party, demanded action. A good example of their attitude was an article on the Monroe Doctrine published in December by John A. Kasson, an Iowa Stalwart who had become alarmed at European imperialism while minister to Austria under Hayes, and who now led the proponents of an active foreign policy in the House of Representatives.

Kasson cited evidences of European political ambitions in Mexico and Chile but declared that the chief danger now lay in commercial rivalry: "Covetous eyes are cast on outlying islands and continental coasts of Central and South America. A steam-ship line is preferred to an army; a canal to a fortification; a good harbor to a strong citadel." Through economic imperialism Europe sought "a flanking position, a military and naval rendezvous, in time of war, and an exclusive commercial position in time of peace." In the past Cuba and Canada had been the most serious danger points, but now Europe was trying to add to these by converting "a weak Central American state into another distracted Egypt, by means of foreign possessory rights in another isthmian canal." Kasson declared that any isthmian project should be an American undertaking, and in the name of the Monroe Doctrine he outlined a broad plan of economic expansion in the hemisphere.

> One million dollars saved from ineffectual interior improvements . . . will open several new [shipping] lines and markets to our agriculture and manufactures. . . . There are islands, and bays, and ports, and lines of communication which it may yet cost us a war to save to our interests, but which could now be peacefully saved. . . . [The changed situation] calls

for a change of our passive policy into one of action, knitting more and more closely our union with our sister republics, and opening wide the doors to the commercial activity of our people. Then shall we have irresistible arguments to sustain our non-colonization policy, and ample returns for our wise and beneficent enterprise.[1]

By no means did all Republicans follow Kasson. Gustave Koerner, for example, suspected him of wanting to "ride into the presidency on a war whoop" and declared that he had twisted Monroe's "original sound declaration" into "an empty catchword, to drive the people into all sorts of foolish adventures."[2] However, in the evenly divided Forty-seventh Congress many Half-Breeds and a sprinkling of Stalwarts like Kasson and Southern Democrats such as Senator John T. Morgan declared that something must be done about Central America. Accordingly, Frelinghuysen could not ignore Blaine's isthmian policies for long.

*   *   *

After Granville's devastating replies to Blaine in January, 1882, it would probably have been better for all concerned if the argument over the Clayton-Bulwer Treaty had been dropped, but Arthur had endorsed Blaine's dispatches in his annual message. The dispatches had then been published, and the British notes could scarcely be kept secret. Consequently on May 8 Frelinghuysen sent off to London a new set of arguments, made up partly of his own ideas and partly of a draft by Bancroft Davis. Abandoning Blaine's demand for changes in the treaty, he now suggested nothing less than its outright abrogation.

Frelinghuysen began by declaring that a European joint guarantee of isthmian neutrality was unnecessary since the Panama Railway had operated for nearly thirty years without it, and that anyway it would violate the Monroe Doctrine, which he described at length. Turning to Davis' draft, he then suggested that Buchanan's statement of 1860 (that the United States was satisfied with the treaty and its enforcement) applied only to the British protectorate over the Nicaragua Indians and not to

---

[1] Kasson, "Monroe Doctrine in 1881," pp. 523-33.
[2] Gustave Koerner to William Morrison, Belleville, Illinois, March 13, 1882, Morrison Papers.

her illegal expansion of lumbering "settlements" at Belize into the crown colony of British Honduras. (Nothing in Buchanan's message substantiated this point.) Finally he argued at great length that the canal provisions of the treaty referred to a specific project for a Nicaragua canal then under consideration, and that they could not have been intended to apply to Panama, for the treaty of 1846 with Colombia established American rights there. Since the bases of the canal provisions had disappeared, Frelinghuysen proposed to do away with the whole treaty. He graciously added that the American government would be happy to sign a separate agreement retaining those articles which restricted British and American colonization in Central America.[3]

Although Bancroft Davis had expected Granville to make mincemeat of the "weak and assailable" passages written by Frelinghuysen, it was Davis' own arguments from the Clayton-Bulwer Treaty which received the full force of the British reply. Granville quoted from the treaty and from contemporary diplomatic correspondence to prove that Clayton and Bulwer had intended to establish general principles applying to all interoceanic transit routes, and he argued that American rights under the Colombian treaty of 1846 did not rule out a more general guarantee of Panama's neutrality. He denied that Britain had illegally converted Belize from a "possession" into a colony and, presumably after research in his own archives, produced a postal convention of 1869 in which the United States had referred to "the colony of British Honduras." He did not need to say at the end that abrogation was completely unacceptable to Her Majesty's Government.[4]

On May 5, 1883, almost exactly a year after his first dispatch, Frelinghuysen turned once more to the breach. Again he had the aid of Bancroft Davis, now out of the State Department, but the note was no stronger than the last and simply repeated the old arguments: that, in the matter of canals, the Clayton-Bulwer Treaty pertained only to a specific situation, no longer existing; and that Britain had forfeited her rights by usurping Belize.

[3] J. C. Bancroft Davis to Hamilton Fish, Washington, June 4, 1882, Fish Papers, CXXXVI. Frelinghuysen to James Russell Lowell, May 8, 1882, No. 368, U.S., *Foreign Relations, 1882,* pp. 271-83.
[4] Lord Granville to Lionel S. Sackville West, December 30, 1882, No. 344, *ibid., 1883,* pp. 484-90.

Three and a half months later Granville replied, once again stating his arguments with a few new pieces of evidence and adding that he could not see in what way the Clayton-Bulwer Treaty was inconsistent with the Monroe Doctrine, as the American government seemed to think. In his final statement on the subject, Frelinghuysen made no important changes.[5] Since neither side had retreated, *status quo* carried the day, but alas, in this case after two full years of argument a return to *status quo* meant British victory.

Many Half-Breeds welcomed Frelinghuysen's discomfiture. At Blaine's urging the *New York Tribune* criticized Bancroft Davis' "tedious and irrelevant" discussion of the Nicaragua Indian question and predicted accurately that Britain would never agree to abrogate the treaty. Even if she did, the British Navy would still be free to seize Central America. Month after month the *Tribune* hammered away at the need to revise the treaty in order to place American rights at Panama on a footing with British rights at Suez.[6]

Newspapers which had opposed Blaine, however, agreed with Frelinghuysen that the treaty was "mere dead diplomatic lumber" and advised him not to try to save any of the still useful parts of it. Other patriotic Americans denounced the treaty as a source of Anglo-American misunderstanding, an obstacle to American expansion to the south, and a memento of bad diplomacy. As one writer asked indignantly, should the United States "withdraw from the honorable and patriotic position of defender and upholder of republicanism on this continent . . . calmly submit to the errors, mistakes, aye, blunders of its aforetime rulers, and under a mistaken sense of honor continue to be bound hand and foot by the terms of that . . . covenant of national disgrace?"[7]

[5]Frelinghuysen to Davis, Washington, April 10, 1883; Davis to Frelinghuysen, uncompleted draft, May 1, Davis Papers, XXXIII. Frelinghuysen to Lowell, May , No. 586; Granville to West, August 17; Frelinghuysen to Lowell, November 22, No. 708, U.S., *Foreign Relations, 1883*, pp. 418-21, 477-78, 529-32.
[6]James G. Blaine to Whitelaw Reid, Washington [April 22, 1883], Reid Papers, Box CIV. *New York Tribune*, June 9, 1882, p. 4; June 23, p. 4; September 28, p. 4; October 10, p. 4; October 12, p. 4; January 27, 1883, p. 6; January 17, p. 4; April 4, p. 4.
[7]George W. Hobbs, "Clayton-Bulwer Treaty vs Monroe Doctrine," *Bay State Monthly*, III (1885), 25. See also *New York Herald*, June 6, 1882, p. 6; and *Harper's Weekly*, XXVI (June 17, 1882), 371; (June 24), 392.

For all the efforts of Blaine and Frelinghuysen, American pa
triots were left to simmer in impotent wrath. In the long rur
the ponderous notes emanating from the State Department ma
have hastened the end of the Clayton-Bulwer Treaty by arousin
American public opinion, but this would be hard to prove. Th
credit for the abrogation of the treaty later went to John Hay
Blaine and Frelinghuysen got nothing for their pains but embar
rassment and a reputation for stubborn refusal to recognize th
obvious.[8]

*   *   *

Another part of Frelinghuysen's Central American inheritanc
from Blaine was American intervention in the boundary contro
versy between Mexico and Guatemala. Blaine's note of Novembe
28, 1881, warning the Mexican government not to attack Guate
mala, and his proposal for an inter-American peace congress wer
supposed to have a neutralizing effect on the controversy. Actu
ally both measures tended to favor Guatemala. Blaine read h
note of November 28 to the Guatemalan foreign minister the
visiting Washington, Lorenzo Montúfar, who was much pleasec
and the Guatemalan government received its invitation to th
peace congress with ecstatic approval.

Montúfar's joy was short-lived, for a few days later when h
proposed a formal treaty, Blaine evasively replied that he was no
politically dead and referred him to Arthur. Somewhat uneasy
Montúfar and representatives of Honduras and El Salvador ap
proached Frelinghuysen and Bancroft Davis with a treaty dra
giving the United States the right to station troops and occup
ports in their countries in return for American protection again
outside attack. At the same time Barrios pressed American Ministe
Logan (soon to leave Central America for Chile) to promise tha
the United States would recognize the union of these thre
countries, even if he could not prevail on Nicaragua and Cost
Rica to join at first. By January, 1882, economic troubles i
Guatemala had grown so alarming that Barrios sent his wife an

[8]For more extended comments on the Anglo-American correspondence se
Travis, *Clayton-Bulwer Treaty*, pp. 220-22, 225-26, 232-39; T. J. Lawrence, *Essa*
on Some Disputed Questions in Modern International Law (2d ed.; Cambridg
1885), pp. 126-42; Henderson, *American Diplomatic Questions*, pp. 147-50, 155, 15
59; and Keasbey, *Nicaragua Canal*, pp. 401-2, 408-9, 415-16.

children to San Francisco for safety.[9] To add to his difficulties, he became involved in a petty quarrel with France over the arrest of a member of the French legation for disorderly conduct. When France sent a warship to the Guatemalan coast as a warning, Barrios requested American good offices, but the crisis subsided before Mexico could take advantage of it.[10]

While Guatemala tried to draw closer to the United States, Mexico was further considering the desirability of American mediation in the boundary dispute. American Minister Morgan discreetly chose to present Blaine's invitation to the peace congress before his warning on the Guatemalan question. Foreign Minister Mariscal replied to the invitation in courteous but vague terms and did not accept until it was clear that the congress would not be held. On December 31 Morgan presented the substance of Blaine's warning and formally proposed arbitration by the President of the United States, recognizing the Mexican title to Chiapas in advance. He made no further progress, however, for by this time the Mexican government had decided to transfer negotiations to Washington by appointing as Mexican minister Matías Romero, who was well acquainted with the border dispute and had many friends in the United States.[11]

In March Romero presented his credentials to Frelinghuysen, who received him cordially and declared that the United States had no intention of forcing its mediation on either Mexico or Guatemala. Much gratified, Romero met Montúfar, who had been appointed Guatemalan minister to the United States. Since the two were personal friends, they began a direct, informal discussion of the principal point at issue—whether Mexican sovereignty over Chiapas should be assumed from the outset or sub-

[9]Cosío Villegas, *Historia moderna de México*, V, 184-85. Draft of agreement presented to Davis, December 27, 1881, U.S., Notes from Foreign Legations, Guatemala and Salvador, VI. *El Guatemalteco*, February 18, in U.S., *Foreign Relations, 1882*, p. 33. Cornelius A. Logan to Blaine, Guatemala City, December 28, 1881, No. 228; Logan to Frelinghuysen, January 25, 1882, No. 252, U.S., Despatches, Central America, XVIII.

[10]Logan to Frelinghuysen, Guatemala City, February 2, 13, 20, 27, 1882, Nos. 250, 264, 265, 271, *ibid*. A. Ubico to Frelinghuysen, February 3, 4, U.S., Notes from Foreign Legations, Guatemala and Salvador, VI.

[11]Philip H. Morgan to Frelinghuysen, Mexico City, January 10, February 6, March 8, 1882, Nos. 335, 354, 372, U.S., Despatches, Mexico, LXXV.

mitted to arbitration. On his own initiative and without instructions, Romero went so far as to submit a draft agreement, dated April 17, by which Mexico would agree to arbitration by President Arthur. At that point, however, he learned that in Mexico City the Guatemalan minister was asking an indemnity of $4,000,000 for the provinces. This news, together with evidence which he uncovered at this time concerning Blaine's earlier private correspondence with the Guatemalan government, made him suddenly cautious, and he decided to break off negotiations and await further instructions.[12]

Stymied in this direction, Montúfar then revived the earlier proposal for an alliance with the United States. On May 6, he suggested a treaty by which Guatemala would offer canal rights and low tariffs in exchange for American protection against outside attack. A few weeks later Montúfar urged Frelinghuysen to take over the job of negotiating for Guatemala, promising to accept whatever he obtained from Mexico. Frelinghuysen wisely rejected both proposals and merely suggested American good offices. Meanwhile he kept up his conversations with Romero, repeated his former assurance that the United States would mediate only at the request of both parties, and refused even to express an opinion on Romero's private conversations with Montúfar. As an extra precaution, Romero prevailed on former President Grant to talk to Arthur, who assured him that he had given up Blaine's interventionist policy.[13]

On July 1 President Barrios left Guatemala on a visit to the United States, probably intending to determine for himself how

[12]Matías Romero to Ignacio Mariscal, Washington, March 9, 24, May 5, 1882; Frelinghuysen to Romero, March 24, México, Ministerio de relaciones exteriores, *Correspondencia diplomática cambiada entre el gobierno de los Estados Unidos Mexicanos y los de varias potencias extranjeras* (6 vols.; México, 1882-1892), IV, 838-39, 855, 862-68. Matías Romero, "Settlement of the Mexico-Guatemala Boundary Question, 1882," *Journal of the American Geographical Society*, XXIX (1897), 130-33. Romero to Frelinghuysen, Washington, June 3, 1882, U.S., Notes from Foreign Legations, Mexico, XXVII. Montúfar to Frelinghuysen, Washington, April 10, 13, 14, 29, *ibid.*, Guatemala and Salvador, VI.

[13]Montúfar to Frelinghuysen, New York, May 6, June 14, 1882, *ibid.* Montúfar to Frelinghuysen, June 9, 15, U.S., Congress, House, 48th Cong., 1st Sess., 1883, House Executive Doc. 154, pp. 165-67. Frelinghuysen to Montúfar, June 5, July 24, *ibid.*, pp. 163-65, 171. Cosío Villegas, *Historia moderna de México*, V, 219. For a more detailed account of the three-way negotiations in Washington and Mexico City during the first half of 1882, see *ibid.*, V, 132-232.

much aid the Arthur administration would give him in acquiring the disputed provinces and unifying Central America. He arrived in Washington in mid-July, and during his first ceremonial visit to Frelinghuysen he lost no time in asking for American protection against Mexico. Rumors of a canal "deal" between Guatemala and the United States began to circulate widely, but Frelinghuysen made it clear once again that the American government would do no more than serve as arbiter, and only on the invitation of both parties to the dispute.[14]

Having made no progress at the State Department, Barrios addressed himself to Romero. At President Arthur's official reception the two Latin Americans, who were personal enemies, met each other with the stiff wariness of two strange dogs, but before long the tension relaxed. Barrios conceded the Mexican title to Chiapas as a basis of negotiations, and after more than a week of discussion, Romero signed a preliminary treaty accepting American mediation, because, as he said, Barrios was about to sail for Europe, and Romero was afraid that on his return he would try to claim Chiapas again. However, the Mexican government, still suspicious of the United States, repudiated the draft and censured Romero.[15]

On September 27, while Barrios was still in Europe, the Guatemalan minister in Mexico City signed a treaty which provided for direct negotiation over the disputed boundary without American aid, and after his return Barrios accepted the settlement. This ended the question for the time being, but after much bickering over details negotiations broke down once again in 1895. As before, both countries approached the United States for good offices. On this occasion the American minister served for a brief time as arbitrator, but he retired from office before completing the job. After years of negotiations "the natural protector" of Central America had no connection with the final settlement of the boundary dispute.[16]

[14]Romero, "Settlement of the Boundary Question," pp. 134-37.

[15]*Ibid.*, pp. 136-59. Cosío Villegas, *Historia moderna de México*, V, 238-48.

[16]Romero to Frelinghuysen, Washington, January 16, 1883, U.S., House Executive Doc. 154, pp. 176-87. Henry C. Hall to Frelinghuysen, Guatemala City, December 20, 1882, No. 47, *ibid.*, pp. 17-18. For the later history of the dispute see John Franklin Sensabaugh, *American Interest in the Mexican-Guatemalan Boundary Dispute*, Birmingham-Southern College Bulletin, XXXIII (Birmingham, Ala-

Although the American press paid less attention to the contro-versy between Mexico and Guatemala than to other problems of American foreign policy in 1881 and 1882, a few anti-Blaine editors joined the *Nation* in criticizing Blaine's "troublesome vi-vacity" which caused him to rush into the argument "with his-torical statements which were not only open to question but also betrayed a bias of mind in favor of the Guatemala side of the case" and which contradicted his "professions of disinterested friend-ship and of 'lofty' purposes." The *New York Tribune* put up a feeble defense of his actions after Frelinghuysen entered the State Department, but the *Herald* opposed any sort of intervention in Central America to promote unification.[17]

It was perfectly proper for Blaine and Frelinghuysen to tender American good offices or mediation to Mexico and Guatemala. Blaine and Logan erred in listening to the various Guatemalan offers without making it quite clear that the United States would not send arms or accept territory, and Blaine compounded the error by the severity of the language with which he warned Mexico against aggression and offered mediation. Since it was impossible to keep the Guatemalan offers secret, exaggerated rumors about American annexations reached Mexican ears and delayed the very settlement for which the American government was working.

More than that: the Mexican press and public, newly recovered from an epidemic of anti-Americanism, relapsed for a time into suspicion and hatred of the *norteamericano*.[18] Blaine should have realized that the United States had two stakes which might be affected by the outcome of the boundary controversy—on the one hand, her existing and growing trade and investments in Mexico and, on the other, her much smaller interests in Central America and her hope for an interoceanic canal across a stable, unified nation. In grasping at the hope in Central America, he endangered the reality in Mexico. The proper policy, as Freling-

bama, 1940), pp. 22-27. See also Jones, *Guatemala, Past and Present*, pp. 78-81, and Cosío Villegas, *Historia moderna de México*, V, chap. iv.

[17]*Nation*, XXXIV (February 16, 1882), 131; (March 16), 219. *New York Tribune*, May 31, 1882, p. 4. *New York Herald*, July 24, 1882, p. 4.

[18]See Romero's judgment in Matías Romero, "Mr. Blaine and the Boundary Question between Mexico and Guatemala," *Journal of the American Geographical Society*, XXIX (1897), 281.

huysen realized, was to protect both interests by holding out to both sides friendship and impartial good offices.

*   *   *

While Frelinghuysen with varying success disposed of Blaine's policies regarding the Clayton-Bulwer Treaty and the Mexico-Guatemalan boundary controversy, Congress was attacking the isthmian question from another angle, by continuing its debates on the rival transit projects. On December 15, 1881, Senator John F. Miller of California introduced a bill similar to one of the preceding session which provided for the incorporation of the Nicaragua canal company and for a government guarantee of profits. Miller, a vigorous Westerner who had made a fortune from an Alaskan fur monopoly, supported the bill in the Foreign Relations Committee, and with the approval of John T. Morgan and the committee chairman, William Windom of Minnesota, reported it favorably with amendments in April. The Nicaragua canal bill then passed to the House, where John A. Kasson, having tried in vain to obtain the reappointment of the special Isthmian Canal Committee, put it through the Foreign Affairs Committee instead. Kasson's favorable report was delivered in July, and a Democratic minority reported against the bill.[19]

Although the Nicaragua canal bill thus reached the floor of both houses, it was not voted on before adjournment, and meanwhile Eads's supporters publicized their project in hearings before the Senate Committee on Commerce, which was friendly to the ship-railway. Convening in December, 1882, the short session of the Forty-seventh Congress devoted its principal energies to the tariff problem (see Chapter 8), but the canal bill was reintroduced into the House (without the request for a guarantee). The Senate Foreign Relations Committee once again recommended

[19]*New York Tribune*, December 16, 1881, p. 1. U.S., Congress, Senate, 47th Cong., 1st Sess., 1882, Senate Rept. 368, as reprinted in 56th Cong., 2d Sess., Senate Executive Doc. 231, Part 5, pp. 107-10. U.S., Congress, House, 47th Cong., 1st Sess., 1882, H. Rept. 1698, *passim. Ibid., Congressional Record*, XIII, 34, 1777. Two dissertations are useful on this subject: Ollen Lawrence Burnette, Jr., "The Senate Foreign Relations Committee and the Diplomacy of Garfield, Arthur, and Cleveland" (Ph. D. dissertation, University of Virginia, 1952), and Sarah Georgia Walton, "The Frelinghuysen-Zavala Treaty, 1884-1885" (M.A. thesis, University of Virginia, 1953). On Senator Miller see *Dictionary of American Biography*, XII, 630-31.

the bill on the floor, but it went no further in either house.[20]

What caused the Congressional deadlock? Undoubtedly a large bloc favored an American-sponsored transit project of some sort, for at one point the House voted 127-76 for immediate settlement of the Nicaragua canal bill. However, for one thing, isthmian enthusiasts were split by the two projects, and although some congressmen voted for both, others were narrowly partisan, so that in a sense Eads and Ammen killed each other off. Some congressmen favored a canal or ship-railway in the future but preferred to settle the controversy with England first, feeling that "what was right, what was reasonable for this country to do when the Clayton-Bulwer Treaty was negotiated is not reasonable now."[21] Others preferred to spend public funds on projects which would more directly benefit their constituents. Still others, especially Northern Democrats, opposed anything smacking of bounties which protectionists might use to justify ship subsidies or which would so deplete the Treasury as to necessitate continued high tariffs. Thus Congress found a variety of excuses to avoid action.

*   *   *

The inconclusive debate in Congress did not prevent the State Department from undertaking its own investigation of the Nicaragua canal project. American observers were reporting "the excessively Frenchy air" in Panamanian society, and occasional wild rumors floated northward to the effect that Chile had designs on the isthmus or that Britain planned to buy from Colombia an island in the Bay of Panama.[22] Although Frelinghuysen lacked Blaine's congenital suspicions of Europe, he gradually came to the conclusion that the United States must strengthen its position

[20]U.S., Congress, House, 47th Cong., 2d Sess., 1883, House Executive Doc. 107, pp. 165 ff. *Report to the Provisional Interoceanic Canal Society, by the Executive Committee, March 16th, 1883* [Washington, 1883], p. 1. U.S., Congress, Senate, 47th Cong., 2d Sess., 1883, Senate Rept. 952, *passim.*

[21]*Ibid., Congressional Record*, XIV, 2133. For Congressional opinions see *New York Tribune*, December 29, 1881, p. 1; *New York Herald*, January 18, 1882, pp. 3-4, and Belmont, *American Democrat*, pp. 337-51, in addition to the *Congressional Record* and committee reports.

[22]*New York Herald*, February 22, 1882, p. 3. Jehu Baker to Frelinghuysen, Caracas, August 18, December 11, Nos. 532, 588, U.S., Despatches, Venezuela, XXX, XXXI. William L. Scruggs to Frelinghuysen, Bogotá, April 5, 1883, No. 78, *ibid.*, Colombia, XXXVII.

in Nicaragua and that Admiral Ammen's Provisional Interoceanic Canal Society did not adequately safeguard American influence over the transit route, because its concession of 1880 gave too much power to private individuals and failed either to exclude European capital or to guarantee the neutrality of the route in wartime.

To Ammen's disgust, the Maritime Canal Company, which his group founded as a permanent corporation, did not satisfy the State Department any better, and even when the Senate Foreign Relations Committee inserted into Miller's guarantee bill a clause allowing the American government to occupy and manage the canal in an emergency, "subject to any sovereign rights of the Government of Nicaragua," Frelinghuysen objected to the restrictive phrase.[23] However, in spite of the Admiral's ill feeling, the Secretary seems to have realized that until the United States could work out its own policy regarding a Nicaragua canal, the company's concession might temporarily forestall European rivalry. He offered no objection when, in May, 1882, Edward P. Lull obtained an extension of the concession for two and a half years. On occasion Frelinghuysen even used the company president, Captain Seth L. Phelps, U.S.N., as his own agent in negotiations with Nicaragua.

During the latter half of 1882 the State Department began to maneuver for control of the Nicaragua canal project. In September Frelinghuysen sent Phelps on a special informal mission to inquire if the government of Nicaragua would allow the United States to establish coaling stations in Lake Nicaragua, at the midpoint of the proposed canal route. Phelps arrived in Managua just at the end of a presidential term of office. The outgoing president, Lorenzo Zavala, welcomed the proposal but declined to act, for fear of opposition from a nationalistic clique in the capital, and because he did not want to commit his successor. After some delay Phelps then laid his plan before the president-elect, Adán Cárdenas, and the three discussed terms for the lease

[23]Frelinghuysen to Henry C. Hall, July 19, 1884, No. 154, U.S., Instructions, Central America, XVIII, 443-45. Frelinghuysen to Logan, March 14, 1882, No. 196, U.S., *Foreign Relations, 1882*, p. 34. For Ammen's view of Frelinghuysen see Daniel Ammen, *The Errors and Fallacies of the Interoceanic Transit Question. To Whom Do They Belong?* (New York, 1886), pp. 58-60.

of islands in the lake. At this point rumors about Phelps's mission touched off a violently anti-American article in one of the nationalist newspapers. Phelps took it upon himself to publish a denial that the United States had any designs on Nicaraguan sovereignty over the canal route. Then he returned home.[24]

Frelinghuysen sent Phelps off to Peru as minister, and for the next year he allowed the transit question to drift. During that time the new American minister to Central America, Henry C. Hall, helped to settle a quarrel between Nicaragua and Britain over coastal rights and prevailed on the Nicaraguan government to make certain favorable modifications in the Lull concession of 1882, but nothing further was said publicly about the canal project, to the discontent of some Nicaraguans, who began to talk of seeking European support.[25]

Frelinghuysen did well to move slowly, for at this time there was an unusual amount of buzzing in the Central American hive. At the end of 1882 the Guatemalan dictator, General Barrios, had returned from his visit to the United States and Europe full of enthusiasm for his plan to unite Central America. El Salvador fell into line readily, and when the president of Honduras tried to offer opposition, Barrios forced him into exile and substituted a more compliant puppet. President Cárdenas of Nicaragua concluded that his turn was next and wired to Admiral Ammen, requesting American aid, which, it turned out, he did not need.[26]

[24]Unsigned instructions to Seth L. Phelps, Washington, September 23, 1882, Special Missions, III, 347-49, Records of the Department of State (National Archives, Record Group 59). Hereafter cited as U.S., Special Missions. Phelps to Frelinghuysen, Washington, December 2. U.S., Special Agents, XXXII. *New York Herald*, January 4, 1883, p. 7. For a brief sketch of Phelps see *New York Tribune*, June 23, p. 2.

[25]F. J. Medina to Frelinghuysen, Managua, September 6, 1883, U.S., Notes from Foreign Legations, Nicaragua, II. Hall to Frelinghuysen, Guatemala City, June 9, No. 122, U.S., Despatches, Central America, XX. Frelinghuysen to Hall, February 24, April 17, No. 62, U.S., Instructions, Central America, XVIII, 310, 340. See also Walton, "Frelinghuysen-Zavala Treaty," pp. 91-92.

[26]Paul Burgess, *Justo Rufino Barrios* (Philadelphia, 1926), pp. 223-25. Adán Cárdenas to Daniel Ammen, Managua, March 8, 1883, copy in Thomas F. Bayard Papers, LXIII (Library of Congress). Frelinghuysen instructed Hall that he might tender his personal good offices if a dispute developed, and asked him to suggest an additional remedy for future quarrels. Frelinghuysen to Hall, December 4, 1883, No. 116, U.S., Instructions, Central America, XVIII, 355-57.

The effects of this rivalry on the canal project became apparent when the foreign minister of El Salvador suggested to the other governments that they urge the United States to construct the canal. Honduras agreed at once, but Nicaragua and Costa Rica found various reasons to decline.[27]

Thus at the end of 1883 American interests in Central America did not seem appreciably more secure than when Frelinghuysen took office, two years before. While the deadlock with Britain over the Clayton-Bulwer Treaty did not increase the real danger of British armed intervention, fears of Europe would remain as long as De Lesseps continued digging and French and British warships cruised in the Caribbean. Frelinghuysen had helped to settle the Mexico-Guatemalan boundary question at least temporarily and had thereby virtually eliminated Mexico from the isthmian question, but the rivalry between Barrios and Nicaragua threatened at any moment to burst into open conflict which would force the United States to make a painful choice. At home, Congress could not decide between the Eads and Ammen-Phelps groups. In Managua the Nicaraguan government could not or would not grant those safeguards which Frelinghuysen felt essential to the success of a canal. Yet, far from despairing, the Secretary was about to renew his efforts for an American transit project, and despite the unpromising circumstances of the preceding year, in 1884 his efforts would bear fruit.

[27]The correspondence arising from the proposal of El Salvador appears in U.S., *Foreign Relations, 1883*, pp. 57-61.

CHAPTER 7

The New Navy

DURING the early 1880's it was impossible for officials, press, or public to penetrate very far into the question of American security without facing the necessity of naval reform. Since the Civil War, economy and inefficiency had eroded the fighting strength of the United States Navy, while Britain, France, and other Powers kept apace of technological changes and little by little pulled ahead of the United States. In 1881 it seemed clear to many that an expansionist foreign policy would require the immediate construction of new warships and the overhauling of the whole Navy Department. During the following year the Arthur administration opened a new chapter in the history of American militarism.

* * *

By almost any imaginable standard of judgment the United States Navy of 1881 was a disgrace to the nation. Through great effort and at a time of rapid change in naval technology the Union government had created a fleet of ships during the Civil War which was one of the strongest in the world, but instead of profiting from the experience gained and from new developments in steam power and iron or steel hulls, the Johnson and Grant administrations rested on their oars. In five years after the war the number of ships fell from seven hundred to two hundred. Traditional methods regained sway, so that a general order of 1869 required "full sail power" for all new vessels. It was even proposed to charge commanding officers for all coal used whenever they started the engines. According to the ruling theory, inherited from Thomas Jefferson, the principal function of the Navy was to prevent hostile ships from entering American harbors and shelling American ports. Cruising beyond sight of American land was coming to be thought unnecessary and wasteful.[1]

[1]Harold and Margaret Sprout, *The Rise of American Naval Power, 1776-1918* (Princeton, New Jersey, 1939), chap. xi.

In 1881 the Navy contained not a single up-to-date warship and less than fifty which could safely fire a gun. According to the departmental report of the following year, the United States had one first-rate ship (the "Tennessee," of 4,840 tons displacement), fourteen second-rates, and twenty-two third-rates, which the Secretary of the Navy described as creditable looking and comfortable to live in but inferior to other navies in steaming, maneuvering, and fire power. In addition the Navy had thirteen single-turreted monitors, built during and immediately after the Civil War for shore defense. They were practically useless even for this purpose, since in order to venture out of harbor they required towing and a quiet sea. What was even worse, the supposedly active ships were actually in wretched condition. When Alfred T. Mahan took command of the "Wachusett" in 1883, he found her boilers and engines run-down and the timbers of her hull shaken and battered from the effects of four years of cruising without repairs. Nine months after the "Alaska" came out of dry dock, a common sailor wrote in his diary: "For all that I can go up on the Berth Deck to day and put my hand into seams that are wide open and wooden knees that cost hundreds of dollars I can pick to pieces like so much *Tinder*."[2]

Even if one of these slow, outmoded tubs had come within range of an enemy without being blown to bits, she could have done little damage for lack of modern artillery. The various ships mounted a variety of smooth-bore, muzzle-loading guns, plus a few converted by the later addition of rifling and a number of the notorious Parrott rifles, which were said to be more dangerous to the firing crew than to the target. While the British worked night and day to develop and manufacture rifled artillery, an American steel manufacturer contracted in 1880 to furnish a single experimental casting; two years later it was still unfinished. A naval officer who had invented several precision devices for range-finding and gun-sighting found to his amazement that while the Navy officials refused to order any, they had no objection to

[2]Entry for May 15, 1880, John Thompson, Journal, Section III, p. 3 (New York Public Library). See also Sprout, *Rise of American Naval Power*, pp. 172, 175. U.S., Congress, House, *Report of Secretary of the Navy, November 29, 1882*, 47th Cong., 2d Sess., 1883, House Executive Doc. 1, Part 3, pp. 5-7. William Dilworth Puleston, *Mahan* (New Haven, Connecticut, 1939), p. 66.

his selling them to European admiralties. The backward condition of artillery was also reflected in the disrepair of harbor fortifications, which the *New York Tribune* thought little better than pasteboard against enemy guns. At the same time, in the internal organization of the department overlapping bureaus duplicated functions and accumulated useless supplies—enough canvas, for example, to outfit both American and British navies for thirteen years.[3]

Most critics of the hapless Navy admitted that American officers and sailors were greatly superior to their ships, but even in personnel critics found room for improvement. One basic difficulty was an oversupply of officers. In 1882, to handle thirty-one ships the Navy had 937 officers on sea duty, 664 on shore duty, and 236 awaiting orders—"a sort of amphibious arrangement," said the Democratic wit, S. S. Cox. The Naval Academy turned out more ensigns than the Navy could accept, while at the other end of the scale elderly admirals resisted retirement and innovation with equal vigor. (Eventually Congress abolished the ranks of admiral, vice admiral, and commodore, and tried to abolish that of rear admiral as well.) The lax discipline lowered morale, and Congress made pets of some officers, such as Robley D. ("Fighting Bob") Evans, who engaged his superior, the Secretary of the Navy, in a needless and insubordinate public argument.[4] A few of the protégés were incompetent drunkards, such as the commander of the leaky "Ashuelot," which sank in the China Sea during February, 1883, with the loss of eleven seamen. After that disaster Consul Charles Seymour proposed that all congressmen be compelled to take a world tour on an American warship as a prerequisite for re-election.[5]

---

[3]John R. Spears, *The History of Our Navy from its Origin to the End of the War with Spain, 1775-1898* (5 vols.; New York, 1899), V, 57-64, 81-84. *New York Tribune*, January 30, 1880, p. 1; May 18, 1883, p. 1. Bradley A. Fiske, *From Midshipman to Rear Admiral* (New York, 1919), pp. 133, 141. Mark D. Hirsch, *William C. Whitney, Modern Warwick* (New York, 1948), p. 264.

[4]U.S., *Report of Secretary of the Navy, 1882*, pp. 7-9. U. S., *Congressional Record*, 48th Cong., 1st Sess., 1883, XV, 1659. *New York Herald*, February 24, 1883, p. 6. Leon Burr Richardson, *William E. Chandler, Republican* (New York, 1940), pp. 317-24.

[5]*Ibid.*, p. 324. *New York Herald*, February 22, 1883, p. 7. Charles Seymour to John Russell Young, Canton, February 22, enclosed with Young to Frederick T. Frelinghuysen, Peking, March 15, No. 152, U.S., Despatches, China, LXIV.

By 1881 many of the factors which were promoting other aspects of American expansionism had begun to stimulate interest in naval reform. Led by a few Navy officers and others possessing technical information, newspapers such as the *New York Tribune* and the *New York Herald* set forth a variety of arguments, seeking to frighten, shame, and persuade a land-based public to review maritime policy. Before long these arguments were appearing in Congressional debates as well. No single writer or congressman dominated the naval reform movement of the 1880's as Alfred T. Mahan did after 1890, but in one way or another these early publicists anticipated many of his ideas.[6]

The most elementary argument was that of fear. Rear Admiral John Rodgers declared that the Navy was "capable neither of inflicting material harm nor of affording us adequate protection from the assaults of either Chile, Brazil, or Buenos Ayres [*sic*], to say nothing of England, France, Germany, Italy, or Spain." Within three weeks after a declaration of war Chile could sweep American commerce from the Pacific and attack San Francisco without material hindrance from American warships. A little later Rodgers likened his country to "a great jelly-fish, huge in bulk but powerless to strike back if assailed."[7]

Other critics, while minimizing the danger of attack, pointed out that the prestige of the United States and its expanding foreign policy demanded the support of obvious physical strength, for the history of every world Power from Phoenicia to the British Empire had demonstrated that a first-class navy was an absolute pre-requisite to national greatness. "We cannot rely solely upon the moral sense of mankind for respect for our treaty rights, or the safety of our citizens abroad," warned an American minister to Germany. In a series of editorials the *Washington Post* embroidered the same theme, reminding its readers that the integrity of the Monroe Doctrine and American control of an isthmian canal rested in the last analysis on force. After publishing Blaine's dispatch of

[6]An excellent analysis of this early agitation is Robert Seager, II, "Ten Years before Mahan: the Unofficial Case for the New Navy, 1880-1890," *Mississippi Valley Historical Review*, XL (1953), 491-512. Most of Seager's evidence comes from the years after 1882, when the reforms had already begun to take effect.

[7]*New York Herald*, December 6, 1881, p. 7. U.S., *Congressional Record*, 48th Cong., 1st Sess., 1883, XV, 1454.

November, 1881, on the Clayton-Bulwer Treaty, the *Post* predicted "a new era in naval construction" if the nation were to be spared the humiliation of backing down.[8]

An argument of special interest to naval reformers was the connection between a strong navy and the spread of American foreign commerce. "We are the great middle kingdom," wrote Lieutenant James D. J. Kelley, "and an analysis of the laws underlying trade expansion proves incontrovertibly that we should rule the commerce of the world. . . . Every [war] ship should become a commercial agent, and . . . [spread] information about the resources of the country, the prices and values of our commodities, [and] the advantages inuring to foreign merchants of dealing with us."[9] Commodore Robert W. Shufeldt, whose thinking often foreshadowed Mahan, agreed: "The man-of-war precedes the merchantman and impresses rude people with the sense of the power of the flag. . . . I believe that our merchant marine and our Navy are joint apostles, destined to carry over the world the creed upon which its institutions are founded."[10]

It goes without saying that these expansionist arguments failed to convince some conservatives that the country needed a new navy. Confident that the United States had ended its last major war and would never acquire colonies or meddle in European disputes, many people, especially in the interior, regarded battleships, like diplomats, as ornaments unsuitable to a simple, clean-living republic. In Congress an important obstacle to naval reform was ignorance of technical details, for, as the *New York Tribune* put it, many of the members hardly knew a frigate from a dugout.[11] Confronted with the necessity of putting blind trust in the expert knowledge of naval officers and committees, some took refuge in opposition. Lastly, the "pork barrel" impeded progress, for, as Grant's secretary of the navy, George M. Robeson, had discovered, repairs were often more profitable than new ships, and under his guidance the

[8]*Ibid.*, 46th Cong., 2d Sess., XII, Appendix, pp. 142-43. A. A. Sargent to Frelinghuysen, Berlin, March 4, 1884, No. 248, U.S., Despatches, Germany, XXXIV. *Washington Post*, February 9, 1881, p. 2; March 9, p. 2; March 22, p. 2; April 8, p. 2; December 19, p. 2.

[9]*New York Herald*, December 12, 1881, p. 4.

[10]Robert W. Shufeldt, *The Relation of the Navy to the Commerce of the United States* (Washington, 1878), pp. 6-8 *et passim*.

[11]*New York Tribune*, February 1, 1880, p. 6.

government spent millions of dollars uselessly. When Robeson left the Cabinet, he entered the House of Representatives to defend himself against Congressional investigations, with the result that whenever the House recommended naval reform, the suspicions of the *Nation* and other exponents of honest government were aroused.[12]

*   *   *

Despite isolationism, inertia, and fear of waste, agitation for a new navy was under way by 1881. Blaine had given lip service to the cause in the Senate, although he regarded revival of the American merchant marine as more important.[13] Garfield's secretary of the navy, William H. Hunt, while mainly a political appointee, surrounded himself with able advisers and set up a planning board which included the forceful and outspoken Commander Robley D. Evans. After a summer of study the board presented a report to Congress, dated November 7, which recommended increasing the effective vessels of the Navy from thirty-two to seventy, including reserve, and the immediate construction of two new steel cruisers, twenty-one other steel vessels, and numerous smaller ships. After suitable debate Congress obliged the Navy Department with a modest compromise between past and future: two steel cruisers carrying full sail power.[14]

By this time Arthur had replaced Hunt with a new secretary of the navy, William E. Chandler, a skilled lobbyist and party organizer from New Hampshire who was a personal friend of Blaine. He had already been rejected by the Senate in 1881 for the position of solicitor-general. Grant opposed this new appointment because Chandler was a Half-Breed, and Democrats and reformers abused him as "a man who never drew an honest political breath," but the Senate confirmed him this time.[15] Although Chandler continued to

[12]Sprout, *Rise of American Naval Power*, pp. 175-82, 190-98. *Nation*, XXXIV (June 22, 1882), 511; XXXVII (November 1, 1883), 371-72.

[13]U.S., *Congressional Record*, 45th Cong., 3d Sess., VIII, 627-28. Mercantile elements sometimes felt the same way. New York *Daily Commercial Bulletin*, December 3, 1881, p. 2.

[14]Sprout, *Rise of American Naval Power*, pp. 186-87. Richardson, *Chandler*, pp. 289-90. U.S., Congress, House, 47th Cong., 1st Sess., 1882, House Executive Doc. 1, Part 3, 28ff.

[15]Richardson, *Chandler*, pp. 281-86. Muzzey, *Blaine*, p. 164. Blaine to William E. Chandler, Washington, January 12, 1882; A. H. Young to Chandler, Dover, New Hampshire, April 7, Chandler Papers (New Hampshire Historical Society).

use the Navy Department as a source of patronage, he also devoted his energy, his gift for organization, and his political connections to naval construction and renovation. He placed the able Commodore Robert W. Shufeldt in charge of a new advisory board, added a number of well-trained engineers, and set them at the task of implementing the will of Congress.[16]

In his first report, of 1882, Chandler surveyed his derelict empire with unpitying eye and transmitted the advisory board's recommendations for three new cruisers (each smaller than the ones recommended in the previous year), a dispatch boat, and a ram. The board was unable to agree on the advisability of completing four half-finished monitors of revised design. Chandler called attention to the problem of harbor defense and as a compromise suggested that money be appropriated to commission one monitor. Even before the preparation of this report Chandler had begun to overhaul his department, and while Congress debated general naval policy, he organized a much-needed Naval War College at Newport, Rhode Island.[17]

During the short session of 1882-1883 the Forty-seventh Congress used up most of its time and energy with the tariff question, but the House devoted a week in January to the Navy, and a handful of senators spoke on the subject. At first the representatives reviewed the dismal realities and tried to dispose of the surplus of officers, but eventually they came to the proposed construction program. Some objected that the proposed appropriation was inadequate, others that no appropriation at all was necessary, since American strength lay, not in her navy, but in her resources and population. In time of crisis, said one, "the great heart and head of the American people will respond, as they have done in the past." When a member ridiculed the "miserable old monitors," Robeson, who had begun their construction, replied with a vision of hemispheric dominion:

> [The monitors] will give us control of the Spanish Main, if need be, and in the waters of the Orinoco, where to-day Eng-

[16]Richardson, *Chandler*, pp. 290, 309-15 *et passim*. For a much less friendly account see Hirsch, *Whitney*, pp. 258-63.

[17]U.S., *Report of Secretary of the Navy, 1882, passim*. New York *Tribune,* June 25, 1883, p. 1. Richardson, *Chandler*, chap. xv.

land is attempting to establish her South American empire; will give us control in the West Indies where to-day England ... is about to establish on the island of Antigua what she calls the Malta of the West ... right in the route of our commerce from New York to New Orleans and the Gulf States. The finishing of these monitors under such restrictions as we have provided will give us power on the Isthmus, if necessary, to assert the dignity and honor of our country and to maintain its policy.[18]

After the House had passed the naval appropriations bill, it went to the Senate for another round of debate. Here the principal opponent was a personal enemy of Chandler, John McPherson of New Jersey, who called the bill "snakish" because it gave the Secretary too much power to experiment with public funds. However, John T. Morgan supported the bill, to strengthen American trade abroad:

We send our commerce into all the different parts of this world, and we are getting so strong now in our industries and in our commercial power that it has become a matter of great importance to the people that our commerce should seek every avenue of trade. ... In order to do that with any degree of success, and in order to impress the people with whom we deal ... with a sense of our power, our strength, and our financial ability, ... we are bound to have a navy.[19]

The final bill was a compromise, as before. Chandler got his three cruisers and a dispatch boat, to be provided with sail power, and Robeson's monitors were also to be completed, while many of the old wooden hulks were condemned to be junked.

As soon as Arthur signed the naval appropriations bill, the advisory board invited builders to submit plans for cruisers and, when this appeal yielded no practical result, drew up its own plans and asked for construction bids. When the bids were opened, it appeared that one firm, John Roach and Company of Chester, Pennsylvania, had submitted the lowest figures for all four ships. Chandler awarded the contracts to the Roach company, thereby touching off a controversy which lasted beyond the end of the Arthur administration. Roach was a tough old Ulsterman in his seventies,

[18]U.S., *Congressional Record*, 47th Cong., 2d Sess., XIV, 1419-20, 1454, 1509, 1559.
[19]*Ibid.*, pp. 3094, 3098.

almost illiterate, who had come to the United States as a penniless immigrant, built up a prosperous business in engines and other heavy machinery, and erected one of the largest shipyards in the country. With a reputation for honesty and good merchandise, he had sought out government contracts, employed lobbyists, contributed heavily to the Republican party, and staunchly defended high tariffs and ship subsidies. In all these things he was typical of his class, but Democrats and reformers claimed to see an unholy connection between Roach and Chandler, who, it is true, were personal friends. Despite Roach's low bids, Chandler should have considered his advanced age and the certainty of criticism and should have made some arrangement whereby several firms could share the four contracts.[20]

Having accused Chandler of corrupt dealings with Roach in permitting him to submit such low bids, his enemies sat back and waited for the inevitable flaws in the new, experimental cruisers. Undoubtedly the Navy could have obtained better ships by buying plans outright from England, but patriotism and the need for experience dictated American design. Although the iron industry was as yet unable to produce the proper type of steel plating for the hulls, Roach's shipyard had ample facilities for the actual construction. The specifications for the vessels, however, caused trouble from the beginning. Their two-thirds sail power, their lack of copper sheathing, the allegedly inadequate protection at the bow, and every unusual detail of the engines received a share of advance criticism. The *London Engineer*, for example, found defects everywhere when it described the "Chicago":

> Her engines are revivals of devices long since obsolete, and all the vices of American marine engineering manifest themselves. No English engineer in his senses would dream of putting in compound beam engines to drive twin screws. Defective as the engines are, they are admirable when compared to the boilers. To go to sea with such boilers is simply to court destruction.[21]

[20]Richardson, *Chandler*, pp. 292-96. For the exact bids see U.S., *Congressional Record*, 48th Cong., 1st Sess., XV, 2803. It is worth noting that, while the second lowest bidder criticized the contracts, the third lowest bidder supported Chandler. Both were American shipbuilding firms of high reputation.
[21]*London Engineer*, n.d., quoted *ibid.*, p. 2764. See also Richardson, *Chandler*,

Shrugging off opposition, Chandler recommended seven additional cruisers and four gunboats in his report for 1883; a year later he requested new appropriations and transmitted the board's advice that sails be omitted.[22] Congress engaged in another bitter argument over the naval appropriation bill of 1883, some Democrats attacking Chandler and Roach personally, while other Democrats and the Republicans tried to demonstrate the need for an expanded navy. In long speeches Senator Miller predicted a "new era" of foreign trade in which Americans might need protection from European envy, and Morgan called for four separate fleets in the Atlantic, Pacific, Gulf of Mexico, and the Great Lakes. All to little avail. Before Congress adjourned in July, 1884, for the presidential campaign, it managed to extend existing appropriations for six months, but it would not entrust Chandler with money for any more construction.[23] The "new Navy" of the Arthur administration never went beyond three cruisers and a dispatch boat.

*   *   *

In December, 1883, while Roach was beginning construction of the four warships which Congress had authorized, Chandler inserted into his annual report a mild recommendation that the United States establish its own coaling stations at Samaná Bay or some harbor in Haiti, and at points in Brazil, Chile, Central America, Liberia, east Africa, and Korea.[24] Obviously, the new cruisers could protect American interests effectively only if they were released from dependence on British fuel and supply depots. It is now necessary to examine briefly the policy of the Garfield and Arthur administrations with respect to the acquisition of such naval bases.

When Garfield came to office, the subject had already received attention in the State Department. In 1878 Hayes sent Commodore Shufeldt, an exponent of commercial expansionism, on a two-year cruise around Africa, across the Indian Ocean, to the Far East, and

pp. 297-98, and Sprout, *Rise of American Naval Power*, pp. 192-95. *New York Herald*, November 21, 1883, pp. 5, 6; March 19, 1884, p. 6.

[22]U.S., Congress, House, *Report of the Secretary of the Navy, 1883*, 48th Cong., 1st Sess., 1884, House Executive Doc. 1, Part 3, *passim. Ibid., 1884*, 48th Cong., 2d Sess., 1885, House Executive Doc. 1, Part 3, *passim.*

[23]Richardson, *Chandler*, pp. 298ff. U.S., *Congressional Record*, 48th Cong., 1st Sess., XV, 1453-54, 1486 *et passim.*

[24]U.S., *Report of Secretary of the Navy, 1883*, p. 32.

home by way of the Pacific, with instructions to report on American trade prospects and the consular service and to attempt the settlement of several troublesome disputes (see Chapters 11 and 12). Along with many other measures for the development of American interests in Africa, Shufeldt recommended coaling stations at Fernando Po and on the west coast of Madagascar, where he went so far as to negotiate a preliminary agreement with the Sakalava tribe. Since this agreement conflicted with other American policies on the island, however, it was never ratified.[25]

Another area of early American strategic interest was the central Pacific. As early as 1867 steamship interests and naval strategists combined to claim Midway Island for the United States, and if Seward's Alaskan and Caribbean ventures had not stirred up so much opposition at home, he would probably have acquired other bases. During the 1870's, while the United States rested from its expansionist labors, the British established the Fiji Islands as a crown colony, and German politicians and businessmen, "tingling with a new consciousness of triumph and unity after the Franco-Prussian War," and seeking raw materials and markets for their expanding industries, sent warships and traders through Melanesia, Micronesia, and parts of Polynesia.[26]

The effect of this increased activity on Blaine's relations with the Hawaiian Islands has already been observed. Another group of islands in which the American government had developed some interest was Samoa. By 1880 the United States, Britain, and Germany had obtained treaties from the Samoans giving them commercial privileges and the right to establish naval bases, the American grant being at Pago Pago. During that year the consuls of the three nations signed a convention establishing a cooperative municipal government over Apia, the principal Samoan town, but in the last weeks of the Hayes administration the death of the Samoan

[25]Charles Oscar Paullin, *Diplomatic Negotiations of American Naval Officers, 1778-1883* (Baltimore, 1912), pp. 353-55. Robert W. Shufeldt to R. W. Thompson, Fernando Po, May 14, 1879, No. 30, Letterbook, pp. 15-19, Box CXCIII; Shufeldt to Admiral Earl English, Tullear Bay, September 21, Letterbook, pp. 164-67, Box CLXXV, Robert W. Shufeldt Papers (Library of Congress).

[26]Brookes, *International Rivalry in the Pacific*, pp. 263-64, 412-17. D. N. Leff, *Uncle Sam's Pacific Islets* (Stanford, California, 1940), pp. 12-15. Sylvia Masterman, *The Origins of International Rivalry in Samoa, 1845-1884* (Stanford, California, 1934), pp. 79, 88-92, 155-58 et passim.

king raised fears of civil war and threatened the precarious balance.[27]

Occupied with diplomatic questions nearer home, Blaine sent no new instructions of importance to the American consul, Thomas M. Dawson, and did not see fit to include Samoa in his "spirited" policy of November and December, 1881. Even without instructions, however, Dawson did what he could to prevent civil war and expand American influence in the islands. In July with the aid of Captain James H. Gillis of the U.S.S. "Lackawanna," he managed to bring the rival chieftains and the foreign consuls together for a conference. On the deck of the "Lackawanna" (where, eight months earlier, the diplomats of Chile, Peru, and Bolivia had signed the abortive convention of Arica) the consuls agreed upon one of the chiefs, Malietoa Laupepa, as king. Dawson advised the State Department that the natives would probably accept an unqualified American protectorate, but just before Blaine left office, he rejected this suggestion and censured Dawson for his frequent quarrels with the British and German consuls.[28]

For three years, therefore, the three consuls, yoked together unwillingly by the municipality convention of 1880, tried to help the docile but incapable Laupepa to govern the islands. In 1883 revolution threatened his rule, but peace was restored. Later in the year appeared a more serious threat to American interests, when a New Zealand adventurer, John Lundon, began to agitate among the natives for annexation of the islands to Britain and New Zealand. Eventually he persuaded Laupepa to send an appropriate petition to Queen Victoria, but although the government of New Zealand

[27]Charles Callan Tansill, *The Foreign Policy of Thomas F. Bayard, 1885-1897* (New York, 1940), pp. 15-16. Masterman, *Origins of International Rivalry*, pp. 127-30, 150-53 *et passim*. George Herbert Ryden, *The Foreign Policy of the United States in Relation to Samoa* (New Haven, Connecticut, 1933), pp. 264-66 *et passim*. For a thorough analysis of the case for an expansionist American policy in Samoa, see two memoranda of Alvey A. Adee, March 30, 1880, Nos. 10, 12, U.S., Reports of the Diplomatic Bureau, IV.

[28]For general accounts of events in Samoa, 1881-1885, see Masterman, *Origins of International Rivalry*, pp. 174-79, and Ryden, *Foreign Policy of United States in Samoa*, pp. 268-93. See also Thomas M. Dawson to Charles Payson, Apia, July 16, 1881, No. 248, U.S., Consular Despatches, Apia, X. Walker Blaine to Dawson, July 25, November 29, Nos. 95, 107, U.S., Consular Instructions, C, 219; CI, 466-67.

received the proposal with enthusiasm, the petition was stifled in the Colonial Office.[29]

Disturbed by Lundon's activities, Dawson's successor, Theodore Canisius, appealed to Washington for instructions, and the State Department replied briefly that the United States would object to the destruction of the independence of any island community to which it was bound by treaty.[30] However, in January, 1885, when the German consul took advantage of a native revolt to seize Apia Arthur and Frelinghuysen, about to leave office, refused to condone any reprisal which might compromise the new administration Even as it was, they bequeathed to Cleveland one of the most tangled diplomatic problems of his presidency.[31]

*   *   *

If the Arthur administration felt that Samoa was too remote for an American naval base or protectorate, similar opportunities presented themselves during the early 1880's in two Caribbean countries, Venezuela and Haiti. The situation in Venezuela was the more complicated of the two, for it involved two separate diplomatic questions: a boundary controversy with Britain and an argument with France about the Venezuelan foreign debt.

After years of desultory correspondence over the jungle boundary between Venezuela and British Guiana, at the end of 1880 the Venezuelan government informed Secretary Evarts that the British had begun to erect telegraph poles on disputed territory at the mouth of the Orinoco River. Evarts expressed disapproval and encouraged Venezuela to keep the State Department informed of British actions. In November, 1881, President Antonio Guzmán Blanco asked the American chargé d'affaires at Caracas if the American government would transmit a Venezuelan brief on the boundary question to Britain. Frelinghuysen replied that although he did not know enough about the question to express an opinion on it, the American government wished to see Venezuelan claims

[29]G. W. Griffin to John Davis, Auckland, October 2, 1883, No. 168; Thomas T. Gamble to Davis, Auckland, January 24, 1885, No. 226, U.S., Consular Despatches, Auckland, VII.

[30]Davis to Theodore Canisius, December 12, 1883, No. 38, U.S., Consular Instructions, CIX, 147-48.

[31]See Tansill, *Foreign Policy of Bayard,* chaps. i-iv.

prevail in every legal manner and would propose arbitration by a third party if Venezuela wished it.[32]

The problem of the Venezuelan debt was more immediately menacing. By the middle of the nineteenth century the improvident nation owed considerable sums to British, French, Dutch, German, Spanish, Danish, and American creditors. In 1864 France and Venezuela had signed a convention setting aside 10 per cent of the principal Venezuelan customs receipts for French bankers and giving the French debt first priority. By 1880 Venezuela had paid nearly one-tenth of the French debt and smaller amounts of the others. In answer to complaints from the less-favored creditors Venezuela reorganized the whole system of payment to give each nation annually about 4.04 per cent of the sinking fund, whereupon Britain and France protested, and the French government threatened to break relations if Venezuela did not return to the old system of differential payments. Venezuela appealed to the United States, whose legation at Caracas was accustomed to distribute the annual payments to the foreign creditors, and submitted a proposal for slightly increased payments to all, but Evarts left office before he could do more than approve it in principle.[33]

At the end of March, 1881, the French government withdrew its chargé at Caracas, and rumors began to drift about the Venezuelan capital that warships would soon appear at the principal ports to enforce the French demands. On May 5 Blaine cabled to Paris suggesting American good offices and asking the French not to act hastily, but they would not retreat from their demands. On July 23, after further pressure by the Venezuelan minister, Blaine sent out one of the few major instructions prepared during Garfield's illness. In it he proposed to the French government that the United States distribute the monthly payments of the Venezuelan debt pro rata to the creditor nations. If Venezuela defaulted for three successive

[32]*Ibid.*, pp. 623-27; map, p. 618. Simón Camacho to Evarts, New York, December 21, 1880, U.S., Notes from Foreign Legations, Venezuela, IV. Evarts to Camacho, January 31, 1881, U.S., Notes to Foreign Legations, Venezuela, I, 216. G. W. Carter to Blaine, Caracas, November 30; Carter to Frelinghuysen, January 26, 1882, Nos. 38, 68, U.S., Despatches, Venezuela, XXVIII, XXIX. Frelinghuysen to Baker, July 15, 1882, No. 169, U.S., Instructions, Venezuela, III, 238-39.

[33]For the early history of the Venezuelan debt see U.S., *Foreign Relations, 1881*, pp. 1191-98; *1883*, pp. 364-68. Camacho to Evarts, New York, February 7, 1881; Evarts to Camacho, February 28, *ibid., 1881*, pp. 1198-1200.

months, an American agent in Caracas would step in and administer
the Venezuelan customs, setting aside the proper portion of the
receipts to service the debt—a customs receivership very similar to
those established after 1904. Guzmán Blanco accepted this arrangement, stating blandly that while *his* government would never de-
fault, he could not vouch for his successors. France, however, continued to insist on preferential treatment.[34]

On December 16, as he prepared to retire from the State Department, Blaine addressed a further plea to France in language remi-
niscent of his invitations to the hemispheric peace congress. All
international debts should be treated alike, he declared, and no
creditor preferred above all others. "Beyond and above the pe-
cuniary interest involved . . . there lies a consideration which appeals
with equal force to . . . France and the United States . . . the
fraternity of feeling and the harmony of relations which should be
maintained between all the republics of the world."[35] Slightly
moved by this high-minded appeal, Premier Léon Gambetta agreed
to place French debts not covered by the treaty of 1864 on an
equal footing with those of other nations. A year later, after a confidential discussion with Bancroft Davis, the French Foreign Office
declared that it was anxious to settle the question, provided that
the United States would agree to distinguish between the two
parts of the French debt, as proposed.[36]

Thus by the beginning of 1883 Venezuela had turned over to the
United States her two most important diplomatic problems, the
British Guiana boundary and the French debt. Frelinghuysen did
what he could within correct diplomatic channels to solve both
problems. In the case of the boundary controversy he offered to
reinforce again the Venezuelan request for arbitration, hinting that
the United States would not refuse to be arbiter. As for the debt,
he sent a circular note to the governments of the various creditors

[34]Camacho to Blaine, New York, March 22, April 18, June 30, August 1, 13, 23,
1881; Baker to Blaine, Caracas, March 23, 30, April 6, 20, Nos. 361, 363, 370, 378;
Blaine to Edward F. Noyes, May 5 (telegram), July 23, No. 402; Noyes to Blaine,
Paris, May 16, No. 467; Levi P. Morton to Blaine, Paris, August 23, No. 15, *ibid.*,
pp. 1202-14, 1216-24.

[35]Blaine to Morton, December 16, 1881, No. 74, *ibid.*, pp. 1226-28.

[36]Morton to Frelinghuysen, Paris, January 18, December 1, 1882, Nos. 103, 262,
U.S., Despatches, France, LXXXIX, XCI. Frelinghuysen to J. C. Bancroft Davis,
July 7, Davis Papers, XXXII.

proposing a pro rata division administered by the United States with an extra annual payment of 720,000 francs to France as *douceur*.[37] Neither suggestion met with much approval in Europe.

Apparently convinced that his only help lay in the United States, Guzmán Blanco went out of his way to cultivate American friendship. He granted new and important concessions to Americans in the disputed area along the Guiana border. He asked the United States to station a warship at La Guayra or Puerto Cabello as protection against imagined hostility from the Chilean navy. In October, 1883, he surprised the American minister, Jehu Baker, with the most sweeping proposal of all: a treaty of alliance which would open Venezuelan ports and rivers to American trade and make the country a "moral protectorate" of the United States. When Baker remarked that he supposed that his country "would assume some undetermined obligations in the matter," Guzmán Blanco replied that his only return would be "the facil [*sic*] potentiality of the United States when referred to by Venezuela as her ally."[38]

Somewhat later, Frelinghuysen reviewed the Venezuelan proposal in a dispatch to Baker. He did not see how Venezuela could expect to benefit from a paper alliance unless the use of American capital in the Orinoco Valley led to American protection during civil disturbances, but this would constitute "intervention in the domestic difficulties of an independent state." Frelinghuysen countered by suggesting a far-reaching commercial treaty under which Venezuela would open her ports and waters to American ships, provide special guarantees for American life and property, reduce import duties, and probably abolish export duties in return for

[37]Frelinghuysen to Baker, January 31, 1883, No. 203, U.S., Instructions, Venezuela, III, 280-84. Baker to Frelinghuysen, Caracas, February 22, No. 638, U.S., Despatches, Venezuela, XXXI. Frelinghuysen to A. A. Sargent, March 31, No. 102½, U.S., *Foreign Relations, 1883*, pp. 364-69.

[38]Tansill, *Foreign Policy of Bayard*, p. 628. Antonio Guzmán Blanco to A. M. Soteldo, Antimano, November 28, 1883, U.S., Notes from Foreign Legations, Venezuela, V. Baker to Frelinghuysen, Caracas, October 31, December 29, Nos. 777, 803, U.S., Despatches, Venezuela, XXXII, XXXIII. However, at the same time Guzmán Blanco stopped payments on certain American claims and resisted all American efforts to settle an outstanding damage case. See U.S., *Foreign Relations, 1883*, pp. 893-933, *passim; 1884*, pp. 597-609, *passim*, and *1885*, pp. 930-39, *passim*.

similar concessions by the United States and a provision for American good offices in future Venezuelan disputes.[39]

It seems clear that the United States could have secured a naval base or bases at Venezuelan ports, along with other controls over the Venezuelan economy amounting to a partial protectorate. However, Blaine did not stay in office long enough to carry his customs receivership beyond a mere suggestion, and Frelinghuysen balked at the idea of an alliance or military commitments, preferring an economic relationship which, as will be seen, fitted better into the rest of his Caribbean policy. Since neither administration would put more than moral pressure on Europe to settle Venezuela's problems, the boundary controversy with Britain remained unsolved, and Venezuela had to concede priority to the French claims.[40] Later, in 1895 and 1902 respectively, the British Guiana boundary and the Venezuelan foreign debt were to cause major crises in American diplomacy, but during the 1880's neither question seemed urgent enough to Blaine or Frelinghuysen to justify a showdown.

*   *   *

Throughout its history the American government has been notoriously sensitive to threats of European expansion in the West Indies. After the collapse of the American projects to annex the Danish West Indies and the Dominican Republic, rumors of French and German interest in these islands bedeviled the State Department during the 1870's. In 1877, when Sweden ceded the island of St. Bartholomew to France, Evarts did not protest, but he kept a close watch on the Danish West Indies and carried on a long argument with Britain over the ownership of the insignificant guano island of Morant Cays. In April, 1881, American Minister Andrew D. White reported from Berlin that a certain Herr Kück, posing as Dominican minister, seemed to be on suspiciously friendly terms with Bismarck. White warned the

[39]Frelinghuysen to Baker, July 25, 1884, No. 326, U.S., Instructions, Venezuela III, 390-99. His proposal closely followed an earlier suggestion by Baker. See Baker to Frelinghuysen, Caracas, May 6, No. 919, U.S., Despatches, Venezuela, XXXIV.

[40]Tansill, *Foreign Policy of Bayard*, pp. 628-31. Frelinghuysen to Morton, June 16, 1884, No. 540, U.S., Instructions, France, XXI, 53-54. Frelinghuysen to James Russell Lowell, July 7, No. 907, *ibid.*, Britain, XXVII, 239-46.

State Department that if American policy in the Caribbean showed
any signs of weakness, Germany would surely try to obtain control of the island. Kück turned out to be a crank, and the German
threat did not materialize, but during the winter of 1881-1882 the
United States Navy sent two warships to take soundings in
Samaná Bay, to the alarm of the Dominican government and
people.[41]

It was in the neighboring republic of Haiti that Frelinghuysen
encountered the most attractive opportunity to forestall European
influence and to advance American control over the Caribbean
through the cession of a naval base. From its origins as a colony
of France, Haiti had retained the French language, law, and re-
ligion; many influential families and professional people were more
French than Haitian. During the late 1870's the government of
Haiti had organized a national bank with French capital and had
granted railroad, lighthouse, and other concessions to Frenchmen.
French ships were almost always in the harbor of Port-au-Prince.
As for other European Powers, German political influence was
negligible as yet, despite large German business interests, but the
British government was carrying on a bitter argument over a
log-cutting concession on the nearby island of Tortuga.[42]

American promoters had also secured concessions in Haiti, and
the State Department had become embroiled over two long-
drawn-out claims cases for breach of contract and unjust imprisonment of an American. In pressing these cases the American
minister, John M. Langston, found it almost impossible to give
his words the same weight as those of European diplomats, for
French and British warships were constantly at hand, while the
American government rarely allowed its flag to be seen in Haitian
waters. At the end of 1881 Langston managed to secure the cancellation of certain irritating Haitian taxes and fees which bore un-

[41]Barrows, *Evarts*, p. 368. Andrew D. White to Blaine, Berlin, April 4, 1881,
No. 196, U.S., Despatches, Germany, XXVIII. Morton to Frelinghuysen, Paris,
January 10, 1882, No. 100, *ibid.*, France, LXXXIX. William Lithgow to Hunter,
Puerto Plata, January 19, No. 3, U.S., Consular Despatches, Puerto Plata, I. Stanis-
las Goutier to State Department, Cape Haytien, February 1, *ibid.*, Cape Haytien,
XIV.

[42]John M. Langston to Blaine, Port-au-Prince, June 18, 1881, No. 388, U.S.,
Despatches, Haiti, XV. Logan, *United States and Haiti*, pp. 367, 371-72.

fairly on American commerce, but in other respects American influence in Haiti seemed to have a limited future.[43]

The dispatch of American warships to survey Samaná Bay in December probably raised the United States in the eyes of Lysius Salomon, the autocratic president of Haiti, and events of 1882 convinced him that he could not afford the luxury of Yankee-phobia. In March a Liberal revolt broke out on the island, which Salomon put down with some bloodshed. Whether the British incited the revolt, as he suspected, they took advantage of his involvement to demand a settlement of their log-cutting claim and a salute to the British flag. The Haitian minister at Washington, Stephen Preston, declared that Britain would seize Tortuga as a base if the United States did nothing, and Frelinghuysen agreed to tender good offices if necessary to forestall further action. Meanwhile, the French minister intervened to bring about a British withdrawal.[44]

As in the case of Venezuela, the slightest indication of Freling-huysen's interest encouraged the Haitian president to make a more extensive proposal. In March, 1883, a more serious revolt broke out, lasting for the rest of the year and raising new fears of British aggression. At the end of May Salomon called in Langston and abruptly offered to cede Tortuga to the United States as a naval base in return for the cancellation of all outstanding claims against Haiti. Naturally, Frelinghuysen realized at once that the extinction of the claims was only part of the purchase price, and that some sort of protectorate would be involved. He replied that American policy did not permit the acquisition of overseas terri-tories and put Salomon off with the further excuse that unless he could discuss the confidential communication with Congress, he could do nothing at all.[45]

Instead of subsiding, the Liberal revolt continued to spread, and

[43]Report of Langston, June 30, 1881, in U.S., *Commercial Relations, 1880-1881*, pp. 542-43. On American claims see L. L. Montague, *Haiti and the United States, 1714-1938* (Durham, North Carolina, 1940), pp. 116-28.

[44]For a more detailed account of Haitian-American relations between 1881 and 1885 see Logan, *United States and Haiti*, pp. 368-85. See also Langston to Freling-huysen, Port-au-Prince, March 10, 1882; March 20, 1883, Nos. 448, 532, U.S., Des-patches, Haiti, XV, XVI.

[45]Langston to Frelinghuysen, May 30, 1883, No. 557, *ibid.*, XVI. Frelinghuysen to Langston, June 20, No. 217, U.S., Instructions, Haiti, II, 339-41.

on September 22 and 23 uncontrollable rioting broke out in Port-au-Prince. After a day of this destruction the principal European diplomatic representatives issued an ultimatum to Salomon's government, and British, French, and Spanish warships landed troops to restore order. Anticipating a new series of foreign claims arising from the disorder, and still suspicious of British intentions, the dictator informed his minister in Paris that, failing aid from France, he must "conclude a *mariage de raison* with the United States."[46] Five days later he held a confidential talk with American Minister Langston and the captain of the U.S.S. "Swatara," then in port. Accusing England of treacherously aiding the rebels, Salomon offered to cede the best harbor in Haiti, the Mole St. Nicolas, or Tortuga to the United States in return for a sum of money, two warships, two gunboats, a guarantee of Haitian independence, and good offices or mediation in quarrels between Haiti and a foreign country.[47]

While lacking the bait of an interoceanic canal, this offer was equivalent, in terms of Caribbean strategy, to the treaty which Frelinghuysen signed with Nicaragua a year later. Nevertheless, Frelinghuysen rejected Salomon's offer after sending an American ship to examine Mole St. Nicolas and submitting the question to Arthur's whole cabinet for discussion. The reasons which he gave were an expanded version of his earlier refusal. The United States, he declared, had a fixed policy not to "attempt territorial aggrandizement which would require maintenance of a naval force in excess of any yet provided for our national uses." Also, "as simple coaling stations such territorial acquisitions would involve responsibilities beyond their utility. The U. S. have never deemed it needful to their national life to maintain impregnable fortresses along the world's highways of commerce."[48]

During 1884 and 1885 rumors circulated between Port-au-Prince and Washington to the effect that, since the American government had rejected his offer, Salomon was making a similar proposal to France. The authenticity of these rumors has never

---

[46]Quoted in Logan, *United States and Haiti*, p. 376.

[47]Langston to Frelinghuysen, November 9, 1883, U.S., Despatches, Haiti, XVII.

[48]Langston to Frelinghuysen, January 21, 1884, No. 617, *ibid.;* Frelinghuysen to Langston, February 1, No. 258, U.S., Instructions, Haiti, II, 380-82.

been proved, but, while they did not affect Frelinghuysen's decision, they made him so uneasy that on two different occasions he sent the American representative in Paris to inquire about them at the Quai d'Orsay. Both times the French Foreign Office assured him that the rumors were false, and on the second occasion, Minister Morton reported the foreign minister had laughed at the idea of a quarrel with the United States over the Monroe Doctrine.[49]

Thus in his relations with both Venezuela and Haiti Frelinghuysen refused to acquire naval bases controlling the approaches to an isthmian canal—and this at a time when he was evolving a policy of American control over a canal itself. How can one explain the apparent inconsistency? Rayford W. Logan attributes the caution of the Arthur administration to lack of naval strength,[50] but it is more likely that the explanation lies in Congress. Confronted by the fire power of anti-imperialists in the Senate who had already riddled the expansionist policies of Seward and Grant, Frelinghuysen was understandably reluctant to abandon cover and make an open declaration for naval bases without the protective excuse of a completed canal and a fleet in being.

[49]Langston to Frelinghuysen, August 5, December 3, 24, 1884; January 23, 1885, Nos. 657, 691, 696, 707, U.S., Despatches, Haiti, XVIII, XIX. Frelinghuysen to Henry Vignaud, October 22, 1884, No. 638; Frelinghuysen to Morton, February 28, 1885, U.S., Instructions, France, XXI, 123, 172-75. Vignaud to Frelinghuysen, Paris, November 26, No. 672, U.S., Despatches, France, XCV. Montague, *Haiti and the United States,* pp. 175-76.

[50]Logan, *United States and Haiti,* pp. 377-79. In 1883, at Chandler's request, Frelinghuysen asked the Mexican government for permission to establish a coaling station at Magdalena Bay, an excellent harbor in Lower California. However, this would not have been a new base, since Chandler proposed only to transfer facilities already established for some time at Pichilingue. The Mexican government refused permission. Chandler to Frelinghuysen, January 29, 1883, U.S., Miscellaneous Letters. John Davis to Chandler, August 14, U.S., Domestic Letters, CXLVII.

Disposing of the Surplus

Chapter 8

The Mongrel Tariff

In March, 1882, while Congress and the public were still hotly discussing the reversal of Blaine's policies, Representative W. C. Whitthorne, a Democrat from Tennessee, used the annual debate on the diplomatic and consular appropriation bill as the occasion for a vigorous attack on the new administration's cautious behavior. Praising Blaine's Clayton-Bulwer notes and his proposal for an inter-American congress, Whitthorne called on Arthur to shake off the timid advice of Wall Street speculators—a familiar target for rural Democrats—and smooth the way for the expansion of American trade into Latin America and the Far East: "The executive department should . . . obtain the friendship, good-will, and kindly disposition of the country with which commercial intercourse is sought; the partial barriers, burdens, and taxation upon trades there prevailing should be modified or removed; reciprocal advantages should be sought and given." With this aid, he predicted, "wherever it is desired to open markets for our surplus wealth, we shall find volunteer pioneers for our trade and willing missionaries for our commerce."[1]

Appreciating the partisan nature of the attack, the Stalwart expansionist, John A. Kasson, quickly defended the administration by minimizing the extent of its changes in Blaine's policies. However, during the months following, the idea of government encouragement to trade and business abroad gained increased support from those in both parties who saw in foreign commerce the only solution to the problem of overproduction. Beset by economic troubles, party divisions, and Democratic criticism, Arthur and Frelinghuysen began to emphasize this goal more and more in their foreign policy. After a resounding defeat in the Congressional elections of 1882, they set out to further hemispheric

[1]U.S., *Congressional Record*, 47th Cong., 1st Sess., XIII, 1553-56.

trade and unity through a system of reciprocity treaties. By helping to dispose of the surplus, they hoped to stabilize the American economy; and by displacing European influence in Latin America, they hoped to silence Blaine and the Democrats.

*   *   *

The background of Arthur's economic foreign policy was the declining prosperity of 1882. During the two fat years which had followed the bumper crops of 1879, overproduction of manufactured goods and speculation in the mounting commodity prices had weakened the resistance of the American economy. In 1881 bad weather cut down both American and European crops, so that, while farm prices remained high, railroad freight receipts fell off. The railroads in turn cancelled some of their orders for steel rails, and these cancellations, together with the fear of others to come, began to force down iron and steel prices as early as December, 1881. During the following year both American and European wheat crops were among the largest in history. Grain prices fell, then prices of cotton, already piled up in British warehouses. Another round of contraction by American railroads and manufacturing industries followed. In the words of David A. Wells, the country seemed to be settling back gradually into a depression, "as if matters were naturally again assuming a normal condition."[2]

During the depression years of the 1870's and now again as business conditions deteriorated, there appeared demands for the government to abandon some of its laissez-faire attitude toward the economy and lend a helping hand to faltering business. The Hayes administration had responded slightly to these calls. In 1880, for example, at the suggestion of the New York Chamber of Commerce, the State Department began to publish selected reports from American consuls as a guide to trade conditions abroad.[3]

[2]Wells, *Recent Economic Changes*, p. 11. Noyes, *Forty Years of American Finance*, pp. 83-87. American Iron and Steel Association, *Report, 1881*, pp. 10-13 *et passim; 1882, passim.* The financial pages of the New York Tribune give much information on the economic slump.

[3]On business pressure for government aid see Milton Plesur, "Looking Outward: American Attitudes toward Foreign Affairs from Hayes to Harrison" (Ph. D. dissertation, University of Rochester, 1954), pp. 209-10.

The Hayes and Garfield administrations also took a tentative step toward active intervention in the field of currency regulation. After Western free-silver agitation and the passage of the Bland-Allison Silver Purchase Act of 1878 had upset his hopes for a domestic policy of "sound money," Hayes sent delegates to an unsuccessful international monetary conference later in the year. The President hoped to negotiate a general agreement for a bimetallic standard, since few nations seemed firmly committed to gold. Three years later the United States and France proposed another international discussion of bimetallism. By this time, however, both the British and the German governments had adopted a single gold standard. They reluctantly accepted the Franco-American invitation on the explicit understanding that they reserved all freedom of action. Despite the small chance of success, Garfield pressed ahead hopefully, interpreting his election to be a victory for sound money.[4]

As most informed observers expected, the Paris international monetary conference of 1881 was a complete failure. The American delegates could not marshal the scattered European sentiment in favor of bimetallism, because they failed to convince their hearers that the American government was not acting solely for the benefit of Western silver producers or that the American Congress would actually stop silver coinage if the conference failed.[5]

American newspapers, few of which had supported the conference, called on the Treasury to stop coining silver for the time being or give up negotiation. Blaine's supporter, the *New York Tribune*, blamed Britain for obstructing the conference.[6] Faced with such a confusion of tongues, the Arthur administration sent

[4]H. B. Russell, *International Monetary Conferences; Their Purposes, Character, and Results* (New York, 1898), pp. 248-49. Jeannette P. Nichols, "Silver Diplomacy," *Political Science Quarterly*, XLVIII (1933), 568-71. Henry M. Wriston, *Executive Agents in American Foreign Relations* (Baltimore, 1929), p. 581. James Russell Lowell to James G. Blaine, London, March 14 (telegram), April 19, 1881, No. 167, U.S., Despatches, Britain, CXLI. Andrew D. White to Blaine, Berlin, March 21, No. 193, *ibid.*, Germany, XXVIII.

[5]*Nation*, XXXII (June 23), 434. See also Russell, *International Monetary Conferences*, chap. vi, and Nichols, "Silver Diplomacy," pp. 571-73. S. Dana Horton to Blaine, Paris, April 22, U.S., Special Agents, XXXI.

[6]*Nation*, XXXII (April 28), 288. New York *Daily Commercial Bulletin*, July 11, p. 2. *New York Tribune*, July 16, p. 8.

a special emissary, S. Dana Horton, to sound out opinion in Europe during 1882. However, since neither the State Department nor the Treasury Department would assume responsibility for Horton's mission, his instructions were garbled, and he accomplished nothing.[7]

*   *   *

During the Hayes and Garfield administrations it was becoming increasingly obvious that any actions to encourage foreign trade would have to be judged by their relationship to the tariff, that great touchstone of American economic policy during the decades after Appomattox. When the fighting was over, American industrialists had quickly secured the repeal of most of the wartime internal excise taxes, but inertia and self-interest preserved many of the high tariff schedules. Gradually a few serious students of the problem, led by the able chairman of the Revenue Commission, David A. Wells, came to the conclusion that high import duties did more harm than good to most American interests. In 1869 Wells set forth his low-tariff arguments in a classic report which led Horace Greeley to declare that he must be a subversive foreign agent. A year later Wells's office was abolished, and he returned to private life as a free-trade pamphleteer and consultant on trade problems.[8]

The chief obstacle to tariff reduction was that wartime industrial production had raised a clutch of lobbyists, determined to extend the measure which had been a leading source of their profits. One of the first formal lobbies organized was the National Association of Wool Manufacturers, presided over by the energetic, knowing John L. Hayes, a Harvard lawyer with more than a decade of experience in Washington corridors. Another, the Industrial League of Pennsylvania, was the work of Peter Cooper, Daniel J. Morrell, Joseph Wharton, and others identified with iron, steel, and related industries. The indefatigable James M. Swank became chief lobbyist for the American Iron and Steel Association, an outgrowth of the Pennsylvania group, and made

[7] J. D. Horton to Chester A. Arthur, Pomeroy, Ohio, June 30, 1882; memorandum of Alvey A. Adee, Washington, August 21, U.S., Special Agents, XXXI.

[8] Fred Bunyan Joyner, *David Ames Wells, Champion of Free Trade* (Cedar Rapids, Iowa [1939]), pp. 33-34, 43-56, 59-75, 82-90.

himself a two-way channel for propaganda, funneling helpful arguments into Congressional offices and Congressional speeches, regardless of party, into newspapers and pamphlets.[9]

During the first postwar years opinion was fairly evenly divided in Congress between high and low tariffs, and even after President Grant came out for protection, his supporters had to fight hard for the tariff act of 1870. Gradually, however, the growth of manufacturing industries in the Middle West, reinforced by the blandishments of lobbyists, changed Congressional opinion, until by 1883 not a single Republican free trader remained in the Senate.[10] Here Justin S. Morrill of Vermont, Chairman of the Finance Committee, officiated as high priest of protectionism, while William D. ("Pig-iron") Kelley devoted his eloquence to the same cause in the House. A few protectionist Democrats, led by Samuel J. Randall in the House, often voted with the Republicans on tariff bills, but most of the party still favored low duties or free trade. The most effective and persistent speaker for this group was Senator James M. Beck of Kentucky, while William R. Morrison, the ranking Democratic member of the Ways and Means Committee offset Kelley in the House.

In general, low-tariff and free-trade men linked tariff reform with the other measures designed to make the United States a major Power: an interoceanic canal, a navy second to none, development of the Mississippi Valley, education, and labor reform. As Senator John T. Morgan put it, all Americans needed to obtain prosperity was "a fair opportunity to visit the nations that are purchasers of goods, with better and cheaper productions than any other nation." If we do not sell abroad, declared Wells, "we are certain to be smothered in our own grease." Others developed the familiar arguments that high tariffs were "legalized plunder"

[9]Ida M. Tarbell, *The Tariff in Our Times* (New York, 1911), 41-42, 86-87. Allan Nevins, *Hamilton Fish; the Inner History of the Grant Administration* (New York, 1936), pp. 571-72. James M. Swank to Justin S. Morrill, May 6 [1883], as quoted in James A. Barnes, *John G. Carlisle, Financial Statesman* (New York, 1931), p. 79.

[10]Nevins, *Fish*, p. 289. Clarence Lee Miller, *The States of the Old Northwest and the Tariff, 1865-1888* (Emporia, Kansas, 1929), pp. 134-40.

and class legislation which made parasites out of industrialists, debased labor, and corrupted law.[11]

For their part, protectionists pointed to American prosperity during the 1860's and the early 1870's as proof that high tariffs fostered economic growth. All of them insisted that tariffs were the only salvation of the American workingman, for without them competitors would "offer the cup of cheap machine labor, filled to the brim, to our lips, and force us to drink it to the dregs." Some high-tariff men, led by Senator Morrill, carried their arguments almost to the extreme of economic isolationism, belittling foreign customers and declaring that American industries needed nothing more than assurance of full control over the domestic market.[12]

Many other protectionists, however, wanted to expand the foreign trade of the United States, as long as this did not involve a general lowering of tariffs. Some, indeed, even argued that high tariffs were a positive encouragement to foreign trade, and that Americans would beat out their competitors in the long run, not by undercutting prices but by offering goods of higher quality.[13] Blaine was one of the principal spokesmen for this expansionist wing, especially after he left office and the prosperity of 1879-1881 began to fade, while his henchman, Whitelaw Reid, filled the columns of the *New York Tribune* with boasts about American sales abroad and advice to exporters. Although Blaine opposed the campaign of the Arthur administration for reciprocal trade treaties, he eventually came to recognize that some concessions

[11]U.S., *Congressional Record*, 47th Cong., 1st Sess., XIII, 2105-6. David A. Wells, *Freer Trade Essential to Future National Prosperity* (New York, 1882), pp. 23-30. Among the many speeches and pamphlets advocating tariff reform for domestic reasons a good sample is to be found in the speeches of Senator Beck in U.S., *Congressional Record*, 46th Cong., 2d Sess., X, 3912-16; *ibid.*, 47th Cong., 1st Sess., XIII, 73-74.

[12]W. G. M., "Foreign Trade No Cure for Hard Times," *Atlantic Monthly*, XLIV (October 1879), 476. [George Draper], *Some Views on the Tariff Question by an Old Business Man. The American Market for the American People* (New York [1886], pp. 7-8 *et passim.*

[13]"How Protection Tends to Increase Our Exports of Manufactured Goods," in American Iron and Steel Association, *Hold the Fort! A Collection of Fresh Facts and Arguments in Support of the Policy of Protection to Home Industry* (Philadelphia [1876]), pp. 14-16. Henry Varnum Poor, *Twenty-Two Years of Protection* (New York [1888]), pp. 171-72.

were necessary, and in the campaign of 1884 favored both high tariffs and a hemispheric *Zollverein* (customs union). Some years later he too embraced reciprocity.

Whether they leaned toward isolationism or expansionism, protectionists also affected American foreign policy by encouraging Anglophobia. An important part of their teachings was the belief that the Cobden Club and other free-trade organizations of "greedy, grasping, never-sated, never-satisfied England" were trying to lure the United States to lower its tariff walls so that British manufactures could monopolize American markets. In spreading their insidious propaganda the British free traders enjoyed "the gratuitous services of [American] book-makers, college professors and leader-writers" such as David A. Wells.[14] Blaine and other expansionists further stimulated Anglophobia by denouncing British commercial competition in Latin America. Although the writings of tariff reformers seldom criticized Britain, many low-tariff supporters, especially in the Middle West, had other motives for suspecting the English and applauded Blaine's Anglophobe sentiments for reasons unconnected with the tariff.

* * *

Much of the confusion in tariff debates arose from the difficulty of generalizing about the multifarious industries and services which made up the American economy. In particular, the interests of those who produced raw materials were often completely opposed to the interests of those who converted them into manufactured goods, so that the same set of duties might ruin one and enrich the other unless a compromise could be found. A good example of this duality was the wool schedule. Since both woolgrowers and textile millowners wanted protection, a specific duty was charged on raw wool and a larger ad valorem duty on woolen cloth—12c and 50c per pound on the average, respectively, under the tariff act of 1867. Eventually the wool schedule became so intricate that no one dared attempt over-all revision, and as long as it excluded the leveling influence of foreign supply, it facilitated

---

[14] *New York Tribune*, May 26, 1883, pp. 2, 4; June 10, p. 6. Thomas Sargent Fernon, *Free Trade Means Serf Pay and Famine Fare* (Philadelphia, 1880), p. 51 *et passim*. Thomas Haines Dudley, *The Cobden Club of England and Protection in the United States* [New York, 1884?], *passim*.

speculation, price manipulation, and "corners."[15]

The problems of tariff reform may be further shown by considering in detail the examples of two commodities whose restrictions most directly affected American foreign policy in the 1880's: sugar and ships. By 1880 Americans were consuming annually between one and a half and two billion pounds of sugar, of which Louisiana cane growers furnished only about 200,000,000 pounds. (Beet sugar production had begun in parts of the West, but few persons foresaw its great growth.) The Civil War had temporarily ruined Louisiana cane growers, who lobbied earnestly for tariff protection, but in their best prewar year they had not produced much above half a billion pounds of sugar, and no one outside Louisiana expected them to reach that level again. Consequently the nation imported most of its raw or partly refined sugar from Cuba, the British West Indies, and Brazil. About 60 per cent of these imports came from Cuba.

Since the United States sold virtually no refined sugar abroad, American sugar refiners and the consuming public stood in practically the same relationship to the sugar tariff. In 1880 the American government derived about one-sixth of its total annual revenue from duties on sugar, molasses, and related products, but the Treasury collected this revenue in an outmoded, clumsy fashion. All sugars were divided into twenty grades of purity, measured roughly by color (the "Dutch standard"), the browner grades paying a lower specific duty than the white. By 1867 a new type of refining machinery had been developed which coated the white crystals with a brownish tinge, disguising their purity. At first the American collectors fought back by pulverizing sugar samples, but this hit-or-miss solution satisfied no one. Treasury officials then suggested the more accurate polariscope test, but producers and importers objected that, being more complex, it would prevent them from computing their duties in advance. For simplicity's sake many of them preferred a flat duty on all grades of imported sugar.

[15]F. W. Taussig, *Some Aspects of the Tariff Question* (Cambridge, 1915), pp. 313, 324-25.

The refiners' concern over the tariff was easy to understand. After a period of overexpansion following the Civil War, the sugar industry had suffered heavily during the depression of the 1870's. Squeezed between rising expenses and the public demand for cheap sugar, refining profits almost disappeared, with the result that only large-scale operators could stay in business. In 1878, after a thorough study of the industry, David A. Wells agreed that the tariff was excessive and the Dutch standard obsolete, but he opposed a flat rate on all sugars, since this would encourage crude refining in the producing country. Instead he favored an ad valorem duty, the values to be determined by the polariscope test, and he urged the government to place sugar collections under the direction of a special bureau of experts. This did not satisfy the refiners, but they could not come to any agreement among themselves during the next four years.[16]

Another complex segment of the tariff question which helped to influence foreign policy was the problem of the merchant marine. In 1855 American ships had carried three-fourths of all American imports and exports, but by 1881 this figure had fallen to about one-sixth. The causes of this sorry decline were many. While shipbuilding costs had steadily risen in the United States, the shift to steam power and iron hulls had made American clipper designs obsolete and enabled Britain to capitalize the enormous advantages of her rich coal deposits and well-developed iron industry. The Civil War interrupted the cotton trade, the staple of American shipping, and Confederate raiders scared shipowners into registering their craft under European flags. During the late 1870's an oversupply of shipping in the California grain trade forced some of the less efficient American carriers to shift to other routes, and the increased use of petroleum dealt a heavy blow to whalers. Meanwhile, European governments were encouraging

---

[16]Paul L. Vogt, *The Sugar Refining Industry in the United States—its Development and Present Condition* (Philadelphia, 1908), chap. iii. David A. Wells, *The Sugar Industry of the United States and the Tariff* (New York, 1878), pp. 5-18, 22-31, 112-19. David A. Wells, *How Congress and the Public Deal with a Great Revenue and Industrial Problem* (New York, 1880), pp. 1-18. *New York Tribune*, February 7, 1882, p. 2; December 11, p. 1.

their merchant fleets with mail contracts, subsidies, and other favorable legislation.[17]

Seeing that many of these trends were irreversible, shipowners, shippers, and the public turned to the American government, demanding reform measures. Since the 1860's high tariffs on ironware and other shipbuilding materials had burdened American shipyards. In compensation, over the years Congress had passed a series of navigation acts, denying American registry to foreign-built ships, ships even partly owned by a foreigner, or ships with a foreigner among their officers. No foreign-registered ship could engage in the American coasting trade, so that if a British or French ship docked at New York without unloading her whole cargo, she had to visit a foreign port en route from New York to Philadelphia or Boston. American laws regarding seamen were even more capricious, so that some captains shanghaied their crews for want of volunteers, while others were held up in foreign ports by unreasonable technicalities and consular whims.[18]

As in the case of the wool and sugar tariffs, protectionists and free traders suggested opposite solutions to the shipping problem. Tariff reformers, led as usual by David A. Wells, proposed to do away with restrictive navigation acts, allow American shipowners to buy modern British-built ships if they wished, and compensate American shipbuilders by reducing or abolishing the duties on shipbuilding materials. Protectionists tried to arouse fears of foreign infiltration into American shipping and advanced their own solution: government subsidies to shipowners which would enable them to buy and operate the high-priced American ships.

One basic objection to ship subsidies was that in the past they had not helped either American shippers or shipbuilders to compete with European rivals. Although the government spent about $14,000,000 in subsidies before the Civil War, only one major line

[17]David A. Wells, *Our Merchant Marine, How It Rose, Increased, Became Great*, [etc.] (New York, 1882), pp. 22-33. John G. B. Hutchins, *The American Maritime Industries and Public Policy, 1789-1914, an Economic History* (Cambridge, Massachusetts, 1941), p. 316 *et passim*. George Walton Dalzell, *The Flight from the Flag; the Continuing Effect of the Civil War upon the American Carrying Trade* (Chapel Hill, North Carolina, 1940), pp. 248-56.

[18]Wells, *Our Merchant Marine*, pp. 75-89. See also report of Consul A. C. Marston, Málaga, April 12, 1881, U.S., Consular Reports, No. 10 (August 1881), pp. 287-88.

survived the war period. This line, the Pacific Mail Steamship Company, established regular connections with the Far East and Hawaii, but after an investigation in 1874 disclosed that the president of the company had spent $1,465,000 in bribes and fees, the government stopped its subsidy. For a time the company continued to flourish, expanding its service to New Zealand and New South Wales, but in 1881 its contract with these governments was about to expire, and British companies were offering faster service.[19]

Another example of the futility of subsidies was furnished by John Roach, the builder of the "new navy" (see Chapter 7), who was one of the leading exponents of the subsidy plan. In 1865 he founded the United States and Brazil Mail Steamship Company under contracts with the American and Brazilian governments for annual subsidies of not more than about $300,000 and set out to provide direct, fast service which would attract Brazilian trade to American shores. Despite his optimism, however, the expected American trade was slow in developing, and British steamship companies, seeing their monopoly threatened, undercut his rates and started a "whispering campaign" against him in Rio de Janeiro. During 1875, probably as a result of the unsavory disclosures concerning the Pacific Mail Company, the American Congress discontinued Roach's subsidy, forcing him at once into financial straits. He and his Republican allies, led by James G. Blaine, fought in vain to renew the subsidy. After operating costs in Brazil had banished all hope of profit, he sold out and devoted his full attention to shipbuilding.[20]

Thus in the sugar and shipping industries the rivalry of producers and manufacturers, shipbuilders and shippers, together with the sporadic, ill-focused public demand for reform, complicated the tariff question as the 1870's drew to a close. Unfor-

[19]Hutchins, *American Maritime Industries*, pp. 367-68, 529-31. *American Protectionist*, I (August 27, 1881), 368-69. Report of Consul G. W. Griffin, Auckland, May 20, U.S., Consular Reports, No. 9 (July 1881), pp. 45-49.

[20]On Roach's Brazilian line see David M. Pletcher, "Inter-American Shipping in the 1880's: a Loosening Tie," *Inter-American Economic Affairs*, X (Winter 1956), 32-34. Muzzey, *Blaine*, pp. 146-48. John Roach to Rutherford B. Hayes, New York, November 15, 1878, Hayes Papers. For Roach's views on protection and subsidies see *New York Tribune*, February 28, 1881, p. 3, and U.S., Congress, House, 47th Cong., 2d Sess., 1883, H. Rept. 1827, Appendix, *passim*.

tunately, these industries were to play a vital role in any program for hemispheric trade and unity during the Arthur administration. Sugar was the staple crop of the Caribbean, and as long as Britain controlled the sea lanes, it was not likely that American manufactured goods could beat the products of Manchester and Birmingham in the race to the Latin-American customer.[21]

*   *   *

The economic distress of the 1870's did not bring about any substantial changes in the tariff but caused enough complaints to worry both political parties. During the presidential campaign of 1880 the Democratic candidate, General Winfield S. Hancock, sought to keep out of trouble by dismissing the tariff as a "local affair," only to have his perhaps unconsciously perceptive formula laughed to scorn by his opponents. For his part, Garfield had once supported low tariffs, but during the 1870's he experienced a partial conversion, as the iron industry moved into his district of Ohio. In the campaign of 1880 his supporters beat the drum for protection, while he said as little as he could on the subject. It is at least arguable that Democratic awkwardness and Republican dexterity on the tariff issue swung the vote of several critical states to Garfield.[22]

Before the beginning of the campaign the iron lobbyist, Daniel J. Morrell, had written to Garfield, then a congressman, urging that the House stop all tariff agitation and let business enjoy its new-found prosperity in peace. However, the very prosperity made tariff revision inevitable, for the Treasury, always in sound condition through the worst years of the depression, received $600,000,000 from the customs offices alone between 1878 and 1880, paid off nearly $100,000,000 of the net debt, and still accumulated an embarrassing surplus. In July, 1881, James M. Swank wrote to Morrell that the time had come for a thorough-going revision, if only to correct abuses and end the everlasting

[21]For evidence on this point see Pletcher, "Inter-American Shipping," pp. 14-41, *passim.*

[22]Edward Stanwood, *American Tariff Controversies in the Nineteenth Century* (2 vols.; Boston, 1903), II, 199-201. Miller, *Old Northwest and the Tariff,* pp. 115-16, 120-21. Tarbell, *Tariff in Our Times,* pp. 94-97. Caldwell, *Garfield,* pp. 193-201. Herbert J. Clancy, *The Presidential Election of 1880* (Chicago, 1958), pp. 218-22 *et passim.*

arguments with Treasury officials over the interpretation of confusing regulations.[23]

At this point the assassination of Garfield postponed serious discussion for several months. When Arthur succeeded to the presidency, both protectionists and reformers counted on his blessing, and tariff conventions met at Chicago and New York late in the autumn to draw up guides for Congress. Fewer than two hundred attended the Chicago convention, however, and at New York low-tariff delegates managed to force proceedings into a deadlock, while the New York *Daily Commercial Bulletin*, representing the importers' point of view, congratulated protectionists on "the exceeding frankness with which they disclosed their preparations for a grand campaign against the public treasury."[24]

Some observers wondered nervously whether it might not be better to postpone further planning until the nation had another good crop to sell abroad, but the discussion had gone too far to stop. The most influential protectionist lobbyists and congressmen concluded that if change were inevitable, the tariff might as well be "revised by its friends." Seeing the growth of reform sentiment in the House, William D. Kelley and a few cohorts revived an old proposal for a special tariff commission and urged it on the Ways and Means Committee to gain time. Surprisingly, the Democrats, who also feared a showdown, supported the measure in the hope that public opinion would put the Republicans on the defensive, and that the by-elections of 1882 would bring new tariff reformers into Congress.[25] The tariff commission

[23]D. J. Morrell to James A. Garfield, Philadelphia, March 23, 1880, as quoted by Senator James M. Beck, U.S., *Congressional Record*, 46th Cong., 2d Sess., X, 3914. Stanwood, *American Tariff Controversies*, II, 201-2. James M. Swank to Morrell, Philadelphia, July 30, 1881, quoted in American Iron and Steel Association, *Report, 1880*, pp. 8-9.

[24]New York *Daily Commercial Bulletin*, September 22, 1881, p. 2; December 2, p. 2. *American Protectionist*, I (October 1), 437. *Nation*, XXXIII (November 24), 403-4. *New York Tribune*, November 30, pp. 1-2; December 2, p. 4.

[25]*Ibid.*, January 28, 1881, p. 1; March 31, 1882, p. 4. Younger, *Kasson*, pp. 310-12. Miller, *Old Northwest and the Tariff*, p. 122. Tarbell, *Tariff in Our Times*, pp. 99-100. Stanwood, *American Tariff Controversies*, II, 202-4. T. F. Bayard to David A. Wells, Washington, June [?] 10, 1882, David A. Wells Papers (New York Public Library).

of 1882 was, therefore, simply a bipartisan device to "pass the buck."

Immediately the competition began for places on the new commission. At Arthur's request Senator Morrill prepared a list of candidates, including a majority of Republicans and protectionists since, as he put it, "the country and Congress are overwhelmingly that way." John L. Hayes, whose name was first on Morrill's list, appealed to Secretary of the Navy William E. Chandler to get him an appointment so that he could "equalize the conditions of labor and capital here with those of our foreign competitors." Joseph Wharton warned Chandler against the economist, Francis A. Walker (not on Morrill's list), as "an embryo David A. Wells." The final list of appointees included lobbyists (representing wool, sugar, and iron), a statistician, a customs administrator, a country lawyer, and a pair of politicians.[26] Neither industrialists nor reformers were satisfied.

At the first meeting of the commission Chairman Hayes told his colleagues that they were forbidden to propose any "radical or subversive change" in the tariff. After a week of preparatory sessions in Washington the commission held hearings for a month at the swank resort of Long Branch, New Jersey, and then traveled around the country for nearly three months, hearing 604 witnesses and taking 2,625 pages of testimony in which industrialists such as Joseph Wharton and John Roach pointed with pride to their accomplishments as examples of what protection could do for infant industries. However, not all evidence favored high tariffs, and an occasional factory owner, such as Abram S. Hewitt, mortified his colleagues by confessing that profits had risen entirely too high.[27]

Long before the commission issued its report, reformers were denouncing it as a pander to wealthy manufacturers, and the *New York Herald* declared it "the most expensive luxury of the

[26]Morrill to Arthur, Washington, May 13, 1882, copy in Justin S. Morrill Papers, XXXI (Library of Congress). Richardson, *Chandler*, p. 337. Joseph Wharton to William E. Chandler, Camden, New Jersey, May 23, William E. Chandler Papers, LIII (Library of Congress). For comments on the final choices see Tarbell, *Tariff in Our Times*, pp. 101-3.

[27]*Ibid.*, pp. 103-6. Stanwood, *American Tariff Controversies*, II, 204-7. Miller, *Old Northwest and the Tariff*, pp. 124-25.

kind which the country has enjoyed in many years. . . . The Commissioners . . . live in a style that only European emperors and American railway magnates can afford." Somewhat to the surprise of these critics, the report of the tariff commission recommended almost no increases and a series of reductions averaging about 25 per cent. The protectionist *New York Tribune*, while recognizing that the report was a compromise, urged Congress to enact it into law. Senator John Sherman, the financial expert of the Republican party, later called the report "clear and businesslike" and "by far the most comprehensive exposition of our customs laws and rates of duty that, so far as I know, had been published [up to that time]."[28]

Alas, too late. Perhaps no amount of tariff concessions could have mollified the electorate, smitten with falling prices and rising unemployment, but Republican campaigners could not obliterate from the public mind the picture of junketing commissioners drinking champagne with factory-owners in their private railway car. The Democrats had many other issues on which to attack the administration: Chinese immigration, the protection of Irish-Americans abroad, civil service reform, the "Star Route" frauds, as well as the vaguer charges of extravagance and centralization of power. James G. Blaine, pleading illness, declined to campaign for the Republicans and stayed on the sidelines, sneering at the administration which had repudiated him. The results of the elections fully confirmed their forebodings, for the Democrats captured the House of Representatives by a comfortable margin. Smugly, Henry Adams pronounced the Republican party "a burst bladder."[29]

*   *   *

When the "lame duck" Congress assembled in Washington at

[28]John Sherman, *Recollections of Forty Years* (2 vols.; New York, 1895), II, 351. See also *New York Herald*, September 12, 1882, p. 6, and *New York Tribune*, December 22, p. 4.

[29]Henry Adams to John Hay, Washington, November 26, 1882, Worthington C. Ford (ed.), *Letters of Henry Adams, 1858-1891* (Boston, 1930), p. 343. For the Democratic platform see *The Campaign Book of the Democratic Party. The Republican Party Reviewed, Its Sins of Omission and Commission. Why a Change Is Demanded by the People* (Washington, 1882), *passim*. Emmons Blaine to Chandler, Augusta, Maine, October 6, 1882, Chandler Papers. James G. Blaine to Whitelaw Reid, October 14, Reid Papers, Box CIV.

the beginning of December to hear the report of the tariff commission, everyone expected action of some sort, if only to forestall the Democrats. Most able-bodied lobbyists assembled with the congressmen, so that they should not lack counsel. Ohio woolgrowers, alarmed at the sharp reduction in wool duties recommended by the commission, sent Columbus A. Delano to urge that no changes be made. John L. Hayes of the wool manufacturers, erstwhile chairman of the commission, lobbied for even higher duties than his commission had thought advisable. A new group, the New York Association for the Protection of American Industry, held a mass meeting at Cooper Institute, where former Secretary Evarts, who had never shown any great interest in the tariff, spoke for more than an hour in support of protection. For several months the *New York Tribune* ran a series of articles by a member of the commission describing the depression of British labor under free trade and the beneficial effects of tariffs in Germany.[30]

Pressed for time by the shortness of the session, Congress turned at once to the intricate, technical business of overhauling the tariff. The result was a parliamentarian's nightmare. William D. Kelley and other protectionists on the House Ways and Means Committee rejected the recommendations of the tariff commission and reported a bill which contained only enough reductions to preserve appearances. Although high-tariff Republicans controlled the House, the face-saving bill bogged down in a morass of oratory and petty amendments, as each representative sought to provide for his own constituents. Meanwhile the Senate, more evenly divided than the House, had resurrected an unused revenue bill from the last session and, through the amending process, was shaping a tariff act of its own. In the Finance Committee Senator Sherman, under strong pressure from smelter-owners, did his best to raise pig iron duties, then carried the fight to the Senate floor,

[30]Tarbell, *Tariff in Our Times*, pp. 113-14. Columbus A. Delano to Morrill, Washington, February 14, 1883, Morrill Papers, XXXI (Library of Congress). *New York Tribune*, January 17, 1883, p. 8; February 2, p. 1. Barrows, *Evarts*, pp. 412-13. For a statement of purpose in the first *Tribune* article by Robert P. Porter see the issue for January 5. The activities of the Louisiana sugar lobby are described in New Orleans *Times-Democrat*, March 9, p. 8.

and finally got his way by threatening to sabotage the whole bill. After this crisis the work proceeded faster, and on February 20 the Senate passed its bill, a combination of moderate reductions.

Disliking the Senate bill but faced with an immovable deadline, the principal Republican strategists in the House racked their wits for an escape. In order to prevent further time-consuming speeches, Representative Thomas B. Reed (later nicknamed "Czar" for just such audacity) found a way to suspend traditional House rules, take up the amended Senate bill, and appoint a joint committee which hastily revised the complicated schedules. On March 2 this committee presented an amended form of the Senate bill with many upward changes in duties—some of them even higher than the House had earlier proposed. At midnight the Senate adopted the committee bill by a vote of 32-31. Next day tariff reformers in the House fought a delaying action, forcing the clerk to read the entire list of duties for several hours, but in vain. Protectionists forced a roll call; after much changing of votes, the bill was passed, 152-116. The President signed it moments before the constitutional hour of adjournment, while the weary congressmen straggled out of the Capitol. "I came home & slept 14 hours yesterday," wrote Senator Beck to the discouraged David A. Wells. "If you quit we may as well all quit."[31]

After weeks of heaving and churning, Congress had managed to reduce duties on the average of 1.47 per cent, and the raised and lowered rates were so illogical that the scornful critics were soon calling the bill "the mongrel tariff." The *New York Herald* inveighed against a measure "which in some clauses increases the duty on raw materials and decreases that on manufactures; which upon one kind of steel imposes three different rates in three different places; which, according to the statement of experts, will lead to more Treasury appeals and general uncertainty than any preceding tariff." Everywhere the bill showed signs of haste in dangling modifiers and other grammatical absurdities, and the

[31]James M. Beck to Wells, Washington, March 7, 1883, David A. Wells Papers, XIX (Library of Congress). Stanwood, *American Tariff Controversies*, II, 207-18. Tarbell, *Tariff in Our Times*, pp. 114-30. Younger, *Kasson*, pp. 316-18. Miller, *Old Northwest and the Tariff*, pp. 127-28.

lobbyist, James M. Swank, called it an open invitation to fraud.[32]

Some protectionists approved the new act. For example, the National Association of Wool Manufacturers voted to thank Senator Morrill for "the wisdom of his counsels" in bringing about "a substantial reduction of duties together with a substantial preservation of the protective feature of our national economical system." (Morrill, too, was complacent about the act.) However, Ohio woolgrowers were angry at Senator Sherman for expending most of his energies on pig iron instead of on wool, and the American Iron and Steel Association regretted that not all duties had been raised. Louisiana sugar planters complained at slightly reduced sugar rates, while refiners objected because they were not reduced further, despite the added tariff enjoyed by refined sugar.[33] Blaine denounced the concessions as playing into the hands of the Democrats. He urged Whitelaw Reid to write further protectionist editorials, but Reid considered the tariff a "triumph." The *Tribune* criticized only minor details, and within a year it was quoting a speech by John L. Hayes which elevated the raggle-taggle law to the eminence of a solemn covenant:

> The act of 1883, he said, was in its nature not unlike a treaty between the Government and the important industries affected. . . . The Government virtually undertook to subject industries to no greater disadvantages and burdens, under existing conditions and until the needs of the Government had materially changed, than those to which the act of 1883 subjected them. . . . For such an enactment implies that the Government . . . will not encourage its citizens to invest their means and enterprise in an industry, and then, without adequate and controlling reason, condemn them to ruin.[34]

[32]*New York Tribune*, February 27, 1882, p. 2. For an example of grammatical fuzziness see *ibid.*, February 26, p. 4. A general summary of reductions appears in *Nation*, XXXVIII (May 8, 1884), 395. *New York Herald*, March 5, 1883, p. 4. *Washington Post*, March 5, p. 2.

[33]Resolution of National Association of Wool Manufacturers. Morrill Papers, XXXII. Morrill to Wharton Barker, Washington, March 10, 1883, Wharton Barker Papers (Library of Congress). Tarbell, *Tariff in Our Times*, pp. 130-31. Swank to Morrell, Philadelphia, May 1, 1883, in American Iron and Steel Association, *Report, 1882*, pp. 7-8. New Orleans *Times-Democrat*, January 22, 1882, p. 4. [Henry E.] Havemeyer to Wells, New York, August 7, 1882, Wells Papers, XIX.

[34]*New York Tribune*, February 15, 1884, p. 4. See also *ibid.*, January 24, 1883, p. 4; February 22, p. 4. Blaine to Reid, Washington, February 19, Reid Papers, Box CIV. Reid to G. W. Smalley, March 8, Reid Letterbook, XLI, 671-88.

Hayes and Reid were indulging in wishful thinking entirely unjustified by circumstances. The "mongrel tariff" was not a lasting solution but a patchwork of compromises, representing the studied convictions of neither administration nor Congress, neither Republicans nor Democrats, neither protectionists nor reformers. If Arthur and the Cabinet learned anything from it, they realized that effective aids to foreign commerce involving the American tariff must originate with the executive. Before the passage of the mongrel act, Arthur and Frelinghuysen had already begun to work for commercial reciprocity through the State Department. The paralysis of Congressional tariff reform could only encourage them to continue this policy.[35]

[35]The Forty-seventh Congress also found it difficult to agree on reforms in shipping laws. A special joint committee tried to combine the most attractive features of bounties and protection by recommending rebates to shipbuilders equal to tariff duties paid on construction materials and supplies purchased abroad, increased mail allowances, and a revision of the troublesome and confusing laws regulating the payment of sailors. Chairman Nelson Dingley introduced a bill embodying this report; a deadlock developed; and after much parliamentary maneuvering Congress passed a compromise bill which, like the "mongrel tariff," satisfied few, since it confined itself to the reform of consular fees, port duties, and seamen's wages, leaving the basic questions of bounties and the navigation acts unanswered. Nothing further of importance was accomplished during the Arthur administration. U.S., Congress, House, 47th Cong., 2d Sess., 1883, H. Rept. 1827, *passim. New York Tribune*, January 13, 1883, p. 1.

CHAPTER 9

The Pork Controversy

THE PHENOMENAL expansion of the American economy and the dominance of American high-tariff policies inevitably helped to encourage economic nationalism in other parts of the world. The influx of cheap farm products from the United States, reducing the profits from European agriculture, reinforced the dislike of conservative landowners for republican America, while the continued growth of American manufactures, protected by tariffs, foreshadowed bitter competition with European industries, the bulwark of the middle classes. Already in the 1870's Russia, Austria-Hungary, Italy, and Germany were turning to protection, more or less on an experimental basis. At the same time British and German manufactures were reaching out for new markets in Asia, Africa, and Latin America, and Russian wheat and oil producers were preparing to contest the European trade with the Americans.

Thus both sides girded for what the New York *Daily Commercial Bulletin* called "the great 'irrepressible conflict' of the nineteenth century."[1] The most overt diplomatic aspect of that conflict during the Garfield and Arthur administrations was a controversy over American pork exports. Although apparently trivial in itself, this controversy suggested that rival tariff systems and economic nationalism might be chronic problems in the future relations of the United States and Europe.

[1]New York *Daily Commercial Bulletin*, March 26, 1881, p. 2. Wells, *Recent Economic Changes*, pp. 264-66. James Henry Smith to J. C. Bancroft Davis, Mayence, February 16, 1882, No. 21, U.S., Consular Despatches, Mayence, I. Allan Nevins, *Study in Power: John D. Rockefeller, Industrialist and Philanthropist* (2 vols.; New York, 1953), I, 115-19. For a later expression of the aristocratic European attitude toward American competition see Alfred Vagts, *Deutschland und die Vereinigten Staaten in der Weltpolitik* (2 vols.; New York, 1935), I, 1, note. See also p. 2.

More than any Continental country, Britain of the mid-nine-teenth century had committed herself to the doctrine of free trade, and even during the depression of the 1870's the British government remained loyal to economic liberalism. The growth of American wheat, flour, and meat shipments might threaten British agriculture with chronic hard times, but the policy-makers of both parties were convinced that British industry could not afford an artificial rise in food prices.

Naturally the British industrialists and financiers were less com-placent about American threats to British manufactures. Some factory-owners made their peace with the American rivals: Joseph Chamberlain, for example, later admitted accepting a subsidy from them for not exporting screws to the United States. Other injured Britons sought solace in discussing retaliatory tariffs, and a segment of the Conservative party, thrown out of power in the elections of 1880, began to campaign for "Fair Trade," which they interpreted to mean moderate tariffs of perhaps 10 per cent on items most threatened by foreign competition. Liberals pointed out, however, that in spite of the American tariff Britain con-tinued to enjoy a favorable balance of trade with the United States and urged the government not to start a tariff war. The gradual improvement of trade during 1881 softened the outcry for protection, and in September James Russell Lowell described the Fair Trade movement as "more noise than substance . . . an ephemeral delusion, like that of the Greenback Party among ourselves."[2]

For a time the British free-trade policy was attractive enough to inspire imitation by France. In 1860 the two countries negotiated the Cobden-Chevalier reciprocal trade treaty, and during the next decade France signed eight somewhat similar treaties with other nations. For perhaps twelve years after the Cobden-Chevalier treaty France prospered, but the heavy burden of the Franco-Prussian War and the generally hard times of the mid-seventies

[2]James Russell Lowell to James G. Blaine, London, September 30, 1881, No. 256, U.S., Despatches, Britain, CXLIII. *Nation*, XLI (November 26, 1885), 435. *New York Tribune*, September 15, 1881, p. 4; January 1, 1882, p. 1. *Westminster Review*, CXII (July 1879), 6-7.

disillusioned many free traders and brought forth protectionist agitation by both agricultural and industrial lobbies.[3]

At this point a group of low-tariff enthusiasts in France started a backfire against the protectionist movement by proposing a commercial treaty with the United States. For many years French exports to the United States had steadily declined because of the high American tariff, especially on silks. Early in 1878 a group of French manufacturers, politicians, and journalists sent the publicist Léon Chotteau to the United States to agitate for a reciprocity treaty. At first he awakened considerable approval, but when he reached the West Coast, Californians began to wonder how the proposal would affect their wine industry. Early in the following year the San Francisco Chamber of Commerce printed a rousing pamphlet against the project, denouncing the French as a provincial, deceitful people and Chotteau as a trickster who wanted to cripple American industry by forcing it to compete with the pauper wages of Europe.[4]

By this time the Democratic majority in the House of Representatives had taken an interest in the Franco-American project. Fernando Wood, then chairman of the Ways and Means Committee, secured the passage of a favorable resolution, and Chotteau made another tour of the United States, met President Hayes, and appeared before Wood's committee. Despite protectionist outcries the Hayes administration might have undertaken negotiations, but to Chotteau's great embarrassment, he could not win over his own government. After the Republican victory in 1880 the likelihood of official support in the United States also faded.[5]

[3]Percy Ashley, *Modern Tariff History: Germany, United States, France* (3d ed.; New York, 1920), pp. 297-314. *Nation*, XXIV (April 12, 1877), 216-17. Edward F. Noyes to William M. Evarts, Paris, March 28, 1878, No. 80, U.S., Despatches, France, LXXXIII.

[4]Benjamin F. Peixotto to F. W. Seward, Lyons, July 1, December 19, 1878, Nos. 37, 58, U.S., Consular Despatches, Lyons, VI. *Nation*, XXX (February 12, 1880), 109. *The Franco-American Treaty of Commerce. Reports and Resolutions Adopted in the United States and France* (Paris, 1879), *passim*. *New York Times*, April 5, 1878, p. 4; August 10, p. 4. *Philadelphia Inquirer*, August 10, p. 4. San Francisco Chamber of Commerce, *Franco-American Commerce. Statements and Arguments in Behalf of American Industries Against the Proposed Franco-American Commercial Treaty* [etc.] (San Francisco, 1879), pp. 91, 112-13, 122 *et passim*.

[5]Léon Chotteau, *Mes campagnes aux États-Unis et en France, 1878-1885. Discours et lettres* [etc.] (Paris, 1893), pp. 213-14, 224-27, 320-27 *et passim*. Lucius Fairchild to Seward, Paris, April 10, 1879, No. 48, U.S., Consular Despatches, Paris, XXI.

Like France the newly created German Empire of the 1870's inherited a liberal free-trade tradition which it soon abandoned. Greatly stimulated by victory over France in 1870-1871, German industry expanded too rapidly and suffered pangs of overproduction and readjustment during the international depression which followed. As in England, the desire of German farming interests for protection conflicted with the demand of the cities for cheap food, but in Germany the protectionist bloc was larger and more unified. By the end of the decade it had convinced Chancellor Bismarck that free trade was bleeding the nation white, and early in 1879 the legislature adopted the German Empire's first protective tariff. Within a few months a strong opposition to the new duties appeared, but at the same time the duties encouraged German agricultural organizations to demand even more protection against American farm products. Also, by giving imperialists a new excuse to demand German colonies, the tariff contributed indirectly to German-American friction in Samoa and Africa.[6]

*   *   *

In the early 1880's the accumulated European resentment toward American competition discharged itself in a series of lightning bolts against the American pork trade. Cheap pork imports furnished a valuable staple food to European cities, but they seemed to rob European producers of their rightful market. Furthermore, the occasional appearance of trichinae in American pork gave protectionist governments a providential opportunity to pose as guardians of the public health. At no time were experts agreed as to what caused trichinae in pork or whether American pork

Noyes to Evarts, Paris, May 16, 1879; July 8, 1880, Nos. 233, 365, *ibid.*, France, LXXXV, LXXXVI. Report of Commercial Agent George Gifford, Nantes, October 31, 1880, U.S., *Reports from the Consuls of the United States on the Commerce, Manufactures, etc. of their Consular Districts* (Washington, 1880-   ), No. 3 (January 1881), pp. 106-7. Hereafter cited as U.S., *Consular Reports.*

[6]Wells, *Recent Economic Changes*, p. 62. Ashley, *Modern Tariff History*, pp. 39-48. Otto zu Stolberg-Wernigerode, *Germany and the United States of America during the Era of Bismarck* (Reading, Pennsylvania, 1937), pp. 140-41. L. L. Snyder, "The American-German Pork Dispute, 1879-1891," *Journal of Modern History*, XVII (1945), 16-17. Report of Consul H. J. Winser, Sonneberg, October 1, 1879, in U.S., *Commercial Relations, 1879*, II, 156-57. Andrew D. White to Blaine, Berlin, June 14, 1881, No. 211, U.S., *Despatches, Germany*, XXVIII. Report of Consul General Kreismann, Berlin, March 14, U.S., *Consular Reports*, No. 11 (September 1881), pp. 369-79.

was actually worse infected than any other, but the economic nationalists never allowed this uncertainty to stand in their way. In 1878 a Viennese doctor published a letter warning that one-fifth of American hams might be infected with trichinae, and this letter started a "whispering campaign" all over western Europe. On June 25, 1880, the German government banned American pork sausage and chopped pork.

In Britain the publication of warnings from Her Majesty's consuls in the United States began to attract attention. The climax of this series was a sensational report from Acting Consul Crump in Philadelphia, declaring that 700,000 pigs had died in Illinois that year from hog cholera, which he confused with trichinosis. Crump quoted a frightful description of a human victim: "Worms were in his flesh by the millions, being scraped and squeezed from the pores of his skin. They are felt creeping through his flesh, and are literally eating up his substance." When the Crump report appeared in an official Blue Book, the panic-stricken British readers felt their own flesh begin to creep. In answer to a question in Parliament the Government then tried to reassure the public. Minister Lowell, suspecting a speculators' plot, did what he could to counteract its effects, while the State Department challenged the accuracy of Crump's information. On Blaine's instructions Lowell delivered a formal protest to the Foreign Office, but inasmuch as the British government did not seem disposed to pass restrictive legislation, Blaine soon let the matter drop.[7]

Across the Channel the pork question caused much more serious trouble in Franco-American relations, since it served to aggravate already existing grievances over the failure of Léon Chotteau's reciprocity project. Cheap American bacon and lard had practically driven French pork products off the market, and even before the appearance of the Crump report there was a strong movement in the French legislature for protective duties against American pork. In February, 1881, as a health measure the min-

[7]Crump's report is quoted in U.S., *Foreign Relations, 1881*, p. 580. Lowell to Blaine, London, March 9, April 9, 13, 1881, Nos. 139, 161, 163; Blaine to Lowell, March 17, June 10, Nos. 130, 180, *ibid.*, pp. 510-11, 515-17, 525-29, 534-35. Snyder, "American-German Pork Dispute," pp. 18-19. Frederick T. Frelinghuysen to Chester A. Arthur, January 31, 1884, in U.S., Congress, Senate, 48th Cong., 1st Sess., 1884, Senate Rept. 345, pp. 3-4.

ister of agriculture and commerce forbade the importation of all American pork products. Interior farm towns rejoiced and urged the government to enforce the decrees rigidly, but there was consternation in the seaports, especially in Bordeaux, where several capitalists had just opened a steamship line to the United States and were even then awaiting the first eastbound steamer, loaded with pork and hams. Immediate protests brought a postponement of the prohibition, but the French government refused to withdraw its decrees altogether.[8]

Blaine at once supplied Minister Edward F. Noyes with all possible information on sanitary conditions in American packing plants, but without effect. When Noyes hinted that the French desire for a reciprocity treaty might have been partly responsible for the decrees, Blaine replied sternly that the United States would not consider any sort of commercial negotiations until the restrictions were withdrawn. On November 25, in the midst of his hurried activity before leaving office, he sent a stiff note to the French Minister in Washington, defending wholesome corn-fed American pork and hinting at retaliation by Congress against French wines, which were not infrequently adulterated.[9]

With Frelinghuysen's full approval, however, the new American minister, Levi P. Morton, abandoned Blaine's sternness and set out to ingratiate himself with the French government and upper classes, trusting that time would eventually soften their prejudices. In November, 1883, President Jules Grévy actually withdrew the decrees of 1881 and agreed to admit American salt pork, but the Chamber of Deputies set aside his action until a French system of inspection, completely unacceptable to American packers, could be established. The French government maintained

[8]Thomas Wilson to John Davis, Nantes, December 4, 1882, No. 12, U.S., Consular Despatches, Nantes, V. Noyes to Evarts, Paris, February 26, No. 439; Noyes to Blaine, March 24, 1881, No. 449, U.S., *Foreign Relations, 1881*, pp. 396-400, 405. R. Gerrish to John Hay, Bordeaux, March 9, No. 114, U.S., Consular Despatches, Bordeaux, VIII. Report of Consul Frank H. Mason, Basle, April 29, U.S., *Consular Reports*, No. 9 (July 1881), pp. 192-94.

[9]*New York Tribune*, May 16, 1881, p. 1. Noyes to Blaine, Paris, March 24, 1881, No. 449, U.S., Despatches, France, LXXXVIII. G. P. Pomeroy to Blaine, Paris, July 23, No. 495; Blaine to Levi P. Morton, August 18, No. 19; Morton to Blaine, Paris, October 6, 13, Nos. 48, 54; Blaine to Max Outrey, November 25, U.S., *Foreign Relations, 1881*, pp. 417-18, 421-23, 430-31, 442-44.

this position for the rest of the Arthur administration, even though the French Academy of Medicine gave a clean bill of health to American pork by an overwhelming vote. On July 4, 1884, in the midst of the argument, however, the French government held a gala celebration and presented the colossal Bartholdi Statue of Liberty to Morton for the United States, as if to say that France appreciated America's ideals, if not her pork.[10]

*   *   *

Before European fears had run their course, the governments of Italy, Austria-Hungary, Spain, Portugal, and even Turkey had shut out American pork products. It was in Germany, however, that the prejudice against American pork did the greatest damage to diplomatic relations. This was so, partly because the powerful German landowners regarded the United States with contempt and envy, and partly because many meat-packers in the United States were German-born and already hated Bismarck. During 1881 and 1882 the Chancellor contented himself with his earlier decree shutting out American sausage, but late in 1882 a new surge of protectionism began, disguised as fear of trichinosis. A member of the Reichstag introduced a bill to prohibit all importation of American pork, while German customs officials invoked every possible technicality against American meats.

Liberal opponents of Bismarck protested that the exclusion of American pork would raise its price, to the detriment of the poor; newspapers printed exhaustive defenses of American meat-packing; and German merchants urged the government to spare their flourishing import trade, which paid generous taxes and gave much business to German shipping. Hoping to forestall action at the last minute, President Arthur sent a telegram inviting the German government to appoint a special commission to inspect American packing plants. All in vain. On March 6 the Reichstag

---

[10]However, Morton did persuade the French government to make important changes in French corporation law, which for years had discriminated unfairly against American companies. His correspondence on these subjects is found *ibid*. *1882*, pp. 148-56; *1883*, pp. 264-72, 283-84, 292-94; *1884*, pp. 128-30, 132-35, 141-42, 158-64. See also Henry Vignaud to J. C. Bancroft Davis [Paris], July 9, 1882, Davis Papers, XXXII.

approved a decree prohibiting the importation of all American pork.[11]

As in the case of France the German prohibition presented two alternative lines of action to the United States: retaliation against German products and the establishment of rigid inspection in American packing plants. The packing companies and many other commercial interests urged the government to shut out French and German wines and other imports. On the other hand, even before the European pork decrees, spokesmen for American stock-raisers had argued that the foreign demand for adequate inspection was reasonable. In November, 1883, the National Livestock Convention drew up a formal petition to Congress along this line. Testimony about the packing plants varied widely. In 1879 and 1880 doctors employed by the Marine Hospital Service and the Bureau of Animal Industry reported filthy conditions and diseased hogs being marketed, but when Blaine sent the chief of the Bureau of Statistics to examine the stockyards, he found nothing censurable. In 1883 a special commission appointed by Arthur declared that existing methods of inspection were adequate. They reported, however, that it was possible for diseased meat to be exported, and that microscopic examinations could be performed if necessary. Naturally such contradictory findings did nothing to reassure the Europeans.[12]

In Congress the debate on retaliation and inspection was soon broadened to tariff policy in general. When Senator H. B. Anthony of Rhode Island introduced a resolution looking toward retaliation, Senator Beck offered an amendment directing the

[11]Aaron A. Sargent to Frelinghuysen, Berlin, November 6, 13, December 11, 18, 1882; January 1, 13, February 17, 24, March 14, 15, 19, 1883, Nos. 74, 77, 85, 87, 90, 96, 109, 111, 121, 122, and telegrams; Frelinghuysen to Sargent, November 28, 1882; January 12, February 15, 16, 21, March 14, 1883, Nos. 66, 74, 87, 88, 99, and telegrams, U.S., *Foreign Relations, 1883*, pp. 305-10, 318-26, 327-30, 335-42, 355-61. Stolberg-Wernigerode, *Germany and the United States*, pp. 150-51.

[12]This aspect of the pork question is well discussed in John L. Gignilliat, "Pigs, Politics, and Protection: the American Pork Boycott in Europe, 1879-1891," an unpublished paper read at the American Historical Association convention, December, 1959. See also *National Livestock Journal* (August 1879), p. 331. U.S., *Congressional Record*, 48th Cong., 1st Sess., XV, 425. U.S., Department of Agriculture, *Report of Commissioner, 1879*, p. 418. U.S., Congress, House, 47th Cong., 1st Sess., 1882, House Doc. 209, p. 190; 48th Cong., 1st Sess., 1883, House Executive Doc. 106, *passim*.

Foreign Relations Committee to investigate discrimination of all kinds against American products by special trade agreements. Beck advocated what amounted to an economic Golden Rule: Do not object to other nations' protectionism while proclaiming it a good thing for the United States. After the Senate had passed Anthony's resolution with Beck's amendment, the problem was turned over to the Foreign Relations Committee, which worked closely with the State Department. Moving cautiously to avoid offending the nationalists in Congress, Frelinghuysen wrote confidentially to the chairman of the committee, Senator Miller of California, to discourage any sort of retaliation, indicating that he preferred to settle commercial questions by bilateral reciprocity treaties. The committee reported in favor of an inspection system, but the Senate refused to pass a bill for this purpose, although it took no further steps toward retaliation.[13]

The failure of proposals for inspection or retaliation should have consigned the German-American pork dispute to the limbo of dormant controversies, like that with France. However, Bismarck's native dislike of republican America had been sharpened by resentment over the steady emigration of German men of military age to the United States.[14] Also, by ill chance the State Department did not have a representative in Berlin as shrewd and persuasive as Levi P. Morton. The American minister to Germany, Aaron A. Sargent, was a former senator from California, not well trained in diplomatic subtleties but anxious to cut a proper figure before the voters at home. On his arrival at his new post, late in 1882, he had shown too little deference to suit Bismarck, and, disturbed at the agitation over pork, he had consulted the liberal opposition too freely. For these offenses he became the principal target of the Chancellor's wrath.

[13]U.S., *Congressional Record*, 48th Cong., 1st Sess., XV, 402-5, 558-64 *et passim.* Burnette, "Senate Foreign Relations Committee," pp. 205-11. Frelinghuysen to Arthur, January 31, 1884, U.S., Congress, Senate, 48th Cong., 1st Sess., 1884, Senate Rept. 345, pp. 3-7. Frelinghuysen to Arthur, February 28, 1884, U.S., Report Book, XV, 317-18. Frelinghuysen to Miller, March 14, Records of the Senate Committee on Foreign Relations (National Archives). Hereafter cited as United States, Senate Foreign Relations Committee Archives.

[14]On this subject see Stolberg-Wernigerode, *Germany and the United States,* chap. ii and especially pp. 185-86.

In Sargent's early dispatches he carried out his duty by reporting frankly that he believed agrarian pressure for protection to
be largely responsible for the pork decrees. Unfortunately he
overstepped both his instructions and diplomatic propriety by
threatening the German government with retaliation, and when
Bismarck's minister at Washington protested, Frelinghuysen had
to disavow Sargent's statement and send him a mild reprimand.[15]
At about the same time the State Department committed an
equally serious blunder by allowing one of Sargent's candid dispatches to slip into the *New York Tribune*, less than a month
after he had written it. The government-subsidized press in Germany burst into denunciations, suggesting that the United States
was trying to force its diseased pork on Germany, and newspapers
in several European capitals criticized Sargent's actions.[16] German
liberals, favoring free trade, naturally defended him, and one of
Bismarck's principal opponents in the Reichstag, Dr. Edward
Lasker, chose this moment to make a lecture tour in the United
States. His attacks on German tariffs and the applause which he
received further grated on Bismarck's nerves.

The sudden death of Lasker on January 5, 1884, in the middle
of his American tour, gave Bismarck the awaited opportunity to
strike back. Representative Thomas P. Ochiltree of Texas, a friend
of the Lasker family, introduced into the House an ill-advised
resolution of regret at the passing of a statesman whose "firm and
constant exposition of and devotion to free and liberal ideas have
materially advanced the social, political, and economic conditions

[15]Sargent to Frelinghuysen, Berlin, February 24, 1883, No. 111; Frelinghuysen
to Sargent, March 14, No. 99; Von Eisendecher to Frelinghuysen, Washington,
May 2, U.S., *Foreign Relations, 1883*, pp. 339-42, 356-57, 404-5. Accounts of Sargent's troubles may be found in Snyder, "American-German Pork Dispute," pp.
23-24; and Stolberg-Wernigerode, *Germany and the United States*, pp. 152-65,
passim. The latter account is very anti-Sargent.
[16]The dispatch in question was Sargent's No. 90 of January 1, 1883, U.S., *Foreign
Relations, 1883*, pp. 324-26. It was first published in the *New York Tribune*, January 27, p. 2. However, its publication in the *New Yorker Handels-Zeitung* for
March 10 seems to have attracted the most attention. Sargent denied having sent the
dispatch to the press, and it is not clear just how the leak occurred. At about the
same time the State Department asked American consuls in France for confidential
information on the adulteration of French wines and then published the replies,
to the great embarrassment of the consuls. Thomas Wilson to J. C. Bancroft
Davis, Nantes, January 12, Davis Papers, XXXIII.

of those people." An almost empty House voted to send this partisan condolence to the Reichstag, but when Sargent presented it to the German Foreign Office, Bismarck refused to receive it and went out of his way to denounce Sargent for not warning the State Department against such an obvious insult. In later dispatches the Chancellor accused Sargent of conspiring with the liberal opposition and pressed for his recall, while the German press heaped up abuse. "He means to drive me away," wrote the unhappy minister, "partly from hatred for my opposition to his prohibition policy, partly desire to show his power, and to teach the Diplomatic Corps that humility is good policy. . . . Future American ministers are expected to learn by my fate."[17]

Although the rest of Europe was probably not sorry to witness a falling-out between the two leading protectionist nations, Sargent received much sympathy, as a soldier obeying orders or as a scapegoat for American tariffs and German liberals. In the United States Carl Schurz, Senator George F. Edmunds, and others urged Frelinghuysen to support a minister who had only done his duty. Several hotheads in the House of Representatives prepared abusive resolutions against Germany, but John A. Kasson and other peacemakers managed to suppress these, advising the House to leave the question to the State Department. Frelinghuysen backed up Sargent loyally and, when the Minister decided that he could not stand any more abuse, recalled him with full approval and appointed him minister to Russia. Sargent wisely declined the new appointment, protesting bad health and the fear that Russia would refuse to receive him.[18]

After the wounded feelings began to mend, the *Nation* commented that the Lasker incident should teach the House never to pass resolutions without knowing what they contained and

---

[17]Sargent to Frelinghuysen, Berlin, February 18, March 3, 11, 15, 1884, Nos. 243, 245, 253, 256, U.S., Despatches, Germany, XXXIV, XXXV. On Lasker's death see *Washington Post*, January 6, 1884, p. 1.

[18]For samples of European opinion see Sargent to Frelinghuysen, Berlin, February 25, 1884, No. 244, U.S., Despatches, Germany, XXXIV, and *New York Tribune*, March 27, p. 5. Carl Schurz to George F. Edmunds, New York, March 9; Edmunds to Schurz, March 14, Carl Schurz Papers, LXXXI (Library of Congress). Younger, *Kasson*, p. 321. For Frelinghuysen's correspondence with Sargent on his resignation see U.S., Instructions, Germany, XVII, 329-30, 333-38, 345-46, and Despatches, Germany, XXXV, *passim*.

suggested that hara-kiri would be a suitable gesture for Ochiltree. Ignoring its own part in the leakage, the *New York Tribune* denounced the "indiscretion and folly" of the State Department in releasing confidential dispatches and urged Frelinghuysen to leave the legation at Berlin in the hands of a chargé for a few months as a sign of displeasure. The Secretary did not follow this advice, but at least he chose a qualified successor, John A. Kasson, who had served as minister to Austria under Hayes and had many friends in central Europe. Within a few weeks after his arrival in Germany Kasson was reporting that he had the situation well in hand.[19]

Some weeks after Sargent's departure the *Berliner Tageblatt* reprinted from a medical journal an article by the renowned bacteriologist, Rudolf Virchow, casting serious doubts on all evidence of trichinae in American pork. Americans welcomed this expert vindication and looked forward to the repeal of the German edict of prohibition, but neither Kasson nor Virchow had the slightest effect on Bismarck. For over five years after the end of the Arthur administration the discriminatory law remained in force. Only in 1891, after American packers had set up a thorough system of inspection and the Harrison administration had promised to exempt German sugar from the American tariff did Berlin repeal the objectionable decree.[20]

[19]*Nation*, XXXVIII (March 27, 1884), 265-66. *New York Tribune*, March 12, p. 4; April 27, p. 6. John A. Kasson to Frelinghuysen, Berlin, November 17, 1884; February 7, 1885, Nos. 70, 158, U.S., Despatches, Germany, XXXVI, XXXVII.

[20]*New York Tribune*, May 3, 1884, p. 3. On the later history of the pork question see Stolberg-Wernigerode, *Germany and the United States*, pp. 165-68, and Snyder, "American-German Pork Dispute," pp. 27-28.

CHAPTER 10

The Growth of Reciprocity

THUS in the early 1880's American producers and merchants faced the dilemma of an irresistible force confronted with two immovable objects, as the outward thrust of American trade met the obstacles of European competition and American protectionism. To Arthur and Frelinghuysen and to many others neither retaliatory tariffs nor general free trade offered any hope of permanent solution. Instead, the only road out of the impasse seemed to them to be by way of reciprocity treaties in which the United States might grant special tariff privileges to potential customers in order to open new markets for the American surplus. For this reason Frelinghuysen continually but tactfully urged Congress to take no drastic action in matters of foreign commerce which might commit the executive branch.[1]

From the beginning the use of the detour of reciprocity around the rocks of economic nationalism was complicated by a fundamental disagreement among those who traveled it. Some, like John A. Kasson, viewed reciprocity as merely a lesser evil, an exception to the general protectionist rule, to prevent "national selfishness" and forestall a general demand for lower tariffs. Others—both reformers such as Edwin L. Godkin and uncompromising protectionists like Senator Morrill—thought of reciprocity as an "insidious way of sapping the foundations of the protective system," the first step toward a general commercial union and free trade for all.[2] Still others were not sure where the detour would lead.

*　　　*　　　*

Praise and denunciation of reciprocity often began with an account of the Elgin-Marcy treaty of 1854, which had set up special

---

[1]See, for example, Frederick T. Frelinghuysen to John F. Miller, March 14, 1884 U.S., Senate Foreign Relations Committee Archives.
[2]Younger, *Kasson*, pp. 288-89. *Nation*, XXV (November 17, 1877), 297-98.

tariff concessions between the United States and Canada for a period of ten years. Some Americans had supported the treaty to encourage annexation, others to prevent it, but when Canadian producers seemed to be deriving more benefits than Americans, the United States let the treaty lapse. For many years thereafter annexationists, producers of various raw materials, and tariff reformers on both sides of the border agitated for a new reciprocity treaty. In 1869 and again in 1874 the Canadian government sent envoys to discuss the matter with the State Department. In 1876 and 1880 committees of the House of Representatives drew up reports favoring reciprocity with Canada, while rumors of annexation occasionally passed through the Grant and Hayes administrations.[3]

The principal American argument in favor of reciprocity predicted that it would provide Canadian business for American railroads and seaports, as well as an outlet for American manufactures. A few American protectionists, such as the industrialist, Wharton Barker, supported an outright commercial union with Canada.[4] On the Canadian side Goldwyn Smith led a tireless group of those who saw in reciprocity the first step toward political union, while others, more cautious, hoped only for a counterbalance to English influence in the dominion and a chance to share in what another Canadian called "the marvelous expansion of the industry, commerce, and population" of the Americans.[5]

Nationalists and orthodox protectionists in both countries, however, opposed the revival of reciprocity. In the United States Senator Morrill and his clique called the Canadians "inferior consumers," and Henry Carey and William D. Kelley saw behind Canadian reciprocity the specter of free trade with the entire

[3]C. C. Tansill, *The Canadian Reciprocity Treaty of 1854* (Baltimore, 1922), pp. 379-82 *et passim*. James Laurence Laughlin and H. Parker Willis, *Reciprocity* (New York [1903]), pp. 65-66, 109-10. C. C. Tansill, *Canadian-American Relations, 1875-1911* (New Haven, Connecticut, 1943), pp. 378-79. Nevins, *Fish*, pp. 150, 212-13, 217, 414-15, 479. Julius W. Pratt, *A History of United States Foreign Policy* (New York, 1955), p. 329.

[4]Wharton Barker to William D. Kelley, Philadelphia, December 16, 1879; Barker to James A. Garfield, December 29; Barker to Chester A. Arthur, February 20, 1882, typed copies in Barker Papers.

[5]Goldwyn Smith, "Canada and the United States," *North American Review*, CXXXII (July 1880), 14-25. P. Bender, "A Canadian View of Annexation," *ibid.*, CXXXVI (April 1883), 326-36.

British Empire. In 1874 James G. Blaine warned his neighbors in Maine that the proposal would be "blighting and disastrous to the last degree," giving Canadians control over some American markets on terms more favorable than those allowed to the Americans themselves.[6] At the same time Canadian nationalism was strengthened by the hostility of some American newspapers, the rise of Canadian manufacturing, and widespread resentment at American "dumping" during the hard times of the 1870's. Sir John Macdonald won the election of 1878, supporting a "judicious readjustment of the tariff" to show the Americans that they must make concessions in order to win the Canadian market.[7]

When Blaine became secretary of state, reciprocity with Canada did not appear on his agenda. Instead he proposed negotiations to settle the fisheries question and develop free navigation on border waters. He did not remain in office long enough to undertake either project, but in 1883, apparently without consulting the Arthur administration, Congress terminated the fisheries articles of the Treaty of Washington. The principal purpose of this sudden and ill-considered action seems to have been to "twist the British lion's tail." If any members of Congress hoped thereby to blackmail Canada into closer commercial relations with the United States, however, they were disappointed, for in 1884, when a member of the Canadian Parliament introduced a resolution urging the government to propose a commercial treaty, Macdonald replied that he had given up paying court to the United States. A subcommittee of the United States House of Representatives under the trade-minded Perry Belmont submitted a report favoring reciprocity with Canada. Congress took no further action, however, while Arthur was president, and Frelinghuysen made no effort to include Canada in his network of reciprocity treaties.[8]

[6] Justin Morrill to Barker, Washington, January 7, 1884, Barker Papers. Henry Charles Carey, *The British Treaties of 1871 and 1874. Letters to the President of the United States* (Philadelphia, 1874), *passim*. William D. Kelley, *The Proposed Reciprocity Treaty* [etc.] (Philadelphia, 1874), *passim*. Blaine, *Political Discussions*, pp. 121-24.

[7] Creighton, *Macdonald, the Old Chieftain*, pp. 119, 208-9, 302-3, 306-7, 420 *et passim*. Edward Porritt, *Sixty Years of Protection in Canada, 1846-1907* (London, 1908), pp. 303-5, 307. A good contemporary summary of the mixed Canadian views on reciprocity is contained in *Bradstreet's*, X (July 12, 1884), 21.

[8] [James G. Blaine] to [Garfield], Washington, December 13, 1880, in Hamilton, *Blaine*, p. 492. Burnette, "Senate Foreign Relations Committee," pp. 80-82, 197-99.

While tariff reformers in the United States and Canada tried in vain to resuscitate the Elgin-Marcy treaty, they had more success in promoting reciprocity with the Hawaiian Islands. On two previous occasions, in 1855 and 1867, Congress had rejected reciprocity treaties with Hawaii. In 1875 Hamilton Fish negotiated a third treaty, in which the United States agreed to abolish duties on a short list of Hawaiian products, including sugar, and Hawaii put a longer list of American products on the free list.

The Hawaiian legislature and the United States Senate approved this treaty at once. When the Grant administration introduced the necessary tariff revision into the House of Representatives, however, it encountered strong protectionist opposition which was dissipated only by blunt, unabashed emphasis on the strategic basis of the treaty. General J. M. Schofield "laid it on the line" in a letter to the chairman of the Ways and Means Committee:

> The Hawaiian Islands constitute the only outpost to the defenses of the Pacific Coast. In the possession of a foreign naval power in time of war, . . . they would afford the means of incalculable injury to the United States. If the absolute neutrality of the Islands could always be insured that would suffice.
>
> But they have not, and never can have the power to maintain their own neutrality; and now their necessities force them to seek alliance with some nation which can relieve their embarrassment.
>
> The British Empire . . . stands ready to enter into such an alliance, and thus to complete its chain of Naval Stations from Australia to British Columbia.
>
> We cannot refuse the Islands the little aid they so sorely need, and at the same time deny their right to seek it elsewhere. The time has come when we must secure forever the desired control over those Islands or let it pass into other hands.[9]

Grudgingly the House agreed, and the enforcement bill passed by a vote of 115-101.

Bradstreet's, IX (February 2, 1884), 66-67. *Washington Post*, April 4, p. 2; June 4, p. 2.

[9] J. M. Schofield to J. K. Luttrell, San Francisco, December 30, 1875, quoted in Elisha H. Allen to William M. Evarts, Bangor, Maine, October 22, 1879, U.S., Notes from Foreign Legations, Hawaii, II. Brookes, *International Rivalry in the Pacific*, p. 358. On the background of the 1875 treaty see Chalfont Robinson, *A History of Two Reciprocity Treaties: the Treaty with Canada in 1854, the Treaty with the Hawaiian Islands in 1876, with a Chapter on the Treaty-making Power of the House of Representatives* [New Haven, Connecticut, 1904], pp. 112-40.

The effects of the Hawaiian reciprocity treaty were more immediate and widespread than its supporters had expected. Between 1876 and 1880 Hawaiian sugar production expanded from 26,-072,429 pounds to 63,584,871 pounds. Hawaiian exports to the United States (over nine-tenths sugar and other articles affected by the treaty) rose from $1,227,191 to $4,606,444; although Hawaiian imports from the United States increased only three-fourths as fast, the American share of all Hawaiian imports rose from 56.3 per cent to 71.56 per cent. Perhaps even more important to the future of American-Hawaiian relations was the increase of American investment in the islands. Before 1876 little new American capital was going into Hawaiian lands because of chronic depression in the sugar industry, but in 1883 a thorough survey of Hawaiian plantations showed that two-thirds of them ($10,-235,464 out of $15,886,800 in value) had passed into American hands.[10] Hawaii had become an economic satellite of the United States.

The greatest beneficiary of the reciprocity treaty was Claus Spreckels, a German-born grocer who had come to California during the gold rush and made himself the largest sugar refiner on the Pacific Coast. Although Spreckels had originally opposed the Hawaiian reciprocity treaty, fearing the competition of Hawaiian sugar, he quickly accepted the inevitable, invested heavily in Hawaiian plantations, and persuaded the native government to grant him invaluable water rights. Independent sugar producers had little choice but to sell their sugar to Spreckels' California refineries, and in 1880 he bought virtually the entire Hawaiian crop.[11]

As the sugar and land booms stimulated other parts of the Hawaiian economy, Spreckels and other Americans expanded into importing, transportation, and politics. Annexationist opinion grew, although nationalists sometimes dominated the Hawaiian government. Britain and Germany, alarmed at the rise of American influ-

[10]Stevens, *American Expansion in Hawaii*, pp. 141-43. U.S., Tariff Commission, *Reciprocity and Commercial Treaties* (Washington, 1919), pp. 122, 131, 133. Laughlin and Willis, *Reciprocity*, pp. 74, 82-83. U.S., Congress, Senate, 48th Cong., 1st Sess., 1884, Senate Rept. 76, *passim*.

[11]Stevens, *American Expansion in Hawaii*, p. 143. Ethel M. Damon, *Sanford Ballard Dole and His Hawaii* (Palo Alto, California, 1957), p. 157. Alexander, *Later Years of the Hawaiian Monarchy*, pp. 3-8.

ence, tried to claim all the benefits of the reciprocity treaty under most-favored-nation clauses in their own earlier commercial treaties, but the American minister, General James M. Comly, kept the native government on his side. Eventually Hawaii formally recognized that the American privileges were exclusive.[12] It was at this time that the British effort to expand their influence in Hawaii through the immigration of East Indian coolies drew from James G. Blaine the vigorous assertion that the islands lay within the American sphere of influence. (See Chapter 6.)

American opposition to the Hawaiian reciprocity treaty hardly slackened after it went into effect. Probably acting as lobbyist for Theodore A. Havemeyer and other Eastern refiners, Henry A. Brown, a former Treasury agent, wrote pamphlet after pamphlet denouncing the treaty as a waste of revenue and an encouragement to fraud. In October, 1881, the *San Francisco Chronicle* began a series of articles, accusing Spreckels of bribing transcontinental railroads to shut out Eastern sugar, so that he could undersell it on the Pacific Coast and as far east as Missouri. A few other anti-Spreckels newspapers in California joined the *Chronicle*, along with practically the entire press of Louisiana and at least half a dozen influential newspapers in other parts of the country. As a result of these attacks Spreckels thought it best to lower the price of sugar on the Coast and end his agreement with the railroads.[13]

During the winter of 1881-1882 Representative Randall L. Gibson of Louisiana and several other congressmen, mostly Southerners, introduced resolutions against the treaty. Brown appeared to testify at committee hearings, and the refiners also organized a publicity campaign to influence the tariff commission during the following summer. Their principal tactics were to deny that the Hawaiian Islands were worth annexing or that the benefits of the treaty outweighed its disadvantages to American producers and the Treasury. Brown reported that Yankee operators on the islands were importing Chinese sugar and reshipping it to the United States

[12]James M. Comly to Blaine, Honolulu, June 6, 1881, Nos. 172, 173, U.S., Despatches, Hawaii, XX. Stevens, *American Expansion in Hawaii*, pp. 156-57. U. S., Tariff Commission, *Reciprocity*, pp. 110-12. Laughlin and Willis, *Reciprocity*, pp. 89-90.
[13]Donald M. Dozer, "The Opposition to Hawaiian Reciprocity, 1876-1888," *Pacific Historical Review*, XIV (1945), 158-67.

under the treaty, but after careful investigation Minister Comly exploded this rumor. Somewhat more accurately Gibson argued that the United States Treasury had given up duties amounting to more than the total increase in American-Hawaiian trade: "We are paying to the Hawaiians one dollar as a bonus on every dollar's worth of goods they buy from us."[14]

The American-born minister of Hawaii in Washington, Elisha H. Allen, operated an efficient lobby in support of the treaty with the experienced aid of George S. Boutwell, a former secretary of the Treasury. These two publicized among protectionist congressmen the exports of their districts to the islands. Boutwell declared that the treaty was worth $20,000,000 in security to the Pacific Coast and that if the United States abrogated it, Britain would immediately negotiate a similar treaty with ultimate annexation in view. As in 1875, this argument convinced many. "Were I an American I would move heaven and earth for having the treaty prolonged . . . ," wrote a friend to Carl Schurz. "Here is a little bit of practical Monroe doctrine, not blustering and crowing, simple and peaceful, but eminently efficient."[15]

When the Forty-seventh Congress convened in December, 1882, to take up the tariff question, Arthur briefly recommended renewal of the Hawaiian treaty in his annual message. Frelinghuysen and Secretary of the Treasury Charles J. Folger submitted cautious statements which admitted some of the weaknesses of the treaty. They advised amendment rather than outright abrogation because of its political benefits.[16] Once again the rival lobbies swung into action.

[14]U.S., *Congressional Record*, 47th Cong., 1st Sess., XIII, Appendix, 29-37. Dozer, "Opposition to Hawaiian Reciprocity," pp. 164-65, 168. Henry A. Brown, *Hawaiian Sugar Bounties and Treaty Abuses Which Defraud the U. S. Revenue* [etc.] (Washington, 1883), *passim*. John M. Kapena to Comly, Honolulu, May 21, 1879, U.S., Notes from Foreign Legations, Hawaii, II. Comly to Blaine, Honolulu, November 19, 1881, No. 202; Comly to William L. Green, December 17, No. 214, U.S., Despatches, Hawaii, XX.

[15]Brice [?] to Carl Schurz, Washington, April 15, 1882, in Schurz Papers, LXXV. *New York Tribune*, September 19, 1881, p. 4. Dozer, "Opposition to Hawaiian Reciprocity," p. 167. A good summary of the case for renewal is Rufus Paine Spalding, *A Birds-Eye View of the Hawaiian Islands, with Some Reflections upon the Reciprocity Treaty with the United States* (Cleveland, 1882).

[16]Letter of Charles J. Folger in New Orleans *Times-Democrat*, January 17, 1883, p. 2. Frelinghuysen to C. G. Williams, January 10, U.S., Report Book, XV, 49-56. Stevens, *American Expansion in Hawaii*, pp. 166-67.

Absorbed in its wrangling over the "mongrel tariff," however, Congress declined to settle the future of the Hawaiian treaty. When Senator Justin S. Morrill introduced a resolution for abrogation, John F. Miller and John T. Morgan of the Foreign Relations Committee opposed it vigorously. Morrill sought to have it referred to his own Finance Committee, which was composed of protectionists, and a heated debate over jurisdiction broke out between the two committees. During the debate Morrill thrust aside strategic considerations as immaterial: "We require no fortified Gibraltar, no halfway houses on any of the highways of the ocean leading to colonial dependencies." However, the Foreign Relations Committee became the official custodian of the resolution and buried it for the rest of the session. At the same time the House Foreign Affairs Committee, after hearing evidence on Hawaiian sugar frauds, recommended further investigation of the treaty and some careful thought about European influences in the islands.[17]

*   *   *

While the country argued over the extension of the Hawaiian treaty, tariff reformers and economic expansionists began to agitate for reciprocity agreements with Latin America. One enthusiast wrote of the area as "a new 'West & South'" and proposed to "Americanize those countries & eventually absorb them, either as integral parts of the Union, or as members of a Grand American Zollverein." While most expansionists would have thought this program a little extreme, they saw in Central and South America a limitless field for American trade and investment, and they wrote of Latin America with the promoter's flair for hyperbole. Thus, for example, the American minister to Colombia described his new home as "a country of singular beauty and inexhaustible natural resources," with fertile soil, producing a variety of temperate and subtropical products, and deposits of coal, iron ore, and petroleum.[18]

[17]Dozer, "Opposition to Hawaiian Reciprocity," pp. 169-71. Burnette, "Senate Foreign Relations Committee," pp. 93-95. U.S., Congress, Senate, 47th Cong., 2d Sess., 1883, Senate Rept. 1013, *passim. Ibid.,* H. Rept. 1860, *passim.*
[18]William L. Scruggs to Frelinghuysen, Bogotá, December 20, 1882, No. 54, U.S., *Foreign Relations, 1883,* pp. 227-30. See also Horace N. Fisher to W. S. Rosecrans, Boston, December 8, 1884, copy in Bayard Papers, LXVII (Library of Congress). *Boston Sunday Herald,* March 6, 1881.

Hitherto, these temptations had left American merchants and investors singularly unimpressed. Accurate statistics of American foreign investments in the 1880's are not available, but a careful survey of trade with Latin America in 1883 revealed that in only one country—Guatemala—did Americans control more than 50 per cent of exports and imports combined. In the case of the major Latin-American nations, the United States accounted for 39.4 per cent of Mexican foreign trade and 26.8 per cent of Brazilian foreign trade, but the figures fell to 6.7 per cent in Argentina and 1.7 per cent in Peru. Europeans did four times as much business as Americans in all Latin America.[19]

Wherein had Americans failed? Sometimes the discouraging statistics were not their fault, for, as a few diplomats correctly observed, the growth of trade and investments must often be painfully slow in an area peopled largely by backward Indians and mestizos, with few conscious wants and even less cash. The fickle, unstable Latin-American governments were another obstacle. In Guatemala, for example, Minister C. A. Logan, despite his friendship with the dictator Barrios (see Chapters 2 and 6), actually came to "regret the inflow of American capital to a country where it has no safeguards whatever."[20] Many other observers, however, blamed Americans themselves for letting Europe take over Latin-American markets. Dishonest measurements, inferior products, faulty labels, and slipshod packing received their share of criticism. The consuls urged their countrymen to learn Spanish and patience, grant longer credit terms, and adapt their styles and models to the taste of their intended customers.

Sooner or later, however, the labyrinth of excuses for commercial failure in Latin America led to the American protective tariff and to the collapse of American shipping, for which the protective policy was partly responsible. American consuls in Rio

[19]Other percentages were as follows: Guatemala, 64.5; Honduras, 21.5; El Salvador, 12.1; Nicaragua, 20.9; Costa Rica, 13.6; Colombia, 36.6; Venezuela, 41.6; Guianas, 17.3; Ecuador, 7.9; Bolivia, 6.9; Chile, 5.1; Uruguay, 13.7; Paraguay, 4.0. U.S., Congress, House, 48th Cong., 1st Sess., 1884, H. Rept. 1445, p. 3.

[20]For accounts of the difficulties of American capital in Guatemala see Cornelius A. Logan to Evarts, Guatemala City, February 1, 1881; Logan to Blaine, April 2, 18, August 2, and Logan to Frelinghuysen, February 4, 1882, Nos. 147, 167, 170, 219, 259, U.S., Despatches, Central America, XVII, XVIII.

de Janeiro and Buenos Aires reminded the State Department again and again that American merchants could not hope to outsell Europeans in those cities if they had to send out their goods by way of Liverpool, for lack of direct steamship lines. David A. Wells asked why Chile bought 55,000,000 yards of cotton cloth from Britain and less than 5,000,000 yards from the United States. Not because of higher British quality, he thought, since the Manchester bolts were often heavily sized with starch or clay. They bought from Britain because Britain would buy Chilean copper in return. A Chilean critic agreed wholeheartedly: "As products are exchanged for products, . . . if we are to purchase theirs, they [Americans] must open the doors of their markets to ours."[21]

From 1865 to 1881 no American secretary of state squarely confronted the problem of commercial reciprocity with Latin America. According to Blaine's statement in September, 1882, the Garfield administration had intended to cultivate hemispheric peace and "such friendly, commercial relations with all Latin American countries as would lead to a large increase in the export trade of the United States." Blaine, like his predecessors, urged his ministers and consuls to aid American trade, but, as has been seen, other evidence of a matured policy of expanding commerce while he was in office is meager.[22]

Thus the field of Latin-American reciprocity was left open to Frelinghuysen. Between 1882 and 1885 he negotiated or informally discussed at least six treaties providing for reciprocal tariff concessions with Caribbean nations or colonial areas (Mexico, Cuba and Puerto Rico, the British West Indies, the Dominican Republic, El Salvador, and Colombia). It has been suggested that Frelinghuysen concentrated on the tropical Caribbean rather than trying to appeal to Argentina, Brazil, and Chile because the latter policy would have required a lower tariff on imported wool, and he feared the Louisiana sugar lobby less than American wool-

[21]Ricardo Becerra, "Commercial Relations of Chili with the United States," translation in U.S., *Consular Reports*, No. 1 (October 1880), p. 54. See also *Nation*, XXV (September 6, 27, 1877), 153, 194-96.
[22]Barrows, *Evarts*, pp. 375-76. Blaine, *Political Discussions*, pp. 411 ff. Blaine to Thomas O. Osborn, October 5, 1881, No. 151, U.S., Instructions, Argentina, XVI, 224-25.

growers.[23] This consideration may have entered his thinking, but one might argue even more logically that he inaugurated his policy in the Caribbean because that area had become the focus of American concern for national influence. Frelinghuysen's reciprocity treaties were more than a solution to American commercial problems. They were an answer to De Lesseps and a reinforcement to the administration's views on the Clayton-Bulwer Treaty—an economic defense of the Monroe Doctrine.

*   *   *

The first Latin-American country with which Frelinghuysen opened negotiations was Mexico. If this was a reasoned judgment, it was well made, for no other Latin-American country held so much attraction for American trade and capital, whether because of Mexico's nearness, her vast resources, or the long era of stable government which she entered in the mid-seventies. During the decade after the Civil War, American railroads, miners, and cattlemen pushed rapidly into the Southwest, and when the panic of 1873 temporarily halted their advance, they were already beginning to cross the border into Sonora and Chihuahua.

Before this could happen, however, American-Mexican relations had to pass through a "time of troubles." After a Mexican general, Porfirio Díaz, seized the presidency in December, 1876, the Hayes administration decided to withhold recognition until he eliminated certain chronic border disturbances along the Rio Grande and clarified his attitude toward American investments. Hayes even ordered American troops to chase marauders onto Mexico territory. For a few weeks there was danger of war, but fortunately the storm blew itself out in a three-year diplomatic correspondence between the Mexican Foreign Office and Hayes's patient minister to Mexico, John W. Foster. To be sure, a number of hotheads along the border felt that the time had come to seize another slice of Mexican territory, but Northerners refused to become excited. The *Chicago Tribune* warned against annexing "a vast body of Mexican Greasers, speaking Spanish—treacherous, illiterate, super-

[23]Henry Parker Willis, "Reciprocity with Cuba," *American Academy of Political and Social Science, Annals*, XXII (1903), 133-34.

stitious, and largely lawless"; and this view (usually expressed more politely) determined Hayes's policy.[24]

In the meantime Mexican nationalists indulged in a riot of anti-Americanism, but Díaz was convinced of the value of American trade and investments. While continuing the diplomatic argument with Foster, he sent agents to the United States to publicize Mexican resources and stability with speeches and newspaper articles. When Minister Foster objected that these agents were misleading the American public by glossing over the existence of banditry and anti-Americanism in Mexico, Matías Romero, then minister of the treasury, replied with a massive tome of over 350 pages, refuting Foster's words and bidding openly for American capital and trade. Díaz and Romero soon received help from American promoters. "There are vast resources there [in Mexico] . . . actually lying dormant, waiting for capital to come and render them profitable business enterprises," declared one of them, and he found willing hearers in the United States as the financial depression loosened its grip.[25]

As a result of the border crisis and the increasing publicity, Mexican affairs were often on Congressional tongues during the Hayes administration. In 1878, for example, Senator Morgan proposed a treaty for the joint protection of railroad projects between the two countries, and during the following year several congressmen suggested reciprocity treaties of one type or another. Unfortunately Morgan's proposal aroused Mexican fears of American domination, and the Democratic majority in the House was too weak to sway the protectionist Republicans in the Senate, so that none of the measures passed.[26]

[24]*Chicago Tribune*, July 15, 1878, p. 4. That this sentiment was not limited to American Protestants is shown by a very similar article in *Catholic World*, XXXIV (March 1882), 721-31. On early American projects in Mexico see David M. Pletcher, *Rails, Mines, and Progress: Seven American Promoters in Mexico, 1867-1911* (Ithaca, New York, 1958), chaps. i-iii. On the border crisis see Cosío Villegas, *Estados Unidos contra Díaz*, (México, 1956), *passim*, especially chaps. vi-x, and James M. Callahan, *American Foreign Policy in Mexican Relations* (New York, 1932), chap. xi.

[25]*Chicago Tribune*, April 8, 1878, p. 3. On the Mexican campaign in the United States see Pletcher, "Mexico Opens the Door," pp. 1-14.

[26]Callahan, *American Foreign Policy*, pp. 484-85. John T. Morgan to John W. Foster, Washington, September 27, 1878, John W. Foster Papers (Library of Congress). Foster to Morgan, Mexico City, July 2, John T. Morgan Papers, X (Library of Congress).

At this point, even without the formal encouragement of the American government, American businessmen won a foothold in the Mexican economy. In September, 1880, Díaz confirmed the grant to American railroad companies of two long-desired concessions extending from the Rio Grande to Mexico City. During succeeding months Díaz and his successor, Manuel González, signed a variety of generous contracts for railroads, mines, and land projects, promising millions of pesos in subsidies. The figurehead of this new crusade of promoters came to be former President Ulysses S. Grant. When Grant failed to obtain the Republican nomination for the presidency in 1880, he went into a variety of business ventures, one of which was a partnership with Romero (an old acquaintance) to build a railroad south of Mexico City. In this project Grant and Romero had the financial backing of Jay Gould.[27]

As Garfield and Blaine took office, American newspapers called on the new secretary to help American capital to take advantage of this new outlet: "The luscious grapes bend low on the Mexican vines and cry, 'Come pluck us.' "[28] Trade with Mexico required prompt consideration indeed, for in November, 1880, the Mexican government had given the required year's notice for the termination of its fifty-year-old commercial treaty with the United States—probably hoping to prick the new administration to action. In June, 1881, Blaine urged Mexico to reconsider certain practices which discouraged American trade: her internal tariffs between states, her laws requiring American companies to become incorporated in Mexico, and the general insecurity. Blaine did not object to Mexican protective tariffs (how could he?), but he suggested that some sort of reciprocal concessions might not be impossible.[29]

Blaine sent no further instructions on American-Mexican trade,

[27]Fred W. Powell, *The Railroads of Mexico* (Boston, 1921), pp. 127-28, 133. Philip H. Morgan to Evarts, Mexico City, June 7, 1880, No. 26, U.S., Despatches, Mexico, LXX. Pletcher, *Rails, Mines, and Progress*, pp. 155-64.

[28]*New York Herald*, March 9, 1881, p. 6. *New York Tribune*, February 18, p. 4. *Chicago Tribune*, March 11, p. 4.

[29]Blaine to P. H. Morgan, June 1, 1881, No. 133, U.S., *Foreign Relations, 1881*, pp. 761-62. Blaine to Morgan, June 16, No. 137, U.S., Instructions, Mexico, XX, 283-96. Blaine suggested "trade regulations of a reciprocal character" affecting Mexican tropical products, such as coffee, sugar, and precious woods, and American manufactured goods, including textiles.

and in November the commercial treaty of 1831 expired. Garfield's sickness and death were partly responsible for the American inaction, but possibly even more important was the fact that Blaine's impulsive interference in the Mexico-Guatemalan boundary question alienated the González government and raised doubts of American good faith.[30] (See Chapter 2.) Although Blaine denied that his peace congress was designed for any existing problem or situation, he may well have expected that once the war clouds had rolled away from the Guatemalan border, sunshine would quicken American-Mexican trade again, and a satisfactory agreement would follow.

Soon after Frelinghuysen entered the State Department, he decided to negotiate a new commercial treaty, and in August he appointed as commissioners former President Grant and the "trouble-shooter" of the State Department, William Henry Trescot, who had just returned from his mission to Chile. (See Chapter 5.) For several months the González government in Mexico refused to take similar action, fearing that the expected American proposals for reciprocal tariff concessions would injure European merchants in Mexico and possibly lead to American demands for territory. As a result of strong pressure from Romero and other progressives in Mexico, González finally gave way in December and nominated him as the principal Mexican commissioner. Romero and Trescot were skilled diplomats with considerable knowledge of each other's countries, but Grant's chief recommendation was his magic name. The coincidence that partners in a railroad company were to negotiate a treaty which might favor that company awakened some adverse comment.[31]

When Romero returned to Washington for the negotiations, he brought with him a draft treaty approved by his government and announced that he was required to communicate any changes

[30]P. H. Morgan to Blaine, Mexico City, June 15, July 12, August 13, 1881, Nos. 208, 229, 254, U.S., Despatches, Mexico, LXXII, LXXIII. On Mexican suspicions of Blaine see, for example, F. Santacilia to Matías Romero, Mexico City, July 1, 26, 1882, Matías Romero Papers, items 30484, 30503, microfilm (Library of Congress).
[31]Badeau, *Grant in Peace*, pp. 351-52. *Nation*, XXXV (November 23, 1882), 431. On the Mexican hesitation see P. H. Morgan to Frelinghuysen, Mexico City, April 24, November 18, 1882, No. 532, U.S., Despatches, Mexico, LXXVI, LXXVII. Romero to Frelinghuysen, Mexico City, November 18, December 21, 1882; January 8, 1883, U.S., Notes from Foreign Legations, Mexico, XXIX.

by mail. Since the Arthur administration hoped at that time to submit the treaty to the "lame duck" Congress for action, Frelinghuysen and Grant set out to arrange conferences between Romero and the Senate Foreign Relations Committee before the negotiations had formally begun or, indeed, before the second Mexican plenipotentiary had even arrived in Washington. Scandalized by such unorthodox proceedings, Trescot refused to take part in any conference, and the plan of securing Congressional approval in advance fell through.[32]

Although Minister Morgan had earlier suggested a long list of American grievances which ought to be remedied in a treaty, Romero's rigid instructions prevented their consideration. Frelinghuysen directed Grant and Trescot to concentrate on the reduction of external tariffs, after calling the attention of the Mexicans to the other matters. In four meetings during January, 1883, the diplomats carried out their assignment, using the Mexican draft as the basis for discussion.

The core of the final treaty consisted of two lists of products to be placed on the free list. The United States agreed to admit twenty-eight categories of Mexican products without duty, including coffee, fresh tropical fruits, henequen and ixtle fibers, uncured hides, the lower grades of sugar, unmanufactured leaf tobacco, and other farm and forest products. In return, Mexico placed seventy-three categories of American goods on its free list. Most of these were manufactures, such as agricultural tools, rails, steam engines, and wire, but minerals such as coal and petroleum and a few agricultural products were also included.

In the midst of the negotiations Grant and Trescot made the embarrassing discovery that the Mexican draft left out the vital word *steel* from its description of American products. Inquiry showed that the omission was not intentional, and the word was later inserted. Another Mexican omission, however, was deliberate— that of textile products—for the González government had no mind to expose its cotton mills to American competition. Grant and Trescot wanted to bind Mexico not to make similar concessions to European countries, but they did not care to restrict the

[32]"The Mexican Treaty," William H. Trescot Papers (South Caroliniana Library, Columbia, South Carolina).

United States as well. After considerable discussion they omitted the qualification. They reported to Frelinghuysen that Mexico had sacrificed more revenue than the United States, and that by the time Mexican sugar and tobacco exports threatened American industries, the treaty would be due for revision anyway.[33]

*   *   *

The Mexican reciprocity treaty was signed too late for consideration by the Senate of the Forty-seventh Congress, then in the toils of tariff debate. When it was released to the newspapers on February 19, public opinion of it was much divided. Grant tried to educate the uninformed in long press interviews, drawing attention to the alarm which the treaty had caused among European merchants in Mexico, predicting a great commercial future for the two countries, but denying that Mexico could ship enough sugar to the United States to affect the price paid to American planters. "We are . . . beginning a new and greater career, hand in hand with Mexico," wrote Senator Morgan, who called the treaty a shining example of democratic cooperation. Matías Romero elaborated similar sentiments at a gala banquet given for him by the principal merchants of Philadelphia, and he did what he could to conciliate New Orleans interests by supporting the city's plan to hold a cotton exposition as a stimulus to trade.[34]

In March and April Porfirio Díaz, enjoying a brief vacation from the Mexican presidency, visited the East Coast for three weeks of banquets at the Union League Club and Delmonico's, complimentary speeches, toasts, and conversation with railroad and commercial magnates. The publicity given Díaz's junket was of doubtful value to the reciprocity treaty, for to some opponents

[33] A draft of Frelinghuysen's instructions to Grant and Trescot, dated January 13, 1883, is in the Frelinghuysen Papers, IV (Library of Congress). For the text of the treaty and the protocol of the four meetings of the commissioners see William M. Malloy (ed.), *Treaties, Conventions, International Acts, Protocols and Agreements between the United States of America and Other Powers, 1776-1909*, (Washington, 1910), U.S., Congress, Senate, 61st Cong., 2d Sess., 1910, Senate Doc. 357, I, 1146-57. See also Romero to Frelinghuysen, Washington, February 4, 1883, U.S., Notes from Foreign Legations, Mexico, XXIX, and Ulysses S. Grant and William H. Trescot to Frelinghuysen, Washington, January 20, U.S., Despatches, Mexico, LXXIX.

[34] New Orleans *Times-Democrat*, January 22, 1883, p. 1; February 21, p. 1; February 23, pp. 5-6. *New York Tribune*, February 12, p. 5. John T. Morgan, "Mexico," *North American Review*, CXXXVI (May 1883), 409-18.

it seemed to confirm the impression that the treaty was only a scheme to line the pockets of Grant and Jay Gould's railroad clique at the taxpayer's expense. The *New York Herald* described Díaz as "escorted by a body guard of notorious American railroad speculators and their attorneys and lobby agents." The New York *Sun* declared that the purpose of the treaty was to bankrupt the Mexican government by cutting off tariff revenue, prevent it from paying the promised subsidies for the new international railroad lines, and force these lines into the waiting arms of Gould and Collis P. Huntington. Others feared that nonpayment of subsidies would furnish an excuse for the American government to seize Mexican territory.[35]

These wild imaginings soon gave way to more rational arguments for or against the Mexican treaty. The *New York Tribune*, which usually favored high tariffs, called the treaty "the most important convention negotiated by the United States government in many years" and urged protectionists to examine it carefully before opposing it: "They must remember that the home industries, which have been built up by the high tariff, . . . will eventually outrun the domestic demand and require foreign markets. If free trade with Mexico implies the development and prosperity of American manufactures, protectionists need have no hesitation about accepting it with good grace." Others valued the treaty chiefly because it tied up loose strings which might otherwise encourage annexationist ambitions along the border and suggested other negotiations to smooth the way for peaceful trade, investment, and travel in Mexico.[36]

From the beginning, however, there was strong sentiment against the treaty. Wharton Barker opposed it because, like the Hawaiian treaty, it was designed to give special privileges to a few speculators and other insiders. What he wanted was a continental *Zollverein*, "absolute free trade in North America with common Commercial Law for all nations." Others objected that the treaty would enrich the southwestern railroads, St. Louis sugar refineries, and foreign

[35]*New York Herald*, April 12, 1883, p. 6. New York *Sun*, as reported in *Chicago Tribune*, February 6, p. 4.
[36]*New York Tribune*, February 21, 1883, p. 4; March 16, p. 4. *New York Herald*, February 27, p. 5.

planters at the expense of the Treasury.[37] The treaty impaled the business interests of Louisiana on a cruel dilemma, for they earnestly desired more trade with Mexico, if only they could protect the sugar planters at the same time. Thus the New Orleans *Times-Democrat* boasted that it printed more Mexican news than all other major American newspapers combined, repeatedly denounced annexationism, praised Mexican progress, and complimented the farsighted Americans who invested capital in Mexico. At the same time it ran "scare" editorials about the future growth of Mexican sugar plantations and demanded protection. As the Forty-seventh Congress adjourned for the last time, the *Times-Democrat* remarked wryly that in the matter of reciprocity treaties the score was about even. The planters would have to endure Hawaiian competition for another year or two, but at least they had kept out Mexican sugar so far.[38]

During the summer recess commercial interests flooded the country with predictions of the flourishing Latin-American trade which the treaty would inaugurate, but despite their efforts further arguments appeared against ratification. For one thing, it was clear that many Mexicans opposed closer relations with the United States. Shortly after the signature of the treaty a leading Mexican daily, *El siglo diez y nueve*, reprinted a prediction of the New Orleans *Picayune* to the effect that the treaty was an annexationist "stalking-horse," and for months Mexican journalists rang changes on this theme. Another newspaper called it a *coup de grâce* for Mexican industry, even if the nation remained nominally independent, and other newspapers combined anti-Americanism with attacks on the González government. The corruption and instability of this government furnished another argument to American opponents of the treaty, who refused to believe that the peaceful election of González in 1880 meant that Mexicans had permanently given up revolutions. A serious riot in Mexico City during December, 1883, which González put down with difficulty, and well substan-

---

[37]Barker to W. E. Chandler, Jenkintown, Pennsylvania, January 21, Chandler Papers (Library of Congress), LIX. *New York Tribune*, January 5, p. 8. *Harper's Weekly*, XXVII (March 3), 130.

[38]New Orleans *Times-Democrat*, January 17, 1883, p. 4; January 23, p. 4; February 2, p. 4; February 19, p. 4; February 27, p. 4; March 1, p. 4.

tiated rumors that his government was near bankruptcy gave body to their skepticism.[39]

Another argument against the treaty was the likelihood that Mexico would extend its benefits to those European nations with which she already had commercial treaties containing most-favored-nation clauses. Mexico had negotiated such a treaty with Germany only a month before the signature of the Grant-Romero treaty, and when American Minister Philip H. Morgan applied to the Mexican Foreign Office for a statement of policy, he received a cautious answer which increased his suspicions. The State Department did not object to most-favored-nation clauses (a common feature of American commercial treaties), but it usually argued that *conditional* benefits, such as reciprocal tariff concessions, should not be extended to other nations unless these nations granted similar concessions in return. Frelinghuysen told Morgan that the Mexican intention, if publicly announced, would probably defeat the treaty in the United States Senate. When Romero learned this, he tried to reassure Frelinghuysen that his government would accept the American interpretation, but a few weeks later he had to admit that his government had overruled him.[40]

The Democratic victories in 1882 and general dissatisfaction with the "mongrel tariff" made it practically certain that the new Forty-eighth Congress would take up the tariff question early in its first session. Before Congress had even convened in December, 1883, the two wings of the Democratic party fought a bitter battle over the speakership of the House, which finally went to the low-tariff leader, John G. Carlisle. Poor discipline and the pressure of other business postponed the tariff debate for two months, but in February William R. Morrison, the chairman of the Ways and

---

[39] *El siglo diez y nueve* (Mexico City), January 29, 1883, p. 1. *El monitor republicano* (Mexico City), February 10, p. 2. The official answers of the Mexican government to these objections appeared in *Diario oficial*, April 2, p. 2. See also Warner P. Sutton to William Hunter, Matamoros, August 7, No. 47, U.S., Consular Despatches, Matamoros, XVIII.

[40] P. H. Morgan to Frelinghuysen, Mexico City, August 27, October 4, 1883; May 7, 1884, Nos. 681, 701, 702, 807, U.S., Despatches, Mexico, LXXX, LXXXII. Romero to Frelinghuysen, Washington, January 2, March 3, 1884. U.S., Notes from Foreign Legations, Mexico, XXXI, XXXIII. Frelinghuysen to Romero, May 2, U.S., Notes to Foreign Legations, Mexico, IX, 1. For the text of the German-Mexican treaty see *Diario oficial*, August 13, 1883, pp. 2-4.

Means Committee, introduced a bill calling for a flat horizontal reduction of 20 per cent in duties on most manufactured goods and placing salt, coal, and lumber on the free list. Once again the lobbyists swung into action, their protests reinforced by the hard times, the approaching election campaign, and the split among the Democrats. Carlisle and Morrison played their cards as well as they could, but their colleagues' habitual longwindedness extended the debate through April. On May 6 a protectionist Democrat offered a resolution to strike out the enacting clause of Morrison's bill, and his clique and the Republicans carried the vote, 156-151. This practically ended tariff reform for 1884.[41]

Needless to say, the collapse of tariff reform complicated the consideration of reciprocity treaties. As in the preceding session of Congress, the Louisiana sugar lobby was much in evidence. Meeting in the largest convention that anyone could remember, the Louisiana Sugar Planters' Association sent a special delegation of twenty-five men to Washington. There they found protectionists from other parts of the country reluctant to support higher sugar duties in view of Louisiana's habitual low-tariff attitude toward other products, and even the Louisiana delegation in Congress refused to promise the lobbyists that they would oppose the Morrison bill. The lobby made no headway whatsoever against the Hawaiian reciprocity treaty, for a special commission of the Treasury reported that it could find no evidence of fraudulent sugar imports. Senator Morgan, speaking for a majority of the Senate Foreign Relations Committee, delivered a strong speech in favor of extending the treaty, taking the opportunity to advertise a policy of economic imperialism.[42] Once again the Senate's failure to act was really a victory for reciprocity.

At the beginning of the session the Senate referred the Mexican reciprocity treaty to the Foreign Relations Committee, which

[41]Stanwood, *American Tariff Controversies*, II, 220-21. James A. Barnes, *John G. Carlisle, Financial Statesman* (New York, 1931), pp. 67-82. Abram S. Hewitt introduced a new bill correcting some of the faults of the Morrison bill but was unable to obtain action before adjournment. Harrison C. Thomas, *The Return of the Democratic Party to Power* (New York, 1919), pp. 120-21.

[42]New Orleans *Times-Democrat*, January 11, 1884, p. 3; January 15, p. 4; January 16, p. 3; February 24, p. 3. *Convention of the Representatives of the Louisiana Protected Industries* (New Orleans, 1884), *passim. New York Tribune*, September 14, p. 2. U.S., Congress, Senate, 48th Cong., 1st Sess., 1884, Senate Rept. 76, *passim*.

reported the treaty unanimously and without amendments on January 10. Protectionists then outlined an orthodox case against it: that the free admission of sugar and tobacco would ruin deserving American industries, and that the Mexican tariff concessions were worth too little in return. Supporters of the treaty defeated all crippling protectionist amendments, but when ratification came up for approval, protectionists and sugar Democrats blocked a two-thirds majority by one vote. The State Department secured a six-month extension from Mexico, and the administration redoubled its efforts. At one point Frelinghuysen and Senator George F. Edmunds cabled to Minister Levi P. Morton in Paris, asking him to persuade Senator J. D. Cameron, then traveling in France, to pair his vote in favor of the treaty. After further heroic measures of this kind, administration senators and Morgan finally obtained approval of the Grant-Romero treaty on March 11, by the narrow, two-thirds vote of 41-20. Despite the outcries of Mexican nationalists, the government majority in the Mexican Congress quietly approved the treaty two months later.[43]

The ratification of the treaty, however, did not end the contest over Mexican reciprocity, for in order to secure votes, administration senators allowed the opposition to attach an amendment to it at the last minute, requiring the passage of implementing legislation before the treaty could take effect. Such legislation, of course, would have to originate in the House of Representatives. The failure of the Morrison tariff bill in May extinguished hope of any action on the implementing bill during that session, but on June 17 Abram S. Hewitt, a low-tariff Democrat from New York, reported favorably on the measure for the Ways and Means Committee, in order that there might be no delay after the Congressional recess. He denied that the treaty posed any serious threat to the sugar and tobacco industries—indeed, the treaty was so limited that he thought it hardly worth the trouble to ratify, except as a prelude to something better:

[43]Burnette, "Senate Foreign Relations Committee," pp. 187-93. *New York Tribune,* January 17, 1884, p. 2; January 19, pp. 1-2. *Chicago Tribune,* January 21, p. 1; March 12, p. 1. Enclosures with Levi P. Morton to Frelinghuysen, Paris, February 6, No. 497, U.S., Despatches, France, XCIII.

The time has already arrived when we must adopt a continental policy, laying its foundations broad and deep in the mutual interests of intimate commercial and political sympathies. The Monroe doctrine must be asserted and enforced. While we ought to welcome the investment of foreign capital on this continent and to make no objection to the construction of highways of commerce, nevertheless it is essential for our safety, as well as our growth, that we shall exercise a controlling influence in the affairs of the Western World. It may not be desirable that we should extend the limits of our sovereignty beyond our own borders, but every measure which tends to establish closer relations with our neighbors . . . should be encouraged.[44]

Thus Hewitt, like Frelinghuysen, linked commercial expansion with security and saw in reciprocity the first step toward the establishment of unchallenged American leadership in the Western Hemisphere.

[44]U.S., Congress, House, 48th Cong., 1st Sess., 1884, H. Rept. 1848, p. 4 *et passim*.

Peripheral Questions

CHAPTER 11

The Far East

WHILE the Garfield and Arthur administrations sought prestige and trade outlets in the Western Hemisphere, they also had to uphold American interests elsewhere. When individual citizens of the United States lost lives or property in the Old World, their sufferings affected national prestige and brought pressure from the American public at home for action by the government. As for trade outlets, Europe had long been the best customer of American exporters, and publicists were giving increased attention to markets in the "Golden East." Asia and Africa, however, were still so remote from the American press and public and from most American businessmen that national policies in these areas lacked solid commercial and strategic foundations. For this reason American expansion in the Far East, the Near East, and Africa was sporadic and less well coordinated than in Latin America.

* * *

During the 1870's and 1880's the Far East resembled a disorganized solar system in which several planets—China, Japan, Britain, France, and Russia—wandered to and fro, drawing satellites out of each other's control.[1] After more than two decades of disastrous wars and rebellions the ancient, hidebound Chinese government had grudgingly opened its domains to foreign merchants, diplomats, and missionaries. The expanding foreign influence naturally aroused much native resentment, encouraged by conservative elements in the Imperial government, but each atrocity against European residents only brought a new round of diplomatic pressure, apologies, indemnities, and trade concessions.

As sprawling China writhed in impotence under Western de-

[1] Tyler Dennett, *The Americans in Eastern Asia. A Critical Study of the Policy of the United States with Reference to China, Japan and Korea in the 19th Century* (New York, 1922), pp. 427-28. For a more detailed account of American policy before 1880 see chaps. iv-xxiii.

mands, the tighter-knit Japanese government was reacting some-what differently to the foreign challenge. During the 1860's the antiforeign feudal leaders tried to expel the Europeans by terrorism as in China, and foreign punitive expeditions resulted in an indemnity and limitations on Japanese tariffs for the benefit of Western traders. In 1868, however, the Emperor Meiji tore through the web of feudal control and, with a group of farsighted advisers, set out to imitate Western trade, industry, and administration. Japan's foreign policy became more ambitious, for in 1871 she negotiated her first treaty on equal terms with China and soon was claiming influence or sovereignty over Korea, the Liuchiu (Ryukyu) Islands, and Formosa.

While the European Powers were pushing their way into the Far East by force or persuasion, the United States usually followed the policy of securing maximum benefits from their actions with minimum obligations. In China the American government cooperated with the Europeans from the outset and secured almost the same trading privileges. In Japan Commodore Matthew C. Perry and Townsend Harris established American leadership for a time, but during the Civil War Secretary Seward also adopted a cooperative policy there. For example, the United States contributed a small rented merchant steamer to the Shimonoseki expedition in 1864 and enjoyed the benefits of the tariff treaty which followed. For some years thereafter Britain's minister to Japan, the clever, tireless, and sometimes domineering Sir Harry Parkes, improved his position at the expense of second-rate American diplomats.

After the Civil War the old American trading houses in the Far East had declined, and their successors were weaker and less well managed. In 1880 the United States took 42 per cent of Japanese exports but supplied only 7 per cent of her imports as against 53 per cent from Britain. It was said that the British sold seventy times as many cotton goods there as the Americans—partly because the Manchester manufacturers sized their shoddy bolts heavily, beat down prices, and capitalized the Oriental love of a bargain. During the late 1870's the Americans partly evened the score by opening a profitable new market for kerosene, so

that by 1881 it was estimated that one out of six homes in the
native quarter of Shanghai burned American oil.[2]

American merchants and promoters in the Far East faced many
obstacles in addition to European competition. In spite of specific
guarantees in commercial treaties, officials, especially in China,
were often uncooperative. As in the case of Latin America, American trade with the Far East suffered from the atrophy of the
merchant marine and the weakness of the Foreign Service and
the Navy. When William H. Trescot visited China on a mission
in 1880, he was shocked to learn that the efficiency of the legation
at Peking depended entirely on one interpreter, Chester Holcombe,
the only available American who spoke Chinese fluently. He
urged the State Department to send out consuls acquainted with
American law, since under the practice of extraterritoriality they
often had to conduct trials. As for the Navy, regular warships
occasionally visited Far Eastern ports, but much of the routine
business of the American government was carried on by two old
paddle-wheel river boats which Trescot declared to be deathtraps.[3]

Despite the haplessness of Foreign Service and Navy, the Americans' obvious lack of interest in colonies and spheres of influence
contrasted so becomingly with ill-concealed European ambitions
that Chinese and Japanese officials frequently confided in American
diplomats and tried to play them off against the British, the French,
or the Russians. The rapid Japanese development after the Meiji
Restoration of 1868 inspired much admiration in the United States,
where sentiment soon appeared in favor of handing back the
Shimonoseki indemnity and giving up the restrictions on the
Japanese tariff. On the other hand, the old American sympathy
toward the Chinese was often marred by impatience and contempt.
"The conception of freedom and of independent thought has

[2]*Ibid.*, pp. 579-81. U.S., *Commercial Relations, 1879*, I, 86, 89-90; *1880-1881*, p. 205.
O. N. Denny to J. C. Bancroft Davis, Shanghai, March 6, 1882, No. 279, U.S., Consular Despatches, Shanghai, XXXIII. *Iron Age*, XXVII (January 20, 1881), 7.

[3]Report of Consul General Bailey, Shanghai, U.S., *Commercial Relations, 1879*,
I, 85-86. Report of Consul General Denny, Shanghai, September 30, 1880. U.S.,
Consular Reports, No. 3 (January 1881), pp. 82-85. William L. Scruggs to Charles
Payson, Canton, April 2, 1881, No. 25, U.S., Consular Despatches, Canton, IX.
Dennett, *Americans in Eastern Asia*, pp. 583-86. W. H. T. [Trescot], Memorandum,
"American Interests in China, Japan & Siam," No. 61½, U.S., Reports of the
Diplomatic Bureau, V.

never reached them, . . ." wrote *Harper's Weekly* in 1884. "The China of to-day is far behind the China of Marco Polo."[4]

Although this duality of American public opinion continued through the early 1880's, an incident of 1879 seemed to foreshadow a new departure in official American policy toward the Far East. In that year former President Grant visited China and Japan at the end of his two-year tour around the world. The trip had gradually broadened his provincialism and impressed him with American potentialities in world affairs; his keen interest in Japanese material progress completed his conversion to a type of internationalism. Fearing that China and Japan would go to war over the Liuchiu Islands and thereby weaken their resistance to European penetration, he wrote to Prince Kung from Japan, urging that the two governments settle the question by private negotiation, since they represented the only hope of the Far East: "With a little more advancement in modern civilization . . . they could throw off the offensive treaties which now cripple and humiliate them, and could enter into competition for the world's commerce."[5]

Grant's magic wore off after his departure, and the two nations resumed their quarrel, but his friendship left pleasant memories among Oriental politicians, and the publicity given his tour awakened new American interest in the Far East. After Garfield's election Grant tried to persuade him to appoint a protégé, John Russell Young, as minister to Japan, but Garfield preferred to leave the experienced John A. Bingham at his post. In the following year, however, Arthur appointed Young minister to China, an even more important and delicate office. Although Half-Breed journals saw in Young only a sycophantic journalist who had talked his way into Grant's esteem, for once the casual American appointive system produced results. Young became one of the three or four most competent American ministers in the Far East during the

[4]*Harper's Weekly*, XXVIII (September 20, 1884), 624. *New York Tribune*, August 13, 1881, p. 4; January 29, 1882, p. 2; December 4, 1884, p. 3.

[5]Quoted in Dennett, *Americans in Eastern Asia*, pp. 444-45. See also John Russell Young to Frelinghuysen, Peking, October 9, 1882, No. 33, U.S., Despatches, China, LXI.

nineteenth century.[6] If the Arthur administration wished to expand American influence in China, it could not have chosen a better instrument.

*　　　*　　　*

At the time of Young's appointment the most serious problem troubling Chinese-American relations was one over which he had little direct influence, for its solution depended on the actions of President and Congress. This was the problem of limiting or shutting off Chinese immigration into the United States. Although Californians had welcomed Chinese labor during the gold rush, sentiment gradually changed during the 1860's. After 1870 a continuous series of inflammatory speeches and editorials recited the case against the immigrants: their strange customs, their filth, their vices, and, above all, the low wages for which they would work. Since treaty commitments and the Fourteenth Amendment to the Constitution seemed to limit local action, the California crusaders determined to seek relief through both state and national government. During the Hayes administration a number of measures were passed curtailing Chinese immigration in one way or another.[7]

Inasmuch as the Burlingame treaty of 1868 had guaranteed Chinese subjects free admission into the United States, Hayes soon realized the necessity of corrective diplomacy. In 1880 he sent a special commission to China, consisting of James B. Angell, president of the University of Michigan, William H. Trescot, and John F. Swift of California. To everyone's surprise, the commissioners concluded their business in less than two months. As it happened, the Chinese government had never paid much attention to the troubles of emigrants, and a diplomatic crisis with Russia made the Yamen (Foreign Office) value American friendship more highly than usual. The Chinese government would not agree to the outright prohibition of further immigration, but

[6]Tyler Dennett, "American Choices in the Far East in 1882," *American Historical Review*, XXX (October 1924), 84-85. *New York Tribune*, March 14, 1882, p. 4.
[7]Elmer Clarence Sandmeyer, *The Anti-Chinese Movement in California*, Illinois Studies in the Social Sciences, XXIV, No. 3 (Urbana, Illinois, 1939), chaps. i-v. Dennett, *Americans in Eastern Asia*, pp. 535-42. Oberholtzer, *History of the United States*, IV, chap. xxviii.

the new treaty recognized the American right to "regulate, limit, or suspend" the immigration of Chinese laborers (although not of other classes) if such immigration seemed to threaten public order.[8]

When the Forty-seventh Congress convened, Senator John F. Miller of California introduced a bill shutting out both skilled and unskilled Chinese laborers for twenty years, denying citizenship to Chinese residents, and setting up an elaborate system of registration with stiff penalties for fraud. He and other West Coast congressmen defended the bill with the traditional California arguments against the Chinese. Southern senators, touched by a familiar chord, sprang to his aid, one of them declaring that "the Constitution was ordained and established by white men" and that he would protect "the white people of the Pacific States . . . against a degrading and destructive association with the inferior race now threatening to overrun them."[9] Miller's exclusion bill aroused instant opposition from Northern senators, pricked by their memories of abolition, their tradition of free immigration, and their concern for Chinese trade. Respected leaders such as George F. Hoar of Massachusetts, George F. Edmunds, and John Sherman denounced the departure from American liberal tradition and the violation of the clear intent of the 1880 treaty before it was two years old. Nevertheless, Congress adopted the Miller bill.

Despite strong pressure from the West Coast, Arthur promptly vetoed the bill in a long, temperate message which argued that since nothing in the treaty suggested that its signers contemplated a suspension of immigration for as long as twenty years, adoption of the act would be "a breach of national faith." He concluded with a eulogy of Oriental trade and suggested that its value required cautious experimentation with measures which might injure it. Eastern journals praised his message as "moderate," "sound, pru-

---

[8]Dennett, *Americans in Eastern Asia*, pp. 542-43. J. B. Angell, *The Reminiscences of James Burrell Angell* (New York, 1912), *passim.* For the commissioners' official account see U.S., *Foreign Relations, 1881,* pp. 168-69, 171-78, 182-90, 195-204, 210. The treaty appears in Malloy, *Treaties,* I, 237-41. The United States guaranteed protection to resident Chinese. At the same time a commercial treaty forbade Americans to engage in the opium trade in China.

[9]*New York Tribune,* March 7, 1882, p. 1. A good summary account of the debates in Congress is M. R. Coolidge, *Chinese Immigration* (New York, 1909), pp. 168-73. For Miller's speech see U.S., *Congressional Record,* 47th Cong., 1st Sess., XIII, 1481-88.

dent and patriotic," and consistent with Republican Reconstruction policy, but labor organizations all over the country and Californians of practically all classes denounced him as "the slave . . . of the Eastern bigots and scared New York merchants." Eight thousand laborers paraded in Philadelphia, and in San Francisco flags hung at half-staff and merchants draped their stores in mourning.[10] After such melodramatics the final disposition of the immigration question was an anticlimax. Failing to pass the Miller bill over the presidential veto, Congress revised it by reducing the term of twenty years to ten and by providing a cumbersome system of registration for Chinese nonlaborers who might wish to enter the United States. These changes did not satisfy the New Englanders, but Arthur signed the new measure.

The Chinese immigration act sat uneasily on the American stomach for several years after 1882. Its vague terminology and awkward enforcement filled the American courts with contradictory cases, and for two decades Congress had to pass supplementary acts, plugging up gaps in the original law. The Chinese government protested against it in vain, and it did not even satisfy Westerners, for in 1885 a new wave of anti-Chinese sentiment broke out. Not until the end of the century did Americans fully realize that in "temporarily" shutting out the despised Chinese, they had passed a turning point in their whole immigration policy and could never return to the freedom of old.[11]

*   *   *

While American diplomats in China exerted almost no influence on the actions of Congress, there was much that they could do to explain American policies to the Chinese and persuade the Imperial government to accept American trade and advice. When John Russell Young arrived in Peking as minister in August, 1882, he was well received. Thereafter Prince Kung, the foreign minister,

[10]*New York Tribune*, April 5, 1882, pp. 1, 4; April 6, p. 4. Other contemporary comment is quoted in Oberholtzer, *History of the United States*, IV, 302-5. See also Sandmeyer, *Anti-Chinese Movement*, pp. 93-94, and Coolidge, *Chinese Immigration*, pp. 174-78. For Arthur's veto message see Richardson, *Messages and Papers*, VIII, 112-18.
[11]Sandmeyer, *Anti-Chinese Movement*, chap. vi. During the Arthur administration Congress also passed legislation to prevent the shipment of opium to China and to return to China the unused portions of the Indemnity Fund of 1858.

and Li Hung-chang, the viceroy of the coastal province adjacent to Shanghai, talked with him most frankly on all kinds of topics. Seizing the advantage offered by Li's interest in Western customs and methods, Young frequently urged on him a policy of peace and economic development. However, the American minister found that Li's natural caution was reinforced by the influence of his enemies in Peking, the "eunuchs in the palace," as Young called them, ". . . pink buttoned censors who read the stars . . . and all that mass of thieving treacherous, cowardly cunning adventurers which surround the throne and live an insectiverous, parasitic existence on this venerable and august monarchy."[12]

Young quickly realized that the United States faced a basic decision in its Far Eastern policy: whether to maintain a solid front with the European nations, expanding influence by rigid insistence on the letter of the old treaties, or to bid for Oriental friendship through a more pliable attitude on American privileges. In some cases he did not hesitate to cooperate with the Europeans. For example, when a series of antiforeign riots broke out in Canton during August and September, 1883, causing much damage to American property, he joined the European diplomats in long negotiations with the Foreign Office and eventually secured indemnities from the Imperial government. On some other occasions Young acted alone, as, for example, when officials at Shanghai tried to forbid the use of kerosene as a safety measure, and officials at Canton restricted its sale by creating a local retail monopoly and imposing a special tax in violation of a commercial treaty. The American minister's protests to Prince Kung brought assurance that the central government had no intention of shutting out American petroleum products, and Young pointed out to the State Department that he could hardly object to reasonable Chinese measures for sanitation or fire-prevention.[13]

Perhaps the most serious test of Young's determination to balance

[12]Young to Davis, Peking, January 31, 1883, Davis Papers, XXXIII. Young to Frelinghuysen, August 8, No. 230, U.S., Despatches, China, LXV.

[13]Young to Frelinghuysen, Peking, August 30, November 8, 1883; January 6, 21, March 21, August 12, 1884, Nos. 244, 277, 319, 326, 387, 495, U.S., *Foreign Relations, 1883*, pp. 209-10; *1884*, pp. 46-47, 52-64, 79-83, 103. Young to Frelinghuysen, October 23, 1882; October 8, November 30, 1883; March 15, 28, 1884, Nos. 46, 267, 284, 297, 398, U.S., Despatches, China, LXII, LXVI, LXIX.

American privileges and Chinese rights arose in connection with Chinese efforts to shut down foreign factories in the port cities. In 1882 officials at Shanghai refused to allow two American firms which were already operating in the vicinity to establish a new yarn factory and a new silk-reeling plant. At the same time officials at Swatow and Amoy threatened several German enterprises in a similar manner.

Acting together, as in the case of the Canton riots, Young and the German minister, Von Brandt, managed to obtain corrective orders from Peking. When the official at Swatow defied the orders and tortured a Chinese foreman at a German foundry, Von Brandt sent warships to both ports, and marines landed to take possession of the disputed property and run up the German flag. Young then asked the admiral commanding the Far Eastern squadron to send American warships to Amoy and Shanghai, but when the Chinese government held firm in the case of the yarn factory, he confined himself to a long correspondence setting forth American treaty rights. In the end the Chinese government refused to allow the factory to be opened.

Throughout the correspondence Young maintained that long-range Chinese interests were parallel to American interests in this matter, and that "a generous commercial and fiscal policy will not only benefit the laboring classes, but add to the wealth of the nation." He confessed to Frelinghuysen that the precedent interested him more than the immediate prospects for American manufactures in China. "The danger," he explained, "is that if we concede [the right to suppress foreign factories], other concessions will be asked and won in the same way, and China will once more become a hidden nation, her ports closed to our ships and her markets sealed to our capital and enterprise."[14] Frelinghuysen approved of Young's stand but cautioned him to act in cooperation with European legations if he had to use the United

[14]Young to Frelinghuysen, Peking, February 4, 1883, No. 120, U.S., Despatches, China, LXIV. A portion of the correspondence on the question of American and German factories is published in U.S., *Foreign Relations, 1882*, pp. 117-20, 134-37; *1883*, pp. 129-41, 180, 187-97, 206-8, 215-17. These dispatches should be supplemented by unpublished communications as follows: Young to Frelinghuysen, December 6, 19, 1882; January 3, 6, February 4, April 2, August 25, 1883, Nos. 69, 79, 93, 97, 120, 189, 242, U.S., Despatches, China, LXIII-LXVI.

States Navy further. Thereby he showed himself less venturesome than Blaine, who believed in a policy of separate action in the Far East but had no opportunity to carry it out.[15]

In Japan John A. Bingham, like Young, had to reconcile Japanese and foreign interests independently or in cooperation with European representatives. In general, however, he faced easier problems than those in China, for at bottom the Japanese government recognized the value of foreign factories and techniques, and Americans, too, respected the Japanese government more highly than the Chinese. A symbol of this respect was the decision of Congress in 1883 to pay over to the Japanese government the sum of $785,000.87, the American share of the Shimonoseki indemnity of 1864. (However, the interest on the indemnity, amounting to about $1,200,000, remained in the American Treasury.)[16]

Far more complex and serious than the return of the indemnity was the question whether the United States should release Japan from the treaty-imposed burdens of extraterritoriality and low tariffs without the concurrence of the European Powers. After revising its penal code and police system, the Japanese government submitted the draft of a new treaty for consideration at a conference during 1882 and presented its case for higher tariffs and legal reforms. The Japanese representatives proposed a transition period of six to ten years during which mixed courts would apply Japanese law, and offered in return to open the whole domain to foreign trade and travel. The European diplomats, led by Sir Harry Parkes, tried to retain the Japanese offer of free travel while yielding as little as possible of the *quid pro quo*, and the conference came to no agreement. In general, Bingham supported the Japanese argument. Frelinghuysen approved his position but added that in his opinion the time was not yet ripe for independent American action. Not until 1888, at the end of the first Cleveland

[15]Frelinghuysen to Young, February 26, 1883, No. 86, U.S., Instructions, China, III, 396-401. Blaine expressed this opinion in a dispatch to John A. Halderman, the American minister to Siam, June 24, 1881, No. 4, cited in Plesur, "Looking Outward," p. 102.

[16]*New York Tribune*, June 13, 1882, p. 1; March 21, 1883, p. 2. U.S., Congress, Senate, 47th Cong., 1st Sess., 1882, Senate Rept. 120, *passim. Ibid.*, H. Rept. 138, *passim*. Frelinghuysen to Bingham, March 21, 1883, No. 724; Bingham to Frelinghuysen, Tokyo, April 30, May 9, Nos. 1671, 1677, U.S., *Foreign Relations, 1883*, pp. 603-7.

administration, did the United States and some European Powers negotiate new treaties with Japan.[17]

While it would be inaccurate to say that the Garfield and Arthur administrations made any new departures in their relations with China, Japan, and the European Powers active in the Far East, the dispatches of Bingham and especially of John Russell Young clarified the issues involved. Under the influence of these two ministers American policy took several steps closer to that independence of action which would identify the United States unmistakably as a Great Power in the Far East.

*   *   *

American expansionism during the 1880's was more obvious in its relation to the Korean question than in the Far Eastern problems discussed so far. Until 1866 the world had generally assumed that the Kingdom of Korea was a dependency of the Chinese Empire, one of several tribute-bearing satellites which revolved lazily in the fluctuating gravitational pull of Peking. In that year, however, Prince Kung denied Chinese responsibility for the murder of French missionaries in Korea, whereupon the French sent an expedition against the kingdom as an independent nation, and Japan, seeing her opportunity, tried to establish formal diplomatic relations. Both efforts failed, and for a few years longer Korea retained her isolation. In 1876, however, Japan negotiated a commercial treaty which gave her a first foothold on the continent of Asia and also recognized Korean independence of China. From that time a cardinal policy of the Japanese government was to uphold Korean independence loudly while expanding Japanese influence in the peninsula.[18]

American concern over Korea began in 1867 with the murder

[17]Dennett, *Americans in Eastern Asia*, pp. 515-20, 522-31. Payson J. Treat, *Diplomatic Relations between the United States and Japan, 1853-1895* (2 vols.; Stanford, California, 1932), II, 145-50 *et passim*, and F. C. Jones, *Extraterritoriality in Japan, and the Diplomatic Relations Resulting in its Abolition, 1853-1899* (New Haven, Connecticut, 1931), pp. 90-106. Frelinghuysen to Bingham, January 16, April 11, 1882, Nos. 707, 730, U.S., Instructions, Japan, III, 153-54, 181-82.

[18]Treat, *United States and Japan*, II, 75-76. Dennett, *Americans in Eastern Asia*, pp. 433-37, 446-47. An excellent discussion of the "elder brother-younger brother" relationship between China and Korea, which Westerners misunderstood, appears in M. Frederick Nelson, *Korea and the Old Orders in Eastern Asia* (Baton Rouge, Louisiana, 1945), pp. 112-19.

of several American sailors from the merchant ship "General Sherman," which had been reconnoitering along the coast. As in the case of France, China denied responsibility, and American Minister Anson Burlingame concluded wrongly that the Chinese-Korean connection was only "one of ceremonial." Acting on instructions from Washington, his successor, Frederick P. Low, led an unsuccessful expedition to Korea in May, 1871, to negotiate a treaty.

Seven years later the Hayes administration instructed Commodore Robert W. Shufeldt to visit Korea for that purpose in the course of his world cruise in the "Ticonderoga." In 1880, when the "Ticonderoga" finally arrived in the Far East, Shufeldt received a cool welcome from the Japanese government, which wished to maintain its monopoly over Korean relations with the outside world. He visited the Korean port of Fusan, but when the Japanese consul put obstacles in his way, Shufeldt returned to Japan and sent a letter to the King of Korea by way of the Japanese Foreign Office, thereby strengthening the impression that the peninsula was independent of China and drifting into the Japanese orbit.

Alarmed at Shufeldt's actions, Viceroy Li Hung-chang invited him to his provincial capital, Tientsin, where he plied him with promises of aid in negotiating a commercial treaty with Korea and hints of an appointment in the Chinese navy. Shufeldt, who had developed an interest in China not unlike that of John Russell Young, and who was irritated by Japanese evasions, received these overtures with pleasure. As 1881 began, he returned to the United States, confident of becoming a force in Far Eastern affairs.[19]

Blaine, now Secretary of State, was so much encouraged by Shufeldt's report that he determined to send him back to Korea at once to press negotiations with the aid of Li Hung-chang. At first he merely told Shufeldt to prepare a report on opportunities for American trade in China, but in November, just before leaving the State Department, he instructed him to seek a treaty with Korea for the relief of shipwrecked sailors. If the government proved cooperative, he might also negotiate a commercial treaty, securing for American goods most-favored-nation treatment as to

[19]Dennett, *Americans in Eastern Asia*, pp. 450-58. Nelson, *Korea and the Old Orders*, pp. 119-26, 135-40. Paullin, *Diplomatic Negotiations*, pp. 282-302.

tariffs, freeing them from all internal taxes, and giving American consuls the same extraterritorial privileges as in Japan and China. Blaine added that if Shufeldt wished to serve in the Chinese navy, he must make his arrangements privately, unless China requested his services officially through her minister at Washington.[20]

After brief visits in Tokyo and Peking Shufeldt arrived in Tientsin late in June, 1881, to begin preliminary talks with Li Hung-chang. He soon realized that Li's interest in the American-Korean treaty had cooled, and that his only purpose now was to make up for past blunders and recreate the old bond between China and Korea. Li pressed him to stay in Tientsin until he could make the proper arrangements with the King of Korea, but to Shufeldt's exasperation he refused to invoke the supposed authority of the Emperor to secure action. Finally at the end of the year, Li declared that the King was ready to negotiate, but the Commodore suspected that he had withheld the news for two months. Shufeldt had received no new instructions from the State Department, and his patience was at an end.[21]

He celebrated New Year's Day, 1882, by "blowing off steam" in a letter to his personal friend, Senator A. A. Sargent of California, who was being talked of for a Cabinet position under Arthur and would surely have much influence in the new administration. In his letter Shufeldt declared that he had always sympathized with the downtrodden Chinese, but that "six months residence in this city . . . has convinced me that deceit and untruthfulness pervade all intercourse with foreigners; that an ineradicable hatred exists, and that any appeal across this barrier, either of sympathy or gratitude is utterly idle." China, he added, "would to-day, if she could, exclude every article of foreign manufacture from her shores." He called Li Hung-chang "the Bismarck of the East" and a despot living at the mere whim of the Empress, "an ignorant, capricious and immoral woman." He concluded that American policy toward the Chinese, whether as immigrants or

[20]*Ibid.*, pp. 303-4, 308-9. Blaine to Robert W. Shufeldt, May 9, 1881, U.S., Senate Foreign Relations Committee Archives. Blaine to Shufeldt, November 14, U.S., Instructions, China, III, 271-77.

[21]Paullin, *Diplomatic Negotiations*, pp. 304-9. James B. Angell to Blaine, Peking, July 16, 1881, No. 187; Chester Holcombe to Blaine, Peking, December 19, 29, Nos. 30, 37, U.S., Despatches, China, LVII, LVIII.

in their homeland ought to be *"purely selfish . . .* by no means governed by the fallacious idea of international friendship, or even the broader ground of a common brotherhood."[22]

Shufeldt's letter to Sargent was perhaps the most serious blunder in his distinguished career of naval leadership and diplomacy. The experienced legation interpreter in Peking, Chester Holcombe, later admitted that he agreed with many of Shufeldt's frank statements about the Chinese character and government. But whether true or false, to send such a letter in the midst of a delicate diplomatic mission was an irresponsible action, and to send it to the leader of the anti-Chinese clique in the Senate seemed spiteful as well. Through a misunderstanding for which Shufeldt was partly to blame, Sargent released the letter to the newspapers, where it created a sensation, especially in California. Grant and Young were appalled, and Li Hung-chang was angry. Frelinghuysen, highly displeased, recalled the unfortunate Commodore, and the Navy denied him the desired post of commander of the Far Eastern squadron, assigning him to a desk job in Washington.[23]

Fortunately, long before this happened, Shufeldt had completed his mission. After receiving further instructions from Washington, he still had to wait two months longer before Li and the Yamen decided to support an American-Korean treaty as a counter to Japanese influence. Between March 25 and April 19, 1882, Li and Shufeldt drew up a full-fledged commercial treaty draft, permitting Americans to trade and live in Korean ports, fixing tariff rates, granting extraterritoriality, and prohibiting the opium trade. Although the treaty did not give American missionaries access to the Korean interior, in many other respects it placed American relations with Korea on the same footing as American relations with China. At one point, however, the negotiations nearly collapsed, when Li insisted on putting into the treaty the phrase

[22]Shufeldt to A. A. Sargent, Tientsin, January 1, 1882, newspaper clipping enclosed with Holcombe to Frelinghuysen, Peking, May 22, No. 108, *ibid.,* LX.
[23]Young to Frelinghuysen, Peking, September 20, 1882, No. 18, *ibid.,* LXI. Young to J. C. B. Davis, New York, April 20, May 1, Davis Papers, XXXII. Frelinghuysen to Young, June 28, No. 11, U.S., Instructions, China, III, 319-20. F. M. Grinnell to Shufeldt, Washington, July 25; Sargent to Shufeldt, Berlin, August 17; Shufeldt to Sargent, San Francisco, October 15; Shufeldt to William E. Chandler, no date (copy), Shufeldt Papers, Boxes 173, 180, miscellaneous.

"Chosen [Korea], being a dependent state of the Chinese Empire. . . ." After much argument Shufeldt threatened to go to Korea alone, whereupon Li deleted the phrase, on condition that Shufeldt recognize the dependent position of Korea in a separate letter.

Except in a ceremonial sense, the actual signature of the treaty in Korea was something of an anticlimax. Arriving in Seoul with Holcombe and a Chinese official, Shufeldt was cordially received by the Korean dignitaries, to whom Li had already sent a copy of the treaty with appropriate instructions. On May 22, after several days of feasts and ceremonies, Shufeldt and the Koreans signed the treaty, only slightly modified from Li's draft. The Koreans then presented the Commodore with a formal letter to President Arthur from the King which proclaimed Korea's dependent status in language strongly suggesting Chinese authorship.[24]

American reactions to the commercial treaty with Korea were very mixed. One of Shufeldt's fellow naval officers called him a second Perry in "opening" Korea to the West, but the publication of his indiscreet letter to Sargent robbed him of much of his deserved credit in the public eye. The *New York Tribune* called the treaty "really of very slight importance to anybody but the Corean King, who has taken this step . . . to defend himself against Russia"; and the *New York Herald* compared it unfavorably to the Mexican reciprocity treaty. After considerable grumbling over Korea's dependent status, the Senate approved the treaty but added an ill-humored resolution opposing the use of executive agents such as Shufeldt who had not received senatorial confirmation. Meanwhile Britain and several European nations negotiated commercial treaties with Korea on the model of the American document.[25]

[24]Paullin, *Diplomatic Negotiations*, pp. 310-24. Shufeldt to Frelinghuysen, Tientsin, March 11, 31, April 12, 28, 1882; Shanghai, May 29; Nagasaki, June 8, Nos. 2, 4, 7, 8, telegram, U.S., Despatches, China, LIX, LX. For the text of the treaty see Malloy, *Treaties*, I, 334-40. Charles O. Paullin, "The Opening of Korea by Commodore Shufeldt," *Political Science Quarterly*, XXV (September 1910), 497.

[25]Paullin, *Diplomatic Negotiations*, pp. 327-28. *New York Tribune*, July 14, 1882, p. 4. *New York Herald*, August 20, 1883, p. 4. Young to Frelinghuysen, Peking, December 26, 1882, No. 85, U.S., *Foreign Relations, 1883*, pp. 172-73. Burnette, "Senate Foreign Relations Committee," pp. 115-21. Wriston, *Executive Agents in Foreign Relations*, pp. 275-78. Dennett, *Americans in Eastern Asia*, pp. 474-75.

The Shufeldt treaty created some sort of legal basis for American trade with Korea, but it certainly did nothing to clarify the indeterminate political status of the kingdom. Frelinghuysen, Shufeldt, and Young disapproved of the Chinese claim to sovereignty over the peninsula, but the mere fact that Shufeldt negotiated the treaty in Tientsin rather than in Seoul effectively recognized a measure of Chinese control. On the other hand, Li Hung-chang, who had hoped to use Shufeldt to re-establish Chinese sovereignty, suffered a major defeat through the exclusion of the phrase "dependent state" from the draft, despite the Korean letter to Arthur. For a time, also, the treaty raised Japanese fears of an informal alliance between China and the United States to shut her out of the continent. Soon after the treaty was signed, the Japanese Foreign Office suggested to Bingham that Japan and the United States come to some understanding as to Korea's legal position, but Bingham professed not to see any need.[26] No one could expect the ambitious Japanese to accept this answer as the last word on the question.

*   *   *

Events soon demonstrated the artificiality of Korean independence. On July 23, 1882, antiforeign mobs attacked and burned the Japanese legation in Seoul, while the reactionary leaders murdered several members of the Queen's pro-Chinese family and launched a *coup d'état*. This violence gave both Japan and China an opportunity to expand their influence on the peninsula. Japan demanded and eventually obtained an indemnity and additional commercial privileges. Li sent troops to Seoul which restored to power the King, who then signed a commercial treaty which declared Korea to be "a boundary state of China" and received P. G. von Möllendorf (formerly an official of the Chinese customs) and other emissaries of Li as inspectors and administrators.[27]

These events did not materially change American views on Korea. John Russell Young, who had just arrived in China at

---

[26]Bingham to Frelinghuysen, August 19, 1882, No. 1547, U.S., Despatches, Japan, XLVII. For unfavorable appraisals of the treaty see Dennett, *Americans in Eastern Asia*, pp. 460-62, and Nelson, *Korea and the Old Orders*, pp. 142-51.

[27]Dennett, *Americans in Eastern Asia*, pp. 466-71. Nelson, *Korea and the Old Orders*, pp. 152-58.

the time of the uprising, sent the decrepit old warship "Monocacy" to Korea as a gesture of defense for foreign interests and wrote to Frelinghuysen that the United States could not preserve peace in the Far East "without taking an active, what might better be called an 'officious' interest in the Corean question and in all questions between China and Japan." During the summer of 1883 Young tried to convince Li that if China disclaimed responsibility for Korean actions, as she had often done in the past, she ought to recognize Korean independence. Li reduced his argument to powder with one question: Why should Westerners assume that their law was the only law? "I am King of Korea," he added, "whenever I think the interests of China require me to assert that prerogative."[28]

Since the State Department chose to regard Korea as independent, its next logical step was to open formal diplomatic relations. As if to emphasize the significance of the action, Congress appropriated funds for a minister plenipotentiary, the highest rank existing in the Foreign Service. In February, 1883, Frelinghuysen appointed to the post Lucius H. Foote, who had served capably as consul at Valparaiso during most of the War of the Pacific, but who, being a Californian, was prejudiced against the Chinese. The Secretary informed Foote that the United States would eventually have to protest against the special commercial privileges which Korea had granted China. He instructed Foote for the time being to do nothing but exchange ratifications of the treaty, inaugurate friendly relations, and send back information on political and commercial matters. Foote went to his post by way of Japan, where he collected information from Bingham, Parkes, and the Japanese Foreign Office and hired Japanese-trained interpreters. The King of Korea welcomed him to Seoul with touching eagerness and was soon consulting him on all kinds of Western innovations, to the obvious jealousy of the Chinese-appointed adviser, von Möllendorf.[29]

[28]Young to Frelinghuysen, Peking, August 19, October 2, December 28, 1882; March 21, 24, August 6, 8, 1883, Nos. 5, 27, 87, 166, 170, 230, U.S., Despatches, China, LXI, LXIII-LXV. See also Nelson, *Korea and the Old Orders*, pp. 159-70.
[29]Frelinghuysen to Lucius H. Foote, March 17, 1883, No. 3, U.S., Instructions, Korea, I, 5-17. Foote to Frelinghuysen, Seoul, May 24, 25, June 29, August 21, 1883, Nos. 6, 7, 10, 24, U.S., *Foreign Relations, 1883*, pp. 241-48. Foote to Freling-

Soon after Foote's arrival the King decided to send a special mission to the United States to confer with the President on Far Eastern relations, observe American institutions, and possibly arrange for a loan and the appointment of American advisers. At its head he placed Min Yong Ik, a member of the Queen's family. At the beginning of September Min and his colleagues were received with much ceremony at San Francisco and taken to Washington and New York, where they visited President Arthur, factories, stores, a hospital, newspaper plants, the Brooklyn Navy Yard, and West Point. Their outlandish costumes attracted much attention, and American merchants flocked around them to inquire about Korean timber, furs, and minerals and to propose sending out exhibits of American merchandise.[30]

When Min asked Frelinghuysen for American military and civil advisers, the Secretary seems to have given an oral assent. Shufeldt agreed to occupy the principal post, but he was not prepared to accompany the Koreans. In his place the American government sent Ensign George Clayton Foulk, U.S.N., a young naval officer already familiar with the Orient, who was to become for several years the main bulwark of American influence in Korea. On December 1, Foulk and the Koreans sailed from New York on the warship "Trenton" bound for Korea via the Suez Canal. While the Koreans made side trips to England and France, Foulk worked diligently to learn their language, and in conversations with them he took every opportunity to contrast European imperialism with American friendship.[31]

In Min's absence the faction of young progressives, led by Kim Ok Kiun, worked to modernize the country's institutions with the aid of Japanese money and guidance. Although Foote complained of the sluggishness of foreign trade, American steamers,

huysen, May 1, July 19, October 19, 23, Nos. 4, 17, 18, 32, 34, U.S., Despatches, Korea, I. Foote to Young, Seoul, September 10, John Russell Young Papers, XVI (Library of Congress).

[30]Foote to Frelinghuysen, Seoul, July 13, August 13, 1883, Nos. 14, 19, U.S., *Foreign Relations, 1883*, pp. 244-45, 248-49. Frelinghuysen to Foote, October 16, No. 27, U.S., Instructions, Korea, I, 33-38. George C. Foulk to Frelinghuysen, New York, November 19, George C. Foulk Papers (New York Public Library). Bingham to Frelinghuysen, September 20, No. 1744, U.S., Despatches, Japan, XLIX. Tyler Dennett, "Early American Policy in Korea, 1883-1887," *Political Science Quarterly*, XXXVIII (March 1923), 86-87.

[31]*Ibid.*, pp. 87-89.

petroleum, flour, machinery, rifles, and notions became common sights, while Dr. Horace N. Allen and other American missionaries contributed an element of humanitarianism. Most Americans leaned toward the Japanese progressive faction in Korea, preferring Japanese diplomats, servants, and even (to Dr. Allen's dismay) Japanese mistresses. The return of the mission did not change this situation, for Foulk, who became naval attaché at the legation, supported the progressives.[32]

During the autumn of 1884 Chinese influence in Seoul continued to decline, and Kim Ok Kiun's party, probably encouraged by the Japanese legation, determined to crush the Mins once for all. On the evening of December 4, during a great banquet to celebrate the opening of a post office at Seoul, Kim and his pro-Japanese cohorts attempted a coup, seriously wounded Min Yong Ik, and made the King a virtual prisoner. Thanks to first aid by Dr. Allen, Min survived, but Kim and the King ordered most of the pro-Chinese leaders beheaded. They decreed a number of progressive reforms, some of them on the advice of Foote, who however, had taken no part in the coup. Once again, local Chinese commanders threw their troops into the city, and soon Kim and his allies were fleeing toward the coast. The King obligingly restored the old form of government and severely punished the remaining rebels, leaving China in control of the situation.[33]

Although Foote, Foulk, and other Americans in Korea tried to play the role of makeweight in the fluctuating rivalry of China and Japan, it does not appear that they were much more than pawns. Indeed, by the end of the Arthur administration, American influence in Korea was rapidly diminishing. To the dissatisfaction of the Koreans, Shufeldt did not arrive in Seoul until 1886 and never actually entered Korean service. Congress reduced Foote's rank to that of a minister resident, and he resigned, unwilling to accept

[32]*Ibid.*, pp. 89-91. Nelson, *Korea and the Old Orders*, p. 170. Fred Harvey Harrington, *God, Mammon, and the Japanese; Dr. Horace N. Allen and Korean-American Relations, 1884-1905* (Madison, Wisconsin, 1944), pp. 3-16. William Elliot Griffis, *Corea, Without and Within* (Philadelphia, 1885), pp. 218-20. Foote to Frelinghuysen, Seoul, April 29, 1884, No. 70, U.S., *Foreign Relations, 1884*, p. 126. For a detailed appraisal of the Korean situation by Foulk see *ibid., 1885*, pp. 335-41.

[33]Nelson, *Korea and the Old Orders*, pp. 171-72. Dennett, "Early American Policy," pp. 91-92. Harrington, *God, Mammon, and the Japanese*, chap. ii.

demotion and a lower salary. Foulk and Allen remained, and American merchants and missionaries continued their activities. A decade later, however, when Sino-Japanese rivalry culminated in war, no American expectations had been substantially realized, and the influence of American diplomats made little difference in the outcome of the war.[34]

*   *   *

While Foote and Foulk played for a balance of power between China and Japan in an independent Korea, John Russell Young was doing all he could to prevent or minimize a war between China and France for the control of Indo-China, to the south. For years the French had gradually expanded their influence, annexing Cochin China, and establishing protectorates over Cambodia and Annam. On December 20, 1882, Li Hung-chang, representing China, signed a memorandum with the French minister, M. Bourée, by which China agreed to withdraw her troops from Indo-China and permit trade across the border, while France recognized the independence of Annam and promised not to conquer the northernmost province of Tonquin. The agreement was a statesmanlike compromise, but unfortunately it displeased both the Chinese nationalists in Peking and the French imperialists, led by Premier Jules Ferry, who repudiated the memorandum and recalled Bourée in disgrace. Both sides prepared for war, using the activities of Chinese guerrillas in Tonquin as an excuse.

At this point Young entered the picture. Early in July Li Hung-chang visited Shanghai to attempt new negotiations with M. Tricou, the French minister to Japan. Young, who happened to be in the city, tried to serve as a buffer between the two men. He spoke quite frankly to Li, warning him that China had neither the munitions nor the transportation system with which to wage war against the second greatest military and naval Power in the world, and that the only results would be military disaster, a large indemnity, and the loss of Canton to the French. At the same time, he pointed out, Russia awaited a favorable moment to move south, and the Japanese army was ready "like a shining blade anxious to leap from the sheath." Li seemed impressed and inquired at

[34]Dennett, "Early American Policy," pp. 93-94, 101-3.

one point whether China could borrow money in the United States for railroads and peaceful public works. However, Young felt that he feared "the thieving eunuch mob" in Peking more than the French.[35]

Li broke off negotiations with Tricou, but when he had returned to Tientsin, he called Young to him and asked him to propose American arbitration of the Franco-Chinese dispute to the State Department. Shortly after this the Chinese minister to France and England, garrulous Marquis Tseng, called on James Russell Lowell in London and made a similar proposal. Frelinghuysen considered the suggestion and replied to Young that the United States could lend its good offices only if both sides agreed. He then instructed Levi P. Morton in Paris to sound out the French government. Morton being away from Paris at the time, the American chargé d'affaires, E. J. Brulatour, transmitted the inquiry to the French Foreign Office. P. Challemel Lacour, the foreign minister, showed interest and might have accepted the offer if Morton had been on hand to apply his persuasion, but Brulatour made the mistake of discussing terms prematurely with Marquis Tseng, who demanded that France evacuate Tonquin and recognize Annamese independence. When Challemel Lacour learned of this, he became indignant and firmly rejected the American offer. Tseng then informed Peking secretly (and quite wrongly) that Britain, Germany, Russia, and the United States had formed an alliance to restrain France.[36]

After a series of French victories in Tonquin, Li Hung-chang once again braved the anger of Chinese nationalists and on May 11, 1884, negotiated a peace treaty with Commandant E. Fournier of the French Navy. By its terms China agreed to recognize the new French regime in Annam and Tonquin and to permit trade across the Kwangsi and Yünnan frontiers, while France waived any claim to an indemnity. Once again a promising settlement

[35]Young to Frelinghuysen, Peking, August 8, 1883, No. 230, U.S., Despatches, China, LXV. This long and very revealing dispatch is one of Young's best efforts.
[36]E. J. Brulatour to Frelinghuysen, Paris, July 18, August 2, 9, 1883, Nos. 372, 383, 391; Levi P. Morton to Frelinghuysen, Paris, July 24, August 22, No. 397, U.S., Despatches, France, XCII. Henry Vignaud to J. C. B. Davis, Paris, November 16, Davis Papers, XXXIV. Henri Cordier, *Histoire des relations de la Chine avec les puissances occidentales, 1860-1902* (3 vols.; Paris, 1901-1902), II, 417.

collapsed, but this time because of Chinese action. When French troops began to occupy the border area of Tonquin, a Chinese garrison at Baclé refused to leave, apparently through a misunderstanding, and in the ensuing battle roundly defeated the French. Ferry and his imperialists, under attack at home, seized the opportunity to deliver an ultimatum, demanding an additional indemnity of 250,000,000 francs for the Chinese violation of the Li-Fournier convention.

The new French demands so alarmed the Chinese that they appealed twice again for American good offices. Frelinghuysen transmitted their requests to Paris, but the only concession which the French offered was to postpone fixing the exact amount of the indemnity until later. Before Young could act further, the time limit fixed in the French ultimatum expired. On August 4, four French warships bombarded Keelung, the principal port of Formosa. A little over two weeks later the principal French squadron destroyed most of the Chinese war fleet and the fortifications at Foochow, and during the next two months the French set up a blockade around Formosa.[37]

Through these trying weeks the moderates at Peking leaned heavily on the American minister, seeking him out at his legation for almost daily conferences. Young lost no opportunity to drive home his favorite moral—that China must adopt Western practices and attitudes in self-defense or disappear as a World Power: "Of what value the teachings of Confucius," he asked, "with a half dozen ironclads belonging to an enemy lying outside of Taku Bar?" However, his most important action in this period smacked more of expediency than of long-range reform. At the suggestion of a member of the important American firm of Russell and Company, he helped to persuade Li to sell to the Americans the great fleet of merchant ships owned by the state-sponsored China Merchants Steam Navigation Company, to prevent their falling into French hands. Li's steamship concern had bought these ships of Russell and Company only a few years before. He was very proud of

[37]Morton to Frelinghuysen, Paris, May 13, July 24, 25, August 6, 1884, Nos. 557, 592, 593, 601, U.S., Despatches, France, XCIV. Frelinghuysen to Morton, July 22, 23, 31, August 13 (telegrams), U.S., Instructions, France, XXI, 76-77, 83-84, 90, 138-39. Young to Frelinghuysen, Peking, August 21, No. 496A, U.S., Despatches, China, LXXI.

them, but at length he consented, and once again the ships flew the American flag.[38]

Ironically, the bombardment and blockade of Formosa led to French overtures for American mediation. The Ferry regime, feeling that France had achieved her goals and fearing that further war taxes would weaken support at home, began to sound out Morton as early as the first week in September. For more than two months the American legation and the French Foreign Office sparred with each other as to armistice terms. After suggesting an indemnity of 80,000,000 francs, Ferry intimated that he would be willing to let the United States determine the amount, and it was soon apparent that the French premier was mainly concerned to "save face." Frelinghuysen then asked Young to inquire informally whether China would agree to pay a nominal indemnity of perhaps 5,000,000 francs and consent to temporary French occupation of two ports on Formosa and certain undefined commercial privileges. When the Chinese government rejected both the indemnity and the occupation, Ferry thanked the Americans for their trouble, and the negotiations ended.[39] During the following year the British inspector-general of the Chinese customs, Sir Robert Hart, brought the two sides together in the Treaty of Tientsin, which omitted any mention of an indemnity.

In attempting mediation between France and China, the State Department showed admirable persistence. Its failure was due more to bad luck than to any error or lack of judgment. Apparently the ill-considered reports of Marquis Tseng in Paris confirmed the suspicions of the Yamen that French concessions were a sign of weakness, and that if China held out a few weeks longer, a disgusted French public would compel retreat. At the same time false rumors circulated in France to the effect that Young

[38] Young to Frelinghuysen, Peking, August 21, September 4, November 20, December 30, 1884; January 7, 1885, Nos. 496A, 501, 558, 614, U.S., Despatches, China, LXXI, LXXII, LXXIV. See also *New York Tribune*, November 12, 1884, p. 3.
[39] Morton to Frelinghuysen, Paris, September 3, 4, 9, 12, 1884; Washington, October 15, 28; Vignaud to Frelinghuysen, Paris, October 2, 3, 4, 7, 8, 9, 11, 13, 14, 20, 23, 30, November 21, Nos. 611, 619, 630, 633, 634, 641, 647, 648, 653, 668, telegrams, U.S., Despatches, France, XCV. Frelinghuysen to Morton, September 6, 17; Frelinghuysen to Vignaud, September 28, October 17, 20, 25 (telegrams), U.S., Instructions, France, XXI, 104-5, 107-8, 125-27. Young to Frelinghuysen, Peking, December 9, 1884, No. 569, U.S., Despatches, China, LXXIII.

and other American legation officials in Peking were encouraging Chinese resistance, and these sapped French confidence in American good faith.[40] Actually, as has been seen, Young repeatedly threw his influence on the side of peace, but his help in engineering the sale of the Chinese merchant fleet to Russell and Company naturally betrayed his lack of real neutrality.

Young based his policy of mediation and pacification in the Franco-Chinese War on the same foundations as his policy toward Korea. It was a foundation of assumptions announced by Grant during his visit of 1879: that European influence was basically opposed to Chinese and Japanese interests; that only through economic progress could the two nations grow strong enough to defend these interests; and that peace was an absolute prerequisite to such progress.[41] In 1884 and 1885 these assumptions seemed valid, but within the next decade it became obvious that Japan had cast her lot with the despoilers of China, in the confidence of being able to outplay the European Powers at their own game.

Furthermore, American Far Eastern policy under Garfield and Arthur—especially the Shufeldt treaty with Korea and Young's efforts at mediation between France and China—presupposed a keener American concern for Chinese integrity than actually existed in the 1880's, after race prejudice and the immigration debates had blunted American sympathies. Except for missionaries and a few merchants and investors, Americans cared little about China, Japan, or Korea. The American public would tacitly permit such noncommittal measures as commercial treaties and peaceful mediation, but it was not yet prepared to see the United States play the role of a Great Power in the Far East.

[40]Morton to Frelinghuysen, Paris, December 3, 1884, No. 678, U.S., Despatches, France, XCV. Young to Frelinghuysen, Peking, December 9, 22, 26, Nos. 571, 583, 591, U.S., Despatches, China, LXXII-LXXIV.

[41]San Francisco Chronicle, March 15, 1881. Ulysses S. Grant to [Young], New York, May 18, 1883, Young Papers, XV.

Chapter 12

The Near East and Africa

I F American commercial, strategic, and humanitarian interests in the Far East were still too inchoate during the early 1880's to serve as the firm basis of a positive, consistent foreign policy, the same was true to an even greater degree in the Near East and Africa. Since trade with these areas was insignificant, and strategic considerations would wait upon the construction of a modern navy, the principal American stake seemed to be the work of missionaries.

Foreign policy, however, is sometimes based on hopes rather than on realities. In the Near East and especially in Africa a few missionaries, strategists, businessmen, and publicists thought that they discerned the outlines of future American interests. Disapproving of colonialism, anxious to preserve an open door into Africa, yet fearful of violating isolationist traditions, they urged the State Department to explore the possibilities of commercial treaties and other manifestations of disinterested friendship through which the United States might expand its influence in obscure corners of the world. The result was much the same as in the Far East: a haltingly expansive foreign policy in which an uncertain State Department experimented with interventionist measures which, for one reason or another, were usually discarded before they involved long-range commitments.

*   *   *

Although some American diplomats discoursed glowingly on American opportunities in the Near East, the official attitude of the Ottoman Empire was unfavorable to Americans. The consul at Jerusalem warned: "The Government does not wish foreign capitalists to enter the country for this purpose, nor does it wish to sell its land to aliens. . . . Individual effort is useless, no matter how great the skill which may direct it or the capital which it can command." There was much evidence to support such pes-

simism. Turkish nationalists resented the competition of American imports so much that they inflicted the gratuitous insult of forbidding American pork shipments into a Moslem country. The Sultan's government levied crushing taxes on foreign-owned real estate, alleging military necessity, and put all sorts of obstacles in the way of storing American petroleum, on the score of public safety. Turkish officials placed an illegal duty on American alcohol and tried to collect it even after they had admitted its illegality. Finally, the government denounced the commercial treaty of 1862 and demanded a higher ceiling on conventional tariffs.[1]

As in the case of China, the State Department usually counseled patient firmness in defense of American trading interests, but it could not remain so passive when Turkish bandits or mobs attacked American missionaries and other residents. After the American chargé had reported a list of robberies and beatings, and one notorious murder had gone unpunished for nearly a year, Blaine sent the new American minister to Turkey, General Lew Wallace, to his post with a stern denunciation of "this state of perversion of the sense of right and justice . . . by practically promising immunity to thieves and murderers for any outrage they may perpetrate upon foreigners." Blaine instructed Wallace to demand that the Turkish government execute the sentenced murderer without further evasion, make every effort to arrest other offenders, and pay indemnities to their victims.[2]

Even before this the Turkish government had thrown the United States on the defensive in matters of individual security by challenging its right of extraterritorial jurisdiction. According to a treaty of 1830, American residents in Turkey, when charged with some offense, were to be tried by the American minister or consul and punished "following . . . the usage observed towards other

[1]Report of Consul Selah Merrill, Jerusalem, October 18, 1883, U.S., *Commercial Relations, 1882-1883*, II, 555. On the real-estate taxes see U.S., *Foreign Relations, 1881*, pp. 1176-77. On petroleum storage see *ibid., 1883*, pp. 822-24, 829-31, 834-35, 842, 844-47, 874-76, 877, 887-88. On the illegal alcohol duty see *ibid., 1882*, pp. 497-98, 499-501, 504-8; *1883*, pp. 819-21, 832. On the commercial treaty see *ibid., 1883*, pp. 841-42, 843, 848, 850, 865-70, 876.

[2]Porter C. Heap to William M. Evarts, Constantinople, October 16, November 8, 1880; Heap to James G. Blaine, May 5, 11, 14, June 25, 1881, Nos. 32, 36, 6, 10, 12, 22; Blaine to Lewis Wallace, June 29, August 8, 1881, No. 3, 8, *ibid., 1881*, pp. 1173-75, 1178-79, 1180-81, 1184-88.

Franks." (This was the term by which the Ottoman Empire loosely described Western Europeans.) Soon after the signature of the treaty a disagreement had broken out between the two countries regarding the English translation of the text, and during the 1870's the Turkish foreign minister began to insist that according to the Ottoman version, American residents must be tried under Turkish law. Since Turkish law rejected the testimony of a non-Moslem against a Moslem, it was apparent that this interpretation would lead to an endless chain of injustices against foreigners.

After a long, exhausting argument with the Turkish minister in Washington, Evarts instructed his minister at Constantinople to consult with European diplomats as to their understanding of the rights of "Franks." Blaine confirmed this instruction but, as has been stated, saved most of his force for the related problem of unpunished Turkish criminals. When Frelinghuysen came to office, he instructed Wallace to concentrate his attention on the former problem, declaring that the American government would "adhere to the rights of the U. S. as they are understood in this Department, until something is substituted with the common consent of the Western powers, which affords equal security and an equal prospect of justice to the citizens of the U. S. in the Ottoman dominions."[3]

Wallace fully agreed with the Secretary and did his best to uphold American rights, but he was no match for the Turkish diplomats, past masters of procrastination, who put him off with all kinds of excuses. At the same time the rest of the diplomatic corps seemed to be waiting to see what the Americans would do. To complicate matters, during the summer of 1883 two missionaries were knifed by a band of Kurds with the apparent connivance of a provincial governor. This egregious case could not be overlooked; for the rest of his tour of duty Wallace had his hands full trying to secure police and court action against Turkish criminals while

[3]Evarts to James Longstreet, March 2, 1881, No. 19; Blaine to Wallace, August 2, No. 7; Frelinghuysen to Wallace, March 3, 1882, No. 44, U.S., Instructions, Turkey, III, 416-30, 472-74, 510-18. Wallace to Blaine, Constantinople, December 5, 1881, No. 38, U.S., Despatches, Turkey, XXXVIII. For the text of the 1830 treaty see Malloy, *Treaties*, II, 1319.

denying Turkish jurisdiction over American residents.[4] On several occasions, at Wallace's suggestion, the United States sent warships from its Mediterranean squadron to visit Turkish ports, but their reception by the Turks, while courteous, did not show much fear. At the end of the Arthur administration the Ottoman government still insisted on its interpretation of the 1830 treaty, and the principal cases of injustices and attacks on Americans remained unrectified.

The efforts of the State Department to uphold American interests in Persia were not much more effective than in Turkey. At the beginning of the decade the United States had no representative in Teheran. When, in November, 1880, a congressman asked Evarts to protect fourteen missionaries (among them his sister and her husband) against the hostile Moslem population, all the Secretary could do was to instruct Minister Lowell to request British good offices. In the following year the Persian minister to Russia suggested to John W. Foster that an American legation at Teheran might lead to profitable trade between Persia and the United States. Congress recommended the establishment of formal relations, mentioning both trade and missionaries, and in February, 1883, Arthur appointed Samuel G. W. Benjamin to be the first American minister. Unfortunately, Benjamin was a bad choice. As an author and painter, he had considerable knowledge of Persia, but he lacked common sense and set out with an exalted opinion of his new importance. He soon became suspicious of Russian influences and disgraced himself by petty quarrels with the Russian and German ministers, so that finally he had to be recalled.[5]

[4]Wallace to Frelinghuysen, Constantinople, March 6, April 14, September 30, 1882, Nos. 67, 87, 128, U.S., Despatches, Turkey, XXXVIII, XL. For the correspondence on the case of the two missionaries and on the unjust imprisonment of an American doctor, another *cause célèbre* of the same period, see U.S., *Foreign Relations, 1883*, pp. 850-65, 881-91; *1884*, pp. 544-46, 548-49, 550-51, 552, 558-59, 563-65; *1885*, pp. 825-26, 827, 842.

[5]Abraham Yeselson, *United States-Persian Diplomatic Relations, 1883-1921* (New Brunswick, New Jersey, 1956), pp. 23-31. John W. Foster to Blaine, St. Petersburg, May 21, 1881, No. 118, U.S., Congress, House, 47th Cong., 1st Sess., 1882, House Executive Doc. 151, pp. 21-22 *et passim. Ibid.,* H. Rept. 1648, *passim.* Frelinghuysen to James Russell Lowell, March 25, 1882, No. 340, U.S., Instructions, Britain, XXVI, 356-58.

In the Near East of the 1880's Americans had to deal with relatively advanced governments and dense native populations already exploiting most of the available natural resources. In Africa, however, the situation was somewhat different. Here, as one American publicist put it in 1877, was a land with "a future as great as our own continent, perhaps greater . . . a land of wonderful abundance, animal, mineral, and vegetable, . . . the greatest of unappropriated treasures on the world's map to-day."[6] Unappropriated still, but not for long. Britain, France, and Germany had already begun to extend their coastal footholds into the interior, drawn by the many explorers' reports of the past three decades. Between 1880 and 1885 Egypt, Tunisia, West Africa, the Congo Valley, Southwest Africa, and Madagascar became the scene of colonial rivalry or of agreements to divide the spoils. Despite Americans' concern with their own hemisphere, it would have been difficult for them to ignore European activities in Africa altogether, and from time to time the State Department was briefly involved in the diplomacy of imperialism.

One of these occasions was the British occupation of Egypt in 1882. After the opening of the Suez Canal in 1869 and Disraeli's purchase of a large block of Canal shares six years later, British interest in Egypt steadily increased. Largely ignoring the overlordship of Turkey, the British and French governments established a loose joint protectorate over Egyptian finances to safeguard the interests of their bondholders. At the end of the decade an Egyptian nationalist movement appeared in protest against the European controls, and early in 1882 its leader, Ahmed Arabi, became minister of war in the Khedive's cabinet. Alarmed at the upsurge of nationalism but unable to agree on a policy of cooperation with Turkey to put it down, Britain and France sponsored a conference of ambassadors at Constantinople in June and sent a joint fleet to Alexandria to cow Arabi, whereupon an outburst of antiforeign riots killed some fifty Europeans. Unwilling to risk war, France withdrew her squadron, but the British remained and sent an ultimatum to Turkey, demanding the deposi-

[6] Gilbert Haven, "America in Africa," *North American Review*, CXXV (July 1877), 149.

tion of Arabi and "the further development of the internal administration" of Egypt.[7]

Up to this point the United States observed events from the outside and even hesitated to approve the Anglo-French plan for liquidating the Egyptian debt, lest this expression of opinion affect the interests of American citizens. On July 4, however, the Turkish Sultan called American Minister Wallace to him, showed him the terms of the British ultimatum, and requested American good offices, as a prelude to formal mediation. On instructions from Frelinghuysen, Wallace held long conversations with the Sultan and the British ambassador to Turkey, Lord Dufferin. He concluded that the only real point of difference was the meaning of the terms "further development" and "internal administration." As the Sultan recognized, the bland phrase really involved the whole question of British control over Egypt, but Wallace was fully convinced that American mediation would lead to an amicable settlement.

Events soon disillusioned him. On July 10 he received word from Dufferin that the admiral commanding the British squadron at Alexandria had threatened that unless the Egyptians stopped work on the city's fortifications, he would open fire on them the following day. Dufferin then demanded a temporary Anglo-Turkish occupation of Egypt, followed by the prompt withdrawal of the token Turkish forces. The Sultan pressed for more time to consider the proposition, and finally Dufferin cabled a request that the admiral postpone firing. The request arrived too late, and British troops proceeded to occupy Egypt. Both Dufferin and the Turks blamed each other for the breakdown of negotiations. It is not clear to this day whether the British proposals were offered in good faith, but Wallace, who served as liaison during the last stages, became convinced that they were not.[8]

American newspapers reacted in different ways to the British

[7]For more details on the background of the British ultimatum see William L. Langer, *European Alliances and Alignments, 1871-1890* (New York, 1931), chap. viii.

[8]Frelinghuysen to Comte Maurice Sala, October 6, 1884, U.S., Notes to Foreign Legations, France, X, 24-25. Wallace to Frelinghuysen, Constantinople, July 20, 1882, No. 110, U.S., Despatches, Turkey, XXXIX. Frelinghuysen to Wallace, July 21, No. 73, U.S., Instructions, Turkey, III, 543-47. Langer, *European Alliances and Alignments*, pp. 275-76.

invasion. Some criticized "this spectacle of the first naval Power in the world bombarding a flea," but the *New York Tribune* supported the occupation as a painful necessity for the safety of the Suez Canal: "The European Powers have undertaken to give civilization and commerce a certain amount of protection within the dominions of 'the unspeakable Turk.' " Former President Grant compared Egypt to the American South before the Civil War and predicted that a British protectorate would improve the condition of the people.[9] In a similar manner leading New York newspapers commented favorably on the French establishment of a protectorate over Tunisia in 1881 and 1882. One declared that "civilization gains whenever any misgoverned country passes under the control of a European race. . . . A torch will be lighted in a benighted quarter of the world." Another defended France by comparing Tunisia to Cuba. Where populations of European descent were concerned, however, the press was less apt to condone imperialism: for example, the *New York Tribune* declared Disraeli's proposal to annex the Transvaal as an "inexcusable and reprehensible act of national piracy."[10]

*   *   *

While the American government and public viewed European imperialism in North Africa with detachment, the State Department took a somewhat more active interest in British expansion on the west coast. The focus of American concern was the negro republic of Liberia, founded by ex-slaves from the American South and regarded, in Frelinghuysen's words, "as an offshoot of this country," although in no sense an American possession.[11] In 1878, when Commodore Shufeldt visited Liberia during his round-the-world cruise, he pronounced it "the *objective* point of American trade on this Coast, and . . . really the garden of Africa."

[9]*Harper's Weekly*, XXVI (July 22, September 2, 1882), 461, 463, 555. *New York Herald*, July 15, p. 6. *New York Tribune*, June 27, p. 4; July 7, p. 4; July 13, p. 4; July 19, p. 1; August 20, p. 6; July 25, 1883, p. 4; November 13, p. 4; December 17, p. 4. Some were interested in the fighting mainly because they hoped that it would create a market for American wheat. *Washington Post*, July 13, p. 2.

[10]*New York Tribune*, January 14, 1880, p. 4; January 21, 1881, p. 4; February 2, p. 4; April 29, p. 4; May 14, p. 4; December 3, p. 4. *New York Herald*, April 29, 1882, p. 6.

[11]Frelinghuysen to Theodore J. Roustan, August 22, 1884, U.S., Notes to Foreign Legations, France, X, 15. See also *New York Herald*, December 27, 1881, p. 4.

He urged the American government to keep a gunboat regularly stationed off the coast to support the Liberian government, to establish a new consulate and a coaling station in the area, and in some way to encourage the opening of steamship companies and a hundred-mile railroad into the interior.[12]

During Shufeldt's visit to West Africa he tried in vain to bring about a settlement of a long-standing boundary dispute between Liberia and the neighboring British colony of Sierra Leone. In 1882 the American Colonization Society, which represented Liberia in Washington, appealed again to the State Department for aid, and the American minister resident in Monrovia reported that in his opinion the British governor was trying to rush Liberia into yielding territory to which Britain had no shadow of a claim.[13] John Davis (Acting Secretary during Frelinghuysen's illness) asked James Russell Lowell to discuss the problem informally at the British Foreign Office and added that the United States "would view with positive disfavor the compulsory alienation of territory . . . without a considerable opportunity being afforded to [Liberia] to make good in other ways according to its ability and resources whatever money claim may be conclusively adjudged to be due to British claimants."[14]

Davis' caution was justified, for when Lowell carried out these sensible instructions, he learned the other side of the case: that many natives in the disputed area opposed Liberian rule, that the claims had originally risen from Liberian efforts to seize the border area by force, and that the president of Liberia had actually accepted a British compromise offer but had not kept his promise to submit it to his senate. Lowell concluded that Liberia already had more territory than her government could rule effectively, and that both parties would benefit from a compromise boundary at the Mannah River. By the time that

[12]Robert W. Shufeldt to Richard W. Thompson, Sierra Leone, February 16, 1879; Monrovia, March 19; Cape Merut, April 25; Monrovia, April 28, Nos. 12, 16, 24, 26, Letterbook, pp. 34-42, 47-51, 68-73, 76-77, Shufeldt Papers.

[13]A. Aenmay to Frelinghuysen, Monrovia, June 23, 1882, No. 9; John H. Smith to Frelinghuysen, Monrovia, October 2, No. 12, U.S., Despatches, Liberia, IX.

[14]John Davis to Lowell, September 15, 1882, No. 460; Frelinghuysen to Lowell, September 22 (telegram), U.S., Instructions, Britain, XXVI, 488-509, 511-12.

Frelinghuysen had approved such a settlement, it had already been put into effect.[15]

About a year later the State Department got wind of a rumor that France intended to occupy Kent's Island in the Mannah River, along the newly created boundary. Frelinghuysen asked the French minister if this were true and declared that any nation which occupied Liberian territory without allowing the United States to interpose its good offices in the question "could not but produce an unfavorable impression in the minds of the Government and people of the United States." Since the French government flatly denied any territorial ambitions in the vicinity of Liberia, Frelinghuysen took no further action, and Liberia was left to vegetate in tropical indolence and governmental confusion.[16]

*   *   *

Another part of Africa in which European imperialism seemed to cut across American interests or sympathies was Madagascar. This large island, inhabited by over five million natives of various levels of civilization, was claimed as royal domain by Queen Ranavalomanjaka of the dominant tribe of Hovas (Malagasy). Queen Rana held effective rule over the eastern and southern parts of the island, including the capital, Atananarivo, and the principal port, Tamatave, but in the northwest another powerful tribe, the Sakalavas, denied her authority. Although at various times past both Britain and France had briefly occupied Madagascar, there seemed to be adequate evidence under international law that they had later recognized the Hovas' rule. However, frequent petty quarrels over the foreigners' right to own land and other similar issues kept consuls and diplomatic agents at odds with the Queen's government. Because the French were more

[15]Lowell to Frelinghuysen, London, January 3, March 14, May 1, 4, 1883, Nos. 472, 512, 537, 542, U.S., Despatches, Britain, CXLVI. Frelinghuysen to Lowell, April 9, No. 567, U.S., Instructions, Britain, XXVI, 625-26.

[16]Frelinghuysen to Roustan, August 22, 1884, U.S., Notes to Foreign Legations, France, X, 15-18. Frelinghuysen to Morton, August 19, No. 599, U.S., Instructions, France, XXI, 94-96. Frelinghuysen to Lowell, August 22, No. 955, *ibid.*, Britain, XXVII, 289-92. Morton to Frelinghuysen, Paris, September 20, No. 622; Henry Vignaud to Frelinghuysen, Paris, November 19, No. 667, U.S., Despatches, France, XCV.

active in pushing the claims of their citizens, the Hovas leaned toward Britain.[17]

By the early 1880's Americans had helped to spread trade and Christianity widely through the islands. In 1867 the Johnson administration negotiated a brief commercial treaty with the Hovas, and during the next thirteen years Americans came to supply half of the imports into the island, estimated at a million dollars annually. Much of this figure represented petroleum and cheap brown cotton cloth, which happened to please the natives' taste. However, the trade of Americans rested on a precarious foundation, for they maintained no general stores on the island, and few American ships called at its ports. The principal element of American strength was the consul at Tamatave, W. W. Robinson, a large, bluff, free-spoken Wisconsiner who urged merchants to establish agencies for machinery and other American goods.[18]

In the summer of 1879 Commodore Shufeldt negotiated an agreement with the Sakalava tribe on the northwest coast, providing for an American coaling station at Tullear Bay. The false rumor spread to Tamatave that Shufeldt had raised the American flag on the west coast, but the Hayes administration did not ratify the agreement, and Robinson managed to stifle the rumor. He was much annoyed at Shufeldt's action, for he feared that it would weaken the Queen's hold on the west coast and prejudice American influence with her government. In an effort to curry favor at court, Robinson began to advise the Queen's officials regarding a proposed military expedition against the Sakalavas, but when they asked him if the United States would send a warship to take troops and munitions to the west coast, he had to tell them to apply to Britain or France. However, he persuaded the foreign minister to sign a new commercial treaty on May 13, 1881.[19]

[17]*New York Tribune*, February 4, 1883, p. 3; March 20, p. 2. Unsigned memorandum, October 14, 1884, No. 152, U.S., Reports of Diplomatic Bureau, VI.

[18]W. W. Robinson to Charles Payson, Tamatave, August 7, October 2, 1880, Nos. 66, 70, U.S., Consular Despatches, Tamatave, III. Memorandum of October 14, 1884, No. 152, U.S., Reports of Diplomatic Bureau, VI. *New York Tribune*, March 4, 1883, p. 1.

[19]Paullin, *Diplomatic Negotiations*, p. 353. Robinson to Payson, Atananarivo, January 15, April 28, 1881; Tamatave, June 9, 27, Nos. 74, 77, 81, 82, U.S., Consular Despatches, Tamatave, III. For the text of the treaty see Malloy, *Treaties*, I, 1061-73.

While Robinson was thus engaged, news arrived from the west coast that the Sakalavas had killed four Arabs in a dhow flying the French flag. The French agent at Atananarivo at once demanded an indemnity and declared that his nation would claim sovereignty over part of the northwest coast. Although a later report from the coast revealed that the Arabs were smugglers and had opened fire first, the Queen reluctantly paid the indemnity. Since she refused to recognize the territorial claim, the French agent left the capital for Tamatave, there to await naval reinforcements. As soon as the trouble began, the Hova government ordered five thousand rifles from an American firm, but only half of these could be delivered, owing to opposition from the French naval commander.[20]

Threatened with French occupation, Queen Rana decided to send a diplomatic mission to Europe and the United States and asked Robinson to accompany it. On his request for instructions, the State Department permitted him to go, provided that he avoided "officious interference" in the negotiations. While Robinson followed the letter of these instructions, there is no way of knowing how much private advice he may have given the Hova mission. Certainly they needed all they could get. After five or six weeks of discussions in Paris, the French foreign minister suddenly demanded a general protectorate over the whole island and special privileges on the west coast—an ultimatum which, as Robinson remarked, the envoys had no time to send home, and which would have cost them their heads if they had. When they refused, the French foreign minister ordered the Malagasy flag removed from their hotel, and the Hovas departed for London, taking Robinson with them. At his behest, Minister Morton directed a mild inquiry to the foreign minister, who exploded against the envoys—"Ce sont des farceurs!"—and asked if the United States were supporting them. At this, Morton denied any knowledge and declared that his only instructions were to work for peace.[21]

[20]Robinson to State Department, Tamatave, June 5, 29, July 31, 1882, Nos. 99, 101, 105, U.S., Consular Despatches, Tamatave, III.
[21]Robinson to State Department, Tamatave, July 28, 1882, No. 104; Robinson to Alvey A. Adee, London, December 3, *ibid*. Adee to Robinson, October 17, U.S.,

Meanwhile the envoys were creating a sensation in London, attending church at Westminster Abbey (where they sang hymns in Malagasy) and being generally lionized, while a special committee, representing missionaries and trading interests, petitioned the Cabinet for action. Wanting no trouble with France, which was already sensitive over the Egyptian question, Lord Granville reluctantly called in Lowell and intimated that Britain thought the French action high-handed and would not be sorry if the United States saw fit to remonstrate. At the same time Robinson appealed for American intervention:

> Does our Government prefer to see our trade either hampered or driven out of all foreign corners by French policy or French force of arms? . . . She is not satisfied with shutting out American pork from France and its colonies, but intends to hamper our trade everywhere she can—by diplomacy when it will answer the purpose, by bluster and force when intrigue fails. Why? Because French goods, and French manner of trading cannot compete, on fair and equal terms, with American goods in barbarous, or semi civilized countries.[22]

When dispatches from Robinson, Lowell, and Morton arrived in Washington shortly after New Year's Day, 1883, Arthur and his cabinet discussed the Madagascar problem. Frelinghuysen assured Morton that his pacific assurances to the French government were perfectly correct. At the same time the Secretary privately urged the Senate to ratify Robinson's commercial treaty of 1881 in order to forestall British traders. The Navy sent a warship to visit the principal ports of Madagascar, while the State Department made ready to welcome the Hova envoys to the United States. On March 3 they arrived in New York, where they received salutes from the harbor forts and an escort to Washington. Since the Senate had hurriedly approved the commercial treaty, the State Department solemnly exchanged ratifications with the envoys. In addition to their official reception, they attracted much attention from merchants and missionaries, and

Consular Instructions, CIV, 651-52. Morton to Frelinghuysen, Paris, November 7, 30, December 5, Nos. 249, 260, 265, U.S., Despatches, France, XCI.

[22]Robinson to Adee, London, December 3, 20, 1882, U.S., Consular Despatches, Tamatave, III. Lowell to Frelinghuysen, London, December 16, No. 464, U.S., Despatches, Britain, CXLVI.

Henry Ward Beecher welcomed them to his Brooklyn church with a sermon against the French intervention. After a tour of New England they left for home at the end of the month.[23]

The visit of the Hova envoys aroused much idle curiosity and sympathy but little genuine sentiment in favor of American action. Robinson, to be sure, acted the role of promoter, praising the island's resources and the Hova civilization, with special emphasis on churches and schools, and denouncing the French. The *New York Tribune* printed his remarks at length, but concluded that since Queen Rana's sovereignty over the island was under dispute, the ratification of a treaty recognizing that sovereignty represented "culpable negligence either in the State Department or in the Senate." Others feared a falling-out with France, which, the *Nation* declared, would be ludicrous: "The American people . . . care very little whether the Queen of Madagascar governs the whole of that island or only a part of it. They would like to extend their trade that way, but it is after all a matter of comparatively small interest to them."[24]

For several months after the departure of the mission Robinson remained in the United States because of ill health. During his absence the French tried to force a showdown in Madagascar by occupying Tamatave and towns on the northwest coast. The Hova forces withdrew into the interior without firing a shot and prepared for guerrilla warfare, leaving the French to occupy the ports and squeeze what tribute they could out of the ruined trade. When the French admiral peremptorily called on all foreign consulates to close their doors, the American vice-consul complied with some bewilderment. By the end of 1883 a stalemate had developed on the island, the French occupying Tamatave in the hope of starving out the natives, and the Hovas supreme in the almost impassable interior.[25]

[23]Frelinghuysen to Morton, January 16, 1883, No. 206, U.S., Instructions, France, XX, 513-14. Frelinghuysen to William Windom, December 20, 1882; February 19, 1883, U.S., Senate Foreign Relations Committee Archives. *New York Tribune*, January 4, p. 4; March 4, p. 1; March 14, p. 5; March 26, p. 2; March 30, p. 5.

[24]*Nation*, XXXVI (March 22, 1883), 248-49. See also *New York Tribune*, March 4, p. 1; March 7, p. 4; March 20, p. 2, and *New York Herald*, March 1, p. 6.

[25]R. M. Whitney to Adee, Tamatave, June 5, 14; August 7, 21, 30, 1883, Nos. 123-125, 129, 130, U.S., Consular Despatches, Tamatave, III, IV. *New York Tribune*, July 13, p. 4.

At this point the Hova officials, apparently misinterpreting the recently ratified commercial treaty with the United States, decided to ask for American aid. In a note of April 25, 1884, the Queen's government appealed to Frelinghuysen, pointing out rather pathetically that although the French disclaimed territorial ambitions, "yet their persistence to have the negotiations based on the parallels is quite to the contrary." Early in May Consul Robinson arrived in Tamatave and was soon urging that the State Department persuade the French to submit their claims to arbitration. In September, 1884, still further letters from the Queen arrived in Washington.[26]

None of these appeals moved Frelinghuysen from his earlier noncommittal attitude. After the French attack on Tamatave he had ordered the American vice-consul to remain at his post, do all he could to help American residents, and await further instructions as to recognition and official status. After full discussion of the question in the State Department, the Secretary sent a formal memorandum to Arthur, dated October 21, in which he denied that anything in the treaty of 1881 might be construed as recognizing Hova sovereignty over the whole island. He declared that to press France for arbitration would place the United States in the position of an interested party. As in the case of China, he added that a request from both parties for friendly mediation would be quite acceptable, since "the impartial attitude of the United States would be amply assured in view of the refusal hitherto to intervene as the friend of Madagascar, or as a party in interest whose treaty rights are prejudiced by the continuance of a state of hostilities."[27]

As Frelinghuysen probably expected, the French did not accept

[26]Whitney to Adee, Tamatave, November 28, December 26, 1883, Nos. 136, 139; Robinson to Adee, Tamatave, May 27, August 14, 1884, Nos. 154, 160, U.S., Consular Despatches, Tamatave, IV. Rainilaiarivony (the Hova prime minister) to Frelinghuysen, Atananarivo, April 25, enclosed with Lowell to Frelinghuysen, London, June 7, No. 791, U.S., Despatches, Britain, CXLIX. *New York Tribune*, September 27, p. 7.

[27]Frelinghuysen to Whitney, August 28, 1883, No. 91, U.S., Consular Instructions, CVIII, 185-87. Frelinghuysen to Arthur, October 21, 1884, U.S., Report Book, XV, 667-73. See also State Department memoranda of October 4 and 14, Nos. 149, 152, U.S., Reports of Diplomatic Bureau, VI. Frelinghuysen to Robinson, October 21, November 22, Nos. 106, 110, U.S., Consular Instructions, CXII, 17-18, 210-11.

his offer, but in the end the result was about the same as if they had. An epidemic of fever among French troops at Tamatave and heavy anti-imperialist attacks in the Chamber of Deputies convinced Jules Ferry that for the moment the game was not worth the candle. France withdrew her troops from Madagascar and accepted an indemnity for real and imagined damages, postponing conquest of the island until the mid-1890's. When the Arthur administration went out of power, Robinson reported that in five years American trade on the island had fallen by nearly four-fifths. The future looked black, for the French occupation had reawakened native fears of foreigners, and the British had begun to penetrate the American textile monopoly. Just before the occupation ended, a Manchester mill shipped out a consignment of cheap brown cotton cloth, identical with the American product and neatly labeled "Massachusetts sheetings."[28]

Frelinghuysen's prudent refusal to act alone was diplomatically correct and accurately reflected the apathy of most Americans. As in the case of the Franco-Chinese war of 1884-1885, he did not care to defy a major Power alone in an area where American commercial interests were uncertain. His refusal to become involved in Madagascar, however, did not mean that he washed his hands of African problems. As will be seen, at the same time that he rejected the appeal of Queen Rana, he was committing the United States to an even more ambitious project for the peaceful development of the Congo Valley, where the future rewards seemed greater than in Madagascar and the immediate danger of a showdown considerably less.

[28]Robinson to State Department, Tamatave, February 12, July 3, 1885, Nos. 170, 179, U.S., Consular Despatches, Tamatave, IV.

CHAPTER 13

The Irish-American Agitators

DURING the latter half of the nineteenth century, as American foreign trade grew, and more American citizens began to go abroad, the State Department was called upon with increasing frequency to safeguard the lives, liberty, and property of these wanderers. The efforts of the Garfield and Arthur administrations to secure justice for harried missionaries in Turkey and Persia have already been observed. They also inherited from Hayes and Evarts the problem of protecting American Jews in Russia from the perennial anti-Semitism of the Imperial government.[1] The wholesale emigration of Europeans to the United States increasingly complicated the work of the State Department, for there was as yet no general international agreement about the transfer of citizenship. When these immigrants, now naturalized Americans, returned to the homeland and got into trouble, the European governments sometimes denied the right of the United States to intervene for their protection. Thus in Germany the government usually allowed returning German-Americans a visit of two years and then drafted them for military service—which, in many cases, they had gone to America to avoid.[2]

The only controversy over naturalized citizens which is important enough to describe in any detail involved Irish immigrants to the United States who returned to the British Isles to agitate

[1] For a summary of State Department policy on this question see William M. Evarts to John W. Foster, March 3, 1881, No. 55, and James G. Blaine to Foster, July 29, No. 87, U.S., *Foreign Relations, 1881*, pp. 1007-8, 1030-36. Frederick T. Frelinghuysen to Wickham Hoffman, April 15, 1882, No. 123, *ibid., 1882*, p. 451. Cyrus Adler and Aaron M. Margolith, *American Intervention on Behalf of Jews in the Diplomatic Correspondence of the United States, 1840-1938* (New York, 1943), chaps. vii, viii.

[2] Jeannette Keim, *Forty Years of German-American Political Relations* (Philadelphia, 1919), pp. 51-62. A similar problem involving Franco-Americans began to arise in 1884. McElroy, *Morton*, pp. 150-53. Neither problem was solved under Garfield or Arthur.

for home rule or who carried on terrorist campaigns against Britain from headquarters in New York or Chicago. The Irish-American problem was more serious than that of the Russo-American Jews or the German-American draft-dodgers, because it caused a wave of anti-American sentiment in Britain, and because the Irish-American vote in New York seemed so important to the Republican party that the State Department had to handle the problem with extreme care. It has no direct connection with other major diplomatic questions of the Garfield-Arthur period, but, perhaps better than any other, it demonstrates the intimate relationship between diplomacy and politics during the 1880's.

*   *   *

Between 1840 and 1880 famines and English oppression drove nearly four million people out of Ireland. Most of them settled in the cities of the United States, where they could whet each other's memories and receive all the latest news from home. Many plunged into politics, especially in the Democratic party. During the 1860's the Irish-Americans not only fought lustily in the Civil War (usually on the Northern side) but joined the Fenian movement by the hundreds. After the war the veteran John O'Neil, defying the efforts of American officials to restrain him, led two hare-brained attacks against the British in Canada.[3]

For a time in the early 1870's the Fenian fiascos and the general prosperity of the British Isles diverted Irish attention from independence to home rule, while Gladstone's first land law of 1870 temporarily quieted agrarian grievances. In America most Irish devoted their energies to local politics, but a few nationalist agitators did what they could to keep alive the old hatreds. The noisiest of these was Jeremiah O'Donovan Rossa, a prolific and fiery pamphleteer who had been sentenced to life imprisonment in Britain for Fenian activities, but amnestied. After being elected to Parliament in 1869, he crossed to the United States and, under the loose regulations of the time, ran for the New York state

---

[3]Eric Strauss, *Irish Nationalism and British Democracy* (New York, 1951), p. 138 *et passim*. Florence E. Gibson, *The Attitudes of the New York Irish toward State and National Affairs, 1848-1892* (New York, 1951), chaps. i-viii. William D'Arcy, *The Fenian Movement in the United States, 1858-1886* (Washington, 1947), chaps. ii-v, ix.

senate two years later. His newspaper, the *United Irishman*, urged its readers to murder and arson in the cause of a free Ireland.[4] Another Fenian and ex-convict, John Devoy, founded the *Irish Nation* to advocate armed revolt and the advancement of Irish culture all over the world.[5]

The third among the principal leaders of Irish-American agitation was Patrick Ford, who, unlike Rossa and Devoy, had been brought to Boston as a child. His newspaper, the *Irish World*, was soon the most influential Irish nationalist organ in America. Ford accepted no compromises; to him home rule was a delusion, Gladstone a scheming opportunist, and England past her prime. In purple periods he described the United States as the proper Irish base of operations:

> Here in this Republic—whose flag first flashed on the breeze in defiance of England—whose first national hosts rained an iron hail of destruction upon England's power . . . we are free to express the sentiments and to declare the hopes of Ireland. It is your duty, revolutionary chieftains, to realize these hopes! If you are but true to this duty—if you are but true to nature— there are those among you who, perhaps, will yet live to uplift Ireland's banner above the ruins of London, and proclaim with trumpet-tongued voice . . . "The rod of the oppressor is broken! Babylon the great is fallen!"[6]

Many of Ford's editorials demanded broad social reforms both in Ireland and in the United States, reflecting the influences of Socialism and native American radicalism.

The prosperous years of the early 1870's were probably the last period in which Britain might have found a peaceful solution to the Irish question through home rule and a program of gradual land reform. After 1876 hard times started a new wave of emigration and reopened all the old Irish wounds. In 1880 the great Irish leader, Charles Stewart Parnell, visited the United States,

[4]John S. Crone, *A Concise Dictionary of Irish Biography* (Dublin, 1928), pp. 184-85. Gibson, *Attitudes of New York Irish*, pp. 242, 254. *Times* (London), June 21, 1882, p. 5.

[5]*Dictionary of American Biography*, V, 264-65. *Times*, June 21, 1882, p. 5.

[6]*Irish World*, September 19, 1874, as quoted in Gibson, *Attitudes of New York Irish*, p. 329. See also *ibid.*, pp. 328-30 for other quotations. *Dictionary of American Biography*, VI, 518. Carl Frederick Wittke, *The Irish in America* (Baton Rouge, Louisiana [1956]), p. 212. *Times*, June 21, 1882, p. 5.

hoping to build a united machine out of "the respectable lawyer, the affluent merchant, the local politician, and the dynamite-loving ex-Fenian soldier." Irish-Americans turned out in droves to hear him and founded an American branch of the Land League, but not even Parnell's oratory could permanently reconcile the violent and the respectable elements in the Irish movement.[7]

At the same time the Irish policy of the British government mixed severity and generosity. During the winter of 1880-1881 the government briefly arrested Parnell, and in March Parliament passed a stiff coercion bill providing for imprisonment without immediate trial in cases of rioting and agitation. Five months later, however, Gladstone secured royal approval for a new, radical land act which created a board to arbitrate questions of rent between landlord and tenant and which otherwise limited property rights. Moderate observers in the United States welcomed the Land Act of 1881, but Patrick Ford's *Irish World* denounced it as "Gladstone's quack remedy" and "babbling abortion" and warned Irish leaders that they would forfeit American support if they accepted it. Rossa threatened landlords with death, but the more conservative *Irish American* reproved him and urged passive resistance.[8]

Thus in the spring of 1881 the governments of Gladstone and Garfield faced a developing crisis in the triangular relationships between Britain, Ireland, and the United States. Gladstone, inclined to moderation in Irish affairs, had apparently not foreseen the agitation of 1880-1881, but he was well disposed toward the United States. His foreign secretary, Viscount Granville, felt less sympathy toward America, but since he was elderly, ill, and burdened with financial worries, he had little stomach for a fight.

[7] Good recent studies of the situation in Ireland are P. S. O'Hegarty, *A History of Ireland under the Union, 1801 to 1922* (London, 1952); Norman Dunbar Palmer, *The Irish Land League Crisis* (New Haven, Connecticut, 1940), and Conor Cruise O'Brien, *Parnell and his Party, 1880-1890* (Oxford, 1957). In the last-named see especially pp. 120, 134-36. On Parnell's visit in 1880 see Gibson, *Attitudes of New York Irish*, pp. 332-35; Wittke, *Irish in America*, pp. 165-66, and Philip Henry Bagenal, *The American Irish and their Influence on Irish Politics* (n.p. 1882), chap. viii, pp. 221-22.

[8] Quoted in Gibson, *Attitudes of New York Irish*, pp. 337-38. See also Palmer, *Irish Land League Crisis*, pp. 235, 258, 282. For American press opinions see, for example, *New York Tribune*, April 10, 1880, p. 4; January 27, 1881, p. 4; February 16, p. 4. *Nation*, XXXII (January 27, February 3, April 14, 1881), 53, 69, 255-56; XXXIII (August 25), 145.

Of the other Cabinet members the home secretary, Sir William Harcourt, favored a stiff policy toward the United States, holding that its toleration of Irish-American publications was "not compatible with the self-respect of a civilized state."[9]

The American minister to Britain, James Russell Lowell, had the thankless task of defending the irrepressible Irish-Americans before their erstwhile sovereign. In this assignment he seldom satisfied them, and to the end of his service Irish-American congressmen denounced him as "the best nickel-plated Englishman" they had ever seen and a typical example of that "school of snobbery," the Foreign Service. This judgment was shallow and unfair, for although Lowell was a scholar and poet and often talked like a college professor, he came to England highly sensitive about American honor and with a reputation for petulant criticism of the British. He became a close personal friend of Granville, with whom he often discussed diplomatic problems in private. Lowell came to recognize that the British were making an honest effort to solve the Irish question, although hampered by extremists, but he favored home rule, predicting that it would "make Conservatives every mother's son of them."[10]

In Washington two factors in particular bore upon Blaine as he prepared his first instructions to Lowell. One was his chronic Anglophobia, of which something has already been said. Another was his sensitivity to party politics. Many prominent congressmen of both parties were of Irish descent or represented districts with large Irish populations, such as New York and Chicago. British Minister Sir Edward Thornton once observed that these men breathed fire to impress their constituents but added: "If they would tell the truth, as they sometimes do to me, they hate the Irish no less than the majority of their countrymen."[11] In 1880

[9]Alfred George Gardiner, *The Life of Sir William Harcourt* (2 vols.; London, 1923), pp. 428-29. Knaplund and Clewes, "British Embassy Letters," p. 83. A. J. P. Taylor, *Germany's First Bid for Colonies* (New York, 1938), pp. 21-22.

[10]Ferris Greenslet, *James Russell Lowell* (Boston, 1905), p. 205. U.S., *Congressional Record*, 48th Cong., 2d Sess., XVI, 613. George W. Smalley, *Anglo-American Memories* (New York, 1910), pp. 181-82. Beckles Willson, *America's Ambassadors to England* (New York, 1929), p. 375. *New York Tribune*, April 12, 1885, p. 3.

[11]Sir Edward Thornton to Lord Granville, Washington, February 22, 1881; Lionel S. Sackville West to Granville, March 7, May 16, December 12, 1882, Knaplund and Clewes, "British Embassy Letters," pp. 116, 164-65, 169-70, 172-73.

the Democratic Irish voters of Brooklyn elected to the House William E. Robinson, a Fenian demagogue who made the most of every opportunity to bring up the Irish question in debate.

Even without Robinson's periodic reminders Blaine could hardly have forgotten that the Irish-Americans were the makeweight of New York state politics. In 1880, 17.4 per cent of the population of New York City and 13.7 per cent of the state population were Irish-born, and thousands more had at least one Irish parent. Over the country Garfield received 215 electoral votes against 155 for Hancock, but he won New York's thirty-five electoral votes by the slim margin of 21,033 popular votes out of 1,103,945 votes cast.[12] Clearly, if there were any way of luring the Irish-Americans of New York City away from their traditional Democracy, it would strengthen Republican hopes for 1884.

*   *   *

A week after Garfield's inauguration Lowell reported his first serious Irish-American case, that of Michael Boyton, who had applied for renewal of his American passport and had then been arrested in Ireland. Upon investigation Lowell learned that Boyton had falsified information on the original passport and was not entitled to American citizenship. When Blaine received these facts, he told the British minister confidentially "that he believed Boyton to be a pestiferous fellow and that he deserved what he had got."

To Lowell he wrote somewhat more formally that, had Boyton's citizenship been established, he would have done all that he could legally do for an American citizen. While he did not claim exemption for Americans merely on grounds of their foreign citizenship, he would not admit in advance that they were automatically subject to "a retroactive law, suspending at will the simplest operations of justice. . . . Immunity would not be asked, but prompt and certain justice, under the usual and unstrained operation of the law, would certainly be expected."[13] This was not

[12]Gibson, *Attitudes of New York Irish*, pp. 321-22. W. Dean Burnham, *Presidential Ballots, 1836-1892* (Baltimore, 1955), p. 249.

[13]James G. Blaine to James Russell Lowell, May 26, 1881, No. 166, U.S., *Foreign Relations, 1881*, pp. 530-31. See also Thornton to Granville, Washington, April 19, 1881, Knaplund and Clewes, "British Embassy Letters," pp. 130. The facts of the Boyton case are set forth in U.S., *Foreign Relations, 1881*, pp. 511-13, 517-23.

enough for the Irish-American press, which opened fire on Blaine and Lowell and painted a pathetic picture of the enfeebled prisoner.[14]

Less than a week after his statement on Boyton, Blaine applied the same principles to the case of Joseph B. Walsh: that the American government had no intention of protecting criminals but would insist on certain minimum guarantees of justice, prompt arraignment, and speedy trial before an impartial judge and jury. Having satisfied himself that Walsh was a bona fide American citizen, Lowell called his case to Granville's attention, whereupon the Secretary hinted that Blaine ought to look for "some exceptional injustice" in Walsh's treatment instead of merely attacking the coercion act. In the end Lowell obtained Walsh's release on grounds of poor health.[15]

From February, 1881, to February, 1882, twelve cases of imprisoned Irish-Americans presented themselves to Lowell. The accused claimed American citizenship. They maintained that they had been living peaceably, minding their own business, and had been falsely arrested; they begged or demanded that Lowell obtain their release. On August 3, in a letter to one of his consuls, which he reported to Blaine, he laid down the policy which he proposed to follow toward the prisoners:

> The only possible case in which it would be proper for me to intervene would be where an American citizen who is in Ireland attending exclusively to his private business, and taking no part whatever in public meetings or political discussions, should be arrested. In such a case it would be proper to appeal to the courtesy of the government upon the ground of mistake or misapprehension, and ask for the release of the prisoner. It does not appear, however, that these reasons exist in any of the cases that have so far been brought to my knowledge.

Blaine tacitly approved of this policy, and as late as 1883 he told the British minister privately that he regarded the Irish-

[14]Gibson, *Attitudes of New York Irish*, pp. 342-44.

[15]Blaine to Lowell, June 2, 1881, No. 172; Lowell to Blaine, London, June 4, July 15, Nos. 193, 218; W. T. Hoppin to Blaine, London, November 14, No. 220, U.S., *Foreign Relations, 1881*, pp. 532-34, 540-44, 552-54. Granville to Thornton, June 24, *ibid., 1882*, pp. 243-45.

American agitators as foreigners. The United States, he added, must not be made "the refuge for the scum of Europe."[16]

Unfortunately, during the summer and autumn of 1881 the Irish question continued to seethe, and when Congress convened in December, Democratic members from Irish districts began to take after Arthur and Blaine. On January 23 and 26, 1882, William E. Robinson delivered a long, rambling tirade in the House of Representatives. Recalling Congressional efforts against the European pork embargoes, he cried, "Oh, that we only had as much . . . protection given to a live American citizen as there [is] given to a dead Cincinnati hog!" At the end he proposed resolutions demanding the release of the prisoners, expressing the sympathy of the House with Parnell, and denouncing the "disgraceful salute of the tyrant [British] flag" at the recent celebration of the Yorktown Centennial.[17]

Robinson's eloquence stirred up a swarm of stinging critics. Newspapers printed appealing letters from the prisoners and their families, and the editors promptly sent clippings to the State Department. Administration Republicans in the House did their best to restrict action to a resolution of inquiry—a "humbug resolution," as Robinson called it. The talkative Irishman, tearing his way through a wilderness of parliamentary rules and exchanging insults with his personal enemies, called on the Attorney General for an opinion as to the legality of the British action in imprisoning American citizens without trial. By the uncomfortably close vote of 117-102 the House tabled his resolution, whereupon Robinson launched into another speech, demanding in the words of Henry Clay that we "let Great Britain hear the roar of American artillery." Then he subsided for several weeks, but on March 2 Abram S. Hewitt introduced the subject of the Irish-American prisoners again.[18] Clearly something would have to be done and quickly.

On March 3 and 4 Frelinghuysen cabled instructions to Lowell to "use all diligence" in the recent cases and ask the British

[16]West to Granville, Washington, April 3, 1883, Earl Granville Papers (Public Record Office, 30/29 154, London). Hereafter cited as Granville Papers. Lowell to Edward P. Brooks, London, August 3, 1881, U.S., *Foreign Relations, 1881*, p. 546.

[17]U.S., *Congressional Record*, 47th Cong., 1st Sess., XIII, 165, 241, 569-70, 654-57, 659-60; Appendix, 6-15.

[18]*Ibid.*, pp. 761-65, 1132-43, 1302, 1557-62.

government under its discretionary powers to order prompt trials for American suspects. After two weeks' delay Granville replied that he did not see how the British government could be expected to treat foreigners better than its own subjects by hastening their trials.[19] Meanwhile the fire continued to rise under the Arthur administration. On March 24 Mayor William R. Grace of New York and a group of Irish-American leaders issued a summons for a mass meeting on April 3 to recall the government to its duty and invoked an old law of 1868 requiring the President to resist the arrest of American citizens abroad. It seemed likely that at any moment the House of Representatives might formally demand the release of the suspects. As Senator George F. Hoar and Bancroft Davis reminded Lowell, such a demand might make it impossible for Gladstone to yield anything, and they urged him to secure a concession while there was still time. At Lowell's urging, Gladstone finally conceded that the men might be released if the American government would pledge that they would return to the United States or behave themselves, but President Arthur refused to authorize such a pledge.[20] Affairs had reached an impasse.

At this point the State Department called on outside aid. Apparently at Bancroft Davis' suggestion, Frelinghuysen authorized him to consult former Secretary of State Hamilton Fish. On April 1 the two friends sat down at Fish's home over a bottle of whiskey and scratched out on the back of a discarded envelope the text of a personal cablegram to Sir John Rose, a retired British diplomat whom Fish knew well from his years in the State Department. Fish urged Rose to persuade the Gladstone government to name a day of trial or discharge the prisoners quietly without conditions. "We cannot understand the hesitation," he concluded. "It strains the relations between the two governments, and looks like throw-

[19]Frelinghuysen to Lowell, March 3, 4, 1882 (telegrams); Lowell to Frelinghuysen, March 29 (telegram), U.S., *Foreign Relations, 1882*, pp. 200, 228. Lowell to Frelinghuysen, April 7, No. 338, U.S., Despatches, Britain, CXLIV.

[20]Gibson, *Attitudes of New York Irish*, pp. 348-49. Davis to Hoppin, March 28, 1882; George F. Hoar to Lowell, March 28, 29 (telegrams); Frelinghuysen to Lowell, April 1 (four telegrams), U.S., Instructions, Britain, XXVI, 359-61, 365-67. Lowell to Frelinghuysen, April 7, No. 338, U.S., Despatches, Britain, CXLIV.

ing away the substance to grasp after the shadow. Pray help to stop it."[21]

Where Lowell had failed, the private word from Fish succeeded. Most willing to help, Rose immediately spoke to Granville and W. E. Forster, the chief secretary for Ireland, and on the following day he set forth the case for compromise in a letter to Forster. Rose pointed out the basic friendliness of the United States and the likelihood of further embarrassing pressure from Congress under the law of 1868. The suspects, he argued, "are *voluntary Martyrs;* and if in playing that role they can succeed in creating trouble betn. the two Govts. the end of their martyrdom will be attained." On the other hand, if Britain released them now and they returned to Ireland later, it would be difficult to arouse sympathy in the United States for them a second time. Even if Lowell had given the required pledge, he added, it probably could not have been enforced under American law.[22]

The next weeks proved the wisdom of Rose's advice. Frelinghuysen had already offered confidentially to advance $200 for each man released, to enable him to return to America. On April 2 the Gladstone government accepted the tacit agreement, and by the following day all but three suspects had been released. On April 4 Arthur sent to the Senate a report from Frelinghuysen on all Irish-American cases to date, emphasizing the releases and the doubtful claims of citizenship. Two days later Granville summed up the new British position in a dispatch to the British minister at Washington. He did not entirely understand the American representations, he said, since the United States had imprisoned British suspects in exactly the same manner during the Civil War. Her Majesty's Government would not admit the right of Irish-Americans to special treatment but would consider releasing any who would promise to leave the United Kingdom at once.[23]

[21]J. C. Bancroft Davis to Hamilton Fish, Washington [April 18 or 19, 1882], Fish Papers, CXXXV. Davis to Hoppin, April 1 (telegram), U.S., Instructions, Britain, XXVI, 364-65. This contains the message from Fish to Rose, the original of which is in the Fish Papers. Davis also wrote a similar letter to H. C. Rothery, recently an official of the British legation in Washington. Granville Papers.

[22]Sir John Rose to Fish, London, April 4, 1882; Rose to W. E. Forster, April 2 (copy), Fish Papers, CXXXV.

[23]Lowell to Frelinghuysen, April 2, 3, 1882 (telegrams), U.S., *Foreign Relations, 1882,* p. 229. U.S., Congress, Senate, 47th Cong., 1st Sess., 1882, Senate Executive

Naturally it was impossible to turn off the Irish-Americans at once like a tap. Thousands attended the scheduled mass meeting in Cooper Union on April 3, to hear Mayor Grace and Democratic congressmen denounce Lowell's "sickening sycophancy to English influence." Arthur's announcement on the following day deflated the Democrats for a while, but ten days later Senator Daniel W. Voorhees returned to the battle with a fiery attack on Lowell's "stupid evasion of duty," and in the House Robinson delivered another long speech of protest. Through May and June a little group of Democrats vainly put forth other proposals to force the President into an ultimatum or at least to secure the recall of Lowell, "nominally our minister to Great Britain but really doing police duty . . . under Lord Granville."[24] These, however, were the last rumblings of a retreating storm.

Since a few suspects remained in prison, and since the British police occasionally arrested new Irish-American agitators, the two governments continued to exchange notes on the subject for months, but without pressure or heat. On April 25, for example, Frelinghuysen admitted that when a naturalized American returned to his former homeland to live and hold office, he must expect to obey the laws of that country just as its citizens must do, but he continued to insist on prompt arraignment and trial. In this dispatch Frelinghuysen fairly epitomized the views of the moderate American press.[25]

A year and a half after the height of the crisis over the Irish-American suspects occurred the last and least creditable of the efforts by the United States government to protect its citizens

Doc. 155, Part 2, *passim. New York Tribune*, April 6, p. 1. Granville to West, April 6, Great Britain, *Sessional Papers* (Commons), LXXX (1882), "Correspondence Respecting the Imprisonment in Ireland under the 'Protection of Person and Property (Ireland) Act, 1881,' of Naturalized Citizens of the United States," pp. 19-20. See also Fish to Rose, April 18, Letterbooks, Fish Papers.

[24]U.S., *Congressional Record*, 57th Cong., 1st Sess., XIII, 2512, 2596, 2886-91, 3183-84, 3223, 3275-97, 3946, 5449-51, 6146; Appendix, 161. Gibson, *Attitudes of New York Irish*, pp. 349-52. *New York Tribune*, April 4, 1882, pp. 1-2.

[25]Lowell to Frelinghuysen, London, April 20, 1882 (telegram), U.S., Despatches, Britain, CXLIV. Lowell to Frelinghuysen, July 14, No. 398; Frelinghuysen to Lowell, April 25, September 22, Nos. 366, 463, U.S., *Foreign Relations, 1882*, 230-34, 285, 293-95. The case which attracted the widest attention was the brief imprisonment of Henry George, traveling as a journalist in Ireland. Frelinghuysen to Lowell, October 3, No. 466, *ibid.*, pp. 296-300.

in Ireland. This concerned the O'Donnell murder case. On May 6, 1882, shortly after Rose's intervention had broken the Anglo-American impasse, a band of terrorists in Dublin knifed two British officials as they walked in Phoenix Park. One of the members of the murdering gang, James Carey, betrayed the others in return for his own freedom. After the trial of his fellows the government hurried Carey on board a ship for South Africa, but another passenger, Patrick O'Donnell, an Irish-American, recognized him and killed him during the voyage. There was no doubt of O'Donnell's guilt, but since the whole Irish world had detested Carey as an informer, his assassin became a hero over night.

Naturally, Irish-American leaders had to do what they could for him. A group of Chicago Irish and their friends, led by Senator John A. Logan, Representative John F. Finerty, and others, collected funds to send two lawyers to O'Donnell's trial. Since foreign aid was not a customary practice in British courts, Mayor Carter Harrison of Chicago asked Frelinghuysen to intervene. After a long correspondence to weigh O'Donnell's dubious claim to American citizenship, the Secretary instructed Lowell to assure the British government of the "high position" of the two lawyers. When the court sentenced O'Donnell to hang, the House of Representatives adopted an officious resolution of Abram S. Hewitt, requesting a stay of execution in order to determine that there had been no error in the trial, and a delegation of congressmen asked Arthur to intervene. Lowell transmitted the request without comment, and O'Donnell was duly hanged.[26]

The *New York Tribune*, which had often before criticized Irish-American excesses, now called attention to the American humiliation and put a period to the case:

> Perhaps one of these days American Congressmen and other officials will awake to the sense that this is an American Government, and that there is a vote still stronger than the Irish vote, in which it becomes them to take a little interest. The Irish influence in questions of an international character is directly hostile to the United States, and it is one of the most

[26]Gibson, *Attitudes of New York Irish*, pp. 360-62. Lowell to Frelinghuysen, November 8, 1883, No. 655, U.S., Despatches, Britain, CXLVIII. Frelinghuysen to Lowell, November 19, December 11, No. 705; Lowell to Frelinghuysen, December 15 (telegram), U.S., *Foreign Relations, 1883*, pp. 475-76, 479.

serious dangers against which we have to provide. . . . If
Irishmen can establish their independence, all right; let them
do it; but they shall not use this Republic as a convenience.
. . . The plain truth is that, where the real or supposed interests of Ireland are concerned, a large and noisy faction of the
naturalized Irish in the United States are disloyal if not treacherous to the adopted country to which they have sworn fi-
delity; but politicians and newspapers are afraid to say so.[27]

*   *   *

Long before the execution of O'Donnell, the problem of the
Irish-American prisoners had been largely supplanted by another,
equally serious. In this second problem Britain was the accuser,
the United States the accused. Not content with gifts to charity
and subscriptions to the Land League, Rossa, Ford, and other
Irish-American publicists had opened "Skirmishing Funds" and
advertised openly that these were intended to buy dynamite and
otherwise subsidize terrorism in England. Could the British legally
and reasonably expect the American government to halt these
subscription campaigns and imprison the editors without explicit
proof of their connection with acts of violence? Was mere incitement enough? At the beginning of 1881 many British seemed
inclined to make generous allowances for Irish-American blather-
ing, but some, such as Sir William Harcourt, were already becoming
impatient, for, as he put it, "the Irish subscriptions are coppers,
but the gold and silver come from Fenianism in America."[28]

During the spring the British government began to take more
notice of Irish-American newspapers, which were advocating
arson in all major British cities, calling for someone to blow up
the Prince of Wales and Gladstone, and claiming responsibility
for explosions and fires which had already taken place. Harcourt
and Granville privately remonstrated with Lowell and suggested
that in a reverse situation the United States would surely have
protested.[29]

[27]*New York Tribune*, December 18, 1883, p. 4. See also *ibid.*, December 10, p. 4.
[28]Gardiner, *Life of Harcourt*, I, 427.
[29]Gibson, *Attitudes of New York Irish*, p. 365. *Times*, April 11, 1881, p. 6.
Thornton to Granville, Washington, January 25, 1881, Knaplund and Clewes,
"British Embassy Letters," p. 114. Gardiner, *Life of Harcourt*, I, 428-29. Lowell
to Blaine, June 25, 1881, Nos. 209, 210, U.S., Despatches, Britain, CXLII. Granville
to Thornton, June 24, Great Britain, *Sessional Papers* (Commons), LXXX (1882),

At the same time, acting without instructions, British Minister Sir Edward Thornton talked to Blaine, who assured him that Americans despised the Fenian press. Blaine promised that the United States government would act energetically if it discovered armed expeditions being prepared or schemes to destroy British life and property. This reply did not satisfy Thornton, but he admitted that he could not single out specific plotters or places where explosives were actually being manufactured. During 1881 and 1882 the British legation hired the famous detective, Allen Pinkerton, and the British consuls in the principal American cities engaged in much espionage work among Irish-Americans, but in vain. One of the consuls uncovered so many false clues that the British under-secretary for foreign affairs finally pronounced him "Princeps Asinorum," and after two years of effort Thornton's successor, Lionel S. Sackville West, had to confess utter failure.[30]

Meanwhile, Irish-American terrorism was gaining momentum in Britain. On June 10, 1881, two Fenians were caught trying to blow up the town hall in Liverpool. About three weeks later British police, warned anonymously, searched the steamer "Bavarian" on her arrival from Boston and found six detonating machines, composed of clockwork to fire cartridges after a six-hour interval. The British consul at Boston cooperated with American authorities, but a search yielded no further discoveries. Later in the month the British chargé in Washington called Blaine's attention to a torpedo boat which Fenians were building in New York to send out against British shipping and asked the United States to prevent its departure. Blaine promised wholehearted cooperation, and the torpedo boat stayed in harbor, carefully watched by British-paid detectives.[31]

During these early months of suspicions and alarms the British

"Correspondence Respecting the Publication in the United States of Incitements to Outrages in England," pp. 1-2.

[30] Thornton to Granville, June 27, 1881, *ibid.*, pp. 2-3. Harcourt to Lord Tenterden, July 11, 1881; Tenterden to H. C. Jervoise, September 2; West to Granville, December 22, 1882, No. 449, Great Britain, Foreign Office, Series 5, Vols. 1776-1778, 1820. Hereafter cited as F. O. 5/1776, etc. D'Arcy, *Fenian Movement*, pp. 401-6.

[31] *Times*, August 3, 1881, p. 10. Lowell to Blaine, July 30 (telegram), U.S., Despatches, Britain, CXLII. Victor Drummond to Blaine, North Hampton, New Hampshire, July 28, Knaplund and Clewes, "British Embassy Letters," pp. 144-46. See also *New York Herald*, April 18, 1883, p. 11.

and American press took a generally cautious, moderate attitude. Some London newspapers complained of American inaction, but the *Daily Telegraph* reminded its readers of the American tradition of a free press. Even after the discovery of the "infernal machines" on the "Bavarian" the *Pall Mall Gazette* doubted that the arrest of the offensive editors would stop the real plotters—"cool, ingenious, calculating, unscrupulous men, who will certainly not let O'Donovan Rossa into their secrets."[32] In New York the *Tribune* and the *Herald* denounced the cold-blooded, cowardly terrorism of the Fenians and called on Congress to tighten the "inexcusably lax" regulations for the shipment of explosives, but the *Nation* pointed out that there was not as yet enough evidence to convict anyone of dynamite plotting. Surely Britain could not expect the United States to abolish trial by jury![33]

It is doubtful that the Irish-American movement ever recovered all the prestige which it lost during the summer of 1881 as a result of the first dynamite discoveries. Over a hundred delegates attended an Irish-American convention in Chicago at the beginning of August, but the planned program was interrupted by ill-tempered questions about misuse of the Skirmishing Funds, and the convention broke up in dissension. The Phoenix Park murders of the following spring produced a wave of horror in the United States, and most Irish-Americans feared that the crime would nullify all the effects of land agitation. The New York State Legislature passed a unanimous resolution of censure, and United States marshals helped British consular officials to search ships arriving at New York from Ireland. (They found no suspects.) In Britain police continued to unearth fragmentary evidence of dynamite plots, and despite American cooperation London newspapers scolded the United States at great length for its unwillingness to arrest agitators.[34]

[32]See British newspaper clippings enclosed with Lowell to Blaine, June 21, 1881, No. 207, U.S., Despatches, Britain, CXLII. *Saturday Review*, LII (July 2), 3-4. *Pall Mall Gazette*, July 27, as quoted in *New York Herald*, July 28, pp. 4-5.

[33]*New York Tribune*, August 10, 1881, p. 4. *New York Herald*, August 5, p. 4; October 15, p. 6. *Times*, July 28, p. 5; August 11, p. 3. *Nation*, XXXII (April 17), 331.

[34]Gibson, *Attitudes of New York Irish*, pp. 357-60. Bagenal, *American Irish*, pp. 233-39. O'Brien, *Parnell and his Party*, pp. 134-35. *Times*, August 9, 1881, p. 5;

For the rest of the year the terrorism subsided, but on the evening of March 15, 1883, an explosion in Westminster shook the walls of the House of Commons and momentarily interrupted the members present without injuring anyone. This time, when the conspirators were captured and brought to trial, one of them testified that he belonged to the Emerald Club, a secret society in New York, and that a Dr. Thomas Gallagher of Brooklyn had sent him to England, where he was assigned to carry explosives from Birmingham to London. The American press reaction to these developments ranged from condemnation to injured innocence. Some denied that Americans were involved and called the explosion "a huge fraud, concocted by the worst elements of the London police," but the *New York Tribune* soon admitted that the United States must assume some responsibility: "These plots were framed in New York; the money was raised here; the agents . . . were not Irish refugees, but Americans." The *Nation* also unhappily admitted partial responsibility but predicted that legislation against such conspiracies would only result in an "uproarious and irrelevant" trial, an acquittal, or a hung jury, and "the shame and regret of every rational and sober-minded person on either side of the water." Britain must protect herself, on her own terms. Many other newspapers, however, agreed with the *Tribune* that the government ought to act.[35]

* * *

For many months British diplomats had been privately saying the same thing to the State Department. In May, 1882, Frelinghuysen admitted to Minister West "that there was no doubt substantial wrong," but several weeks later, after further pressure, he asked despairingly what West wanted him to do, knowing that the American government had no statute covering the case. Thinking this plea an evasion, West sought more objective advice from an eminent lawyer, Calderon Carlisle, who told him that authors

August 11, p. 5; May 9, 1882, p. 5; May 15, p. 7; May 18, p. 5; May 24, p. 9; July 5, p. 5; July 21, p. 5; July 24, p. 9.

[35]*Ibid.*, March 16, 1883, p. 5; March 31, p. 5; April 20, p. 9. Gibson, *Attitudes of New York Irish*, pp. 401-2. *New York Herald*, April 6, 1883, p. 6; April 20, p. 6. *National Republican* (Washington), March 17, p. 1; April 21, p. 4. *New York Tribune*, March 17, p. 1; April 9, p. 4; April 20, p. 4. *Nation*, XXXVI (April 26), 356. Other newspapers quoted in *Times*, April 11, p. 7.

of public incitement against a friendly Power were liable to suit in state courts, but that the federal government had no clear-cut jurisdiction over the matter except in the District of Columbia.[36]

After the explosions of March, 1883, West decided that he had had enough of unofficial, oral sparring with Frelinghuysen. Acting without instructions, he sent a formal note to the Secretary protesting against Irish-American newspaper articles as "open incentives to murder, arson, and outrage, coming from the shores of a friendly Power." With considerable reluctance and fumbling Frelinghuysen replied that although the President was very anxious to preserve Anglo-American friendship, neither the American government nor the American people were responsible for the outrages, and that the nation had no laws to forbid the expression of unfriendly sentiments. Since it was obvious that the agitators were working for Anglo-American dissension, the President hoped that Britain would not gratify them by asking for action against them which it must know that the American government could not undertake.[37]

In a later conversation with West, Frelinghuysen admitted that extreme editorials might call for action but insisted that news articles, even subscription lists, must have wider latitude. Granville, now entering the discussion, objected to this distinction and reminded Frelinghuysen of Blaine's promise in 1881 that the American government would take energetic measures against armed expeditions or plots to destroy British life and property. After six months Frelinghuysen replied that no evidence yet presented would justify action. He added that the British government would refuse to act on such flimsy evidence as the newspaper clippings which West had collected; why should Granville expect the United States to do more? The American government and people detested

[36]West to Granville, May 12, July 1, 1882; April 15, 1883, Nos. 210, 271, 118; Calderon Carlisle to West, Washington, September 14, December 9, 1882, Great Britain, F. O., 5/1863.

[37]West to Frelinghuysen, March 17, April 7, 1883, U.S., Notes from Foreign Legations, Britain, CIX. Frelinghuysen to West, April 14, *ibid.*, Notes to Foreign Legations, Britain, XIX, 284-90. Lowell to Frelinghuysen, London, May 1, No. 539, U.S., Despatches, Britain, CXLVI. According to Bancroft Davis, Frelinghuysen originally intended to send a much milder reply but unwillingly combined his draft with a stronger one by Davis. Davis to Fish, Washington, April 20, Fish Papers, CXXXIX.

the Irish-American press, but their greatest concern was to avoid arousing Anglophobia among the peaceable majority of Irish-Americans.[38] In the rest of his correspondence on the subject Frelinghuysen remained close to this position, despite Granville's efforts to impress him with evidence.

Such evidence was not long in appearing. On February 25, 1884, a bomb concealed in a portmanteau exploded in Victoria Station, doing serious damage, and London police found more bombs in other railroad stations, ready to explode. These bombs consisted of American cloth bags, containing American clockwork and dynamite, and the *Times* pronounced the plot "clearly of Irish-American origin. . . . There is really no secret in the matter, except as to details." The British press lashed out against the American government more furiously than ever, and Lowell received anonymous threats. Harcourt minced no words in his account to Parliament: "It would be no hard task for the American government to put an end to the whole thing. . . . It is time indeed that a strongly worded remonstrance should be addressed to the Government of a country which connives at all this."[39]

While not carrying out Harcourt's full prescription, Granville stiffened his language, insisting that a provocative newspaper article constituted incitement whether signed or anonymous, whether printed as news or on the editorial page. He cited new examples and declared that this evidence surely justified action by the United States. Upon receiving news of the February explosions, Arthur issued a special order to federal marshals, directing them to use special vigilance in preventing the transportation of explosives. However, as the *Nation* had already pointed out, such measures would probably accomplish little, for one man in a hall bedroom could hatch a plot to blow up the whole royal family and sail undetected for England with a can of nitroglycerine in his pocket. Other American newspapers embroidered the theme

[38]Frelinghuysen to Lowell, December 4, 1883; January 17, 1884, No. 720 (telegram), U.S., Instructions, Britain, XXVII, 69–82, 167. See also Granville to West, May 12, 1883, No. 102, printed copy in U.S., Notes from Foreign Legations, Britain, CIX.

[39]Gibson, *Attitudes of New York Irish,* p. 367. *Times,* February 29, 1884, p. 10; April 12, pp. 9, 11; April 14, p. 9. *Saturday Review,* LVII (March 8), 303–4. *New York Herald,* March 2, p. 21. Other explosions occurred on May 30.

that preventive legislation would be impossible to enforce, and showed mounting irritation at "these continuous curtain lectures from London." The *New York Tribune* added that the American government was not "called upon to [do] detective work for either England or Europe, nor to institute impracticable trials for secret conspiracies, nor to augment the evil by mischievous press trials and interference with public meetings."[40]

As in the case of the Irish-American prisoners, Britain and the United States had worked themselves into an impasse. This time, however, there was no question of turning to Hamilton Fish and Sir John Rose for extrication, since the American presidential campaign was about to begin, and no one dared to jostle the Irish voters. During the summer of 1884, Lowell, Alvey A. Adee (then traveling in England for his health), and the British government carried on confidential discussions about revising the provisions for extradition of criminals laid down in the Webster-Ashburton Treaty of 1842. The specification of incitement as an extraditable crime would have tightened the overly loose provisions of the treaty. Adee, Lowell, and the British agreed upon a new draft, but for reasons of domestic politics the Gladstone government did not wish to press Parliament for the necessary legislation at the moment, so the matter was postponed.[41]

As will be seen, in the election campaign James G. Blaine reversed the reasonable stand which he had taken on the Irish-American question during 1881, and the Republicans launched an emotional appeal for the Irish vote. After such a campaign it was practically impossible for Frelinghuysen to admit further American responsibilities in the conspiracy question.[42] Although the administration could not change its attitude, however, the

[40]*New York Tribune*, March 14, 1884, p. 4; April 13, p. 6. *Nation*, XXXVIII (March 6), 202-3. *New York Herald*, March 3, p. 4. Gibson, *Attitudes of New York Irish*, pp. 367-68. See also Granville to West, March 13, 1884, printed copy in U.S., Notes from Foreign Legations, Britain, CX.

[41]Frelinghuysen to Lowell, July 15, 1884, No. 915; September 15 (telegram), U.S., Instructions, Britain, XXVII, 251-63, 308-9. Lowell to Frelinghuysen, July 30, November 11, December 3, Nos. 820, 894, 911, U.S., Despatches, Britain, CL. The most important Irish-American case illustrating loopholes in the extradition provisions was that of Patrick J. Sheridan. See *Times*, March 1, 1883, p. 5; *Nation*, XXXVI (March 8), 200-201, and *New York Tribune*, May 8, p. 4.

[42]Frelinghuysen to Lowell, November 24, 1884, No. 1029, U.S., Instructions, Britain, XXVII, 349-64.

removal of campaign pressures affected American public opinion. On the afternoon of January 24, 1885, two dynamite bombs exploded in Westminster and one in the Tower of London. Since the buildings were crowded with visitors at the time, and since the blast partly wrecked the House of Commons, public opinion in both Britain and the United States was more outraged than on any previous occasion, and American newspapers denounced the brutality of the dynamiters in strong language.[43]

At last Congress took action. Senator Edmunds introduced a bill enforcing strict punishments against dynamite criminals, Senator Bayard proposed a resolution of regret and sympathy at the disaster in London, and the House called for information on American involvement. Leading Irish-Americans in Washington held a public meeting to protest against the Edmunds bill, but many of the Irish bloc in Congress supported it—out of hatred of crime, they explained.[44] However, Granville made no effort to repeat his protests to an American administration which would soon leave office, and the quarrel was not resumed by the Cleveland administration.

The two-headed problem of protecting and restraining Irish-American agitators might have seriously embroiled Britain and the United States if the British government had insisted on holding the Irish-American suspects indefinitely without trial or had demanded that the American government close down the Irish-American newspapers. Neither Blaine nor Frelinghuysen could take major credit for bringing about the British concessions, for Blaine left office before the British government made clear that the trials would be long delayed, and when Congressional opinion turned ugly during the first months of 1882, it was not Frelinghuysen but Fish and Rose who persuaded the Gladstone government to back down. As for the Irish-American conspiracies in the United States, Frelinghuysen's insistence on lack of evidence was probably sound, and the jurisdiction of the federal government was by no means certain. However, he weakened his case with a transparent concern for what peaceable Irish-Americans

[43]*Times*, January 26, 1885, pp. 10-11; January 27, p. 5; January 29, p. 5; February 12, p. 3. *New York Tribune*, January 26, p. 4.
[44]*Washington Post*, January 31, 1885, p. 1. The Edmunds bill died in committee.

would think, and Blaine let the cat entirely out of the bag during the campaign of 1884.

No matter what Blaine and Frelinghuysen might tell Britain, the administrations of Garfield and Arthur would not or could not secure any sort of effective action from Congress. Had Arthur launched an earlier or stronger campaign for new extradition laws, it is unlikely that the Irish-oriented representatives in the House would have permitted much intelligent discussion of incitement or conspiracy. Considering the amount of irresponsible demagoguery which emanated from Congress, one ought not to be surprised that Arthur's State Department handled the Irish-American question with narrow and literal-minded caution.

Climax and Collapse

CHAPTER 14

The Campaign of 1884

WHEN 1884 began, the Arthur administration had been in office more than two years. After a slow start in foreign affairs it seemed to be moving cautiously toward an expansionist policy in several parts of the world. The Mexican reciprocity treaty signified its willingness to barter low tariffs for increased American economic influence to the south, and it was seriously considering active intervention in the isthmian canal question. Frelinghuysen's futile argument with Britain over the Clayton-Bulwer Treaty and his resistance to British pressure for prosecution of the Irish-American newspaper editors reassured the country that he was no less zealous than Blaine in defending American rights against the national rival. The activities of Young in China betokened an awakening concern for the Far East, and there was already evidence that the administration felt a similar interest in central Africa. By placing orders for four warships it reinforced this expansionism with the pledge of a new navy.

Now, however, Arthur had to submit the future of his foreign policy to the judgment of American politicians and the people. Although an administration can seldom obtain a clear referendum on any given issue in an American election, it would have been more absurd than usual to hope for such a referendum on foreign policy in 1884. Most of the electorate viewed foreign affairs with apathy anyway, and a variety of emotional, partisan views on domestic issues and personalities were bursting for expression. Neither Arthur nor anyone else could keep them under control. Consequently, the campaign of 1884 became a classic demonstration of American politics at its worst.

*　　*　　*

Arthur eagerly desired renomination, if only as recognition that he had been a better president than anyone had expected in 1881.

Most reasonable persons admitted this—faint praise, indeed—for he had shaken himself free from Conkling, had prosecuted the Star Route postal frauds (inherited from the Hayes administration) with some vigor, and had allowed Congress to lay the foundations of a civil service system. But careful as he was to avoid widening the serious splits in the Republican party, he suffered the common fate of compromisers and displeased almost everyone. Spoilsmen criticized him for not opposing civil service; reformers criticized him for appointing spoilsmen. In 1882 he tried to regain control of the New York state machine by securing the election of his secretary of the Treasury, Charles J. Folger, as governor, but his maneuverings only increased Republican dissension. When the Democratic candidate, Grover Cleveland, defeated Folger, professional politicians began to whisper ominously that the President could not even carry his home state.[1]

An important factor working against Arthur was the onset of a new depression, much milder than that of 1873 but quite enough to erode public confidence. During the spring the money market became increasingly tight. In the iron-and-steel industry prices of all types and grades of products continued the precipitous decline which had begun in 1882; at the end of April it was estimated that 50 out of 140 furnaces in eastern Pennsylvania had been "blown out." Since 1881, it was reported, stocks on the New York exchange had declined on the average by over one-third, occasioning paper losses of well over one billion dollars. Between 1880 and 1884 the rate of business failures increased from 63 per thousand concerns to 121 per thousand, while in some areas as many as one-third of the working population lost their jobs.

In the late spring conditions became even worse, for within one week four major financial frauds rocked the exchanges to their foundations. Ferdinand Ward, one of former President Grant's business associates, embezzled the funds of their brokerage firm,

[1]See, for example, Walter Q. Gresham to John W. Foster, Washington, February 27, 1884, John W. Foster Papers. Gresham to David Davis, February 11, March 9, David Davis Papers (Chicago Historical Society). Gresham was Arthur's postmaster general and might have been a reform candidate himself but for his loyalty to the President. On Arthur's campaign for renomination see George F. Howe, *Chester A. Arthur, a Quarter-Century of Machine Politics* (New York, 1934), chap. xxiii.

ruining Grant and many who had trusted in him and, as Bancroft Davis remarked, forcing his friends "to set up that he is a fool to parry the charge that he is a knave." John C. Eno, President of the Second National Bank of New York, fled to Canada with $3,185,000 of the bank's securities. Two other large New York firms closed their doors as a result of the dishonesty or outrageously bad judgment of their presidents, and these failures weakened other banks. Stock quotations fell 20 per cent further, and during the summer enormous grain crops in both America and Europe forced the price of wheat to the lowest level ever recorded.[2]

In spite of these depressing omens, a considerable section of the business class supported Arthur's renomination, especially those identified with foreign trade. In May a group of them held a mass meeting at Cooper Union in his support, endorsing among other things his judicious foreign policy, "in keeping with the teachings of Washington," and his general opposition to internal revenue taxes. Others praised his middle-of-the-road attitude toward tariffs, as shown by the Tariff Commission of 1882. The *New York Herald* replied sarcastically that no one knew where he stood on this question: "It is not often that a party in difficulties on . . . a 'burning question' has a candidate ready to its hand who is . . . as good on one side as on the other."[3] As early as December, 1883, Carl Schurz and a number of Republican Independents, including many low-tariff men, organized a movement to find a fit man for the presidency. They made it clear that they would not be satisfied with the incumbent.

From the beginning, Arthur's chief rival for the nomination was his former secretary of state, James G. Blaine. Although the two kept up some appearance of personal friendship in public,

[2]*New York Tribune*, February 19, 1883, p. 4; March 12, p. 4; April 22, p. 2; May 26, p. 5; August 10, p. 4; December 17, p. 1; December 30, p. 6; January 4, 1884, p. 4. American Iron and Steel Association, *Report, 1883*, pp. 10-13 *et passim; 1884*, pp. 9-11 *et passim*. Thomas, *Return of the Democratic Party*, pp. 123, 137. Noyes, *Forty Years of American Finance*, pp. 96-102. O. C. Lightner, *The History of Business Depressions* (New York [1922]), pp. 94-101, 175-80. U.S., *Historical Statistics*, p. 570. *New York Herald*, May 10, 1884. *Nation*, XXXVIII (May 15), 420. J. C. Bancroft Davis to Hamilton Fish, Washington, June 8, Fish Papers, CXLIV.

[3]*New York Herald*, February 28, 1884, p. 6. See also *New York Tribune*, May 12, p. 4; May 21, pp. 1, 3, 5, 7. James M. Swank to Justin S. Morrill, Philadelphia, June 3, Morrill Papers.

Blaine had been greatly displeased when Frelinghuysen abruptly
reversed his South American policies, and the Chile-Peruvian investigation by the House of Representatives did nothing to soothe
his feelings. Blaine early chose the tariff as a leading issue in
the campaign, and in the midst of the Congressional debates on
the "mongrel" bill of 1883, he called on Whitelaw Reid for one
of his "old-fashioned bugle-blasts in the Tribune for the protection
interest," lest the Republicans lose the initiative. Later in the
year he proposed to solve the problem of reducing the Treasury
surplus without lowering the tariff by distributing the receipts
from liquor taxes to the needy state governments. The *Tribune*
loyally praised this ingenious plan, the "mongrel" tariff, and
shipping bounties, while industrial lobbyists cranked out protectionist pamphlets, and his other supporters "waved the bloody
shirt" and kept up a steady attack on Arthur.[4]

The only chance for Blaine's numerous but scattered opponents
to defeat him lay in uniting behind some vigorous leader, but
the reformers could not stomach Arthur, who controlled the
official machinery, and Arthur was his usual lethargic self. The
veteran Illinois politician, David Davis, called the President's campaign managers "idiotic"; the nominating speech in his honor
was tedious; and although Arthur, Senator George F. Edmunds,
and Senator John Sherman controlled an easy majority of votes
on the first ballot, they could never get together. In the end,
remarked a spectator, "Blaine's regular troops beat the raw militia
in larger numbers." Another declared that when he looked at
the convention he "could think of nothing but a lassoed steer."[5]

*   *   *

Blaine might have lassoed the convention, but many angry,
disillusioned delegates left Chicago, determined to bolt the party

[4]Muzzey, *Blaine*, pp. 273-77. Oberholtzer, *History of the United States*, IV,
159-71. James G. Blaine to Whitelaw Reid, Bar Harbor, February 19, 1883, Reid
Papers, Box CIV. Varying comments on Blaine's distribution scheme appear in
New York Tribune, November 29, 1883, and *Nation*, XXXVII (December 6),
462-63.

[5]Leonard Swett to David Davis, Chicago, June 10, 1884; Davis to [Gresham],
Bloomington, Illinois, June 25; J. E. H. [Harvey] to Davis, Washington, July 3,
David Davis Papers. However, Harrison C. Thomas concludes that Blaine's choice
represented the real will of the convention. Thomas, *Return of the Democratic
Party*, pp. 159-67. See also Muzzey, *Blaine*, pp. 277-86.

or at least stay home for the rest of the year. "If the democrats don't nominate Jeff Davis or old Tilden [New York] is sure to go against Blaine," declared Benjamin H. Bristow, adding with disgust: "Gould & all the scamps who have given Wall street a bad name are for him." When the Democrats nominated the reform governor of New York, Grover Cleveland, a friend of David Davis predicted their sure victory: "The Republican party is rotten to the core as an organization, and people want a change. . . . Corruption and rascality run all through the public service." This sort of feeling was strongest among young reformers such as Theodore Roosevelt, who regarded Blaine as "by far the most objectionable" candidate in the running but reluctantly kept his party membership, and respectable conservatives and moderates such as Hamilton Fish, who sighed to a friend: "Blaine is charming and most attractive *as a companion*, but—I wish that some one else had been nominated."[6]

The campaign of 1884 has always held an irresistible fascination for historians, and they have dealt in great detail with its highlights: the "Mugwumps," the "tattooed man," Cleveland's bastard, and all the rest.[7] This study will confine itself to the issues and arguments having some bearing on foreign relations. Since Cleveland had had no previous contact with international affairs, all discussions in this field tended to revolve around Blaine. His many campaign biographies usually devoted about one chapter out of fifteen or twenty to the hero's deeds of valor in the State Department, and occasionally they added another chapter or two on such issues as Chinese immigration, shipping, and the Irish question, stringing together excerpts from Blaine's speeches and diplomatic dispatches. The *New York Tribune* and other pro-Blaine organs also gave attention to foreign policy. For its part, the opposition published several long and bitterly critical pamphlets excoriating Blaine's actions of 1881 in Latin America and the

[6]Hamilton Fish to William M. Evarts, July 10, 1884, Fish Letterbooks. See also B. H. Bristow to Davis, New York, June 11, and Harvey to Davis, Washington, July 1, Davis Papers. Theodore Roosevelt to Anna Roosevelt, St. Paul, Minnesota, June 8, E. E. Morison *et al.* (eds.), *The Letters of Theodore Roosevelt* (8 vols.; Cambridge, Massachusetts, 1951-1954), I, 70.

[7]For detailed accounts see Muzzey, *Blaine*, chap. xii; Oberholtzer, *History of the United States*, IV, 182-212; and Allan Nevins, *Grover Cleveland, a Study in Courage* (New York, 1933), chap. xi.

Irish question, and a group of normally Republican newspapers joined the Democratic press in answering the *Tribune* blow for blow.

At the beginning of the campaign Blaine laid greater stress on the tariff than on any other issue in foreign affairs. He devoted half of his letter of acceptance to proving that America owed most of her prosperity since the Civil War to Republican protectionism. He evidently hoped that concentration on this question would divert attention from the perennial charges of corruption, for he wrote to Whitelaw Reid in July: "I would advise that you keep a steady flow in editorial columns on Tariff—protection—*wages*—especially *wages*. The opposition dread this. They want to keep up a howl about Mulligan & confine the discussion to that kind of *hog-wash*. . . . The Tariff treated as you are treating [it] with short sharp illustrations quite steadily will drive them mad."[8]

As usual, Reid followed instructions, and a survey of the *Tribune's* editorial columns during the campaign gives the full range of Blaine's arguments on the tariff. High tariffs were reviving German industry and raising the condition of the German laboring classes, while "the misery, squalor and absolute starvation that stare one in the face on a visit to the garrets and cellars of London is almost beyond belief." Holland, also burdened with free trade, was " a country bristling with the monuments of dead manufactures." True, it was a pity that American shipping had languished under the protectionist regime, but the growth of manufactures more than compensated for the loss. The *Tribune* denounced Cleveland as a free trader in disguise—as witness his long list of free trade supporters—and declared that the Democrats were too cowardly to come out in the open and oppose protection. Later in the campaign, as economic conditions continued to deteriorate, it blamed the depression on the growth of free trade influence following the Democratic victory in 1882.[9]

While defending high tariffs, Blaine and his supporters vigorously outlined a policy of economic expansion in Latin America

[8]Blaine to Reid, Bar Harbor, Maine, July 27, 1884, Reid Papers, Box CIV. Blaine's letter of acceptance appears in his *Political Discussions*, pp. 420-34.

[9]*New York Tribune*, September 2, 1884, p. 4; September 18, p. 2; October 1, p. 5; October 3, p. 4; October 29, p. 7.

and even spoke vaguely of a hemispheric *Zollverein* without explaining exactly how it could be reconciled with protection. The *Tribune* declared that the development of trade required the United States to intervene in Latin America and put an end to destructive wars:

> Spanish America must, therefore, be pacified and taught financial science and honor. . . . The mission is certainly not one which the monarchies of Europe can perform. . . . The United States, which proved her friendship and disinterestedness by rescuing Mexico from the clutches of Napoleon III, and which invited a conference of all the republics on this continent in the cause of honorable and lasting peace, is alone entitled to undertake this delicate work.[10]

One of the Republican pamphlets, whose title referred to Mexico as "America's Egypt," pronounced Blaine's Clayton-Bulwer notes "perfectly right and perfectly patriotic" and praised his peace congress and his opposition to De Lesseps with the familiar appeals to security: "Will Central America share the same fate [as Egypt] or have we a Monroe doctrine?" As for the Democrats, the *Tribune* complained that instead of defending American interests abroad, they had weakened foreign policy by opposing the new navy and cutting down diplomatic and consular appropriations "in order to have more money to expend in helping the elections of Democratic candidates in Congressional districts."[11]

The Republican press devoted much space to reprints of articles from British journals which expressed horror and suspicion at Blaine's candidacy, and drew the conclusion that the British feared him because he threatened their world-wide commercial monopoly. Reid also accused the Southern Democratic oligarchy of conspiring with "the selfish zeal and heavy moneyed contributions of foreign traders and manufacturers" and self-righteous snobs in New York and Boston to secure majorities in a few critical cities, win the election, and institute free trade. He asked: "Is an American statesman to be ostracized and hunted to death because he cares for his country more than for Great Britain?"[12]

[10]*Ibid.*, July 27, 1884, p. 6.
[11]*Ibid.*, July 6, 1884, p. 6. James Morris Morgan, *America's Egypt. Mr. Blaine's Foreign Policy* (New York, 1884), pp. 3-4 *et passim*.
[12]*New York Tribune*, June 13, 1884, p. 4; June 21, p. 4; June 25, p. 4; October 22, p. 4.

Blaine cultivated his Anglophobia with special attention to the Irish-American vote, which might decide the election in the pivotal state of New York. Although he had earlier criticized pro-Irish demagogy, he now praised Patrick Ford's "unselfish devotion" and energy. By the middle of the campaign his followers had pulled out every stop in the Irish-American calliope. The *Tribune* published long-winded efforts to reconcile Irish-American rights with diplomatic propriety and explained that Blaine would have obtained the release of more suspects but for the strong evidence against them and their stubborn refusal to leave Ireland. On July 28 a large Irish-American rally at Chickering Hall in New York heard speeches by Patrick Ford and others and passed a firm resolution in Blaine's favor. Throughout the campaign Ford's *Irish World* and John Devoy's *Irish Nation* told their readers that Cleveland was a "Presbyterian bigot" and the enemy of labor, and that as long as the Democrats could count on automatic support, the Irish-Americans would have no influence on party decisions.[13]

With Blaine's record in the State Department as a target, his enemies produced more campaign literature on foreign policy than his supporters. As Blaine suspected, however, many of his opponents were trying to avoid the battleground of the tariff. Carl Schurz admitted its importance but declared that it was only part of the larger question of good government. The Democratic platform contained a wordy and vague tariff plank which meant less than the party's forthright adoption of tariff for revenue in 1880. At the same time the *New York Herald* accused the Republicans of using the tariff issue as camouflage to hide needless taxes, wasted revenue, monopolies, public land swindles, Peruvian "jobs," and truckling to British officials in Ireland.[14]

[13]Lionel Sackville West to Lord Granville, Washington, November 17, 1884, No. 333, Great Britain, F. O. 5/1929. *New York Tribune*, June 26, 1884, p. 4; July 29, pp. 1, 2, 4; August 27, p. 4. Wittke, *Irish in America*, p. 175. Thomas, *Return of the Democratic Party*, pp. 221-22. For a detailed account of the campaign from the Irish-American point of view see Gibson, *Attitudes of New York Irish*, pp. 382-91.

[14]Schurz's viewpoint on the tariff is succinctly expressed in an undated speech draft in Volume LXXXII of his papers. Schurz favored the nomination of Edmunds, who was also a protectionist. Stanwood, *American Tariff Controversies*, II, 222-24.

At the same time low-tariff elements in both parties seized the opportunity to unite behind Cleveland and to press their favorite panacea on the American electorate. *Bradstreet's*, a moderate commercial journal, early declared that the tariff would provide a real issue between the two parties for a change and thus arrest the demoralization of politics. It deplored the existing "system of restrictions and antagonisms" confronting merchants and declared that the day had long passed when the United States could afford an isolationist, anti-British commercial policy. Others criticized the failure of the Forty-eighth Congress to encourage foreign trade, rejecting Blaine's hastily sketched *Zollverein* as unlikely to overcome European opposition and warmly endorsing Arthur's proposal for reciprocity treaties.[15]

The most popular argument against Blaine's foreign policies, in which protectionists and tariff reformers could both join, was that they were too warlike. "His record in the State Department," declared the New York *Evening Post*, "is one continued series of bullyings and blunderings, all calculated to bring us into difficulties with foreign nations, and this at a time when we were in no sense prepared for such difficulties." The *Herald* predicted a war with Spain over Cuba if Blaine were elected, and the commercial press in New York argued for peace with self-confident isolationism:

> This country has a dignified consciousness of its own greatness which has for twenty years saved it from the folly of offensive bluster and self-assertion. . . . There is no more reason to expect a foreign war in the next twenty years than there was in the last twenty years unless we go out of our way to provoke it. . . . [However,] if we take pains to provoke a foreign war we can be accommodated with one.
> . . . Peace is our normal condition, and it will not be broken save by the recklessness or mad ambition of politicians. Therefore we distrust and oppose all schemes for undue increase of fortifications and of additions to the army and navy which

Oberholtzer, *History of the United States*, IV, 184. *New York Herald*, July 26, 1884, p. 4; October 16, p. 6.

[15]David A. Wells to Manton Marble, Norwich, Connecticut, January 7, April 25, July 27, August 27, September 28, 1884, Manton Marble Papers, LV, LVI (Library of Congress). See also David A. Wells, "Evils of the Tariff System," *North American Review*, CXXXIX (September 1884), 274-82. *Bradstreet's*, IX (January 19, March 22, 1884), 34, 178. *New York Journal of Commerce*, July 9,

are beyond the obvious needs of a peace establishment. . . . If allowed to be gratified it can only lead to increased extravagance and corruption in all branches of Government and if it should finally plunge us into war we should be the ultimate sufferers from the revival of the military regime whatever victories we might gain over foreign foes.[16]

This slightly smug satisfaction, disapproving alike Blaine's bluster and Chandler's new navy, did not prevent its authors from supporting the economic expansionism of the Arthur administration.

Blaine's enemies directed heavy fire at his Latin-American policies. Scornfully they characterized his treatment of Colombia in the isthmian question as meddlesome and his Clayton-Bulwer notes as illogical and naive. Somewhat less convincingly, they professed themselves unable to understand how a hemispheric peace congress could possibly advance American trade interests in Latin America. However, they reserved their choicest adjectives for the War of the Pacific. The *Herald*, for example, stated with brutal bluntness: "Blaine was ready to use the whole power of the United States in bullying Chile and oppressing Peru, only that he might enrich himself and his cronies through that shallow pretext, the Landreau claim."[17] William Henry Hurlbert, the half-brother of Blaine's swashbuckling minister to Peru, Stephen Hurlbut, set out to clear the family name (of which he had already altered the spelling) by placing full responsibility for all actions on the Secretary of State and by reviving the old rumor that Blaine had given Hurlbut confidential oral instructions.[18]

At the same time that these critics damned Blaine as too aggressive in South America, they denounced his failure to act decisively in the problem of the Irish-American suspects. Hurlbert re-

p. 2; July 25, p. 2; September 24, p. 2. *New York Herald*, July 26, p. 4. *Washington Post*, June 25, p. 2; July 15, p. 2.

[16]*New York Journal of Commerce*, July 7, 1884, p. 2. See also New York *Evening Post*, October 13, p. 2. *Harper's Weekly*, XXVIII (October 25), 696. *New York Herald*, June 17, p. 6.

[17]*Ibid.*, September 24, 1884, p. 6. For extensive criticism of Blaine's South American policies see [Edward H. Strobel], *Mr. Blaine and His Foreign Policy* (Boston, 1884), pp. 7-20, 26-62 *et passim*, and Thomas H. Talbot, *The Proudest Chapter in His Life. Mr. Blaine's Administration of the State Department. His Conduct of South American Affairs* (Boston, 1884), pp. 10-13, 18-25, 28-36 *et passim*.

[18]William H. Hurlbert, *Meddling and Muddling—Mr. Blaine's Foreign Policy* (New York, 1884), pp. 51-71.

examined the diplomatic correspondence, which had all been published by order of Congress, and proclaimed that the great paladin
of American citizenship had carelessly neglected to read the British
coercion bill, had made no effort to stiffen Lowell's feeble protests,
and, as a result, had obtained the release of exactly one suspect.
Hurlbert capped the climax by quoting a report of British Minister
Thornton to the Foreign Office, saying that "a trustworthy source"
had informed him that the State Department would not press
the cause of the suspects too warmly.[19]

When Blaine fought back by parading his Roman Catholic rela-
tives and by organizing Irish-American rallies, his opponents jeered
at his insincerity. The Irish, remarked one, "may be deplorably
gullible, but . . . [at least] they have never yet taken a joint
interest with anybody else in a demagogue. All their demagogues
have been their own exclusively." When the campaign was over,
and sanity had returned, the *Nation* reproached Blaine for implicitly condoning Irish-American terrorism by accepting the
support of Ford's *Irish World*:

> You knew that in the same issues of his paper in which he
> was supporting Blaine he was announcing every week contri-
> butions to his "Emergency Fund," and was openly avowing
> the object of that fund to be dynamite warfare on England.
> Knowing all this, you quoted from his paper with admiring
> comments.
> This was not mere toleration—it was direct encouragement.
> It was the first time in history that the *Irish World* had re-
> ceived respectful recognition from decent Americans.[20]

No one expected that the aggressive nationalism of Blaine's campaign would arouse much support abroad, and when foreigners
commented on the election, it was usually in Cleveland's favor.
British newspapers, for example, generally assumed that Blaine
intended to make all of Latin America a protectorate of the
United States through expansion of the Monroe Doctrine, rough-

[19]*Ibid.*, pp. 1-39 *et passim. Washington Post*, July 12, 1884, p. 2. *New York Herald*,
September 2, p. 3; September 10, p. 3; September 16, p. 3; October 17, p. 10. New
York *Evening Post*, August 9, p. 2. *Times* (London), September 30, p. 5; October
14, p. 5.
[20]*Nation*, XL (January 29, 1885), 83. See also *ibid.*, XXXIX (August 7, 1884),
101; *Harper's Weekly*, XXVIII (August 16), 541.

handed diplomacy of Hurlbut's type, and fine-sounding devices like the peace congress. Some objected and called on Britain to defend her interests, but others felt that "it would not be an unalloyed evil if the United States were to absorb some of the wretched little South American Republics who are always fighting among themselves, and give them some sort of stable government." Still others doubted shrewdly that the American nation would tolerate much of Blaine's jingoism. Six weeks before the election the *Nation* took a survey of British opinion and reported much apathy and ignorance about the American campaign.[21]

*   *   *

When the ballots were counted, it was found that Cleveland had beaten Blaine by an electoral vote of 219-182. This margin was much closer than it looked, however, for Cleveland's popular plurality in New York was only 1,143 votes out of a total of 1,167,175 votes cast, and New York's electoral count of thirty-six, as had long been expected, decided the election. Since the Republicans had carried New York by 21,033 votes in 1880, historians have been tempted to place the state under a microscope, hoping to find an easy solution to a complex problem by isolating some local group or interest whose shift of support dragged Blaine down to defeat.[22] The emphasis of textbooks on the Reverend Samuel D. Burchard's unfortunate alliteration about "rum, Romanism, and rebellion" is an extreme example of this type of thinking.

It would be impossible to prove that any issue or event related to foreign policy changed enough votes to influence the outcome of the election. To be sure, the normally Republican German-Americans of the Middle West turned out for Cleveland. Some of them bore a grudge against Blaine because he had attacked Prussia while in the Senate, but it seems certain that the decisive factors were their personal loyalty to the Mugwump Carl Schurz and their concern for honest, orderly government, which Cleveland seemed to represent.[23] As for the Irish-American voters,

[21] Quotations from British newspapers appear in *New York Tribune*, June 25, 1884, pp. 2-3; July 8, p. 2. An amused tolerance of Blaine's Anglophobia is shown by the *Times* in an editorial of November 3, p. 9. For a survey of British opinion see *Nation*, XXXIX (October 16), 328-29.

[22] For a breakdown of the presidential vote in 1880 and 1884 see Burnham, *Presidential Ballots*, pp. 249, 639.

[23] Muzzey, *Blaine*, p. 308. [Harvey] to David Davis, Washington, June 2, 1884,

most of the pamphlets and editorials prepared for their edification probably counteracted each other, and it is likely that Blaine got at least his share of their votes. After the election Schurz wrote to Cleveland that he was surprised at the extent of the Irish defection from their usual Democratic allegiance, and that he suspected the Roman Catholic hierarchy of using its influence to divide the Irish vote so as to have a foot in both camps.[24]

In the case of agitation about the tariff question and about the wisdom of a "spirited" foreign policy, one may readily admit that the heated arguments changed some opinions without having any idea of the final gain or loss, since good government and other domestic issues almost invariably entered the discussions too. In New York state any one of several factors—the temperance issue, Cleveland's local record, Irish-American caprice, Burchard's blunder, the "boodle banquet" at Delmonico's, and, not least of all, election-day rainstorms in many upstate counties—could have changed several thousand votes at the last moment.

If one must dispose of the campaign in a sentence, it would be safest to conclude that James G. Blaine lost the presidency simply because he was himself—well-known and charming, but woefully vulnerable to charges of daredevil chauvinism, irregular honesty, and impetuous partisanship. In New York Hamilton Fish, who cast a reluctant vote for Blaine, believed that the party was riddled with the dry rot of factionalism and that Cleveland owed his election to the "strong, ardent, uncompromising Republicans" who had stayed home from the polls. He felt that this was just retribution for Blaine's feuds with Arthur and the Stalwarts:

> So the struck eagle, stretched upon the plain,
> No more through rolling clouds to soar again,
> Viewed his own feather on the fatal dart,
> And winged the shaft that quivered in his heart.[25]

David Davis Papers. New York *World*, September 30, 1884.

[24]Carl Schurz to [Grover Cleveland], January or February 1885. Draft in Schurz Papers, LXXXIV.

[25]Fish to J. C. B. Davis, Glenclyffe, New York, November 13, 1884, Bancroft Davis Papers, XXXVI. See also *Nation*, XXXIX (November 20), 428. However, Whitelaw Reid (who probably represented many others) blamed the defeat largely on a free trade conspiracy. Cortissoz, *Whitelaw Reid*, II, 93-94. On the role of the Mugwumps see Claude M. Fuess, *Carl Schurz, Reformer (1829-1906)* (New York, 1932), pp. 285-99, and Thomas, *Return of the Democratic Party,* pp. 229-31.

CHAPTER 15

The Nicaragua Canal Treaty

ABOUT a month after Blaine's defeat he sent to Whitelaw Reid several statements and editorials for publication in the *New York Tribune*. One of them was a formal announcement disclaiming any interviews which the press might print as coming from him. The others were letters and articles to be published under assumed names. Two of these last protested bitterly that Arthur and his cabinet had openly refrained from supporting his campaign. The President would not meet with members of the national committee, and Frelinghuysen had even refused to come in to Newark, New Jersey, from his country home a few miles away to attend a Blaine rally. The Chairman of the Republican National Committee added that he knew of only one speech made by any Cabinet member and declared that if Arthur had supported the ticket warmly, Blaine would have been elected.[1]

Whether this was so, it is clear that Republican factionalism penetrated to the heart of the Arthur administration, for the President, disappointed at the outcome of the nominating convention and probably chagrined at Blaine's earlier criticism of his policies, took his revenge in characteristic fashion by blandly doing nothing for the candidate. Instead, he and Frelinghuysen devoted their energies to the development of an expansionist foreign policy—energies redoubled by the knowledge that the administration had less than nine months to run. Some parts of their foreign policy outdid even the aggressive Blaine, extending American interests and influence in areas which he scarcely mentioned. One of these measures was the Nicaragua canal treaty, which set

[1]James G. Blaine to Whitelaw Reid, Washington, December 13, 1884, Reid Papers, Box CIV. *New York Tribune*, December 19, p. 5. *Washington Post*, November 19, p. 2. The *Tribune* also accused Frelinghuysen of delaying publication of consular reports which would have helped Blaine's campaign. *New York Tribune*, February 19, 1885, p. 2.

up for the United States a new type of protectorate, at that time more European than American, and proposed a closer association with Central American affairs than Blaine had hitherto thought feasible.

*   *   *

As has been seen, by the end of 1883 the relations of the United States with the nations of the Central American isthmus had reached an impasse. After the quarrels and recriminations of 1881 the State Department had patched up an uneasy truce with Colombia, but the American consul at Panama continued to report rumors that the government in Bogotá intended to lease part of the isthmus to France or allow De Lesseps to found official French colonies along the canal route.[2] The undoubted fact behind the rumors—that French influence in Panama was rising—heightened the value to the United States of the rival Nicaraguan canal route. Realizing this, the Nicaraguan government had circulated proposals in Central America asking aid in getting support for a canal, and the ministers of Guatemala and Costa Rica responded by asking the United States to take part with their countries in a joint guarantee of profits. There was some reason to believe that if the United States did not respond, Central America might turn to Britain or Germany.[3]

At this time, when it seemed that the State Department must act or give up its objections to European intervention, Congress refused to offer guidance, for it could not yet determine whether the Ammen-Phelps canal project in Nicaragua or the Eads ship-railway in Tehuantepec deserved its support. Early in the session of 1883-1884 Representative William S. Rosecrans of California introduced a bill guaranteeing profits to the Maritime Canal Company of Nicaragua but failed to secure the necessary two-thirds majority, largely because of opposition from Eads's supporters.[4]

[2] Thomas Adamson to William Hunter, Panama, August 24, September 3, 1883; March 19, May 13, 1884, Nos. 39, 42, 70, 77, U.S., Consular Despatches, Panama, XVI.
[3] Henry C. Hall to Frederick T. Frelinghuysen, Guatemala City, January 21, 1884; Managua, February 11, 18, 21, 29, Nos. 197, 200, 201, 203, U.S., Despatches, Central America, XXII. Memorandum submitted by Antonio Batres, January 17, U.S., Notes from Foreign Legations, Guatemala and Salvador, VI.
[4] Keasbey, *Nicaragua Canal*, pp. 387-88. Another bill was introduced in behalf of the Eads project but made no more progress. *New York Tribune*, March 2, 1884, p. 2.

The continued deadlock in Congress placed the Maritime Canal Company in an embarrassing situation, for it could not obtain enough capital to begin operations without some sort of approval by the American government. Unless it began excavations before September, 1884, the Nicaraguan government would probably cancel its concession. While Congress debated, Admiral Ammen and the board of directors took out articles of incorporation in the state of Colorado, and the rumor gained currency that they were about to seek capital in Europe. Frelinghuysen later declared that this rumor convinced him once for all that the government must step in and take over control from the company. At one point Ammen asked the Secretary for aid in smoothing the company's relations with Nicaragua, but, according to the Admiral's outraged account, Frelinghuysen refused point-blank and declared that he would oppose the company with all the power of the government.[5]

Ammen may have exaggerated his story, for Frelinghuysen was quite willing to come to terms, if the promoters would sell out to the American government. In January, 1884, he cabled to the president of the company, Captain Seth L. Phelps (then serving as American minister to Peru), asking him if he thought that the Nicaraguan government would cede a strip of territory for a canal, and also how much the concessionaires would ask in return for their interest in the project. Phelps tried to persuade the Secretary to let him organize a special subsidiary under the secret control of the State Department, saying that the open intervention of the American government might alarm the timid Nicaraguans, but Frelinghuysen insisted on a formal transfer, and Phelps agreed to sound out the Nicaraguan government. At the beginning of April Frelinghuysen offered Phelps the purchase price of $12,000

[5]Frelinghuysen summarized the background and origins of his proposals to the company and to Nicaragua in two formal communications. See Frelinghuysen to Hall, July 19, 1884, No. 154, U.S., Instructions, Central America, XVIII, 443-52, and Frelinghuysen to Chester A. Arthur, September 1, U.S., Report Book, XV, 697. For Ammen's side of the story see Ammen, *Errors and Fallacies*, pp. 58-60. Keasbey gives Arthur prime credit for the decision but without citing specific evidence. Keasbey, *Nicaragua Canal*, pp. 423-24.

cash and 1.2 per cent of the eventual construction cost of the canal. He instructed Phelps to go at once to Nicaragua and take part in the negotiations.[6]

Meanwhile Frelinghuysen had already begun to dicker with the Nicaraguans. On February 12 he cabled to the American minister to Central America, Henry C. Hall, instructing him to ask the government at Managua if it would agree to let the United States build a canal and to cede the waters and islands of Lake Nicaragua, together with a five-mile strip of land on either side of the canal route. In return the United States would promise Nicaragua one-fourth of the profits from tolls, free use of the waterway, civil jurisdiction over the canal strip, and a defensive alliance. When Hall approached President Adán Cárdenas, he seemed delighted to learn that American interest in the canal project had revived. It soon appeared, however, that what Cárdenas had in mind was a joint guarantee of profits for a private canal company. When he realized what Hall wanted, he declared that his congress would never consent to alienate land permanently. Instead he offered a 3 per cent guarantee for the Maritime Canal Company, a defensive alliance, and permission for the United States to occupy the canal strip temporarily if war threatened.[7]

As it happened, the rest of the Nicaraguan government would not go even as far as its president, for a junta of notables (including four former presidents) soon rejected Cárdenas' last point, and one of them suggested sending a minister to Britain at once in order to "arrest the absorbing influence of the United States." Hall tried to tempt Cárdenas by suggesting that the American government would be willing to purchase the needed land. He reported that the Nicaraguan president vacillated day by day between the American proposals and the stern nationalism of

[6]Frelinghuysen to Seth L. Phelps, January 23, April 3, 16, 28, 1884 (telegrams), U.S., Instructions, Peru, XVII, 129-30, 131-37. Phelps to Frelinghuysen, Lima, January 25, February 10, April 5, 15 (telegrams), U.S., Despatches, Peru, XXXIX, XL. (The first is filed wrongly under 1885.)

[7]Frelinghuysen to Hall, January 29, February 8, 12, 1884, No. 128 (telegrams), U.S., Instructions, Central America, XVIII, 441-43, 453-56. Hall to Frelinghuysen, Managua, February 18, No. 200, U.S., Despatches, Central America, XXII. As a special mark of favor Congress authorized the Secretary of War to admit the sons of Barrios and former President Zavala of Nicaragua to West Point. *Ibid.*, March 3, No. 204.

his advisers. Frelinghuysen quickly agreed to offer as much as $5,000,000 for political jurisdiction over the canal strip "in the sense of the law of Nations for the protection and management of the Canal" and emphasized that the United States wished to cooperate with Nicaragua in building and operating the canal. "It has no desire to interfere in any way with the sovereignty of Nicaragua," he added, "but to prevent an invasion of that sovereignty to the detriment of Nicaragua, any other Central American State or of the United States." He thought that it ought to be easy enough to find some wording which would satisfy Nicaragua and still permit the United States to protect the canal.[8]

Frelinghuysen was too optimistic, for the negotiations still had months to run. Cárdenas returned to his guarantee plan and then, on April 16, startled Hall by suggesting that the United States build the canal, divide the profits evenly with Nicaragua, allow Nicaragua to pay off the construction cost in installments, and then turn over ownership of the canal, retaining only a share in its management and defense. Hall declared this proposal completely unacceptable. At this point Phelps arrived in Managua from Peru and proposed that his company lend the Nicaraguan government enough money to pay half of the construction cost of the canal, after which the United States government might buy out the company. Eventually the two countries and individual minority stockholders would receive income from the canal and choose its management. Cárdenas now tentatively accepted the principle of joint ownership of the canal, provided that the United States recognize Nicaraguan sovereignty, grant a defensive alliance, and advance her money for public works. The Nicaraguan price seemed too high, and late in May the American diplomats decided to break off negotiations for a time. Phelps went to Washington to report, while Hall returned to his base of operations in Guatemala City.[9]

[8]*Ibid.*, March 6, 22, 1884, No. 205, 208. Frelinghuysen to Hall, March 8, April 3 (telegrams), U.S., Instructions, Central America, XVIII, 457-59.

[9]Hall to Frelinghuysen, Managua, April 22, May 20, 29, June 3, 11, No. 213 and telegrams, U.S., Despatches, Central America, XXII. The text of Phelps's proposal is filed out of order in miscellaneous papers contained in U.S., Notes from Foreign Legations, Nicaragua, II. The changes proposed by Nicaragua, dated May 26, are in the same volume.

One explanation for the reluctance of Cárdenas may be found in a reckless letter from Admiral Ammen to a friend in the Nicaraguan Foreign Office. Apparently angered at Frelinghuysen's opposition to the company, Ammen accused the State Department of declaring that the Maritime Canal Company held its concession only as an agent of the United States government. (There is no other proof that Frelinghuysen said this, and in any case it was not true.) The Foreign Office was understandably disturbed and warned Ammen that the company must not expect an extension of its concession when it expired in September.[10] Shortly before this the Nicaraguan government also let it be known that it was pushing forward its own project to deepen the San Juan River, dig a short canal between Lake Nicaragua and Lake Managua, and build a railroad across the Pacific mountain range as an alternate transit route. The announcement mentioned the use of both American and British engineers, but it may have been largely bluff.[11]

Phelps arrived in Washington to find his company in desperate straits, for ex-President Grant's brokerage firm, which was handling the company securities, had failed just as it was about to issue new stock, and quotations on the old series were sagging badly. At this point occurred an event which was never adequately explained to the public and which, as a result, gave much unfavorable publicity to the Nicaragua project. In the middle of June the *New York Times* reported that the administration had asked Congress to appropriate a secret fund of $250,000 for expenses in connection with the project. Frelinghuysen later explained that the idea of such an appropriation had originated in the Senate, but he appeared before several Congressional committees to defend it. Suspicious congressmen and journalists wondered aloud whether the "slush fund" was intended to buy up a concession which was about to expire and called attention to the official connections of many company members. Others suggested bribery in Nicaragua.

Frelinghuysen eventually informed Minister Hall that the State

[10] Ammen, *Errors and Fallacies*, pp. 58-60. Alejandro Canton to Daniel Ammen, Managua, April 23, 1884, No. 6, copy in U.S., Notes from Foreign Legations, II. See also Walton, "Frelinghuysen-Zavala Treaty," pp. 100-102.
[11] Hall to Frelinghuysen, Managua, March 24, 1884, No. 209, U.S., Despatches, Central America, XXII.

Department would have used the money to publicize the treaty in Central America and to extinguish private claims along the canal route. This explanation, even if made public, might not have pacified the critics for long, since Hall soon learned that Cárdenas and his cronies were hastily buying up land in this area. After some deliberation Congress decided that the fund was not good politics in an election year and defeated the appropriation, whereupon the *Nation* remarked with satisfaction: "Millions for defence, but not one cent for a job."[12]

During the recess in the negotiations President Cárdenas sent Lorenzo Zavala, a veteran diplomat and the most recent ex-president of Nicaragua, on a tour of Central America capitals to confer on the canal question. He also wrote a series of letters to President Justo Rufino Barrios of Guatemala, asking for advice. Barrios took full advantage of this chance to curry favor with the United States. He showed the correspondence to Hall, furnished him with a written opinion that Nicaragua was not entitled to a share in the management or the profits of a canal, and drafted an open letter to Cárdenas, rebuking his fears and preaching gratitude for American progressivism: "The indolent who do not wish to go forward would fall behind, but the active and laborious would be stimulated by the example [of American immigration]. . . . The only danger I can conceive is that in time we should become a people as efficient and hard-working as the North American whose traits we should be compelled to imitate." Barrios' ally, the president of El Salvador, also urged Cárdenas to accept the American terms, and the Costa Rican minister to the United States informed Frelinghuysen that his government supported the American position.[13]

[12]*Nation*, XXXIX (July 10, 1884), 21-22. *Washington Post*, June 20, p. 2; July 4, p. 2. U.S., *Congressional Record*, 48th Cong., 1st Sess., XXII, 2975. Frelinghuysen to Hall, July 19, No. 154, U.S., Instructions, Central America, XVIII, 448-50. Hall to Frelinghuysen, September 4, No. 255, U.S., Despatches, Central America, XXIII. For comments on this episode see also Burnette, "Senate Foreign Relations Committee," pp. 163-66, and Walton, "Frelinghuysen-Zavala Treaty," pp. 117-24, 130-31.

[13]Rippy, "Barrios and the Nicaragua Canal," pp. 193-94. Hall to Frelinghuysen, Guatemala City, June 26, 27, 1884, Nos. 218-220, U.S., Despatches, Central America, XXII. Frelinghuysen to Hall, July 19, No. 154, U.S., Instructions, Central America, XVIII, 451.

Hoping that this pressure from the rest of Central America had flattened Nicaraguan scruples, the American secretary instructed Hall in a telegram of July 26 to return to Managua and offer new terms. Frelinghuysen now proposed that the canal be built by the United States, jointly owned by that country and Nicaragua, and administered by a board of five directors, three to be appointed by the United States. Nicaragua would receive one-fourth of the profits and furnish a strip of territory two and a half miles wide, running up the San Juan River and around the south shore of Lake Nicaragua. She would retain civil jurisdiction along the route in peacetime, but the United States would have enough power to build the canal. The two countries would form a defensive alliance. These American proposals resembled Cárdenas' plan of joint ownership, but the details were considerably less favorable to Nicaragua. When Hall presented them to Cárdenas on August 12, the Nicaraguan president seemed well disposed. Other state matters claimed his attention, however, and when he next conferred with Hall, he had returned to his wavering, pettifogging self. Eventually he demanded equal representation for Nicaragua on the board of directors, one-third of the profits, and a different basis for the concession of territory.[14]

By the time he made these demands, however, Cárdenas had decided to send former President Zavala to complete the negotiations at Washington, whether for fear of Barrios' pressure or in hope of better terms. The Guatemalan president continued to support the United States and even offered to carry American terms in person to Managua, but it developed that he expected the State Department to ratify his actions in advance. Frelinghuysen politely declined his offer.[15] In the meager records of the negotiations at Washington it does not appear that Barrios' influence was needed or felt.

Upon arriving in the United States, Zavala registered Cárdenas'

[14]Rippy, "Barrios and the Nicaragua Canal," p. 194. Frelinghuysen to Hall, July 26 (telegram), August 27, 1884, No. 173, U.S., Instructions, Central America, XVIII, 452-53, 461-63. Hall to Frelinghuysen, Managua, August 21 (telegram), U.S., Despatches, Central America, XXII.

[15]Rippy, "Barrios and the Nicaragua Canal," pp. 194-96. Hall to Frelinghuysen, Guatemala City, October 15, 17 (telegram), 22, November 6, 1884, Nos. 268, 272, 277, U.S., Despatches, Central America, XXIII.

principal demands and requested a loan of $4,000,000 for public works, to be repaid out of the Nicaraguan share of canal receipts. He also inserted a requirement that the company buy up the rights of one Francisco A. Pellas, who had taken out a concession in 1877 for a steamboat line on the San Juan River. (By an odd coincidence Pellas was then serving as Zavala's private secretary and was reported to be a relative of the young lady whom the ex-president was planning to marry.) These provisions all appeared in the final treaty, which was signed on December 1. By its terms the United States obtained a protectorate of sorts over a canal strip two and one-half miles wide, promising to complete the canal within ten years and receiving full facilities for construction and broad exemptions from taxation or other Nicaraguan interference. However, Nicaragua retained civil jurisdiction over the strip in peacetime, and American governmental rights in wartime were not specified. Also Nicaragua received equal representation on a six-man board of directors and one-third of the net profits.[16] If she had sold her virtue, she had obtained a good price for it.

*   *   *

As soon as the Frelinghuysen-Zavala Treaty was signed, garbled versions of it appeared in the American press, but the administration chose to keep the official text secret until December 18, when, to Frelinghuysen's annoyance, it leaked into the columns of the *New York Tribune*.[17] Scarcely a month after one of the most bitterly fought presidential campaigns in the country's history, Arthur could not have expected to avoid controversy over a treaty involving millions of dollars and ill-defined commitments in the future. If one may judge from coverage in the press, the whole country joined in the debate on ratification.

[16]Keasbey, *Nicaragua Canal*, pp. 423-27. The comments of Zavala are contained in a memorandum dated October 24, 1884, U.S., Notes from Foreign Legations, Nicaragua, II. The text of the Pellas contract is enclosed with H. H. Leavitt to John Davis, Managua, January 5, 1885, U.S., Consular Despatches, Managua, I. See also Walton, "Frelinghuysen-Zavala Treaty," p. 81. The text of the treaty is contained in File Y-2, "Unperfected Treaties," Records of the Department of State (National Archives, Record Group 59). Hereafter cited as United States, Unperfected Treaties.

[17]Frelinghuysen to Hall, December 18, 1884 (telegram), U.S., Instructions, Central America, XVIII, 438.

Opinions ran the full gamut from blind praise to accusations of fraud and treachery. The *Springfield Republican* called the treaty "the boldest feat of American diplomacy since the acquisition of Texas or the purchase of Louisiana," while the *New York Herald* hailed it as an earnest of America's determination to play her proper role in international affairs. The *Herald* reprinted over two dozen clippings from other newspapers, most of which gave qualified support. Liberal publications such as the *Nation* and *Harper's Weekly* opposed ratification, however, and even in the South, which was keenly interested in isthmian transit routes, many leading newspapers came out against the treaty. The New York Chamber of Commerce favored the canal in a general way, but two commercial publications, the *New York Journal of Commerce* and *Bradstreet's*, criticized the project as impractical and extravagant. The *New York Tribune*, long a supporter of Blaine's energetic diplomacy, blew hot and cold on the treaty for several weeks, approving the idea of a canal but objecting to details of the plan. Finally, on February 3, the *Tribune* printed anonymously a biting attack by Blaine himself, who sent it to Whitelaw Reid in his own handwriting, exhorting him to secrecy: "Pray be careful not to let my manuscript go to the compositor."[18]

Supporters of the canal project declared that it would stimulate American commerce and bind together the divergent sections: "It is a grand project of national development. . . . Indeed, it should be classed more as a patriotic than a financial enterprise." If England objected, they added, this would be a good time to settle the question of the Clayton-Bulwer Treaty, with the country prosperous and the presidential campaign finished. Once American honor was involved, some exponents of the treaty felt that the

[18]Blaine to Reid [Washington, February 1, 5, 1885], Reid Papers, Box CIV. The changes in the *New York Tribune's* attitude may be followed in these issues: December 18, 1884, p. 4; December 19, pp. 2, 4; December 20, p. 4; December 22, p. 4; December 24, p. 4; December 25, p. 4; January 2, 1885, p. 4; January 14, p. 3; January 19, p. 4; January 23, p. 2; February 3, p. 4; February 7, p. 4. See also *New York Herald*, December 9, p. 6; December 20, p. 6 (reprinted from *Springfield Republican*), and December 26, p. 4. The *Herald's* summaries of other press opinion appear *ibid.*, December 20, p. 6; December 21, p. 6, and December 22, p. 6. For the position of the *Nation*, *Harper's Weekly*, the *New York Journal of Commerce*, and *Bradstreet's* see subsequent footnotes. The attitudes of Southern newspapers are reviewed in New Orleans *Times-Democrat*, January 1, 1885, p. 4.

whole country would support the government, and a British protest would only insure the success of the project. Indeed, the canal would help to revive the Monroe Doctrine and rebuild the United States Navy. Not all supporters were jingoists, however, for some argued persuasively that Britain had little to fear from American control of the canal, since all but Nicaraguan ships would pay equal tolls under the treaty.[19]

Many who opposed the Frelinghuysen-Zavala Treaty objected to any plan for building a Nicaragua canal. For example, Commodore Robert W. Shufeldt, who was doing his best to expand American influence in Africa and the Far East, predicted that any isthmian canal would break the transcontinental monopoly of the American railroads and allow Britain and France to dominate the commerce of the Pacific. *Bradstreet's* agreed: "Our need of [merchant] ships is a more pressing one than our need of ship canals." Other business-minded critics doubted that the canal would ever earn a steady profit, especially in competition with Panama, and advised canal enthusiasts to buy stock in De Lesseps' company if they envied his prospects. Pacifists and economizers further argued that we would need a larger navy if we hoped to defend a canal without England's aid.[20]

Opponents of the treaty used the argument of British power in different and sometimes contradictory ways. Some declared that decency and respect for our international reputation required the settlement of our obligations under the Clayton-Bulwer Treaty before undertaking any new ones; others dreaded a long, bitter argument with Britain, even if reasons for the abrogation of the old treaty were "potent, if not overwhelming." There was no point in antagonizing the British, since we might wish to negotiate another canal treaty with them in a few years. One pamphleteer warned that British expansion was much more to be feared in Canada than in Central America: "Whilst this splendid seat of empire is gradually enlarging, almost at our doors, and daily

[19]*New York Herald*, December 9, 1884, p. 6; December 26, p. 4. *New York Tribune*, December 25, p. 4. See also the surveys of newspaper opinion in *New York Herald*, cited in note 18.

[20]*Nation*, XXXIX (December 11, 1884), 496; XL (February 12, 1885), 128. *Bradstreet's*, X (December 20, 1884), 385. *New York Journal of Commerce*, December 16, 1884, p. 2.

growing into rivalry with us, we are counselled to turn our eyes away to distant and remote regions, upon the pretext that . . . [Britain] may revive her dominion over a few unlettered Indians . . . and thereby obtain the 'exclusive control' over a canal, for the construction of which she never has, and never will, expend one dollar from her treasury."[21]

A considerable section of isolationist opinion stood on guard against involving the United States in Central American affairs. Some doubted that the Constitution would permit the government to hold land in any foreign country and predicted that such an arrangement would lead inevitably to the absorption of Nicaragua, which would convince the world that the policy of self-government was a delusion and encourage Europe in her colonialism. The *Nation*, much exercised over good government, dreamed a nightmare of fifteen million "slightly Catholicized savages, who are still ruled by chiefs and priests under a simulacrum of civilized government" becoming American citizens. "Fancy a close Presidential contest," shuddered Edwin L. Godkin, "in which the Anglo-Saxon States were pretty evenly divided, with the vote of Honduras, or Guatemala, or Nicaragua still uncounted, with plenty of 'visiting statesmen,' of the Chandler, Brady, and Dorsey type, on the ground, keeping watch against 'fraud.' "[22]

However, it was not necessary to look into the future for possible corruption. Other critics of the treaty, remembering the $250,000 "slush fund" of the past summer, examined the proposed loan to Nicaragua, the provisions for buying up right of way, and the obscure reference to the Pellas steamship concession and smelled a nest of rats. Several journalists interviewed Pellas but came away still suspicious. The *New York Tribune*, the *Nation*, and many others declared that Nicaragua had "skinned" the Arthur administration in a sharp deal, because its time was short. They predicted that the United States could obtain much better terms if it waited a year. Blaine's unsigned editorials suggested that the proposed loan was really a "corruption fund" and that the

[21]*Nation*, XXXIX (December 18, 25, 1884), 516, 539. *Harper's Weekly*, XXVIII (December 27), 852. *Reflections on the Nicaragua Treaty. Is It Constitutional? Is It Expedient?* [no publisher, about 1884], p. 40 *et passim.*

[22]*Reflections on the Nicaragua Treaty*, pp. 3-4, 24-25, 38-39 *et passim.* *Nation*, XXXIX (December 25, 1884), 538.

canal project might prove "a running sore" on the body politic.[23]

When the canal treaty was signed, many Americans were naturally anxious to observe the reactions of the British, protected as they thought they were by the Clayton-Bulwer Treaty. The *Times*, usually rather friendly to the United States, expressed amazement at the first rumors that Nicaragua had ceded territory outright and doubted that American public opinion was ready for the responsibilities of operating a canal. However, when its editors read the official terms, they suggested that perhaps the Republicans had acted for purposes of publicity and hoped that Cleveland would see fit to honor the Clayton-Bulwer Treaty. The *Daily Telegraph* advised Britons not to object to a canal so obviously valuable to their interests, but the anti-American *Saturday Review* sputtered indignantly about "bumptious" behavior and "cool presumptuousness" and called on the Empire to protest against "a crime, not only against Canada and our other colonies, but against the whole world."[24]

Central American reactions to the canal treaty were mixed. Nicaraguans seem to have accepted it willingly enough, although the legislature took its time about ratification, perhaps to avoid losing face if the Congress of the United States failed to act. Frelinghuysen was nervous about Barrios' feelings, since the treaty did not mention him or Guatemala, but Barrios welcomed the news of its signing and again offered his help in securing ratification. Sudden and apparently unexpected opposition appeared in Costa Rica, whose government resented being ignored, since the canal route ran along a still-disputed boundary with Nicaragua. The government demanded a share of the profits and threatened to embarrass the United States by calling for arbitration of the whole canal question, while the president and other officials foresightedly bought all the land near the canal route on which they could lay their hands. In February, 1885, after the whole

[23]*New York Times*, December 29, 1884. New York *Sun*, January 13, 1885. Both are cited in Walton, "Frelinghuysen-Zavala Treaty," pp. 157-58. *New York Tribune*, January 6, p. 5; February 3, p. 4; February 7, p. 4. *Nation*, XL (January 1), 1.

[24]*Times* (London), December 17, 1884, p. 9; December 25, p. 7. *Daily Telegraph* (London), n.d., as summarized in *New York Tribune*, January 19, 1885, p. 4. *Saturday Review*, LVIII (December 20, 1884), 784-85.

matter had become merely academic, Frelinghuysen sent soothing reassurances to Costa Rica.[25]

As for the officials of the French canal company, the United States consul at Panama reported that the treaty gave them "a chill which would not yield to quinine." Newspapers in France pooh-poohed the American action, declaring that the persistence of the Nicaragua promoters only proved the validity of the Panama project all the more, and that De Lesseps would finish his canal by the time Cleveland came to office. Together with these absurd reassurances, a few French journalists suggested wishfully that perhaps Congress would refuse to ratify the Frelinghuysen-Zavala Treaty.[26] Considering the widespread American opposition to the treaty, the recent defeat of the Republican party, and the fast-approaching end of the Arthur administration, their hope was not at all unreasonable.

[25]Hall to Frelinghuysen, Guatemala City, December 5, 1884, No. 292; H. Remsen Whitehouse to Frelinghuysen, San José de Costa Rica, January 8, 10, 25, February 23, U.S., Despatches, Central America, XXIII. Frelinghuysen to Whitehouse, February 10, U.S., Instructions, Central America, XVIII, 474-77. James Russell Lowell to Frelinghuysen, London, January 1 (telegram), 2, No. 924, U.S., Despatches, Britain, CLI.

[26]Adamson to Hunter, Panama, January 31, 1885, No. 134, U.S., Consular Despatches, Panama, XVI. For excerpts from French newspapers on the treaty see *Bulletin du canal interocéanique,* V (December 16, 1884; January 1, 1885), 1117-22, 1131-35.

CHAPTER 16

The Caribbean Reciprocity System

DURING most of 1884, while Frelinghuysen was negotiating with Nicaragua for a treaty which would enable the American government to sponsor the canal project, he was also engaged in developing another part of the administration's expansionist policies. This was a system of reciprocity treaties extending across Mexico, Central America, the northern coast of South America, and the West Indies—an economic application of the Monroe Doctrine to the Caribbean basin, which would dispose of the American surplus while at the same time counterbalancing European influence in an area vital to American security. Early in 1883, as has been seen, former President Grant and Matías Romero had signed a model treaty for the improvement of Mexican-American trade, and after some hesitation the Senate approved this treaty in March, 1884. By that time, however, protectionists of both parties were drawing together with Louisiana sugar interests to oppose the extension of the Hawaiian reciprocity treaty of 1875 and the spread of reciprocity to American trade in other parts of the world. To most observers, therefore, it was apparent that Arthur and Frelinghuysen had their work cut out for them.

* * *

As in the case of the canal negotiations with Nicaragua, the President could point to strong if badly focused sentiment in Congress favoring expansionist commercial measures. In 1882, after the withdrawal of invitations to Blaine's Latin-American peace congress, Senator John T. Morgan and others introduced resolutions and bills outlining new plans for a congress, for a commission to tour Latin America and discuss economic problems, and for the construction of an elaborate inter-American railroad. This last project was the "brain-child" of Hinton R. Helper, the noted antislavery pamphleteer, who had become in his old age

a monomaniac on hemispheric trade and who besieged Congress and the executive departments with petitions and pamphlets for his Three Americas Railway.[1] Expansionists both in and out of Congress kept alive the question of inter-American commerce during 1883 and were largely responsible for bringing about senatorial approval of the Mexican reciprocity treaty. (See Chapter 10.)

Frelinghuysen was delighted to find expansionist support in Congress for his reciprocity treaty, but his enthusiasm did not extend to other Congressional proposals, notably that for an inter-American conference. When the protectionist Senator John Sherman introduced a conference bill into the Forty-eighth Congress of 1883-1884, Frelinghuysen wrote to the chairmen of the Senate and House committees on foreign relations, discouraging the idea, since it would be difficult to secure general attendance, and since the smaller states would probably use their freedom of speech to demand a formal alliance which the United States could not grant. Instead, he argued for bilateral reciprocity treaties in which Americans might obtain special treatment for their manufactured exports, together with navigation privileges and other concessions, giving preferential tariffs in return so as not to violate the most-favored-nation clause of other treaties. Reciprocity, he went on, would be better business than indiscriminate tariff reductions. He also favored bringing Latin Americans to agree upon an international silver coin of some sort so as to provide for the mounting American silver surplus and outmaneuver Britain, still clinging to the gold standard.[2]

In place of a general conference, therefore, Frelinghuysen urged Congress to appropriate funds for a special commission which would visit the Latin-American nations and sound them out privately, while he continued his negotiations for reciprocity treaties. His proposal was designed to reserve the greatest possible

---

[1]Wilgus, "Blaine and the Pan-American Movement," p. 678. The Senate Foreign Relations Committee Archives contain letters from Helper to the committee chairman, William Windom, dated May 1, 15, 19, 22, 1882, and January 26 and February 1, 1883, all urging support for his railroad project, and several undated memoranda in Helper's handwriting. See also *Washington Post*, March 20, 1884, p. 2.

[2]*New York Herald*, December 26, 1883, p. 4. Frederick T. Frelinghuysen to John F. Miller, March 26, 1884, U.S., Congress, House, 49th Cong., 1st Sess., 1886, House Executive Doc. 50, pp. 13-14. Frelinghuysen to John H. Reagen, March 26, 1884, U.S., Senate Foreign Relations Committee Archives.

freedom of action for the State Department and to appeal to free traders and silverites without entirely scandalizing orthodox protectionists. The House Foreign Affairs Committee gave its blessing to his commission and suggested that it also investigate the possibilities of a great hemispheric railroad. After slight discussion Congress voted the necessary money for the commission on July 7, and Arthur appointed as its members George H. Sharpe, a personal friend of Grant, and two obscure lawyers, Thomas C. Reynolds and Solon O. Thatcher.[3]

By this time Arthur had failed to secure renomination for the presidency and knew that the commission could not possibly complete its work while he was still in office. Nevertheless, Frelinghuysen's instructions to the three commissioners set forth his policy of hemispheric economic solidarity at its zenith. At no time since the foundation of the United States, he began, had there been a deeper conviction of the need for unity with the Latin-American republics. Pointing out that close economic relations were an absolute prerequisite of closer political relations, he proposed reciprocity treaties and an international currency as unifying forces, encouraged Latin Americans to develop their merchant fleets, and urged them not to shackle their economies with export duties and monopolies. Convinced that, in the long run, Latin America could advance only with the aid of foreign capital, he read the commissioners a lesson on the principal complaints of American investors against Latin-American governments. As for political union, he reminded them of the Monroe Doctrine and carefully distinguished between American guidance and American dictation:

> This Government cannot assume any control of or authoritative influence over those countries. . . . But it cannot overlook the concurrent interest of all the American states in avoiding and averting all pretext for foreign interference in the affairs of the American continent. It would unhesitatingly favor any common understanding whereby the evils of war among them might be securely warded off by a resort to peaceable arbitration of differences not adjustable by diplomatic means. . . . This Government might even be prepared to consider the practicability of instituting a consultative council of repre-

[3]U.S., Congress, House, 48th Cong., 1st Sess., 1884, H. Rept. 1445, *passim.* U.S., Tariff Commission, *Reciprocity*, p. 141.

sentatives ... whose views as to international questions among them might have respectful heed. Beyond this necessarily inconclusive expression of general views we cannot at present go.[4]

While not one of the great American state papers, Frelinghuysen's instructions to the commissioners deserve as much attention as Blaine's better-known invitations of 1881. Frelinghuysen's debt to Blaine is obvious, but he added an emphasis on economic measures which his predecessor did not proclaim until he had left office. Also, in his list of specific measures Frelinghuysen went far beyond Blaine. Perhaps most important of all, the instructions of 1884, while retaining the explicit warning against European intervention, managed to avoid the air of dogmatism and paternalism toward Latin America with which Blaine had offended many readers throughout the hemisphere when he placed his proposal for a peace congress in the context of American intervention in the War of the Pacific.

*   *   *

While Frelinghuysen sent out the three commissioners to tour Latin America, he directed his main energies to negotiating a treaty with Spain for reciprocal trade concessions covering Cuba and Puerto Rico, for he realized that without Spanish cooperation Cuba would soon be the weakest link in the proposed Caribbean economic chain. Since the stormy days of Narciso López and Pierre Soulé the island had seldom been far from American thoughts, and during the Ten Years' War (1868-1878) only the determination and discretion of Hamilton Fish had prevented imperialists in the Grant administration from securing the recognition of Cuban belligerency and war with Spain over the "Virginius" question. During the Hayes administration Spain had finally put down the Cuban revolution, but with true Bourbon obstinacy the Spanish government made no important concessions for the sake of peace.

[4]Frelinghuysen to George H. Sharpe *et al.*, August 27, 1884, U.S., Congress, Houses, 49th Cong., 1st Sess., House Executive Doc. 50, *passim*. Frelinghuysen gave special instructions for each country, laying greatest emphasis on Mexico, Central America, Colombia, Venezuela, and Chile. William E. Curtis joined the commission before it sailed. A journalist, he had much information and interest in Latin America and became the most active member of the commission. *Dictionary of American Biography*, IV, 620-21.

As before, greedy officials with little control over policy enforced restrictive laws capriciously and squeezed taxes out of the few profitable industries.[5]

The condition of Cuban-American trade was both symptomatic of Spanish reaction and crucial for the future development of the island. In order to favor Spanish shipping, the tariff for Cuba and Puerto Rico contained four separate schedules of duties on Spanish and foreign products imported in Spanish and foreign vessels respectively, and other "differential flag duties" gave further preference to Spanish merchantmen. Spanish goods in Spanish ships enjoyed an advantage of as much as 250 per cent over American goods in American ships. Thus the import duty on American flour, for which Cuba offered a large natural market, was about equal to the whole cost of the flour in New York plus freight to Havana, and other American products paid similar duties. Spanish customs officials levied arbitrary and unreasonable fines for the slightest irregularities in invoices and cargoes, and Spanish consuls in American ports charged high fees which, as Blaine complained, amounted to an export tax. For its part, the United States collected not only a general tariff duty on sugar but also a special retaliatory tax of 10 per cent on Cuban products in Spanish vessels.[6]

Despite the exorbitant duties the total trade of Cuba and the United States in 1881 was $82,585,476 as against only $12,674,157 between Cuba and Spain. Four-fifths of the Cuban-American trade represented Cuban exports to the United States. A few optimistic Americans were buying up sugar plantations and iron mines on the island, but in general, profits and land values declined steadily

[5]On the Grant-Fish diplomacy concerning Cuba see Nevins, *Fish*, chaps. ix, xi, xxviii *et passim*. Even Blaine once admitted to the British minister that Cuba was the one area which he would like to see the United States annex. Lionel S. Sackville West to Lord Granville, Washington, December 8, 1881, No. 335, Great Britain, F.O. 5/1756. For an exceedingly unfavorable picture of the Spanish regime in Cuba during the 1880's see a confidential memorandum of Adam Badeau, Havana, October 23, 1883, U.S., Consular Despatches, Havana, XC.

[6]*Ibid*. Frelinghuysen to John W. Foster, August 28, December 19, 1883, Nos. 64, 108, U.S., Instructions, Spain, XIX, 422-25, 460-67. Foster to Frelinghuysen, Madrid, December 24, 1883, No. 129, U.S., Despatches, Spain, CVII. Same, March 3, 1884, No. 184, U.S., *Foreign Relations, 1884*, pp. 480-81. John Davis to Foster, June 23, 1883, No. 24, *ibid.*, *1883*, pp. 779-81. C. C. Andrews, "Our Commerce with Cuba, Porto Rico, and Mexico," *Atlantic Monthly*, XLIV (July 1879), 81-96. *New York Tribune*, November 11, 1880, p. 5.

during the early 1880's. To many observers the spread of beet sugar in Europe augured ill for the future. Cuban members of the Spanish legislature petitioned the government for a commercial treaty with the United States as the island's only salvation, while American publicists denounced Spanish oppression and declared Cuba a natural part of the American coasting trade. However, the Spanish government hesitated, fearful of rebellion in Cuba and annexationism in the United States.[7]

For a time during 1881 and 1882 American relations with Spain were also complicated by an argument over a long list of claims, some of them dating from the beginning of the century. Under an agreement of 1871 the two countries had submitted these claims to the arbitration of a three-man board, sitting in Washington. Since many claims were presented by naturalized Cuban-Americans (some of them as dubious as the naturalized Irish-Americans), the arbitration board often had to examine evidences of American citizenship. When the chairman of the board, Count Lewenhaupt (the Swedish minister to the United States), decided to go behind the certification of American courts, Blaine balked and refused to submit any more cases. Although he had taken a realistic attitude toward the inflated claims of Irish-Americans in British jails (see Chapter 13), he demanded that Lewenhaupt accept American certificates without question. After some hesitation, Frelinghuysen took the same attitude, to the approval of American nationalists.[8]

In June, 1882, before Frelinghuysen announced his position on Spanish-American certificates, the Spanish minister to the United States, Francisco Barca, inquired on what terms the United States

[7]See the sources cited in the last footnote. Statistics of profits and land values appear in a clipping from the Havana *Weekly Report* enclosed with Ramon O. Williams to Davis, Havana, August 27, 1884, No. 12, U.S., Consular Despatches, Havana, XCIII. *New York Herald*, March 7, 1881, p. 7. David A. Wells, *The Equities in the (Customs) Taxation of Sugar* (New York, 1894), p. 3. American Iron and Steel Association, *Report, 1882*, p. 16. For a Cuban argument in favor of reciprocity see Henry C. Hall to John Hay, Havana, February 24, 1881, No. 987, U.S., Consular Despatches, Havana, LXXXIV.

[8]James G. Blaine to Hannibal Hamlin, December 6, 1881, No. 3; Frelinghuysen to Hamlin, April 4, September 22, 1882, No. 98, U.S., Instructions, Spain, XIX, 17-52, 113-14, 175-93. *New York Herald*, April 23, 1881, p. 4; April 25, p. 3; May 24, p. 6; October 19, 1882, p. 8. *Nation*, XXXII (April 28, 1881), 289. Frelinghuysen to Charles C. Suydam, September 25, 1882, reprinted in *New York Tribune*, October 19, p. 2.

would consider withdrawing its retaliatory duty on Cuban imports in Spanish vessels. Frelinghuysen replied that Spain must first abandon her own discrimination against American products and ships. Six weeks later the Spanish Cortes passed a law authorizing a general reform of Cuban and Puerto Rican tariffs. In February, 1883, about a month after the signature of the Mexican reciprocity treaty, Arthur and Frelinghuysen sent an envoy to Madrid to open similar negotiations. For this important mission they chose John W. Foster, one of the few first-class diplomats whom the patronage system had produced during the 1870's—a Republican journalist and campaigner for Grant in 1872, who had served capably as minister to Mexico during the serious border troubles between 1877 and 1880.[9]

Even before he left the United States, Foster was waylaid by agents of claimants against Spain—one of them insisting that he had a presidential promise of an ultimatum, on the authority of Arthur's dentist! Foster did what he could for the more deserving claimants, but he soon recognized that the Spanish treasury was nearly empty, and, as he remarked dryly, "the Spanish temperament does not admit of celerity in the dispatch of public business." The hubbub of a Carlist revolt and the King's visit to Austria and Germany also delayed negotiations on commercial problems, but by the end of the year Foster had persuaded Prime Minister Antonio Cánovas del Castillo to move American products from the fourth column to the third column of the Cuban differential tariff, effecting a reduction of 30 to 60 per cent in duties. Having thrust in a wedge, Foster then improved his advantage by threatening reprisals if Spain went no further. Although annoyed at Foster's plain language, Cánovas consented on January 2 to remove differential levies altogether from American commerce, as well as most of the consular fees. In return, Foster promised that the American government would remove its retaliatory duty of 10 per cent.[10]

[9]Frelinghuysen to Arthur, January 15, 1884, in U.S., Congress, Senate, 48th Cong., 1st Sess., 1884, Senate Executive Doc. 58, pp. 1-7. John W. Foster, *Diplomatic Memoirs* (2 vols.; New York, 1909), I, 3-5 *et passim*. *New York Tribune*, February 26, 1883, p. 1. Foster had also served briefly as minister to Russia and had then retired to private law practice.

[10]Foster, *Diplomatic Memoirs*, I, 239-57. Foster to Frelinghuysen, Madrid, De-

Far from settling anything, this agreement led only to further negotiations. The Spanish government decided that the whole question should be submitted to the legislature for debate. In order to secure the abrogation of the American duty, however, the foreign minister signed a temporary agreement on February 13 which repeated most of the earlier concessions and looked forward to a full-scale reciprocity treaty. As soon as the new agreement was published, Spanish wheatgrowers and millers held public meetings to protest that the competition of American flour in Cuba would ruin them. (Foster pointed out that Spain customarily imported flour, and that much of the flour which it shipped to Cuba had originally come from the United States.) The British minister to Spain, alarmed at the special duties conceded to the United States, quizzed Foster carefully about details of his agreement, while in the Canadian House of Commons representatives of the wheat provinces called for information on the American negotiations and urged Britain to obtain the same privileges for Canada.[11]

Despite the objections to his provisional agreement Foster advised the State Department to proceed with its plan for a reciprocity treaty. Foreseeing that the Democratic-controlled House of Representatives would probably propose substantial tariff reductions in 1884, he urged the government to retain existing sugar duties, so that the United States might use them as a bargaining counter in negotiations for more trade with semitropical countries, in the manner of the Mexican reciprocity treaty. "This I believe to be the true *American commercial system*, as it combines the best elements of 'protection' and of 'free-trade,' " he added. Foster felt that Cuba and Puerto Rico were ripe for reciprocity, and that in return for lower duties on sugar and a few minor concessions, the United States might obtain "such a treaty with Spain as will secure to us almost the complete monopoly or control of the rich commerce of these Islands." Frelinghuysen agreed whole-

cember 17, 27, 1883, Nos. 107, 131, U.S., Despatches, Spain, CVII, CVIII. Same, January 3, 4, 1884, Nos. 134, 135, U.S., *Foreign Relations, 1884*, pp. 471-72.

[11]Foster to Frelinghuysen, Madrid, January 15, February 14, 15, 1884, Nos. 142, 168, 170, U.S., *Foreign Relations, 1884*, pp. 472-73, 477-80. Same, January 10, 11, February 8, 21, March 27, April 4, Nos. 139, 140, 166, 173, 194, 202, U.S., Despatches, Spain, CVIII, CIX. Malloy, *Treaties*, II, 1681-82.

heartedly with these views and, knowing the dilatory ways of Spanish diplomats, authorized Foster to initiate negotiations in Madrid, to save time.[12]

Meanwhile events in Cuba were complicating the problem. During February and March the American financial distress spread to Havana, where the price of sugar fell more than 50 per cent, and five banks failed within a month. At the end of March the Cuban revolutionary, Carlos Agüero, gathered a few conspirators around him at Key West and launched a small filibuster against the Cuban coast. He had no chance of success, but to protect American residents against possible retaliation, the United States sent two warships to Matanzas. Meanwhile the Spanish minister at Washington started up a lively correspondence with Frelinghuysen over the alleged negligence of Florida officials.[13]

Perhaps even more disturbing to the Secretary, however, was the sudden eruption of Adam Badeau, his consul general at Havana. Appointed largely to please former President Grant, Badeau had continually urged on the State Department the advantages of economic diplomacy: "Cuba stands to day ready to yield us a rich harvest. All that she needs to develop her resources is free access for our capital, enterprise, energy and labor." Of course the Arthur administration sympathized with these beliefs, but because Frelinghuysen was playing a cautious game at Madrid, Badeau, who was thin-skinned like many another amateur diplomat, jumped to the conclusion that the Department was neglecting him. From February to April he complained directly to the President of Frelinghuysen's "vacillating and ignominious policy," accused the Secretary of protecting a dishonest clerk in the Havana consulate, and tried to blackmail Arthur with threats of exposure. Getting no satisfaction from Washington, Badeau then resigned his post and released his complaints to the press, just in time for

---

[12]Foster to Frelinghuysen, Madrid, January 11, February 28, 1884, Nos. 140, 177, U.S., Despatches, Spain, CVIII. Frelinghuysen to Foster, March 14, No. 146, U.S., Instructions, Spain, XIX.

[13]*New York Tribune*, March 25, 1884, p. 4; April 18, p. 4. Badeau to Davis, Havana, March 6, No. 379, U.S., Consular Despatches, Havana, XCII. David Vickers to Davis, Matanzas, April 15, 18, May 16, Nos. 87, 89, 90, *ibid.*, Matanzas, XIV. For Frelinghuysen's views and correspondence see U.S., *Foreign Relations, 1884*, pp. 493-95, 502-21.

the Republican nominating convention and the beginning of the presidential campaign.

On March 28, before Badeau had issued his public challenge, Frelinghuysen instructed Foster to come home for consultation with the President and Congress before continuing the negotiations.[14] With the House of Representatives still deadlocked over the Morrison tariff bill, a business depression spreading over the country, and both parties girding themselves for the campaign, reorientation would have been advisable even without complications in Spain and Cuba.

* * *

For lack of written memoranda in the State Department records, one can only speculate as to the conversations which Foster carried on with Frelinghuysen and other members of the administration. It is not apparent that Badeau's "disclosures" had much effect on Arthur's chances in the convention, on the campaign, or on the administration's policy toward Spain.[15] Several other factors, however, urged haste in the completion of a reciprocity treaty: the continued disintegration of the Cuban economy, the appearance of a groundless rumor that Spain was about to sell the island to Germany, and, above all, the approaching end of the Arthur administration. Frelinghuysen did not draw up elaborate written instructions for Foster but approved his tentative draft, modeled on the Mexican treaty, and sent him back to Spain with full powers to abandon some sections of the draft if necessary. What Arthur and Frelinghuysen wanted was a treaty which would confirm the Spanish abandonment of differential duties on all American products and favor some but not necessarily all American exports. As Foster put it: "We need no special treaty advantages to be able to possess those [Cuban] markets for our provisions and agri-

[14]Badeau to State Department, Havana, October 23, 1883; Badeau to Chester A. Arthur, March 22, April 10, 1884, U.S., Consular Despatches, Havana, XC, XCII. *New York Tribune*, April 29, p. 5; May 3, p. 5. For Foster's views on Badeau's criticism of American policy see Foster to Frelinghuysen, Washington, April 22, Separate A, U.S., Despatches, Spain, CIX. Frelinghuysen to Foster, June 7, U.S., Instructions, Spain, XIX.

[15]For editorial comment on Badeau's criticism see *New York Tribune*, May 25, 1884, p. 6; *New York Herald*, May 26, p. 6.

cultural products. It is in respect to our manufactures that we need the favoring duties."[16]

Foster arrived in Madrid during June and immediately arranged conferences with the ministers of state and of the colonies, to whom he presented the free lists of the Mexican treaty as a basis for discussion. When they objected that Spain, a poor country, could not afford the proposed loss in revenue, Foster pointed out that the United States stood to lose five times as much as Spain ($50,000,000 as against $10,000,000 in duties, if the sugar trade developed as expected). He also predicted the dire consequences of Spanish refusal to negotiate: American reciprocity treaties with Caribbean nations, more claims against Spain, and increased discontent in Cuba, leading to inevitable rebellion. At Foster's suggestion the Spanish cabinet appointed a special negotiator, Salvador de Abacete, to continue the discussion.

From August to November Foster and Abacete held more than twenty conferences before they could agree on the terms of the reciprocity treaty. The Spanish negotiations lasted longer than those with Mexico, partly because Foster inserted into his draft several provisions which had nothing to do with reciprocity but were intended to modernize the outmoded Pinckney treaty of 1795. However, Spanish suspicions of American intentions also delayed the proceedings at many points. Once, in September, Foster became very pessimistic and wrote to his friend, Postmaster General Walter Q. Gresham, suggesting "a little energetic action" at home:

> If we fail in the treaty, I am pretty sure President Arthur will be disposed to "growl" a little, and I hope you and Chandler will back him up, as you know Secy. Frelinghuysen is naturally conservative and not fond of a row. Cuba lives off the United States, . . . and if Spain away off here in Europe is not willing to make a fair treaty with us relative to that trade, it will be to our interest to see the Island independent in the hands of natives who are and will be our friends. And that can [surely] be brought about by a little sympathy or indifference to neutrality matters on our part. We have plenty of

[16]Frelinghuysen to Foster, June 7, July 2, August 29, 1884, Nos. 197, 246, U.S., Instructions, Spain, XIX. Foster to Frelinghuysen, Madrid, July 17, August 4, Nos. 226, 237, U.S., Despatches, Spain, CX. *New York Tribune*, July 9, p. 4.

grounds to quarrel with Spain, but I do not think we want Cuba, although a war might not be the greatest evil that could befall us just now.[17]

The question which caused Foster most concern during the three months of negotiation was not the free list but the extension of Spanish concessions to other European countries. After the provisional agreement of January 2 the British minister had protested to the Spanish government that since Britain had always admitted Spanish products without restriction, Spain ought to extend her the same treatment that she gave the United States. Inasmuch as no pertinent treaty existed between the two countries, Spain could easily refuse, but she had earlier negotiated a commercial treaty with Germany containing a most-favored-nation clause, and when Germany protested, Prime Minister Cánovas gave in. On August 28 a royal decree extended to Germany the same freedom from differential tariffs which the United States had obtained in its agreements of January 2 and February 13.[18]

Anticipating that Germany would also claim any further concessions which the United States might win in a reciprocity treaty, Foster asked the Spanish government at the beginning of his negotiations for an explicit statement of policy. After considerable delay Abacete answered him indirectly by referring to the concessions which Mexico had made to Germany and by suggesting that perhaps the privileges granted to Americans would not benefit German merchants anyway. Foster replied with the American formula for interpreting most-favored-nation clauses—that *conditional* benefits be extended to other nations only if these nations met all the conditions attached. When Abacete seemed to waver,

[17]Foster to Walter Q. Gresham, Madrid, "September 31, 1884" (actually written earlier—probably on September 1), Gresham Papers, XXX (Library of Congress). Foster, *Diplomatic Memoirs,* I, 257-58, 261-63. A full account of each conference between Foster and the Spanish officials is enclosed with Foster to Frelinghuysen, Madrid, November 25, 1884, No. 299. See also his "progress telegrams" to Frelinghuysen, September 24, October 4, 7, 10, 12, 17, 26, 29, November 5, 11, and 18, and his despatch Separate D, Washington, December 8. U.S., Despatches, Spain, CX-CXII.

[18]Sir R. B. D. Morier to Minister of State, Madrid, January 9, 1884, Great Britain, *Sessional Papers* (Commons), LXXXIII (1884), "Correspondence Respecting the Commercial Convention Concluded between Spain and the United States Relative to the West India Trade," pp. 2-3. Williams to Davis, Havana, September 10, No. 24, U.S., Consular Despatches, Havana, XCIII.

he proposed that the new treaty copy the wording of the most-favored-nation clause in the Prussian-American commercial treaty of 1828, which Germany had recognized. Abacete refused, but Foster broke the deadlock by a direct appeal to the prime minister, who accepted a cumbersome formula which, in effect, defined the American position.[19]

By the time this question was settled, the diplomats had agreed on the free lists and the amount of other tariff reductions. At first Foster tried to retain an American tariff on all Cuban sugar above the fineness of No. 14, Dutch standard, in order to placate American sugar refiners, but eventually he retreated two notches to No. 16, as specified in the Mexican treaty. In return, the Spanish government risked the displeasure of its own producers by reducing the tariff on American flour from $4.70 to $1.65 a barrel and on cotton textiles by over 50 per cent. For a time Foster kept tobacco off the list altogether, but at the end of the negotiations he agreed to a reduction of 50 per cent in the American tariff. All in all, the American free list extended to thirty-two categories of Cuban and Puerto Rican products, mostly agricultural, while the Spanish placed on the free list, in exchange, fifty-six categories of American goods, including most types of cast and wrought iron, machines, cotton, wool, and woods. Spain also substantially reduced duties on an even larger list of products and confirmed the removal of the discriminatory flag duties. In addition, the treaty cleared up many doubtful points about the security of American property in Cuba.[20]

Almost a month before he signed the treaty on November 18, Foster predicted to Gresham that it would be "the most perfect reciprocity treaty our Government has ever made. . . . I am quite

[19]Frelinghuysen to Foster, June 28, 1884, No. 193, U.S., Instructions, Spain, XIX. Foster to Frelinghuysen, Madrid, September 9, 25, November 5, 1884, Nos. 254, 267, 299, U.S., Despatches, Spain, CX, CXI. Foster, *Diplomatic Memoirs*, I, 258. The final draft specified most-favored-nation treatment on both sides, "it being understood that the favors or concessions granted to said third power shall be enjoyed gratuitously, if the concession shall have been gratuitous, or said other contracting party giving the same or other equivalent compensation if the concession be conditional."

[20]Foster to Frelinghuysen, Madrid, September 24, October 7, 10, November 11, December 8, 1884 (telegrams), Separate D, U.S., Despatches, Spain, CX, CXII. The final version of the treaty appears in U.S., *Congressional Record*, 48th Cong., 2d Sess., XVI, 148-56.

confident it will result in giving us the almost complete commercial monopoly of the commerce of Cuba. . . . It will be annexing Cuba in the most desirable way." At Foster's suggestion Frelinghuysen recalled him to Washington to stand by during the debate on ratification. Foster's pride in his handiwork was marred, however, by a note of venality, for on the day of his arrival in New York, before Arthur had even submitted the treaty to the Senate, its text appeared in full in the *New York Times*. The secretary of the Spanish senate, the Conde de Romero, who had signed the treaty as an official witness, had then proceeded to sell it to an enterprising journalist for $2,000.[21]

*　　*　　*

During the negotiation of the Spanish treaty the State Department started several other reciprocity treaties along the assembly line. Four days before Foster docked in New York, Frelinghuysen signed a similar agreement with Manuel de Jesús Galván, the minister of the Dominican Republic to the United States. At the beginning of 1883 an American consul in Santo Domingo, H. C. C. Astwood, had discussed "a medium reciprocal treaty" with President Ulises Heureaux, hoping, as he said, to diminish French commercial and political influence. After securing the approval of the Dominican congress, Heureaux's foreign minister formally proposed reciprocity to Frelinghuysen as a means of mitigating the depression in the sugar industry. Upon inquiry from Frelinghuysen, John M. Langston, the American minister to Haiti, also urged a treaty for the benefit of American influence in the West Indies.[22]

Active negotiation began in June, 1884, when Galván presented his credentials in Washington and submitted a draft treaty, largely copied from the familiar Mexican model. Since Foster was then in Washington to settle the details of the proposed treaty with

[21]Foster to Gresham, Madrid, September 28, October 26, 1884, Gresham Papers, XXX, XXXII. Dwight T. Reed to Frelinghuysen, December 29, 1884; January 3, 14, 1885, Nos. 278, 281, 282, U.S., Despatches, Spain, CXII.

[22]H. C. C. Astwood to William Hunter, Santo Domingo, February 16, October 8, 1883; July 25, 1884, Nos. 76, 111, 178, U.S., Consular Despatches, Santo Domingo, X, XI. S. Imbert to [Frelinghuysen], Santo Domingo, October 6, 1883, No. 662, U.S., Notes from Foreign Legations, Dominican Republic, III. John M. Langston to Frelinghuysen, Port-au-Prince, August 4, 1884, No. 11, U.S., Despatches, Dominican Republic, I.

Spain, he had a talk with Galván, examined the Dominican draft, and commented on it to Frelinghuysen. Foster felt that, inasmuch as the Dominicans were more eager to negotiate than the Mexicans, they ought to offer a longer free list. He suggested such additions as cereals, dairy products, building lumber, and rice—the last in order to conciliate Louisiana. Frelinghuysen took Foster's advice and also insisted firmly on the American interpretation of conditional most-favored-nation clauses, which Galván conceded without much argument. In all respects the Dominican government proved considerably more pliable than that of Spain.

The final treaty with the Dominican Republic, signed on December 4, was less complicated than the Spanish treaty, because the existing commercial treaty of 1867 was still adequate in most respects. The new treaty was also more favorable to the United States than either the Mexican or Spanish treaty. The United States agreed to place twenty-nine Dominican products on the free list, including tobacco and sugar refined up to No. 16, Dutch standard, while the Dominican Republic promised to admit, duty-free, sixty-eight American items and (unlike Mexico) lowered the tariff on many other products, including cotton, woolen, and linen textiles, by 25 per cent. Perhaps most striking of all, the Dominican government agreed to make the American dollar its unit of currency in international trade and legal tender up to $100.[23] Thus, as in his instructions to the South American commissioners, Frelinghuysen recognized the power of the American silver bloc and supported the doctrine that unity begins with the pocketbook.

During the summer and autumn of 1884 this doctrine gained followers also in the British West Indies and British Guiana, as these sugar colonies lost their former customers in Europe to the beet growers and realized that the Hawaiians, the Mexicans, the Cubans, and the Dominicans were preparing to elbow them

[23]Frelinghuysen to Manuel de Jesús Galván, July 9, October 28, November 20, 1884, U.S., Notes to Foreign Legations, Dominican Republic, I, 47-69, 71-75. Galván to Frelinghuysen, Washington, June 16, July 17, September 11, October 2, November 4, U.S., Notes from Foreign Legations, Dominican Republic, III. Frelinghuysen to Foster, July 9, No. 204, U.S., Instructions, Spain, XIX. Foster to Frelinghuysen, Madrid, July 25, August 4, Nos. 231, 237, U.S., Despatches, Spain, CX. For the text of the treaty see *New York Herald*, December 18.

out of the American market. In July a mass meeting on Antigua passed resolutions in favor of reciprocity with the United States and Canada, and the chairman of the West India Committee led a group into London for urgent discussions at the Board of Trade and the Colonial Office. A West Indian correspondent of the *Times* even advocated annexation to the United States, crying in despair: "Practically, you say that you can do nothing to help us, though with us it is a matter of life or death. Stand alone we cannot, and hanging on to your skirts means destruction. Give us, then, leave to apply . . . to our big brother who 'bosses' the Western Hemisphere, to take us under his protection."[24]

Several months before these complaints appeared, the British colonial secretary, Lord Derby, had already begun to discuss the plight of the British West Indies with Lord Granville. On May 28 Granville instructed the British minister at Washington, Sir Lionel Sackville West, to point out to Frelinghuysen that since, "as a matter of fact," American products enjoyed most-favored-nation treatment in the Indies, it was only fair to ask the United States to extend the proposed new tariff rates to West Indian exports. Frelinghuysen replied cordially that the American purpose in negotiating the reciprocity treaties was to secure, not most-favored-nation treatment, but special privileges which would not immediately be granted to rival producers. He added that before Britain could hope to see West Indian products on the American free list, she must at least remove existing customs and export duties affecting American trade with the islands. He concluded by wondering if Granville was contemplating a reciprocity treaty like that of 1854, concerning Canada.[25]

After several months of bombardment with pleas from colonial interests, the Foreign Office decided to explore the possibilities

[24]Chester E. Jackson to Davis, Antigua, July 22, 1884, No. 177, U.S., Consular Despatches, Antigua, VI. Philip Figyelmesy to Davis, Demerara, September 27, No. 882, *ibid.*, Demerara, XV. *Times* (London), August 15, n.p.; August 29, p. 7. Albert P. Marryat to editor, London, August 19, *ibid.*, August 22.

[25]Granville to West, May 28, 1884, No. 4; West to Frelinghuysen, Washington, June 10, Frelinghuysen to West, July 16, Great Britain, *Sessional Papers* (Commons), LXXI (1884-1885), "Correspondence Respecting the Negotiation of a Treaty Regulating Trade between the British West India Colonies and the United States," pp. 3-5. Frelinghuysen to James Russell Lowell, December 8, No. 1039, U.S., Instructions, Britain, XXVII, 373-78.

of reciprocity and sent the chairman of the West India Committee, Nevile Lubbock, to join West in Washington. On November 7 West informed Frelinghuysen that in return for free admission of West Indian sugar into the United States, the islands and British Guiana would abolish import duties on nine American agricultural products, and that the islands would add one or two more. West and Lubbock began two weeks of discussion with Alvey A. Adee, who quickly pointed out that Britain would have to raise the ante, and showed them the free lists of the other reciprocity treaties. Later in the month West reported to Granville that the United States would admit West Indian sugar on the same terms as that from Hawaii or Mexico (i.e., duty-free up to the fineness of No. 16, Dutch standard) but wanted other American products such as coal, wood, lumber, machinery, and some textiles added to the free list. Also the United States insisted on its own interpretation of conditional most-favored-nation treaties.

As West added realistically, the Americans were trying to "attach the West India Colonies, by the creation of commercial interests, to the United States," placing them for all practical purposes within the domestic coasting trade. When, at Granville's suggestion, Frelinghuysen drew up a draft treaty for West, it resembled the other treaties except for details. It proposed thirty-five categories of West Indian products for the American free list, including the lower grades of sugar and many other agricultural products, but not tobacco. In return it proposed eighty-four categories of American products for free admission into the Indies, including machinery, a vast array of manufactures, and many provisions, but not textiles. Other American products were to be admitted at half of the prevailing duty, and a ceiling was placed on British export duties on sugar products, coffee, asphalt, and a few others. The draft also restated the American interpretation of conditional most-favored-nation treaties and required Britain to place all American trade with the West Indies on the same footing as her own. West declared that these terms were the only hope of the islands, for, he added, if the Spanish and

Dominican treaties pass the Senate, "the British Colonies will indeed be left out in the cold."[26]

While the Foreign Office was negotiating, one West Indian leader tried another solution. In August Michael Solomon of the Jamaican legislative council went to Britain to discuss with the Colonial Office the possibility of annexing Jamaica to the Dominion of Canada. After securing the Canadian high commissioner's approval, Solomon visited Ottawa and talked to Prime Minister Sir John Macdonald, who cautiously refused to commit himself. As it turned out, Solomon's proposal was soon voted down at home. The interior provinces of Canada were also opposed, but the maritime provinces expressed much concern for their lumber and provisions market in the West Indies. Indeed, when Solomon's project collapsed, the Board of Trade in St. John's, New Brunswick, passed a resolution in favor of union with the United States as a protest.[27]

In addition to the completed treaties and the well-matured negotiations with Britain, the State Department received proposals for reciprocity with three or four other Latin-American nations. During the autumn the president of El Salvador discussed reciprocity with Frelinghuysen while on a visit to Washington, and soon after his departure his foreign minister presented a draft which, he intimated, might be acceptable to Guatemala too. At about the same time a new minister from Colombia arrived in Washington and began informal talks with Frelinghuysen on the same subject. The government of Venezuela, which Frelinghuysen had earlier sounded out on reciprocity in connection with the problem of the Venezuelan foreign debt (see Chapter 7), also showed interest at this time, but action was delayed by the death of Antonio L. Guzmán, who was to have taken charge of the negotiations.[28]

[26]Ibid. West to Frelinghuysen, November 7, 1884; West to Granville, November 20, December 5, 6, Nos. 14, 16, 17, Great Britain, "Correspondence Respecting Negotiation," pp. 8-10, 18-19. West to Granville, December 8, in Knaplund and Clewes, "British Embassy Letters," pp. 179-80. The text of the draft treaty is in Great Britain, "Correspondence Respecting Negotiation," pp. 11-18.

[27]Bradstreet's, X (October 4, 1884), 213-14. St. John's (New Brunswick) Daily Telegraph, November 12, pp. 1-2; November 25, pp. 2, 3; November 27, pp. 1-2.

[28]Antonio Batres to Frelinghuysen, Washington, October 25, 1884, U.S., Notes from Foreign Legations, Guatemala and Salvador, VII. Frelinghuysen to Batres,

As if the erection of a new commercial system in the Caribbean were not enough, Frelinghuysen also chose this time to call for a decision on the continuation of the Hawaiian reciprocity treaty of 1875. In April the Hawaiian government had submitted to Frelinghuysen a draft, simply extending the existing treaty for another period of seven years. Three months later the Senate Foreign Relations Committee reported in favor of extension but asked Frelinghuysen to expand the list of American products to be admitted duty-free and to secure for the United States Navy the right to establish a naval station near Honolulu, presumably in order to emphasize the strategic advantages of Hawaii. The request for an expanded free list brought objections from the Hawaiian minister, H. A. P. Carter, and Frelinghuysen abandoned it. On December 6 the two men signed a new treaty based on the Hawaiian draft, without any mention of a naval base.[29]

Thus when the United States Congress convened after the election, it had four completed reciprocity treaties to consider: one with Hawaii, due for extension; one with Mexico, ratified but not yet legally in force; and two with Spain and the Dominican Republic, newly signed and sealed. Britain was still hesitating, but other Caribbean countries were ready to fall into line. Although Blaine would not admit it, a system of tariff reductions not much different from his vaunted *Zollverein* seemed about to take effect.

*   *   *

The signature of each new reciprocity treaty brought a rush of speeches and editorials, for after the campaign of 1884 nearly

November 25, U.S., Notes to Foreign Legations, Guatemala and Salvador, II, 128-48. Parks, *Colombia and the United States*, pp. 265-66. [Foster] to Abbott, Washington [October 12, 1891], draft, in U.S., Unperfected Treaties, File N. Jehu Baker to Frelinghuysen, Caracas, September 10, December 4, 1884, Nos. 1007, 1063, U.S., Despatches, Venezuela, XXXIV, XXXV.

[29]U.S., Tariff Commission, *Reciprocity*, pp. 114-15. H. A. P. Carter to Frelinghuysen, Washington, April 18, June 3, November 17, 1884, U.S., Notes from Foreign Legations, Hawaii, II. Rollin M. Daggett to Frelinghuysen, Honolulu, July 16, No. 175, U.S., Despatches, Hawaii, XXII. Frelinghuysen to Carter, May 31, U.S., Notes to Foreign Legations, Hawaii, I, 101-3. Frelinghuysen to John F. Miller, June 17, in U.S., Congress, Senate, 56th Cong., 2d Sess., Senate Executive Doc. 231, Part 8, pp. 242-43. Malloy, *Treaties*, I, 919-20. During the winter the legislature of Liberia voted to authorize a reciprocity treaty with the United States, but negotiations never began. John H. Smith to Frelinghuysen, Monrovia, March 6, 1885, No. 118, U.S., Despatches, Liberia, IX.

everyone had an opinion to voice on the much-belabored tariff question. Consequently, although protectionist and free trade leaders planted their pennants at vantage points and sounded their trumpets, they were sometimes drowned out in the confusion.

Even today the historian has a hard time drawing up the lines of battle. For example, some members of the New York produce and metal exchanges went on record in favor of the Spanish treaty, but other members of the same exchanges opposed it just as heatedly. Samuel Gompers, speaking for the cigar-makers' union, called the reduced duty on Cuban tobacco "a deathblow to the tobacco trade of this country," but a cigar-manufacturing firm, Stratton and Storm, welcomed the new duty and promptly shut down its factory (throwing 2,300 men out of work) to await the ratification of the treaty. New Orleans was about to open its great Cotton Centennial Exposition, hoping to attract customers from Mexico and the Caribbean, but it denounced the free admission of Mexican sugar as uncompromisingly as ever. Sugar refineries in New York opposed the Spanish treaty, while in San Francisco newspapers were waging their own private war against the Hawaiian treaty on the ground that it encouraged the Spreckels sugar monopoly. During November Adolph B. Spreckels, son of the redoubtable Claus, contributed to the general excitement by walking into the offices of the *San Francisco Chronicle* and putting a couple of bullets into its publisher, M. H. de Young.[30]

A considerable number of administration newspapers and those identified with low tariffs and the import trade supported all the treaties with slight qualifications. During January, for example, the *National Republican* (Washington) published a series of editorials urging Americans to judge the reciprocity treaties together as a system which might revive depressed industries by providing new markets, and declaring that the country could well afford to experiment with the Louisiana sugar industry, since it was unprofitable anyway. Citing quotations from Blaine in support of more exports to Latin America, the editorials tried to prove that

[30]*New York Herald*, December 13, 1884, p. 3. New Orleans *Times-Democrat*, November 28, p. 3; November 29, p. 4; December 8, p. 1; December 9, p. 4. *San Francisco Chronicle*, November 20, p. 3. For other sample opinions of individuals and newspapers see *New York Tribune*, November 27, p. 2; December 9, p. 2; December 10, p. 2.

reciprocity was not party heresy. Commercially-minded news-papers of New York, Philadelphia, and Washington also defended the treaties for the new markets which they would open to American products. The more imperialistic *New York Herald* declared that the Spanish treaty "makes Cuba for all practical purposes of commerce a part of the United States, without charging us with the political responsibility of its government in time of peace or its protection in time of war." Eventually, it predicted, we shall have "a commercial protectorate over all the West India Islands." Increased trade, whether with or without the visions of empire, appealed also to a great many individuals, both in the United States and in Cuba.[31]

Even a cursory survey of the American press, however, would indicate that opponents of the reciprocity treaties were more numerous or at least more vociferous than their supporters. Since the case against the Hawaiian and Mexican treaties was already familiar to the public, and since some regarded them as compara-tively unobjectionable, opponents of reciprocity concentrated their aim on Foster's Spanish treaty. After about a month of the cam-paign the *New York Herald* listed a motley group of adversaries: protectionists, some free traders, Cuban filibusters, Spanish claims agents, European governments, "pork barrel" politicians, and liquor interests trying to secure repeal of excise taxes. Behind the scenes the vengeful Blaine spoke privately to his friends in Washington against the treaty, while lobbyists and other special interests published catalogues of arguments in the newspapers and circulated private propaganda among members of Congress.[32] The

[31]*National Republican* (Washington), January 8, 1885, p. 2; January 10, p. 4; January 17, p. 4; January 21, p. 2. *Washington Post*, January 9, 1884, p. 2; January 21, p. 2; November 21, p. 2; November 29, p. 2. New York *Commercial Advertiser*, *New York Times*, and *Philadelphia Times*, as quoted in *New York Tribune*, De-cember 10, 1884, p. 2. *New York Herald*, November 19, p. 3; November 20, p. 4; January 13, 1885, p. 8. The *San Francisco Chronicle* favored reciprocity treaties with Mexico and Central America but not with Hawaii. *San Francisco Chronicle*, November 22, 1884, p. 2; November 25, p. 4. Others favored the Mexican treaty but not the Spanish. *Nation*, XXXIX (December 18), 511. *Mexican Financier*, December 27, pp. 194-95. *New York Tribune*, December 26, p. 4. Some doubted that the Dominican Republic was important enough for a treaty. *Ibid.*, December 19, p. 4. For Cuban opinion see Datus E. Coon to Davis, Baracoa, January 10, 1885, No. 95, U.S., Consular Despatches, Baracoa, I.

[32]*New York Herald*, January 6, 1885, p. 6. Muzzey, *Blaine*, p. 452. Foster to Gresham, Washington, December 14, 1884, Gresham Papers, XXXII.

fact that the Arthur administration was trying to secure approval of the Nicaragua canal treaty at the same time only added to the confusion, for opponents of the canal sometimes supported reciprocity and vice versa.

The very number and timing of the treaties provided the opposition with the telling argument that Arthur, a "lame duck" president, was using his declining weeks to embarrass Cleveland and the Democrats and to rush through measures which required closer examination. The *Nation* compared the reciprocity treaties with Blaine's inter-American peace congress, conceived three years earlier under somewhat similar circumstances, and concluded: "President Arthur is not sinning in this respect to the same degree, but he is sinning on the same lines." The secrecy of the treaty and its unfortunately premature revelation in the *New York Times* called forth the familiar demand for more public diplomacy or a popular referendum on the treaty, and some revived the perennial suggestion that the House of Representatives be given a share in approving treaties.[33]

Opponents of the Spanish treaty placed great emphasis on its immediate material defects and objected that it set a precedent for other low-tariff measures. A declaration circulated by the New York Chamber of Commerce and signed within two days by over six hundred prominent businessmen predicted that the treaty would hurt or destroy the sugar and tobacco industries and throw thousands out of work without opening markets to American products in any way comparable to the sacrifices involved. As in the case of the Mexican treaty, skeptics doubted that Cuban purchasing power could be increased: "High civilization and its complex wants will not suddenly appear where semi-barbarism now exists. . . . If the poor people there go without clothes, more or less, the climate favoring, they will go naked still." The American loss of revenue resulting from the treaty was estimated as high as $53,000,000 a year and the increased trade with Cuba as low as $5,000,000. "Really, Mr. Editor," wrote one

---

[33]*Nation*, XXXIX (December 25, 1884), 538. New Orleans *Times-Democrat*, December 13, p. 4. The *New York Tribune* accused Foster of carelessness and haste but a few days later "ate its words." *New York Tribune*, December 28, p. 6; January 2, 1885, p. 4.

man to the *Nation*, "is Mr. Foster a Yankee? Did he ever learn to *kalkerlate?*"[34]

While the treaty failed to benefit Americans, the argument continued, it would provide "a respite for Spanish misrule in Cuba and Porto Rico . . . relief from the American treasury and the purses of the American people for the bankruptcy their [Spanish] pillage has caused those islands." Adam Badeau declared in a letter to the *New York Tribune* that for sixteen years the State Department had been trying to refasten Spanish shackles on Cuba. He predicted that in spite of the article specifying conditional most-favored-nation treatment Spain would promptly extend the new tariff privileges to the rest of Europe as well and thus nullify our advantage. Other pessimists expected Cuban sugar planters to raise their prices, replacing the vanished duties. "In fine," they declared, "[the treaty] will surrender every American interest, take from our national treasury, damage our home interests, the refiners, the sugar planters, the farmers, the manufacturers and the workingmen, in order to support the tottering slave power of Cuba."[35]

Although the sugar and tobacco interests used traditional high-tariff arguments against the Spanish treaty, the *New York Tribune* and some other pro-Blaine organs tried to uphold their candidate's position in the recent campaign by demonstrating that a general *Zollverein* would accomplish more than bilateral reciprocity at less cost: "Instead of a string of complex and separate bargains with each State it would give us one common and simple agreement for the whole Continent." Furthermore, they added, members of a *Zollverein* could not share the special privileges with Europe—unless, presumably, they wanted to risk expulsion. At the same time a committee of the New York Free Trade Club

[34]*Nation*, XXXIX (December 18, 1884), 521. *Harper's Weekly*, XXVIII (December 20), 836. *New York Tribune*, December 10, p. 4; December 11, p. 4; December 12, p. 4; January 20, 1885, p. 3. *Iron Age*, October 2, 1884, p. 24; November 27, p. 16. New York Chamber of Commerce, *Annual Report, 1885*, pp. 100-23. *Commercial and Financial Chronicle*, XXXIX (December 13, 1884), 667-68.

[35]New Orleans *Times-Democrat*, December 10, 1884, p. 4; December 19, p. 4. *The American*, IX (December 6), 131. *New York Tribune*, November 22, p. 7; December 10, p. 2. Germany actually did announce that she would claim all the benefits of the American-Spanish treaty under her own commercial treaties with the two countries. John A. Kasson to Frelinghuysen, Berlin, February 16, 1885, No. 173, U.S., Despatches, Germany, XXXVII.

muddied the debate still further by arguing against the treaty as a deterrent to more thoroughgoing tariff reform. According to its report, the only way to improve foreign trade was to lower duties on raw materials, such as ores, coal, lumber, and wool. By reducing the Treasury surplus or creating a deficit, the reciprocity treaty would make this impossible.[36]

If Congress regarded the press as an index of public opinion or a guide to action, the journalistic auspices on reciprocity must have been even more bewildering than those on the Nicaragua canal treaty. In signing the reciprocity treaties, the State Department had intended to take a single step forward toward more foreign trade. However, if the various groups of critics were to be believed, the Department should have taken three or four steps forward, several steps backward or sideward, or should have remained standing on one foot, waiting for better times or the inauguration of Cleveland.

[36]*New York Tribune,* December 17, 1884, p. 4. *The American,* IX (December 20), 164. New York Free Trade Club, *The Spanish Treaty Opposed to Tariff Reform* (New York, 1885), *passim.*

CHAPTER 17

The Berlin Congo Conference

WHEN the Nicaragua canal treaty and the reciprocity treaties with Spain and the Dominican Republic were signed, Frelinghuysen had already committed the United States to participation in a conference on West African affairs, soon to open at Berlin. The canal treaty and the reciprocity system had evolved out of widely recognized American interests and concerns in Latin America, but the United States possessed few political, economic, or sentimental connections with Africa strong enough to overcome the traditional isolationism toward European diplomatic meetings. Indeed, even while Frelinghuysen was making up his mind to send delegates to the Berlin Congo Conference, he was refusing to intervene in Madagascar, unless France would willingly accept American mediation in her quarrel with the Hovas. (See Chapter 12.) However, although American missionary and trading activity in the Congo Valley was less than in Madagascar, promoters and journalists managed to convince certain key members of the government that the Congo was "a channel through which civilization and all its attendant advantages will be introduced into a region inhabited by 50,-000,000 of people."[1] More than perhaps any other part of the Arthur administration's foreign policy, its actions in the Congo represented a triumph of wishful thinking, propaganda, and well-placed personal influence.

*　　*　　*

At the outset American interest in the Congo was stimulated by patriotic pride in the explorations of Henry M. Stanley, a Welshman whom everybody, including himself, mistakenly thought to be a naturalized American citizen.[2] After migrating to America

---

[1]U.S., Congress, Senate, 49th Cong., 1st Sess., 1886, Senate Executive Doc. 196, p. 166. Hereafter cited as "Independent State of the Congo."

[2]Stanley wrongly believed that because he had taken an oath of allegiance in order to join the Union army, he was a naturalized citizen. After realizing his

as a boy and fighting on both sides in the Civil War, Stanley drifted into journalism. In 1868 he became a foreign correspondent for the *New York Herald*. Drawn to the unknown jungles of central Africa like many other adventurers, he made himself both hero and laughing-stock by tracking down the Scottish missionary-explorer, Dr. David Livingstone, whom the world had given up for lost. Rival newspapers enviously pronounced Stanley an imposter, but the *Herald* boasted of his feat for weeks and sent him back to Africa to continue Livingstone's explorations. For over eight months in 1876 and 1877 he followed the mysterious Lualaba River around a great arc to the north and west until he had proved that it was identical with the Congo and not the Nile, and that it flowed through a lush land of presumably limitless resources.

When Stanley emerged once more into civilization, he found himself on the edge of a diplomatic jungle hardly less bewildering than the one which he had left. At this time the only existing European colony near the Congo was Portuguese Angola to the south. Seeing that the Great Powers were temporarily distracted by the Near Eastern crisis of 1876-1878, the ambitious Leopold II of Belgium had determined to exploit his opportunity. In 1876 he had called a conference of explorers to create a front for his colonialism, the African International Association, with the announced purpose of furthering exploration and civilization in tropical Africa. Leopold sent an agent to meet Stanley at Marseilles, and after the explorer had tried in vain to arouse British interest in his discoveries, he visited the "generous monarch" in Brussels and took service with the Association. Apparently unaware of Leopold's political and economic ambitions, Stanley returned to the Congo and spent five years negotiating native treaties and planting the blue-and-yellow flag of the Association at twenty-two stations along the lower Congo and its tributaries.

The activities of Leopold and Stanley soon created jealous rivals. In 1880 Savorgnan de Brazza, an Italian-born explorer representing France, slipped in ahead of Stanley to secure treaty

mistake, he underwent naturalization in 1885 to protect his copyright, but seven years later he resumed British citizenship. Frank Hird, *H. M. Stanley, the Authorized Life* (London, 1935), pp. 41, 202-3, 295-96. The account of Stanley's early life is summarized from *ibid.*, chaps. i-x.

rights in a large area immediately north of the Congo. About two years later Portugal, alarmed for her shadowy claim to the south bank of the river, pressed Britain to recognize this claim and to resist the encroachments of both France and Leopold's association. The clever Leopold grew apprehensive lest French, British, and Portuguese combine to close the river mouth and shut him out of the rich valley. In order to raise the prestige of his anomalous association in diplomatic circles, he determined to seek recognition from the United States.[3]

Leopold's plan may well have originated in the mind of his friend and agent, Colonel Henry S. Sanford, one of the growing tribe of American ex-diplomats turned promoters. Sanford was the son of a wealthy Connecticut manufacturer, energetic and shrewd, but also, according to Gideon Welles, "fond of notoriety" and meddlesome. During the Civil War he served the Lincoln administration ably as minister to Belgium, propagandist, and purchasing agent. In 1869 he resigned from the Foreign Service and plunged into all kinds of political and business ventures, such as real estate in Florida. He continued to spend part of his time in Belgium, where he owned an impressive chateau, and he served as Leopold's factotum in the African International Association from its creation. It was he who first approached Stanley at Marseilles with the Belgian offer and who undertook to sever the explorer's connections with the *New York Herald*.[4]

Another of Leopold's agents, Colonel William Strauch, also

[3]*Ibid.*, chaps. xi-xxiv, *passim*. For the diplomatic background see Arthur Berriedale Keith, *The Belgian Congo and the Berlin Act* (Oxford, 1919), chaps. ii-iii; and S. E. Crowe, *The Berlin West African Conference, 1884-1885* (London, 1942), chap. i. Younger, *Kasson*, pp. 322-25, covers the ground briefly, with special emphasis on Kasson. During its evolution Leopold's organization was called by several titles, of which African International Association lasted the longest. See also Willard P. Tisdel to Frederick T. Frelinghuysen, London, November 23, 1884, U.S., *Foreign Relations, 1885*, pp. 285-89.

[4]Younger, *Kasson*, pp. 326-27. *Dictionary of American Biography*, XVI, 348. *The Diary of Gideon Welles* (3 vols.; Boston, 1911), III, 39. For an appreciative account of Sanford's war work see Harriet Chappell Owsley, "Henry Shelton Sanford and Federal Surveillance Abroad, 1861-1865," *Mississippi Valley Historical Review*, XLVIII (September 1961), 211-28. On Sanford's early work for the Association see Robert S. Thomson, "Léopold II et Henry S. Sanford," *Le Congo: Revue générale de la Colonie belge*, XI, Part II (October 1930), 295-96; and Thomson, "Léopold II et le Congo, révélés par les notes privées de Henry S. Sanford," *ibid.*, XII, Part I (February 1931), *passim*.

contributed to the campaign for recognition. Sanford and Strauch based their appeal on American interest in Stanley, American sympathy for Liberia, American desire for more foreign trade, and the Southern hope of solving the race problem by settling Negroes in Africa. Soon after the Association was founded, John H. B. Latrobe and other enthusiasts established a branch in the United States. In 1879 Sanford suggested that Commodore Shufeldt stop at the Congo after visiting Liberia on his world tour, and later he urged Blaine and then Frelinghuysen to oppose any European efforts to secure exclusive control of the Congo Valley, since "it is to that vast river . . . that we are to look for relief from the overproduction which now threatens us in some of our manufactories." In April, 1883, President Arthur and a group of friends spent several days visiting him at his mansion in Florida.[5] Thus when American recognition became necessary, Sanford had already laid the foundations.

In June, 1883, he opened his campaign with letters to President Arthur from himself and Leopold II, suggesting that the United States recognize the neutrality of Stanley's new river stations and send a warship to the mouth of the Congo for observation. Leopold was careful to emphasize that the Association proposed to admit American products duty-free, and he even suggested that if Arthur cared to send a consul to the Congo, the Association would pay part of his salary. Arthur took no immediate action, but Frelinghuysen replied for him in an encouraging tone, declaring that he himself favored neutralizing the river posts. By late autumn Sanford had completed his plans, and in November he sailed for the United States, his luggage full of drafts, maps, and a special secret code for cables to Strauch.[6]

[5]Younger, *Kasson*, pp. 326-27. Tisdel to Frelinghuysen, London, November 23, 1884, U.S., *Foreign Relations, 1885*, p. 287. Henry S. Sanford to James G. Blaine, Brussels, June 27, 1881, U.S., Miscellaneous Letters. Sanford to Frelinghuysen, Sanford, Florida, December 30, 1882, in Thomson, "Léopold II et Sanford," p. 297. See also Robert W. Shufeldt to R. W. Thompson, August 2, 1879, No. 45, Letterbook, pp. 123-30, Box CLXXV, Shufeldt Papers. On Arthur's visit to Sanford see entries for April 7-13, 1883, in the diaries of William E. Chandler, Chandler Papers.
[6]Thomson, "Léopold II et Sanford," pp. 298-99, 301-3, 307-9. Frelinghuysen also asked the Navy Department to send a warship to reconnoiter the mouth of the Congo. Frelinghuysen to William E. Chandler, February 2, 1883, U.S., Domestic Letters, CXLV, 424-29.

Sanford arrived in Washington on the morning of November 28, less than a week before Arthur was due to send his annual message to Congress. After an audience with the President, Sanford and Frelinghuysen got down to business at once. The Secretary soon concluded that he could not recommend outright recognition of the new Association without more evidence that the Congo "states" could sustain themselves. At Frelinghuysen's suggestion Sanford drew up a favorable description of Leopold's "philanthropic" project which Arthur incorporated almost verbatim into his message, concluding with a cautious endorsement:

> The United States cannot be indifferent to this work nor to the interests of their citizens involved in it. It may become advisable for us to co-operate with other powers in promoting the rights of trade and residence in the Congo Valley free from the interference or political control of any one nation.

Even this mild language infuriated the Portuguese, but Leopold read the message with much pleasure.[7]

After the opening of Congress Sanford began to develop his campaign along several lines at once. With the aid of the chief justice of the New York Supreme Court, an active member of the Association, he influenced the New York Chamber of Commerce to pass resolutions in favor of recognition. He gave elaborate banquets, granted interviews, and, wherever necessary, paid newspapers out of his expense fund to publish favorable articles and editorials. He circulated thousands of reprints of the New York resolutions. Most important of all, he aroused the interest of Senator John T. Morgan, an influential member of the Foreign Relations Committee and a confirmed expansionist, who was particularly attracted to a venture which would dispose of Southern textiles and Negroes at the same time.[8] During January and February

[7]Sanford's correspondence is reprinted in Thomson, "Léopold II et Sanford," pp. 309-14. For Arthur's message see U.S., *Foreign Relations, 1883*, p. ix. John M. Francis to Frelinghuysen, Lisbon, December 20, 1883, No. 102, U.S., Despatches, Portugal, XXXI.

[8]Younger, *Kasson*, pp. 327-28. Thomson, "Léopold II et Sanford," pp. 315-17. A good later example of the Negro colonization argument is a letter from a Negro, George W. Williams, to John T. Morgan, Boston, April, 1884, enclosed with Williams to Frelinghuysen, May 24, U.S., Miscellaneous Letters. Morgan set forth the plan in "The Future of the Negro," *North American Review*, CXXXIX (July 1884), 81-84.

Morgan read up on the Congo and exchanged ideas with Sanford and Frelinghuysen. On February 23, he reported out of committee a joint resolution to recognize the African International Association. On the following day, however, he presented a supplementary resolution, merely urging prompt action to protect American commercial opportunities. Morgan explained that others had requested the second resolution; quite possibly Frelinghuysen still had doubts about recognition.[9]

During the next month, Sanford continued to work on the Secretary and the Senator, and on March 13 Frelinghuysen wrote to Morgan that he was convinced of the Association's viability and worth. At the end of the month Morgan submitted another report for the Foreign Relations Committee which was one long testimonial to Sanford's effectiveness as a lobbyist. It began by recounting the activities of the American Colonization Society in Liberia as "a recognized precedent in favor of the right of untitled individuals to found states in the interests of civilization in barbarous countries, through the consent of the local authorities." Morgan then described the Association's policies as "in the direction of the civilization of the negro population of Africa" and "intended, in the broadest sense, for the equal advantage of all foreign nations seeking trade and commerce in the Congo country." With some irony he cited the precedent of Confederate raiders during the Civil War, flying a self-created flag, but he placated his Northern colleagues by devoting much more space to the spontaneous generation of the New England colonial governments. He declared that Portugal had forfeited all claims by failing to occupy the Congo Valley, and stated that the trade of the valley already amounted to two million pounds a year.[10]

[9]William W. Halligan, Jr., "The Berlin West African Conference of 1884-1885 from the Viewpoint of American Participation" (M.A. thesis, University of Virginia, 1949), pp. 56-63. Frelinghuysen to John T. Morgan, January 18, 1884, U.S., Report Book, XV, 209-11. Sanford to Frelinghuysen, Washington, February 9, U.S., Miscellaneous Letters. U.S., *Congressional Record*, 48th Cong., 1st Sess., 1884, XV, 1339, 1378. U.S., Congress, Senate, 48th Cong., 1st Sess., 1884, Senate Miscellaneous Doc. 59, *passim*.

[10]*Ibid*., Senate Rept. 393; Frelinghuysen to Morgan, March 13, 1884. Both are found in U.S., "Independent State of the Congo," pp. 161-69. For a more detailed account of Congressional action on the recognition question see Burnette, "Senate Foreign Relations Committee," pp. 217-28.

On April 10 the Senate passed Morgan's resolution, and Frelinghuysen quickly followed with formal recognition. In Brussels
Leopold and his henchmen were overjoyed at the American action and sent Sanford message after message of thanks for his great
services. The British, against whom Leopold, Sanford, and Morgan
had deliberately aimed their arguments, were affronted by the
recognition. The *Times* called it "a piece of very sharp practice—
an act of immorality, in fact," and contrasted Leopold's honeyed
assurances to the Americans with the shrewd, realistic treaty
which he signed at about the same time with France. In the United
States the *New York Herald* and Sanford's claque hailed the action as a piece of constructive diplomacy, but the *New York Tribune* regretted the administration's haste in compromising the nation's traditional isolationism and the Monroe Doctrine, instead
of waiting for Europe to act first. The State Department, it added,
had been "duped and placed in a false position."[11]

The *Tribune* did not greatly exaggerate. The resemblance between the African International Association and the American
Colonization Society, between Stanley's stations and the New
England colonies was more apparent than real. Commercial and
political domination were Leopold's true goals, philanthropy a
secondary concern. At the same time that Sanford was offering
Frelinghuysen and Morgan the lure of the free trade in the Congo
Valley, the King's agents were drawing up new treaties with the
chiefs along the river, giving his stations exclusive commercial
monopolies.[12] The United States had not risked anything except
loss of face, but it had not gained anything either, for Sanford's
inducements were as illusory as Henry M. Stanley's American
citizenship.

*   *   *

The American decision to recognize the African International
Association gave it status among nations which was strengthened
by a recognition treaty with France on the day after Frelinghuy-

[11]Thomson, "Léopold II et Sanford," pp. 326-30. *Times* (London), May 5, 20,
1884. The latter is quoted in *New York Tribune*, May 21, p. 1. A good sample of
the *New York Herald's* propaganda is found in its issue for December 30, 1883,
p. 5. *New York Tribune*, May 27, 1884, p. 4. On the French treaty see also Crowe,
West African Conference, p. 82.
[12]*Ibid.*, pp. 80-81.

sen's action. However, the Congo remained at the center of a diplomatic hurricane among the European Powers for the rest of 1884. In February Britain and Portugal had signed a treaty, establishing Portuguese rights south of the river, but the treaty remained unratified, for Britain was soon embroiled with Germany and France in other parts of Africa. In April, the month when Frelinghuysen recognized the Association, Bismarck at last threw off his opposition to colonies and announced a German protectorate over part of Southwest Africa, thereby arousing much ill-feeling in Britain. At the same time British supervision of Egyptian finances, much criticized by the other Powers, was approaching a crisis.

As a result of these complications, Britain abandoned her treaty with Portugal, and Bismarck went to the point of discussing an entente with France. Realizing, however, that any increase of French interests in the Congo would be harmful to German trade (because by 1884 France was committed to protective tariffs), the German Chancellor decided in September to call a general conference on political and commercial problems in the Congo Valley. Far from threatening Leopold's stations on the river, the Berlin Congo Conference signified general European approval of the Association, although Britain did not formally recognize its flag until after the conference had opened.[13]

When Bismarck issued official invitations for his conference to the United States and interested European Powers, American-German relations were just emerging from the crisis over the Lasker letter and Bismarck's campaign against Aaron A. Sargent, who resigned as American minister in May. (See Chapter 9.) During the summer Sargent was replaced at Berlin by John A. Kasson, a leading Stalwart expansionist in the House and a personal friend of Sanford, who was well acquainted with the promoter's plans and even visited his Belgian chateau on his way to Berlin. Soon after Kasson arrived at his post Frelinghuysen received Bismarck's invitation, which specified that the conference would consider only three subjects: free trade in the Congo Basin, free navigation of the Congo and Niger rivers, and the rules to be followed in es-

[13]*Ibid.*, chaps. ii-viii.

tablishing future African colonies. Asked for his opinion, Kasson declared the three objectives to be laudable and safe. On October 17, therefore, Frelinghuysen accepted the German invitation on the understanding that the United States would discuss only the announced topics and reserved the right to reject the conclusion of the conference.[14]

Appointing Kasson American delegate to the Berlin conference the Secretary left most matters to his discretion. Frelinghuysen indicated that the United States would not recognize anything but completely free trade in the Congo Valley, and that it would favor some sort of neutral political control, such as that of the Association. One of Kasson's first actions was to propose that the State Department appoint Sanford and Stanley to be associate members of the American delegation, both for their expert information and for the publicity value of Stanley's name. Frelinghuysen agreed warning Kasson that he had no funds with which to pay them.[15]

Whatever the value of their presence at Kasson's elbow, the decision was unwise, for both Sanford and Stanley remained agents of Leopold and acted on his orders. During the conference Stanley shuttled between Berlin and Britain, where he was trying to arouse support for the Association with visions of export markets. On one occasion, for example, he told a group of Manchester industrialists that if each Congo native bought one Sunday dress, this access of modesty would consume 320,000,000 yards of cotton cloth. Meanwhile Sanford was conducting negotiations for the Association with the French government in Paris and urging the American minister, Levi P. Morton, to resist exclusive French claims to a section of the Congo. Before long it was apparent to nearly everyone that Kasson's delegation represented both the United States and Leopold II.[16]

[14]Younger, *Kasson*, pp. 322-23, 329-30 *et passim*. The correspondence on the German invitation is reprinted in U.S., "Independent State of the Congo," pp. 7-12 Frelinghuysen made his decision on the basis of a telegram from Kasson (October 14) and before receiving Kasson's longer dispatch by regular mail (October 15 No. 40).

[15]Younger, *Kasson*, p. 330. Frelinghuysen to John A. Kasson, October 17, 23 1884, No. 37 (telegram); Kasson to Frelinghuysen, Berlin, October 23, 24, 28 No. 47 (telegrams), U.S., "Independent State of the Congo," pp. 13-14, 16-17.

[16]Hird, *Stanley*, pp. 196-98. Stanley's Manchester speech is quoted in U.S., *Foreign Relations, 1885*, p. 289. Stanley was not recognized as an associate delegate

One more American had a finger in the Congo question. In September Frelinghuysen had appointed as commercial agent for the Congo Valley Willard P. Tisdel, a friend of Senator Morgan and a former South American explorer and agent of John Roach's ill-fated Brazilian steamship line. Tisdel's instructions emphasized the importance of avoiding entanglements on the Congo and the need of knowing what American products could be sold there: "Both the people and the Government of the United States will be much better satisfied with the early extension and increase of our commerce there than by any other result of your mission," concluded Frelinghuysen. Tisdel set out for the Congo by way of Belgium, where Leopold received him formally, and Sanford out-lined the commercial plans of the Association and hinted that a favorable report on the resources of the Congo would be most welcome. Frelinghuysen soon ordered Tisdel to Berlin to contribute what he could to the American delegation's fund of information before proceeding to his post. During the first weeks of his mission Tisdel accepted Stanley's enthusiastic predictions about the future of the Congo, but his private letters to Morgan show that he was also well aware of Sanford's influence at Berlin. Sanford, declared Tisdel, "was Master of the situation—Of course always yielding the first place to Mr. Kasson."[17]

The Berlin Congo Conference convened on November 15 and after the usual opening formalities proceeded at once to consider the problem of free trade in the Congo Basin. Somewhat puzzled as to how he could further American commercial interests without becoming involved in the territorial rivalries of Britain, France, and Portugal, Kasson determined to confine his remarks strictly to economic and social problems, avoiding anything that smelled

but only as an advisory expert. On Sanford's activities during the conference and his influence on Kasson see Robert S. Thomson, "Léopold II et la Conférence de Berlin," *Le Congo; Revue générale de la Colonie belge*, XII, Part II (October 1931), 328-49, *passim*.

[17]Younger, *Kasson*, p. 328. Frelinghuysen to Tisdel, September 8, 1884, No. 1; Tisdel to Frelinghuysen, London, November 23, U.S., *Foreign Relations, 1885*, pp. 282-89. Tisdel to Frelinghuysen, Berlin, October 29; London, November 25, U.S., Special Agents, XXXII. Tisdel to Morgan, London, November 25, J. T. Morgan Papers, I. William Hunter to Kasson, October 31, No. 43, U.S., Instructions, Germany, XVII, 424-26. Nicholas Fish to Frelinghuysen, October 10, No. 272, U.S., Despatches, Belgium, XXI. Henry Vignaud to Frelinghuysen, Paris, October 14 (telegram), *ibid.*, France, XCV.

political. This policy was agreeable not only to Leopold and Sanford but also to Bismarck, with whom Kasson had established most
cordial relations. Unfortunately it led him in his first speech to
the conference to overpraise the "high and philanthropic European
patronage" of the Association, "dictated by the principles of civilization and humanity," and to declare that the conference must support the Association's actions as the only alternative to chaos.[18]
Leopold's neighbors, who knew him better than did the Americans,
might well have wondered whether Kasson was being credulous,
sarcastic, or merely polite.

Despite his original intentions the American delegate found it
impossible to distinguish sharply between economic and political
issues and to confine himself to the former. One of the first questions, for example, that of tracing the boundaries of the Congo
Basin in order to establish free trade there, at once aroused the
land hunger of the European rivals, especially France and Portugal.
Kasson supported the widest possible definition of the "conventional basin," which eventually included much territory not drained
by the Congo. On November 20, apparently at the suggestion of
the British Foreign Office, Stanley proposed that the conference
decree free trade in a broad belt extending across the whole continent from the Indian Ocean to the Atlantic and including French
and Portuguese colonies as well as the conventional basin. Encouraged by both Bismarck and Sanford, Kasson supported Stanley's proposal against strong French opposition, and with some
modifications it was adopted.[19]

In December the conference proceeded to consider the free
navigation of the Congo and Niger rivers. Kasson had little to say
about the Niger. His principal contribution during this period of
the sessions was a comprehensive proposal to neutralize the whole
conventional basin of the Congo in time of war, forbid the sale

[18]Younger, *Kasson*, p. 331. The text of Kasson's speech of November 19 is
given in U.S., "Independent State of the Congo," p. 34. The protocols of conference sessions are reprinted in the same document, *passim*. For a detailed narrative
account of the discussions see Crowe, *West African Conference*, Part II.

[19]*Ibid.*, Part II, chap. ii, especially p. 110. Younger, *Kasson*, p. 332. Sir Henry
Morton Stanley, *The Congo and the Founding of Its Free State* (New York, 1885),
pp. 394-95. Kasson to Frelinghuysen, Berlin, November 24, 1884, No. 79, U.S.,
"Independent State of the Congo," pp. 42-44.

of contraband, and require disputants to present their cases to a court of arbitration. Once again the representatives of Germany and Belgium supported the American plan, but the Portuguese and especially the French delegates burst into loud opposition to this infringement on their sovereign rights. The final act of the conference provided merely that signatories might neutralize their own territories, if they wished, and must agree to mediation (but not arbitration) before making war. Near the end of the conference Kasson declared hopefully that the French proposals put her "on the same road with us, but at some distance in the rear."[20]

When the conference, despite its announced agenda, turned to a discussion of territorial boundaries, Kasson took little part in the proceedings. During the later weeks of the meetings he tried in vain to prohibit the liquor trade among the natives of the Congo and managed to strengthen a declaration against the interior slave trade. These actions won the approval of many humanitarians in the United States, but they did not represent Kasson's real interest in the conference. On January 12, after opposition to the conference had begun to appear at home, he wrote to Frelinghuysen that the principal concern of the United States was to prevent some colonial Power from closing the gateway to the Congo and shutting out American merchants and missionaries:

> . . . American interests, both material and moral, were equal to those of any other of the enlightened nations of the globe, excepting always the interest in its colonial possession. Not having, nor intending to have, such possessions there, the American interest . . . was to secure equal rights for Americans and American commerce in that country, which had in fact been opened by the daring enterprise of an American citizen, and to secure these privileges, whatever foreign Government might have, or in the future obtain, colonial or other sovereign control of it.

Instead of playing a waiting game, he had done his best to secure common consent to these principles. He believed that he had suc-

[20]Crowe, *West African Conference*, Pt. II, chap. iii, especially pp. 135-39. Younger, *Kasson*, pp. 332-33. Younger is considerably friendlier to Kasson's proposal than Crowe. The text of Kasson's proposal for neutrality and arbitration appears in U.S., "Independent State of the Congo," p. 147. See also Kasson to Frelinghuysen, Berlin, February 16, 1885, No. 171, U.S., Despatches, Germany, XXXVII.

ceeded, and without committing the United States to any entanglements or guarantees, for, he added, the noncolonial Powers
"are in fact mere beneficiaries of the proposed declarations."[21]

Although the United States was not a colonial Power, Kasson
was willing to imitate some of the tactics of those nations which
were. Early in December, at his urging, Secretary of the Navy
Chandler sent the warship "Kearsarge" to the mouth of the Congo
to reconnoiter for a "commercial resort . . . not already lawfully
appropriated by another Power" and directed Admiral Earl English to make a later visit in the "Lancaster." Kasson then pressed
for the establishment of a coaling station, "a general American
factory with dependencies, supported by the presence of an intelligent consul," and "an American association of merchants,
specially devoted to the African trade." Frelinghuysen had approved nearly everything which Kasson proposed until now, but on
receiving this dispatch, he pointed out that the establishment of a
coaling station would be completely inconsistent with Kasson's
original instructions concerning territorial claims. Kasson backed
down quickly and said nothing more about naval bases.[22]

Several weeks later, on February 25, the conference held its
final meeting and formally recognized Leopold's association as
the Congo Free State. Despite their differences the delegates had
managed to draw up a general act providing free trade, free
navigation, and (with some limitations) neutrality for the heart-
land of central Africa, together with declarations in favor of
religious freedom and against the slave trade. Well satisfied with
their contributions, the American delegates did not hesitate to
sign the act.[23]

*   *   *

Long before the close of the Berlin Congo Conference the
American press had begun to debate the pros and cons of American

[21]Younger, *Kasson*, pp. 333-34. Kasson to Frelinghuysen, Berlin, January 12, 1885,
No. 131, U.S., "Independent State of the Congo," pp. 142-45.

[22]Younger, *Kasson*, p. 334. Kasson to Frelinghuysen, Berlin, November 3, December 29, 1884; January 17, 1885, Nos. 60, 115, 138, U.S., Despatches, Germany,
XXXVI, XXXVII. Chandler to Rear Admiral Earl English, Washington, December 5, 1884, U.S., Miscellaneous Letters, December 1884, Part I. Frelinghuysen to
Kasson, January 15, 1885 (telegram), U.S., Instructions, Germany, XVII, 447.

[23]For the text of the general act see U.S., "Independent State of the Congo,"
pp. 297-305.

intervention in central Africa. A sampling of press opinion does not show any marked sectional bias for or against American participation in the conference. At first the *New York Herald* praised both the work of the African International Association and the aims of the conference, as befitted the erstwhile employer of Henry M. Stanley, but early in December the *Herald* suddenly shifted to typical isolationist arguments against diplomatic involvement, finally sneering that the conference was dwindling into "a side show, for the season of court balls is at hand, when . . . the members will do more dancing than discussing."[24] Among New York newspapers the *Journal of Commerce* and the *Times* gave mild support to the conference, but before long the *Times* followed the *Herald* into opposition. Important newspapers in both New England and the Middle West defended American participation.

Criticism of American actions was also widespread from the beginning of the conference. Since Blaine opposed American participation (like most of Arthur's other actions at the end of his administration), it is not surprising to find the *New York Tribune* reporting the meetings at Berlin first with condescension, then with suspicion, and finally with outright hostility, and declaring that Arthur and Frelinghuysen had wantonly violated American diplomatic traditions and interests. The *Nation* had attacked American involvement in the Congo for months before the conference was announced, and *Harper's Weekly* occasionally revealed the same sentiment. Outside New York such newspapers as the *Chicago Tribune* and the Louisville *Courier-Journal* also criticized American participation.

Supporters and opponents of the Berlin Congo Conference differed on the question of its contribution to the peace of the world. At its inauguration the *New York Herald* expected it to teach England and Portugal that rapacious imperialism was "altogether out of date" and to "prove that the methods of peace are far more potent than those of war." Six weeks later, however, the disillusioned *Herald* was predicting that it was "only a question of time

---

[24]*New York Herald*, January 11, 1885, p. 10. Samples of the *Herald's* opinions, illustrating its shift, are found in the issues for November 17, 1884, p. 4; November 20, p. 4; November 23, p. 10; December 1, p. 4; December 10, pp. 4, 5; December 11, p. 4, and later issues.

as to when we shall be called upon to keep men-of-war on the African coast." Others feared a major quarrel of the European Powers and called Africa "the carcass of a sheep among a lot of hungry wolves." Many agreed that Bismarck and France were only awaiting the proper moment to spring upon the weak Association, and others found England "desirous of special, rather than general, advantages, as usual." Why should the United States help to convert the Congo into "a monarchy for some of the impecunious European princes?"[25]

A few defenders of the Berlin Congo Conference laid great emphasis on the humanitarian articles of the general act: "All Christendom is now a unit against the slave trade." Even more significant to them was the prospect of free trade in central Africa. The *Herald* foresaw "an empire as mighty as Hindostan" whose Clive might well be Henry M. Stanley. By breaking the Portuguese tariff monopoly, declared another newspaper, the conference had made possible a new trade route across Africa which "next to the Isthmus canal . . . offers the greatest saving of time to the commerce of the world." Some felt that Stanley's explorations and other American contributions entitled the United States to a share of this wealth:

> It would be somewhat strange if, in view of all this worldwide competition for the new markets of Africa, in view of the over-production that is so much deplored, . . . and in view of the seven millions of American negroes, whose future is such an unsettled problem, there should not be many more Stanleys, white and black, to seize the opportunities which this wonderful continent offers with such tempting promises.[26]

Against every argument of this sort there was an equally vigorous argument on the other side. The *Nation*, for example, declared that the practicability of white settlement in central Africa was by no means proved, and that even if it were, the European Powers

[25]*Ibid.*, November 17, 1884, p. 4; December 24, p. 4. *New York Tribune*, January 1, 1885, p. 4. *Chicago Tribune*, January 30, p. 4. *Chicago Times*, November 13, 1884, p. 4; November 25, p. 4. Louisville *Courier-Journal*, October 19, p. 12; November 12, p. 4. *Nation*, XL (January 8, 1885), 27.

[26]*Cincinnati Commercial Gazette*, January 26, 1885, p. 4. *New York Herald*, December 1, 1884, p. 4. New Orleans *Times-Democrat*, December 4, p. 4. *Springfield* (Massachusetts) *Republican*, January 23, 1885, p. 4.

would only play over again "the game of treaties, war, and mock philanthropy as a cover for treachery, stratagems, and systematic spoiling of the easily deceived natives." Others took a jaundiced view of the sudden humanitarianism of Portuguese slave traders: "Probably they think that just now virtue pays better than the slave trade." These skeptics declared that the Southern plan of settling Negroes in the Congo region was absurd, since "the American negro has never taken kindly to the idea of emigration." Low-tariff editors predicted that as long as protectionists controlled American laws we should have "a precious small share" in African trade or laughed at the idea of a Republican diplomat endorsing a general act which provided for free trade.[27]

"What have the American people gained by taking part in this conference . . . ?" asked the *New York Tribune*. "Nothing but a mischievous precedent at variance with the oldest traditions of their diplomacy." Of all the bugbears raised by the Berlin Congo Conference diplomatic entanglement seemed the most formidable. Many newspapers declared that the main purpose of the meeting was to lure Americans out of their secure isolation: "European diplomatists laughed in their sleeves at the *empressement* with which the gilded pill was swallowed." The *Tribune* quoted British newspapers congratulating the United States upon its new foreign policy and proposing an Anglo-American alliance and permanent American membership in "the European areopagus" whenever it dealt with colonial affairs. The *Tribune* replied with a sniff: "As for the United States, its areopagus is on the American Continent."[28]

The real focus of isolationist fears was the Monroe Doctrine. If Europe welcomed American discussion of African questions, would it not insist on a voice in matters affecting the Western Hemisphere? "Some fine morning," predicted the *Herald*, "we may wake up to find a Berlin, London, Paris, or Madrid conference— to which we may or may not be invited as one among fifteen—

[27]*Nation*, XXXVIII (June 19, 1884), 521-22. *New York Tribune*, November 30, p. 6; December 7, p. 8. *Chicago Times*, December 12, p. 4. *Nation*, XL (January 1, 1885), 8-9. Another editor predicted overspeculation in Africa and resulting panic and depression. *Chicago Tribune*, December 24, 1884, p. 4.

[28]*New York Tribune*, February 28, 1885, p. 4. *New York Herald*, December 10, 1884, p. 4. *New York Tribune*, December 25, p. 4; February 4, 1885, p. 1; February 5, p. 4.

sitting in solemn conclave and settling the internal affairs and local administration of Mexico, Panama, or Nicaragua." Several newspapers reprinted an article from the *Neue Prussische Zeitung* which actually declared that the isthmian canal question would soon be open to an international conference like that at Berlin; and *Harper's Weekly* published a cartoon of Bismarck sticking his nose into Central America.[29]

To the press the question of American participation in the Berlin Congo Conference appeared somewhat less complicated than that of the Nicaragua canal treaty or the Caribbean reciprocity system. It did not involve the violation of previous legal commitments or the technicalities of tariff schedules and production statistics. Like the other actions of the Arthur administration, however, it rested upon a fanciful projection of the American future— a vision of commercial development and international power which many thought to be a wild and dangerous fantasy. Others, however, remembering the prodigious flowering of the West, wondered if these new dreams might not prove within American capacities too.

[29]*Ibid.*, December 25, 1884, p. 4; January 31, 1885, p. 4. *New York Herald*, December 10, 1884, p. 4. *Nation*, XL (January 8, 1885), 21. *Harper's Weekly*, XXIX (January 17), 48. Blaine agreed with this point of view. Muzzey, *Blaine*, p. 425, note 1. However, many other newspapers denied that the Monroe Doctrine was endangered. *New York Journal of Commerce*, March 10, 1885, p. 2. *Boston Evening Transcript*, January 30, p. 2. *Chicago Daily News*, January 8, p. 2; January 9, p. 2. *Chicago Times*, February 11, p. 4. Louisville *Courier-Journal*, February 2, p. 4.

CHAPTER 18

The Repudiation of Arthur and Frelinghuysen

THUS during the six weeks after Election Day, while the country suffered from the hangover caused by campaign excesses, the Arthur administration sprang to life and offered Congress three controversial treaties—with Nicaragua, Spain, and Hawaii—and the first draft of the general act of the Berlin Congo Conference. (Arthur withheld the Dominican treaty for the time being, pending approval of reciprocity with Cuba and Puerto Rico.) The Constitution required senatorial consent to the treaties, and if they were to mean anything, the House would also have to vote on an appropriation for the loan to Nicaragua and on acts to implement the new reciprocal tariffs. Because Congress had not yet passed an enforcing law for the Mexican reciprocity treaty, that question could not be kept out of the debate. As for the general act on the Congo, this was regarded as a treaty requiring senatorial approval, but since it did not impose any immediate concrete obligations on the United States, its main importance was symbolic. If the Senate rejected it, Europe would probably conclude that the American government had no further interest in the development of central Africa.

The "lame duck" Forty-eighth Congress had almost exactly three months in which to settle the fate of the treaties, from the first week in December to midnight on March 3. Even without the obstacle of party feuds, the time would have been too short for the easygoing lawmakers to discuss the many implications and effects of Arthur's new foreign policy. The press made abundantly clear in December and January that the Nicaragua treaty involved unprecedented financial and political commitments in Central America, and that the reciprocity system would un-

doubtedly reopen the whole complicated tariff question, while approval of the Berlin general act might signify abandonment of America's isolation from Old World diplomacy. All three measures called for reappraisal of the Monroe Doctrine. As Blaine in 1881, about to leave the State Department, had tried to bind his successor to a series of new departures, so now Arthur and Frelinghuysen seemed to have even broader commitments in mind.

*   *   *

Although the administration had no time to spare, the complex political makeup of the Forty-eighth Congress required a careful approach. In the Republican-controlled Senate Arthur and Frelinghuysen dealt most directly with the Foreign Relations Committee, of which a majority were favorable to their views. When Frelinghuysen entered the State Department, the Half-Breeds on the committee, resenting his reversal of Blaine's Latin-American policy, had criticized his caution and tried to urge him into expansionism. During 1883 and 1884, however, as Frelinghuysen developed an expansionist policy of his own, a bipartisan coalition on the committee, consisting of Chairman John F. Miller, George F. Edmunds, E. G. Lapham, John T. Morgan, and three others, regularly supported the administration, as in the debates on the Mexican reciprocity treaty, the recognition of the Congo association, and the inspection of American pork products.

Throughout the session of 1884-1885 Senator Miller "went down the line" for the Arthur-Frelinghuysen foreign policy, defending the Nicaragua canal as "the nation's opportunity, and the turning point in the destiny of the Pacific States" and urging America "to peacefully assert its power and utilize its influence among the nations of the West." The second-ranking Republican on the committee, John Sherman of Ohio, was considerably more influenced by Blaine's opposition to the Arthur administration and had serious misgivings on reciprocity, but his leanings toward imperialism tended to neutralize his position. Even after the election, only one of the Democratic members of the committee deserted the coalition, and the ranking Democrats, Morgan and George H. Pendleton of Ohio, consistently supported the administration. As has been seen, Morgan threw his influence behind the Nicaragua

treaty and the recognition of the Congo association months before the treaties were submitted to the Senate. Thus, in spite of Sherman's defections, the Foreign Relations Committee seldom made trouble for Arthur and Frelinghuysen.[1]

Unfortunately, the committee did not represent an accurate cross-section of the Senate, so that when Miller reported a treaty or resolution on the floor, the administration had not won even half of the battle. In the first place, the Democratic minority, which controlled more than one-third of the votes, was not disposed to form a coalition. Although the Democrats had failed to win the Senate in the recent election, they had every reason to delay action on foreign policy until Cleveland took office; and when it became known that one of their number, Thomas F. Bayard of Delaware, might be the new secretary of state, Democratic senators looked to him for indications as to Cleveland's wishes. It seems likely that Bayard was at least partly responsible for Cleveland's later decision to withdraw the treaties for reconsideration.[2]

Among the Republican senators the presidential campaign left deep wounds which had only begun to heal. As already indicated, Blaine felt that he had lost the election in large part because Arthur had refused to support him, and he set out at once to sabotage the President's program. His unsigned editorials in the *New York Tribune* dropped veiled hints of official corruption and bribes to the Nicaragua canal company. He told the British minister that American participation in the Congo conference was utterly inconsistent with the Monroe Doctrine and repeatedly denounced the reciprocity treaties to his friends in Congress, adding in disgust, "There are too many treaties before the Senate just now." Most Republicans could agree with this last sentiment, for after the humiliating electoral defeat they would have preferred to let the Democrats assume the dangerous responsibility of initiating

[1]Burnette, "Senate Foreign Relations Committee," pp. 132-34, 137, 139-40, 200, 264-68, 503-6 *et passim*. Miller's views are quoted from John F. Miller, *Nicaragua Canal: Address Delivered before the Chamber of Commerce, . . . San Francisco, June 17, 1885* (San Francisco, 1885), pp. 18-20.

[2]Burnette, "Senate Foreign Relations Committee," p. 200. Examples of letters putting pressure on Bayard may be found in the Bayard Papers; for example, one in Volume LXXI from Sidney Webster, dated March 3, 1885, urging Bayard to have the reciprocity treaties withdrawn from the Senate.

policy. One of them remarked plaintively: "We could then antagonize them, if necessary, with much greater ease and more
chances of success."[3]

In the House of Representatives a deep split between the high-
tariff and low-tariff factions of the Democratic party reduced the
strength of the party's majority. However, although the defeat
of the Morrison tariff bill in May, 1884, had caused much resentment against Samuel J. Randall, the leader of the protectionists,
Speaker John G. Carlisle and his reform faction could not jeopard-
ize their recent victory at the polls by joining hands with low-
tariff Republicans to support the reciprocity treaties, especially
since Cleveland was maintaining silence on most issues. Democrat
Abram S. Hewitt continued to work for the Mexican reciprocity
treaty in the Ways and Means Committee, but no outstanding
champions appeared for the other measures. Faction-ridden and
disorderly, the House accomplished little of importance during
the session, for, as one journalist wrote: "It takes a two-to-one
vote to pass anything in the House to-day and it is more than
two-to-one that no bill can pass under such circumstances."[4]

*   *   *

When Arthur sent the Nicaragua canal treaty to the Senate on
December 10, he accompanied it with a long message, describing
the canal as "primarily a domestic means of water communication
between the Atlantic and Pacific shores of the two countries
which unite for its construction, the one contributing the territory and the other furnishing the money therefor." He called
the project a partnership and emphasized its political and commercial benefits to the United States, binding California more firmly
to the Union and opening the west coast of Latin America and
the Far East to American trade. Although he thought finances a
secondary consideration, he expected the canal to be "immediately
remunerative." Arthur managed to avoid any indication that
American control over the canal zone represented a new type of
domain, and he completely ignored the Clayton-Bulwer Treaty.
Without waiting for the Senate to act, he commissioned Aniceto

---

[3]*New York Tribune*, December 20, 1884, p. 2. For Blaine's opposition, see
Muzzey, *Blaine*, pp. 425 (note), and 452.
[4]Quoted in Barnes, *Carlisle*, p. 85. On the session in the House see *ibid.*, pp. 84-90.

G. Menocal of the Maritime Canal Company to lead a surveying expedition into Nicaragua.[5]

Although the treaty and Arthur's message were secret, rumors about the contents started the first wave of editorials about the treaty, and opposition appeared at once within the Senate. One senator tried in vain to have the usual bond of secrecy removed from the debate over such an important measure. When this maneuver failed, G. G. Vest of Missouri, for years a sponsor of the Eads ship-railway, offered a resolution disapproving of the survey expedition, which served as an excuse for several days of open debate. At this time the first scruples over the Clayton-Bulwer Treaty appeared, but Edmunds declared that he was in favor of the conflicting Nicaragua treaty, regardless of the British reaction. Representatives of an earlier canal project, long dormant, submitted petitions against the treaty, and there was evidence of opposition even within the Maritime Canal Company, but down to the day of his departure on the surveying expedition Menocal lobbied effectively in its behalf. In answer to an inquiry from Miller, Frelinghuysen remarked that if former concessionaires had any grievances, they must apply for relief to Nicaragua, not to the United States.[6]

On December 18 the pirated text of the Nicaragua treaty appeared in the *New York Tribune*, and disgruntled senators set in motion a resolution of inquiry which was halted when Morgan suggested that the President himself might have released the text. (Since the *Tribune* was an antiadministration newspaper, and since reports of executive sessions continued to leak out, this suggestion seems dubious.) During the remainder of December the case against the treaty was fully developed: that it required unnecessary money payments to the Maritime Canal Company and to Nicaragua which would probably be wasted on bribes; that it was an unconstitutional or dangerous extension of American jurisdiction; and that, as a

[5]Richardson, *Messages and Papers*, VIII, 256-60. Mack, *Land Divided*, p. 217.
[6]Burnette, "Senate Foreign Relations Committee," pp. 170-73. Walton, "Frelinghuysen-Zavala Treaty," pp. 148-49. A. L. Blackman to S. M. Cullom, New York, December 10, 1884, U.S., Senate Foreign Relations Committee Archives. Blackman to [Frederick T. Frelinghuysen], December 10, U.S., Miscellaneous Letters, December 1884, Part I. Frelinghuysen to John F. Miller, December 26, U.S., Report Book, XVI, 54-55.

violation of the Clayton-Bulwer Treaty, it would embroil the United States and Great Britain. Seeing the rising opposition, Arthur and Frelinghuysen summoned the Foreign Relations Committee to a private meeting. At this meeting Arthur appears to have defended the payment to the canal company and the notorious "slush fund" of the preceding summer (see Chapter 15), and appointed Edmunds, Lapham, and Miller as a special subcommittee to secure ratification at all costs.[7]

On January 14 Frelinghuysen provided the Foreign Relations Committee with a long defense brief for use in subsequent debates. He repeated his views on the Clayton-Bulwer Treaty—that it had lapsed, and that the canal would benefit Britain in the long run anyway. He declared that few private lands along the canal route would need to be purchased, that the loan to Nicaragua would go for useful public works, and that it would be fully secured by a mortgage on the canal. He enclosed an explicit denial by former President Zavala of Nicaragua (cosigner of the treaty) that the "slush fund" had been intended for bribes. He added letters to prove that the canal was mechanically practical, and that the Costa Rican government fully approved of it. Then he concluded with a recital of the advantages of the canal project:

> It tends to prevent alien control or encroachments upon this continent, without interfering in any way with the free and independent sovereignty of Nicaragua and without discriminating against any other nation. It knits our own country more closely together . . . ; it opens the markets of Asia and the west coast of South America to the manufacturers of the Atlantic seaboard . . . ; it provides a new field for our coasting trade, and incidentally tends to the increase of the American steam merchant marine. . . .

Declaring that all nations would benefit from the canal, he pronounced the treaty "conservative and tending to the continuance of that amity and friendship which it is our desire to cultivate with all nations."[8]

Since by this time senatorial opposition centered in the question

[7]Burnette, "Senate Foreign Relations Committee," pp. 175-78. *Washington Post,* January 20, 1885.
[8]Frelinghuysen to Miller, January 14, 1885, U.S., Senate Foreign Relations Committee Archives.

of the Clayton-Bulwer Treaty, the Foreign Relations Committee reported out amendments by Sherman making canal tolls equal for ships of all nations and requiring both contracting parties to secure the abrogation of all existing treaties which might conflict with the canal treaty. (Inasmuch as Britain had shown no willingness to change or cancel the Clayton-Bulwer Treaty, this provision alone might have delayed the construction of the canal indefinitely.) Sherman's first amendment on canal tolls was defeated, but despite a long speech by Edmunds, denouncing the Clayton-Bulwer Treaty, the second and more important amendment was adopted, 33-19. In this part of the debate Bayard, the leader of the Democratic opposition, upheld the entire validity of the Clayton-Bulwer Treaty and later introduced another unacceptable amendment deleting from the treaty the pledge to defend Nicaraguan territory from outside attack.[9]

On January 29 the treaty came to a vote and received a majority of nine—too few for ratification. Since all Republicans but one and only one Democrat outside the Foreign Relations Committee voted in its favor, it seems likely that the rejection of the treaty was a party affair, organized by Bayard. During the last week of the session Frelinghuysen sent to the Senate dispatches from Minister Kasson in Berlin calling attention to German and French interest in Central America and a dispatch from Consul Thomas Adamson in Panama describing the opposition of the French canal company to the American treaty. Frelinghuysen urged the Foreign Relations Committee at least to bring the treaty to a vote again before the session closed, but this was impossible.[10] At the end of Arthur's term it was floating in senatorial limbo on a motion to reconsider the original vote.

As Arthur and Frelinghuysen gave up hope for their treaty and prepared to leave office, affairs in Central America boiled up to a climax which would have forced them to reconsider most of

[9]Burnette, "Senate Foreign Relations Committee," pp. 179-82. This account makes use of the Senate *Executive Journal* to trace the course of the largely secret debate. *New York Tribune*, January 27, 1885, p. 4. *Washington Post*, January 30, p. 1. Thomas F. Bayard to George Gray, April 28, 1894, as quoted in Tansill, *Foreign Policy of Bayard*, p. 676.

[10]Burnette, "Senate Foreign Relations Committee," pp. 182-86. *New York Herald*, January 30, p. 2. Frelinghuysen to Miller, February 25, March 2, U.S., Senate Foreign Relations Committee Archives.

their policy, had they stayed in power. On February 28 President Barrios of Guatemala proclaimed the union of Central America under his leadership. Honduras accepted the decree; the president of El Salvador refused; and Barrios invaded his neighbor. But the beginning of the campaign was also its end, for he was killed in action on April 2 at the Battle of Chalchuapa, and with his death the movement for unification collapsed.[11]

Meanwhile, in January internal rivalries in Colombia led to a full-scale revolution against Bogotá in the cities along the Caribbean coast and on the Isthmus of Panama. At the request of the Colombian government, a small detachment of American marines landed in Colón and spent one night there, protecting the Panama Railway. A few days earlier the opportune arrival of an American warship at Cartagena on a routine cruise saved the city and its American residents from attack by the rebel forces. After a lull of several weeks civil war broke out again in Panama, and on April 14 Bogotá once again requested American intervention under the treaty of 1846. The Navy had already ordered the Atlantic Squadron to Colón, and other troops arrived at the same time. From early April to the middle of May two battalions of marines with a few pieces of light artillery maneuvered on the isthmus until order was restored.[12]

Had the Senate approved the Nicaragua canal treaty and had either Arthur or Blaine occupied the presidency after March 4, 1885, it is difficult to say how these events would have shaped their isthmian policy. Certainly no one could have capitalized them less than Cleveland. When he appointed Bayard secretary of state, it was clear that he would not press for the ratification of the canal treaty. Instead, a few weeks after his inauguration he recalled the treaty for "reconsideration," and it was never seen

[11] The dispatches of United States Minister Henry C. Hall and others describing these events appear in U.S., *Foreign Relations, 1885*, pp. 73ff. Nicaragua appealed in vain for the United States to mediate. F. Castellon to Bayard, Managua, March 7, 1885, U.S., Notes from Foreign Legations, Nicaragua, II.

[12] Parks, *Colombia and the United States*, pp. 228-30. Edmund W. P. Smith to John Davis, Cartagena, January 29, 1885, No. 134, U.S., Consular Despatches, Cartagena, X. R. K. Wright, Jr. to William Hunter, Colón, January 20, No. 19, *ibid.*, Colón, XI. For an eyewitness account of the marine occupation see Captain Richard S. Collum, "The Expedition to Panama (March-May 1885)," typed manuscript in New York Public Library.

again. During May he withdrew the marines from Panama, and in his first annual message he opposed the imperialistic alliance with Nicaragua and endorsed a neutralized canal. Thereafter the Cleveland administration stayed out of Central American affairs.

For all their experience in the lobbies of Congress and the State Department, the canal promoters could not rekindle the extinguished flame. James B. Eads continued to seek Congressional support for his ship-railway until his death in 1887. Ammen's Maritime Canal Company quietly disintegrated, for its concession had expired in September, 1884, and its financial backing had vanished as a result of the failure of Grant's banking firm. During the late 1880's Menocal and a group of prominent men organized a second Provisional Canal Company, secured another concession from Nicaragua, put out new propaganda, and bought up some of De Lesseps' dredging equipment. Once again, however, Congress failed to pass any supporting legislation, and in 1893 the company failed. By that time De Lesseps' company had gone bankrupt too, relieving the American public of most of its fears, so that it could resume its complacency about the isthmian question for a few more years.[13]

*   *   *

On the same day that Arthur sent the Nicaragua canal treaty to the Senate he also submitted the reciprocity treaty with Spain. Nearly everyone anticipated a fierce struggle over this treaty, for the tariff question was a familiar battleground of the 1880's, and the debates on the Mexican treaty had clarified the principal arguments for and against reciprocity. Business groups in more than twenty states pelted Congress with petitions, mostly against the treaty. John L. Hayes and the National Association of Wool Manufacturers, although not directly affected by the proposed new rates, drew up a formidable protest against all commercial treaties which might threaten the protective system. Wharton Barker, the Louisiana sugar planters, and industrialists of all description echoed Hayes's sentiments in letters to John Sherman of the Foreign Relations Committee and other senators susceptible to business

[13]Dorsey, *Road to the Sea*, pp. 289-94. Keasbey, *Nicaragua Canal*, pp. 437-38. Mack, *Land Divided*, pp. 217-22. For Cleveland's remarks on the canal see Richardson, *Messages and Papers*, VIII, 327-28.

pressure. In particular, they concentrated their advice and ex-
hortations on Justin S. Morrill of Vermont, author of the original
Civil War tariff and chairman of the Senate Finance Committee,
a position of great strategic importance in tariff debates.[14]

Since Blaine and most prominent business leaders opposed the
reciprocity treaty, Arthur had to depend on loyal proadministration Stalwarts, such as Miller on the Foreign Relations Committee,
who managed to hold a precarious majority of his committee for
the treaty. Bayard and the Democrats were subjected to the same
sort of pressure as protectionist Republicans, and even J. B. Beck
and his low-tariff contingent opposed the treaty as an inadequate
makeshift which would benefit Spain unduly and lessen the chances
of genuine tariff reform.[15]

Facing these discouraging prospects, Miller called the Foreign
Relations Committee to begin preliminary discussion of the Spanish treaty and, doubtless remembering the debates over the Hawaiian treaty in 1875, asked Frelinghuysen if there were not
some "political considerations important to this country" behind
the negotiations which might be useful in attracting votes. In a
long reply the Secretary denied that the administration had the
slightest intention of annexing Cuba or Puerto Rico. The treaty,
he said, "by bringing the islands into close commercial connection
with the United States confers upon us and upon them all benefits
which would result from annexation were that possible." It was
intended to be "one of a series of international engagements"—
reciprocity treaties with Mexico, Santo Domingo, Central America,
and Colombia and the canal treaty with Nicaragua—"which bringing the most distant parts of our country into closer relations,
opens the markets of the West coast of South America to our

[14]New Orleans *Times-Democrat*, December 6, 1884, p. 4. *New York Tribune*,
December 9, p. 2; January 8, 1885, p. 2. U.S., *Congressional Record*, 48th Cong.,
2d Sess., XVI, Index, p. 160. Wharton Barker to Benjamin Harrison, November 21,
1884; Barker to Justin S. Morrill, Philadelphia, December 8, Barker Papers. John
L. Hayes to Morrill, Boston, December 8, Justin S. Morrill Papers, Box II (Baker
Library, Harvard University). Hayes to Morrill, Boston, January 6, 8, 1885;
C. W. Sheldon to Morrill, Rutland, Vermont, November 24, 1884; Morrill to Sheldon, Washington, November 27, Morrill Papers, XXXIV (Library of Congress).
[15][Rodman Gibbons] to Bayard, New York, January 12, 1885; John H. Allen
to Bayard, Brooklyn, January 15, Bayard Papers, LXIX. J. B. Beck to David A.
Wells, Washington, December 13, 1884; William R. Morrison to Wells, December 14, Wells Papers, XXI.

trade and gives us at our doors a customer able to absorb a large portion of those articles which we produce in return for products which we cannot profitably raise." Instead of security (as in the original defense of the Hawaiian treaty), Frelinghuysen offered Miller primarily economic ammunition.

The rest of his letter attempted to answer the leading arguments against the treaty which were already springing up in Congress and the press: that it sacrificed too much tariff revenue, that it would ruin the domestic sugar and tobacco industries, and that it was unconstitutional. The letter appears to have made few converts, for the press denounced Frelinghuysen's arguments as loose and illogical and suggested that if the language of the treaty were no better chosen, the United States had probably been outmaneuvered.[16] For the first month of the session the Senate continued to discuss the treaty in secret, even though its text was public property.

On January 7 Morrill brought the discussion into the open for a time by introducing a resolution condemning "so-called reciprocity treaties, having no possible basis of reciprocity with nations of inferior population and wealth." He followed up at once with a long speech which ably summarized the protectionist case. In the first place he denied the legality of reciprocity treaties—a "limping subterfuge, designed to escape a plain provision of our Constitution"—because they encroached upon the power of the House to initiate money bills. Secondly, he declared them "everywhere incurably wrong" and unalterably at war with the most-favored-nation principle. Thirdly, he denied that any prospect of foreign trade justified the sacrifice of local markets:

> The time is long past when nations can be enormously enriched by any excessive profits upon foreign trade. . . . It is only those articles produced by cheaper labor than anywhere else, or specialties not to be found elsewhere, that are even tolerably sure of a remunerative market, and then largely dependent on the cheapest transportation. National wealth must now and hereafter be mainly created by labor at home; and

[16]Burnette, "Senate Foreign Relations Committee," pp. 157-59. Frelinghuysen to Miller, December 26, 1884, U.S., Senate Foreign Relations Committee Archives. *Nation*, XXXIX (December 18), 511. *New York Tribune*, December 28, p. 6.

the home market is the only one of value over which any nation now has absolute control.

To economic imperialists he quoted Disraeli's disillusioned remark: "These wretched colonies . . . are a millstone around our necks."

Morrill then proceeded to draw and quarter the Mexican treaty as a horrible example. Mexico, he admitted, was a beautiful country with many natural resources, but since her Indian-Spanish population could never become good customers for our manufactured goods, reciprocity would be like trading "the American Lexington or Morgan horse . . . for the Mexican mustang and stump-tail mule." He ridiculed the treaty's "pretentious padding" and added, with a suspicious glance at former President Grant: "There is, perhaps, something too much of railroads in [its] warp and woof." Leaving the Mexican treaty in pieces, he turned to the "jug-handled" Hawaiian treaty and belittled the machinations of naval strategists: "We flatter ourselves with having American ascendancy in the Pacific Ocean, but it is an ascendancy incapable of withstanding the slightest aggression, . . . which a modern gunboat, or a few Old World guineas, might extinguish in forty minutes." Then he swept on into a peroration bristling with warnings against executive encroachments and imperialist wars.[17]

While protectionists applauded Morrill's words, E. G. Lapham, an administration supporter on the Foreign Relations Committee, tried to answer his constitutional arguments, and after a parliamentary tug-of-war Miller managed to snatch Morrill's resolution for his own committee, where it was quietly smothered. Frelinghuysen let more than a month pass before supplying the administration senators with an answer to Morrill's speech. When it arrived, it was a bit too windy and stodgy in places, but it contained statistics to prick some of Morrill's too-simple generalizations. Since American imports from Cuba and Puerto Rico already outweighed American exports to these islands by more than four to one, Frelinghuysen thought that any change must be for the better. Under reciprocity the annual Hawaiian consumption of American goods had increased $37.34 per capita. If the results were one-tenth as favorable in Latin America, our total annual exports there might

[17] U.S., *Congressional Record*, 48th Cong., 2d Sess., XVI, 506-13.

increase from $150,693,000 to $226,081,600. At the end he restated the credo of economic expansionism in terms fully as emphatic as anything in Morrill's speech:

> The resources of the countries with which such treaties may be concluded are practically without limit, and their governments and people are fully alive to this fact. It follows that the superior nation which aids in such development can monopolize the greater portion of the import trade of each and all. . . .
>
> To attain such a consummation some revenue will have to be surrendered, and, perhaps, some home trade displaced; but for every dollar of revenue surrendered, and for every dollar's worth of home trade displaced, we will receive equivalent in our enlarged exports, and the impetus given to our various industries from the field to the factory and from the foundry to the ship yard.[18]

Inasmuch as the remainder of the Senate debate was confined to executive session, it is impossible to determine the effect of Frelinghuysen's arguments, when passed on by Miller and his committee, but by the middle of February the chances of the Spanish treaty were fading fast. On February 24 Arthur amended the treaty, extending the time limit for implementing legislation, and on March 2, as a final inducement, he sent to the Senate four additional articles, obtained from Spain, removing tobacco from the free list and allowing a token tariff on Cuban sugar. All in vain; the treaty remained unratified. After his inauguration Cleveland withdrew it, with the Nicaragua treaty, to enter the State Department's morgue of "unperfected treaties." Late in February the British minister, Lionel S. Sackville West, received instructions from Lord Granville rejecting the American terms of reciprocity with the British West Indies, but West tactfully withheld the bad news until after Inauguration Day, and Cleveland did not resume negotiations. The Dominican treaty and the draft treaties which the governments of Colombia and El Salvador had prepared also went to the morgue.[19]

[18]Frelinghuysen to Miller, February 12, 1885, in U.S., Congress, Senate, 48th Cong., 2d Sess., 1885, Senate Miscellaneous Doc. 45, *passim. Ibid., Congressional Record,* XVI, 548-51. Burnette, "Senate Foreign Relations Committee," p. 157.

[19]*Ibid.,* pp. 159-60. Frelinghuysen to Arthur, March 2, 1885, U.S., Senate Foreign Relations Committee Archives. Grover Cleveland to Senate, March 12, U.S., Report

Since the Mexican reciprocity treaty was already ratified, postponement did not immediately extinguish its prospects. The opponents of the treaty, however, received aid and comfort from a report of January 12 on Mexican commerce, made by a special agent of the Treasury, who described in full detail the tortuous complexities of the Mexican customs service, the backwardness of the Indian population, and the despotic government. In a speech to the House of Representatives Hewitt did what he could to dissociate the Mexican treaty from that with Spain, emphasizing an estimate by the Bureau of Statistics that it would cost only $89,658.59 in revenue as against estimates for the Spanish treaty running from $10,000,000 to $40,000,000. He bid for Southern support by describing Mexico as "the reservoir into which their products will be poured" and warned that Britain and Germany eagerly awaited a chance to fill the reservoir themselves: "If we reject the Mexican treaty we practically reject the Monroe doctrine." However, he could secure no further action from the House.[20]

The later history of the Mexican reciprocity treaty is soon told. When the Forty-ninth Congress convened in December, 1885, Hewitt was given a subcommittee to reconsider his bill, but to his chagrin he found that the entire committee opposed him, the Republicans because they favored high tariffs, and the Democrats because they feared that Mexican reciprocity would interfere with more general tariff reform. In the name of party unity Hewitt appealed to Speaker Carlisle ("a milk-and-water sort of man," he later called him) but got no satisfaction.

The hostile majority of Hewitt's subcommittee then submitted a report which paraphrased most of the protectionist arguments in Morrill's speech of the preceding session—that the treaty would ruin the American sugar and tobacco industries and that it could not benefit American trade since Mexico was too poor to make

---

Book, XVI, 268-69. Lord Granville to Lionel Sackville West, February 12, No. 18; Lord Edmond Fitzmaurice to Sir R. Herbert, February 12, No. 19, Great Britain, "Correspondence Regarding Negotiation," pp. 20-24. Bayard to James Russell Lowell, April 22, No. 1127, U.S., Instructions, Britain, XXVII, 456-58.

[20]U.S., *Congressional Record*, 48th Cong., 2d Sess., XVI, Appendix, 168-76. For the Treasury report by J. F. Evans and Matías Romero's comments on it see México, Secretaría de fomento, *Reciprocidad comercial entre México y los Estados Unidos* (México, 1890), pp. 28-35.

a good customer. The report stirred up a whirlwind in Mexico, and Matías Romero, who privately thought it a libel against his country, renewed his propaganda campaign in Mexican newspapers. Although Mexican criticism eventually died down, Hewitt could not arouse further support of reciprocity in Congress. During June, 1886, the House approved a motion to pass over the reciprocity bill, 162 to 51, and he made no further effort to keep the bill alive. The vote was largely sectional, Southern Democrats (excepting some Louisianians) supporting reciprocity and Northerners of both parties voting to bury the issue.[21]

There remained the extension of the Hawaiian treaty, which Frelinghuysen and the Hawaiian minister, H. A. P. Carter, had signed on December 6, 1884, without reference to senatorial proposals for a naval base or an extension of the free list. Despite these omissions Miller presented a memorial from citizens of California reciting the benefits conferred by the treaty, and West Coast interests applied further pressure during the session. Others on the Foreign Relations Committee, however, refused to accept the administration's draft, and Edmunds inserted a provision for a naval base during the committee discussion. In any case, Morrill's blast against Hawaii unified the protectionists. Democratic leaders were divided, Bayard supporting extension and Morrison in the House opposed, so that the session ended without any action.[22]

During the first year of the Cleveland administration the opponents of reciprocity, having practically disposed of the Mexican treaty, intensified their campaign against Hawaiian sugar. John E. Searles and H. A. Brown, Eastern merchants who were fighting the San Francisco importing interests and who had visited the Hawaiian Islands as Treasury agents to collect facts, published pamphlets crowded with statistics to prove that the Treasury was losing millions of dollars annually, only to support a petty increase in general trade, and that the Spreckels monopoly was the chief beneficiary of reciprocity. With the aid of Senators R. L. Gibson

[21]*Export and Finance*, II (January 18, 1890), 58. Mexican reactions appear in México, *Reciprocal comercial, passim.* For the final vote in the House see U.S., *Congressional Record*, 49th Cong., 1st Sess., XVII, 7341.

[22]Tansill, *Foreign Policy of Bayard*, pp. 372-73. H. A. P. Carter to Frelinghuysen, Washington, February 27, 1885, U.S., Notes from Foreign Legations, Hawaii, II. Burnette, "Senate Foreign Relations Committee," pp. 247-49.

of Louisiana and Nelson W. Aldrich of Rhode Island (the spokes-
man for Eastern refiners), they put pressure on both Congress and
the State Department to counteract the desire for a naval base.

Although Sherman on the Foreign Relations Committee also
opposed Hawaiian reciprocity, Miller and Morgan cooperated with
Bayard, now Secretary of State, to obtain the eventual victory.
Bayard would have preferred to delete the naval base at Pearl
Harbor, substituting one at Midway Island, as a concession to
Hawaiian scruples, but he agreed to put the necessary pressure
on the Hawaiians, and after a seven-month delay engineered by
Sherman, the Senate approved the treaty extension and a naval-
base amendment early in 1887 by a vote of 43 to 11. Since no
new grant of funds was involved, the House did not need to be
consulted. As Bayard had feared, the Hawaiian government was
most reluctant to lease Pearl Harbor, but after further hesitation
and correspondence, it approved ratification in October.[23]

Another fragment of commercial expansionism which survived
the change of administrations was the three-man commission which
Arthur had appointed during the summer of 1884 to visit Latin
America and report on prospects for trade and other economic
connections. Like the ill-fated tariff commission of 1882, this
one began its work by interviewing American businessmen in
New York, Philadelphia, Baltimore, New Orleans, and San Fran-
cisco. The commissioners then set out to look for their Golden
Fleece in the Caribbean countries, Mexico, and part of Central
America, before Barrios' civil war interrupted their search. After
Cleveland's inauguration they proceeded down the west coast of
South America and returned home by way of the Plata Basin
and Brazil, arriving in New York at the end of 1885.

The rejection of Arthur's reciprocity system weakened the commissioners' prestige, but they managed to bring home with them
a great deal of information about Latin-American resources—some
of it highly colored—and an assortment of more or less frank

[23]Tansill, *Foreign Policy of Bayard*, pp. 373-95. Stevens, *American Expansion in Hawaii*, pp. 170-72. U.S., Tariff Commission, *Reciprocity*, pp. 114-16. Burnette, "Senate Foreign Relations Committee," pp. 368-90. John E. Searles, Jr., *A Few Facts Concerning the Hawaiian Treaty* (Washington, [1886]), *passim*. [Henry Alvin Brown], *Revised Analysis of Hawaiian Treaty Blunders. And the Profound Foreign Policy Humbug* [Washington, 1887], *passim*.

opinions by Latin-American political leaders. President Barrios of Guatemala, whom they interviewed a few weeks before the campaign in which he was killed, enthusiastically supported the idea of an inter-American conference and suggested the union of Central America (under his leadership, of course) as the first item on its agenda. The foreign minister of Costa Rica also supported a conference to discuss the arbitration of disputes (such as Central American unity), uniform currency and measurements, and the encouragement of trade. On the other hand, the president of Chile, remembering American intervention in the War of the Pacific, declared himself opposed to all proposals for joint action excepting the suggestion of an international currency, which might provide a market for Chilean copper. The president of Uruguay put his finger on one of the weakest parts of the American argument when he pointed out that any substantial increase of Uruguayan trade would require a lower wool tariff in the United States.[24]

Several of the Latin-American interviews actually magnified the obstacles in the way of closer trade relations, but the commissioners submitted an optimistic report to Cleveland, declaring that the underlying Latin-American admiration of the United States would be decisive. "Our advances toward a more perfect understanding and greater confidences will meet with a quick and true response," they continued. ". . . The only estrangement possible between [the Latin-American governments] and us will flow from our own indifference and neglect." They urged the American government to send better ministers and consuls to Latin America, encourage the establishment of new steamship lines, and simplify customs regulations. In principle they approved of both Arthur's reciprocity treaties and Blaine's plan for a hemispheric conference to discuss trade and a common currency.[25] Early in 1886 Senators Sherman and William P. Frye introduced bills for a Pan-American

[24]U.S., Congress, Senate, 49th Cong., 1st Sess., 1886, Senate Rept. 941, as reprinted in U.S., Congress, Senate, 56th Cong., 2d Sess., Senate Executive Doc. 231, Part 6, pp. 312-14, 316-20, 330-31, 335-39 *et passim*. For general comments see Laughlin and Willis, *Reciprocity*, pp. 121-24.

[25]U.S., Congress, House, 48th Cong., 1st Sess., 1884, House Executive Doc. 226, p. 4. *Ibid.*, 49th Cong., 1st Sess., 1886, House Executive Doc. 50, pp. 21-33. *Ibid.*, 56th Cong., 2d Sess., Senate Executive Doc. 231, Part 6, pp. 278-88, 296-303.

conference, a customs union, regular steamship service to Latin America, a common silver coin, and other unifying devices proposed by the commission. However, all proposals were adversely reported from committee, and the Forty-ninth Congress took no action to carry out the commissioners' report.[26]

*   *   *

The repudiation of the Arthur-Frelinghuysen canal and reciprocity treaties leaves only the general act of the Berlin Congo Conference to be discussed. When Congress convened in December, 1884, Arthur called attention in his annual message to the desirability of free trade in the Congo Valley and promised further information about the progress of the Berlin conference. On December 5 Frelinghuysen supplied the Senate Foreign Relations Committee with a preliminary report which was carefully examined for signs of diplomatic entanglements, but the general act of the conference was not available in final form until late in February, and the committee made no effort to introduce it on the floor of the Senate.[27]

Although the House of Representatives had no authority to approve or forbid ratification of the general act, it seized the initiative from the Senate six weeks before the end of the conference. On January 5 two House Democrats, H. A. Herbert of Alabama and Perry Belmont of New York (Blaine's nemesis in the Peruvian investigation), presented resolutions of inquiry about the instructions given to the American delegates at Berlin. Belmont accompanied the resolution with a suggestion that American participation might give Europe an excuse to violate the Monroe Doctrine. After a delay of several weeks, apparently in order to give the overworked clerks in the State Department time to copy the pertinent documents, Frelinghuysen submitted two full reports on the Berlin Congo Conference and its background. He denied that the case of Africa presented any sort of parallel with the Monroe Doctrine, since civilized nations held every square

[26]Burnette, "Senate Foreign Relations Committee," pp. 283-86. U.S., Congress, House, 49th Cong., 1st Sess., 1886, H. Repts. 1645-47, *passim.*

[27]Richardson, *Messages and Papers*, VIII, 236. Burnette, "Senate Foreign Relations Committee," pp. 235-36, 347. Frelinghuysen to Miller, December 5, 1884; Miller to Frelinghuysen, December 22, Senate Foreign Relations Committee Archives.

foot of South America, whereas "in 1884, the whole of the heart of Africa remained to be opened up to occupancy and control of civilization."[28]

The House Foreign Affairs Committee considered Frelinghuysen's reports and submitted two resolutions disapproving of American participation in the Berlin conference. Andrew G. Curtin, speaking for a majority, tactfully declared the action "unfortunate in so far as it is a departure" from traditional American isolationist policy, but four members, led by the irrepressible Belmont, insisted on submitting a bald dissent which accused the State Department of jeopardizing the Monroe Doctrine without any hope of effective gains to the United States. Americans needed only markets for their surplus products, and they could best secure these, not in general negotiations in European conferences but independently through revision of American tariff, currency, and financial laws. Belmont called for "a maximum of peaceful, friendly intercourse, commerce and trade . . . but a minimum of political arrangements or alliances or treaties or understandings of any sort."[29]

The most important recipient of Belmont's warning was President-elect Cleveland, who requested a copy of his report and suggested minor changes in the phraseology of his resolution. In its final form, a little wordier than the original but no less blunt, Belmont's resolution, therefore, may be taken to represent the views of the incoming administration. When rumors of Bayard's appointment to the State Department began to circulate, his friends warned him to have nothing to do with "the diplomatic flea, Sanford" and to "stop flirting with foreigners and in that way keep our house in order." In his first annual message Cleveland declared that American signature of the general act did not impair our freedom of action and that "to share in the obligation of enforcing neutrality in the remote valley of the Kongo [*sic*] would be an alliance whose responsibilities we are not in a position to assume."[30]

[28]U.S., Congress, House, 48th Cong., 2d Sess., 1885, House Executive Doc. 156, p. 9 *et passim*. Halligan, "Berlin West African Conference," pp. 136-37. *New York Herald*, January 6, 1885.

[29]U.S., Congress, House, 48th Cong., 2d Sess., 1885, H. Rept. 2655, *passim*.

[30]Richardson, *Messages and Papers*, VIII, 330. Halligan, "Berlin West African Conference," pp. 141-44. Belmont, *An American Democrat*, pp. 312-14. [William

Here the matter ended for all but a few die-hards. In the Senate Foreign Relations Committee Morgan occasionally revived the Congo question, and soon Kasson returned from Berlin, out of a job and convinced that Cleveland's policy was a great mistake and a personal affront to him. He had filled his last dispatches from Germany with warnings of German colonial ambitions, hoping thereby to furnish the State Department with ammunition in behalf of both the general act and the Nicaragua canal treaty. After his return he continued his efforts to "smoke the Congo Treaty out of the White House" with letters to influential friends and an article in the *North American Review*, a copy of which he took pains to send to Cleveland. Kasson never became completely reconciled to the failure of his Congo policy, but by the time Cleveland left office in 1889, he had recovered his aplomb and was ready for new diplomatic assignments under Benjamin Harrison.[31]

Democratic fears for the Monroe Doctrine and preference for tariff reform over quasi-commercial agreements such as the general act may have smacked of party politics, but the Republican case for intervention in the Congo was weakened from the beginning by ignorance of trade conditions in tropical Africa. Stanley's panegyrics about African modesty and textile sales were frail evidence on which to base a new foreign policy. After that policy had collapsed, Arthur's special agent in the Congo, Willard P. Tisdel, submitted a pessimistic opinion of the valley as a commercial entrepôt in a series of letters during 1885 and 1886. He found it rich in raw materials of many kinds but unsuited to regular agriculture, with natives too poor to buy imported goods, a climate deadly to the white man, and all good commercial sites at the mouth of the river already controlled by European companies. When Stanley challenged his gloomy descriptions, Tisdel poured out his disillusionment to Bayard: "I have travelled where Mr. Stanley never thought of travelling . . . and I cannot yield the

Henry Hurlbert] to Bayard, Rome, January 14, 1885; [Sidney Webster] to Bayard, March 3, Bayard Papers, LXIX.

[31]Younger, *Kasson*, pp. 337-43. For samples of Kasson's pleading from Berlin see U.S., Congress, Senate, 49th Cong., 1st Sess., Senate Executive Doc. 196, pp. 139-40, 142-45, 186-92. John A. Kasson, "The Congo Conference and the President's Message," *North American Review*, CXLII (February 1886), 119-33.

evidence of my senses to his gorgeous descriptions, which are unsupported by other evidence." He then related how Stanley and Sanford had tried to extract a favorable report from him with promises and threats, and concluded flatly: "I do not believe that Americans want or should want anything to do with Central Africa."[32] Although Kasson continued to grumble for a time after this, in effect it was Tisdel who had the last word on the Congo.

*   *   *

Not content with defeating Arthur's treaties, the new administration trained its guns on his "new navy" as well. Neither Congress nor the President could sink the three cruisers and the dispatch boat for which Secretary of the Navy Chandler had contracted, but he got no more funds with which to continue construction and only a temporary appropriation for routine expenses. Even after Cleveland's victory the Democratic opposition refused to relax, and after the appropriation ran out, the Navy had to do without any funds for nearly a month. Just before the "lame duck" session ended, when there was no chance for Chandler to award a new contract to John Roach or any other Republican ship-builder, Congress approved the construction of two more cruisers and two gunboats.[33]

After Cleveland's inauguration his secretary of the navy, William C. Whitney, set out after Roach, who was about to present the completed dispatch boat, the "Dolphin." There were many faults in her amateurish design for which Roach was not responsible. During her first test the engines broke down; later, her shaft snapped; and soon Whitney was pointing out her inability to keep up the required horsepower. His refusal to pay any further installments until the "Dolphin" had passed her tests eventually drove Roach into a nervous breakdown and bankruptcy, for the old man had overstrained his resources in undertaking four ships at once. Democratic newspapers gloated, while the *New York*

[32]Willard P. Tisdel to Bayard, Lisbon, April 25, 1885; Washington, June 29, U.S., *Foreign Relations, 1885*, pp. 294-315. Tisdel to Bayard, Ilsenburg am Harz, August 10; Brussels, August 25; Buenos Aires, March 20, 1886. U.S., Special Agents, XXXII. See also Daniel De Leon, "The Conference at Berlin on the West African Question," *Political Science Quarterly*, I (1886), 137-39.

[33]Richardson, *Chandler*, pp. 298-302. *New York Tribune*, July 4, 1884, p. 4; January 3, 1885, p. 4.

Tribune and its colleagues stormed and rationalized. Finally in December, 1885, Whitney capped the climax with a devastating report which ignored Chandler's work of reorganization, patronized the advisory board, and played up abuses such as the disorganized purchasing system and the everlasting ship repairs, which Chandler, always watchful for patronage, had failed to correct. Ironically, during the next four years Whitney was to display most of the outstanding qualities of his predecessor: energy, organizing ability, political dexterity, and vulnerability to criticism.[34]

[34]Richardson, *Chandler*, pp. 303-4, 370-81. Hirsch, *Whitney*, pp. 274-88. For Whitney's annual report of 1885 see U.S., Congress, House, 49th Cong., 1st Sess., House Executive Doc. 1, Part 3, *passim*.

CHAPTER 19

Conclusion

THUS by the end of 1885 Congress and the Cleveland administration repudiated the principal expansionist measures which
Arthur and Frelinghuysen had brought forward during their last
year in office: the Nicaragua canal treaty, the Caribbean reciprocity
system, and the general act of the Berlin Congo Conference. The
South American commissioners were allowed to make their tour,
but it seemed likely that the State Department would merely file
away their report to gather dust. The arguments over Irish-American agitators, pork products, and the Clayton-Bulwer Treaty sputtered out for lack of fuel. Recriminations over party patronage
and unfulfilled contracts dimmed the luster of the "new navy."
The commercial treaty with Korea remained on the books as a
monument to American ambitions in the Far East, but Korea was
still a pawn in the Sino-Japanese struggle for power, and American
influence grew too slowly to change the course of events. Only
the reciprocity treaty with Hawaii continued to occupy the position planned for it, as a foundation stone of expanding American
interests, and this treaty was not really the creation of the Garfield or Arthur administration.

Blaine had lived down his earlier repudiation of 1881-1882 to
become the Republican candidate for president in 1884. Even
after his defeat he retained enough power in the party to help
determine the candidacy of Benjamin Harrison in 1888 and to
become Harrison's secretary of state. Arthur and Frelinghuysen,
however, did not long survive the collapse of their foreign policy.
Throughout Frelinghuysen's term of office he had suffered intermittent illness, and four days before Cleveland's inauguration
his doctor diagnosed an attack of hepatitis. The disease progressed
rapidly: a month later Frelinghuysen was confined to bed, his heart
weakened by the strain, and on May 20 he was dead. Former Presi-

dent Arthur tried to return to his law practice in New York, but at the beginning of 1886 Bright's disease and heart trouble forced him into semi-invalidism. On November 17 he died of a stroke.[1]

The polite comments of the press when the Arthur administration left office could not disguise the fact that in foreign policy, at least, it had fallen short of its principal objectives. The *New York Tribune*, recalling the dismal expectations of the country (and especially the Half-Breeds) at Garfield's death, called the administration "in some respects a pleasurable disappointment to the country," but deplored its foreign policy as a warped version of Blaine's expansionism, which Arthur himself had repudiated in 1882. When Frelinghuysen died, the *New York Herald* praised him as conscientious rather than brilliant and predicted that his canal and reciprocity treaties would "secure for him a lasting reputation for the highest qualities of American statesmanship."[2] It seems unlikely that the author of this editorial really believed what he was writing. In any case he was not much of a prophet, for Arthur and Frelinghuysen dropped out of sight immediately, and no major historian has rediscovered them.

*   *   *

Why did the expansionism of the Garfield and Arthur administrations collapse and give way to the more negative, essentially defensive foreign policy of the first Cleveland administration? A superficial explanation of the failure of the Republican foreign policies was awkwardness. Inheriting an amateurish, spoils-ridden Foreign Service from their predecessors, Blaine and Frelinghuysen did nothing to improve it but entrusted delicate assignments to ill-qualified politicians such as Stephen J. Hurlbut or Aaron A. Sargent, who proceeded to create unnecessary diplomatic crises. At home the State Department magnified their indiscretions by allowing confidential documents to slip into print; even treaties could not be kept secret for long. By such blundering the Garfield and Arthur administrations made enemies both abroad and in the United States and endangered the success of their policies.

More serious than an occasional gaucherie was the apparent

[1]*New York Herald*, May 21, 1885, p. 3. Howe, *Arthur*, pp. 286-87.
[2]*New York Herald*, May 21, 1885, p. 6. *New York Tribune*, March 4, p. 4.

weakness of positive planning at the upper levels of the State Department. Evidence on this point is necessarily sparse, since most of the private papers of Blaine and Frelinghuysen have been lost, and aside from a few memoranda by Alvey A. Adee—able enough but usually dealing with questions of minor importance—the State Department archives contain no records for this period outlining policies for the future or weighing the merits of the alternatives in view. Blaine published his only general statement on the foreign policy of the Garfield administration after he left office, when circumstances had greatly changed; and apparently Frelinghuysen never drew up a general synthesis of any sort. During the autumn and winter of 1884 he explained the background of his treaties in long letters to Arthur and Senator Miller without entirely clarifying the bases of decision. Perhaps the lack of forceful planning at the highest level was reflected in the loose communications between the administration and its leaders in Congress during the session of 1884-1885. Frelinghuysen waited weeks before answering some inquiries, and one of the administration newspapers commented in bafflement that Arthur seemed to be putting no pressure on his friends in the Senate to approve the treaties.[3]

The treaties themselves furnish further evidence of faulty planning, for they contained flaws which made them all the more vulnerable to criticism. In the Nicaragua treaty, for example, the loan to Nicaragua and the likelihood that friends and hangers-on of the Nicaraguan president would "make a killing" by selling lands and second-hand concessions to the Americans deserved further scrutiny in the State Department. In the reciprocity treaties the heavy emphasis on sugar and tobacco seemed to place unfair burdens on producers of these commodities in the United States, and the failure to settle the status of most-favored-nation treaties showed either wishful thinking or lack of foresight. Similarly, Blaine's instructions to the Trescot mission of December, 1881, suggested that Blaine had not clearly considered the danger that Chile might be driven to declare war.

Not only did the treaties and policy declarations of the State Department contain weaknesses, but they were sometimes sharply

[3] *New York Journal of Commerce,* January 19, 1885, p. 2.

inconsistent with each other. Thus, for example, Blaine proposed his peace congress, which depended for its success on Latin-American stability and good will, at the very moment of his most tactless intervention in the War of the Pacific. As for Frelinghuysen's policies, Senator Bayard pointed out cogently that the Nicaragua treaty would lead the government to spend millions of dollars on an interoceanic canal, while at the same time the reciprocity treaties reduced the tariff revenue.[4] Others objected that both Blaine and Frelinghuysen intended to elbow Europe out of the Central American isthmus, but that Frelinghuysen showed no reluctance to play a role in the Congo, where Americans had fewer material interests than Europe in Central America. At many points critics advised the administration that to negotiate canal or reciprocity treaties before developing the American merchant marine and navy was putting the cart before the horse.

If the flaws and inconsistencies in the principal measures of Blaine and Frelinghuysen show inadequate planning by the State Department, their timing suggests that the lack of coordination and foresight was largely due to haste. For all practical purposes Blaine and Frelinghuysen were both "lame ducks" when they undertook wholesale revision of American foreign policy within a few weeks or months. At the time of Garfield's assassination Blaine had begun to outline policies covering the isthmian question and the War of the Pacific, but after he decided to resign, he tried to crowd into a few dispatches measures which needed two or three years to unfold properly. Similarly, in the spring of 1884 Frelinghuysen had secured the ratification of his first reciprocity treaty (with Mexico) and had made preliminary reconnaissance for the canal treaty, when the nomination of Blaine impressed upon him that he must present his completed policy to Congress in December or give it up forever. Both secretaries drew up their dispatches and signed their treaties with one eye on the calendar.

The need for haste which afflicted Blaine and Frelinghuysen and flawed their measures arose from the condition of party politics during the early 1880's (for Garfield's assassination was as much a political action as Arthur's rejection by the Republican

[4]*New York Tribune*, January 13, 1885, p. 4.

convention of 1884 and Blaine's defeat in the election). Although the economic and social make-up of the two major parties did not present sharp contrasts, a series of differences on problems of Reconstruction, currency, and the civil service had been artificially inflated into major quarrels, and the twenty-year exile of the Democratic party had made its leaders hungry for power and patronage. As a result, Democrats (excepting a few renegades like John T. Morgan and Abram S. Hewitt) stood ready to use any problem of foreign relations to attack the President or his secretary of state. Thus Perry Belmont made a field day of the Chile-Peruvian investigation at Blaine's expense, while the issues of naval construction and Irish-American agitators degenerated into demagoguery and name-calling. Throughout the whole period the tariff issue divided the parties, despite internal differences. During the final session of 1884-1885 the unwillingness of the victorious Democrats to concede diplomatic laurels to the outgoing administration—a natural impulse in view of the struggle just ended—stiffened their opposition to the canal and the reciprocity treaties.

But if the Republican foreign policies suffered from the bitterness of Democratic rivalry and criticism, they were still further weakened by schism within the Grand Old Party itself. When voices cried out in 1881 against Blaine's jingoism or Hurlbut's corruption or warned that the country was headed for war, it was difficult to distinguish the Stalwarts from the Democrats. After Blaine retired from office, he retaliated with a steady fire of criticism against Arthur and Frelinghuysen from the editorial columns of the *New York Tribune* and other Half-Breed organs. His comments on diplomatic issues such as the War of the Pacific, the peace congress, and the Clayton-Bulwer notes clearly showed his ill feeling. As the tariff question grew more serious and Frelinghuysen began negotiations for reciprocity, Blaine's protectionist strictures seriously hampered the Arthur administration.

The feud between the Republican factions rose to a climax in 1884 and 1885. Flattened by Blaine's "steam roller" at the convention and stung by his earlier criticism, Arthur denied him support in the campaign which might have given him the crucial vote of New York. The election lost, Blaine then returned to his sniping and encouraged Half-Breeds and Democrats in Congress to join

hands against Frelinghuysen's treaties. Justin S. Morrill and the protectionists needed no encouragement to attack the Spanish reciprocity treaty, but Blaine's aid probably added to the votes at their disposal.

The rivalry between Republicans and Democrats and the feuds within the Republican party, however, cannot conceal the existence of a strong tide of public isolationism and conservatism which might have overwhelmed the foreign policies of the Garfield and Arthur administrations without any aid from the politicians. Blaine, Frelinghuysen, and their advisers rightly discerned a rising popular concern for American prestige, security, and trade abroad, but they sometimes tended to underestimate the persistence of continental thinking and introverted instincts. The impetuous Blaine soon gained the undeserved reputation of warmonger. Frelinghuysen, the more cautious of the two secretaries, rejected several opportunities for expansionism out of concern for public opinion, as in his relations with Venezuela, Haiti, and Madagascar, but even he finally aroused conservative opposition with his canal and reciprocity treaties.

The isolationists' brief was to be familiar for decades to come. In the first place they argued that the State Department had shown no convincing need for expanding American influence abroad. "Romance and dramatic incidents," declared one editorialist, "should not make us forget that a neutral policy, wherever we have no national interest at stake, is the only wise policy for this country to follow and the only way of keeping free from dangerous European entanglements." Not two months after Blaine entered office an opponent was recommending to him the example of Hamilton Fish: "Let Mr. Blaine confine his activity to home politics. Our foreign affairs are well enough."[5] According to such citizens the United States needed no more ships as long as the British navy and merchant marine did their jobs, and the transcontinental railroads made isthmian canals redundant. As for the Congo, leave that to Europe and the unhappy natives.

One variation of this theme was the reassurance that reports of European threats to the Western Hemisphere were absurdly over-

[5] *New York Herald*, May 2, 1881, p. 6; December 10, 1884, p. 4.

drawn and merited no violent reaction: "Americans have always been most effective when least sensational."[6] Others, however, admitted the possibility of danger to the Monroe Doctrine but argued that this was all the more reason for America to husband her resources, keep her ships close to home, and stay out of Old World affairs. As has been shown, this argument appeared most prominently in the discussion of the Berlin Congo Conference. Oddly enough, it was largely absent from the debate over the Korean commercial treaty, which suggests either that the public did not realize the political overtones of the treaty and the degree of British involvement in Sino-Japanese relations or that the American pledge not to meddle in the Old World did not apply to the Far East.

It is hardly necessary to elaborate once again the antipathy of many protectionists to Frelinghuysen's system of reciprocity treaties, but it is worth emphasizing that some tariff reformers also disapproved of them as sugar pills which would satisfy the patient without curing the disease. At the same time a group which included both conservatives and liberals opposed measures such as the canal treaty which might lead to colonies or protectorates over backward peoples. During the campaign of 1884 a writer in *The Economist* tried to calm British fears of Blaine's jingoism with a shrewd prediction that he would run afoul of this anticolonialism:

> They would have great difficulties in merely occupying Mexico and the Isthmus without a large increase to their regular army, which they view with dread and dislike, and if they annex, they must give to the new territories the power of voting. . . . The Americans who govern do not cordially like even white men who do not speak English, and do not intend to learn it, whose ideal is not industrial, and who are sincere Catholics, while they distinctly dislike copper-colored persons who claim all privileges like themselves. . . . Amidst such checks it is hard to be a Jingo in America.[7]

Opponents of expansionism found other rationalizations to support their position. As on many previous occasions, the Constitution provided a convenient refuge for the conservatives, who de-

[6]*Harper's Weekly*, XXVI (January 7, 1882), 2.
[7]Quoted in *New York Tribune*, June 25, 1884, pp. 2-3.

clared that a canal zone would require an amendment, and that for the Senate to ratify reciprocity treaties without consulting the House was an infringement of the latter's control over money bills. (Since the Mexican treaty provided for an enabling act, this scruple was not insuperable.) Some who accepted the extension of the national government's constitutional powers objected that this extension would cost too much—that colonies would require a larger army and navy, which, in turn, would lead to higher taxes. Others raised the specter of war.

The prevalence of these conservative, isolationist arguments in the press of the early 1880's suggests that the American public was still largely unprepared to make its entrance upon the world stage as a major Power. A farsighted administration, planning carefully and carrying out these plans slowly and systematically in a period of relatively mild party rivalry, might have persuaded Congress and the public to accept most of the new policies of Blaine and Frelinghuysen, but none of these conditions existed. The foreign policies of the Garfield and Arthur administrations failed, therefore, because too many Americans thought them dangerous, extravagant, and unnecessary, and because the administrations—awkward, hurried, and disunited—could not convince them otherwise.

*   *   *

Garfield and Arthur left behind no great monuments to diplomatic achievement, but the atmosphere of frustration in the spring of 1885 should not obscure the smaller contributions which the two administrations made to American foreign policy. In the first place, for a period of several months during the winter of 1881-1882 and again in 1884-1885 the hue and cry after Blaine and the treaty debates in Congress brought foreign affairs once again to the attention of the public after nearly a decade of concentration on domestic scandals and internal development. The ill-managed intervention in the War of the Pacific and the canal diplomacy in Central America called public attention to the growing economic interests of the United States in Latin America. Frelinghuysen's reciprocity system represented a serious effort to encourage these new interests and place them on a regular basis, developing them by methods which were already successful in the Hawaiian Islands.

Even in their failure the policies of the Garfield and Arthur administrations sometimes rendered a service by clarifying alternatives among which Americans must eventually choose. This was particularly true of the isthmian canal question. In March, 1880, when Hayes pronounced his determination to have an American canal, he and many others jumped to this conclusion without much thought of the expense or planning which such a policy would entail. The clumsy relations of Blaine and Frelinghuysen with Mexico, Guatemala, and Nicaragua demonstrated the entanglements awaiting in Central America, while the three-cornered pamphlet war between De Lesseps, Eads, and the Ammen-Phelps company set forth the merits and demerits of the rival routes. At the same time, the discussion of action to neutralize the Panama canal showed that Europe would not stand by indefinitely while the United States made up its mind. The Senate might reject the Frelinghuysen-Zavala Treaty, but sooner or later Americans would have to "fish or cut bait." Lastly, the construction of the three cruisers and the "Dolphin," for all their mechanical shortcomings, inaugurated a new navy which would hasten the settlement of the canal question and, indeed, revolutionize much of American foreign policy.

In a striking number of cases the foreign policies of the Garfield and Arthur administrations foreshadowed attitudes and expedients of later imperialist years. For example, during the Harrison administration Blaine was able to carry out his plans of 1881 and hold a Pan-American conference, largely because the Fiftieth Congress had finally acted on the report of Arthur's South American commissioners in 1888 and voted an appropriation for such a gathering. During 1890 Blaine prevailed upon Congress to insert into the McKinley Tariff a provision making possible reciprocity treaties with Latin-American nations. He actually negotiated several treaties before he retired from Harrison's cabinet. The protectionist bloc in Congress eventually nullified the effect of most of these treaties, but they and the earlier Frelinghuysen treaties foreshadowed the "dollar diplomacy" of the twentieth century. In particular, Frelinghuysen's negotiations with Spain over Cuba and Puerto Rico formed a link between the crises of the Ten Years' War and the revolution of 1895 on that island which led to the

Spanish-American War, the American occupation, and a special tariff schedule for Cuban sugar.

However, the peace congress and the reciprocity treaties were not the only prophetic measures of the early 1880's. The Freling-huysen-Zavala canal treaty set forth the type of protectorate which Theodore Roosevelt, Taft, and Wilson were to reproduce with variations in several parts of the Caribbean and Central America. The arguments over canal routes foreshadowed the lobbying of the French canal company during 1901 and 1902, and when the isthmian question came to life again, John T. Morgan was still in the Senate to supply continuity and uphold the cause of the Nic-aragua canal as before. Similarly, the argument with Britain over the Clayton-Bulwer Treaty prepared the American public for the negotiations between John Hay and Lord Pauncefote which re-leased the United States from its tiresome obligation.

Outside Latin America the extension of the Hawaiian reci-procity treaty led directly toward the annexation of the islands, whose inhabitants had grown accustomed to American economic domination through the export of sugar to San Francisco and the import of American manufactures. In the Far East the Korean treaty of 1882 and the attempt to mediate between China and France bring to mind John Hay's Open Door notes, based like the Korean treaty on the principle of equal commercial access, and Theodore Roosevelt's mediation in the Russo-Japanese War. Dur-ing the 1880's, as again after 1898, the American policy in the Far East outstripped material American interests in that area.

So many foreshadowings and anticipations can hardly have been due to coincidence alone. They suggest that the "new" imperialism of the 1890's actually germinated before the first Cleveland adminis-tration, and that the outwardly stagnant years of Garfield and Arthur were actually a period of preparation and crude testing in response to impulses which, though strong, were still vaguely formed and not clearly understood. The foreign policies of the early 1880's contain little glory, but in their awkwardness and fail-ure they add plausibility to the heroics of 1898. Like an early stum-bling rehearsal of a play, this apparently futile diplomacy made possible greater self-confidence and seemingly spontaneous deter-

mination a few years later. Like the rough draft of a book—scratched out, scribbled over, and nearly forgotten after publication—these policies represent a few of the ideas and actions which helped to shape the early twentieth century.

Bibliography

I. MANUSCRIPT SOURCES

1. United States Official Papers, National Archives
   Foreign Affairs Section, Department of State
      Instructions to United States Ministers
      Consular Instructions
      Instructions to Special Missions
      Despatches from United States Ministers
      Consular Despatches
      Reports from Special Agents
      Reports of the Diplomatic Bureau
      Notes to Foreign Legations
      Notes from Foreign Legations
      Report Book
      Domestic Letters
      Miscellaneous Letters
      Unperfected Treaties
   Legislative Section, Senate
      Committee on Foreign Relations, papers

2. Great Britain Official Papers, Public Record Office, London
   Foreign Archives, Series 5 (United States)

3. Private Papers
   Allen, Elisha H. Papers. Manuscripts Division, Library of Congress.
   Arthur, Chester A. Papers. Library of Congress.
   Barker, Wharton. Papers. Library of Congress.
   Bayard, Thomas F. Papers. Library of Congress.
   Blaine, James G. Papers. Library of Congress.
   Chandler, William E. Papers. Library of Congress.
   Chandler, William E. Papers and diaries. New Hampshire Historical Society, Concord, New Hampshire.
   Davis, David. Papers. Chicago Historical Society, Chicago, Illinois.
   Davis, David. Papers. Illinois State Historical Society, Springfield, Illinois.
   Davis, J. C. Bancroft. Papers. Library of Congress.
   Evarts, William M. Papers. Library of Congress.
   Fish, Hamilton. Papers. Library of Congress.
   Foster, John. Papers. Library of Congress.
   Foulk, George C. Papers. Manuscripts Division, New York Public Library.
   Frelinghuysen, Frederick T. Papers. Library of Congress.
   Garfield, James A. Papers and diaries. Library of Congress.
   Granville, G. L. G. Gower, Earl. Papers. Public Record Office, London.
   Gresham, Walter Q. Papers. Library of Congress.
   Hay, John. Papers. Library of Congress.

Hayes, Rutherford B. Papers. Hayes Memorial Library, Fremont, Ohio.
Logan, John A. Papers. Library of Congress.
Lowell, James Russell. Papers. Houghton Library, Harvard University.
Marble, Manton. Papers. Library of Congress.
Morgan, John T. Papers. Library of Congress.
Morrill, Justin S. Papers. Baker Library, Harvard University.
Morrill, Justin S. Papers. Library of Congress.
Morrison, William. Papers. Illinois State Historical Society.
Morton, Levi P. Papers. New York Public Library.
Reid, Whitelaw. Papers. Library of Congress.
Romero, Matías. Papers (microfilm). Library of Congress.
Schurz, Carl. Papers. Library of Congress.
Shufeldt, Robert W. Papers. Library of Congress.
Thompson, John. Journal, 1879-1880. New York Public Library.
Trescot, William H. Papers. South Caroliniana Library, Columbia, South Carolina.
Wells, David A. Papers. Library of Congress.
Young, John Russell. Papers. Library of Congress.

4. Dissertations and Articles

Beck, William Freer. "A Comparison of British and United States Relations with Chile, 1879-1883: a Study in Diplomatic History." Ph.D. dissertation, University of Pittsburgh, 1942.

Burnette, Ollen Lawrence, Jr. "The Senate Foreign Relations Committee and the Diplomacy of Garfield, Arthur, and Cleveland." Ph.D. dissertation, University of Virginia, 1952.

Collum, Richard S. "The Expedition to Panama (March-May 1885)." Type-written manuscript, New York Public Library.

Crosby, Kenneth W. "The Diplomacy of the United States in Relation to the War of the Pacific, 1879-1884." Ph.D. dissertation, George Washington University, 1949.

Gignilliat, John L. "Pigs, Politics, and Protection: the American Pork Boycott in Europe, 1879-1891." Paper read at the convention of the American Historical Association, December, 1959.

Halligan, William W., Jr. "The Berlin West African Conference of 1884-1885 from the Viewpoint of American Participation." M.A. thesis, University of Virginia, 1949.

Mathews, Sidney T., "The Nicaragua Canal Controversy: the Struggle for an American-Constructed and -Controlled Transitway." Ph.D. dissertation, Johns Hopkins University, 1947.

Plesur, Milton. "Looking Outward: American Attitudes toward Foreign Affairs from Hayes to Harrison." Ph.D. dissertation, University of Rochester, 1954.

Radke, August Carl, Jr. "John Tyler Morgan, an Expansionist Senator, 1877-1907." Ph.D. dissertation, University of Washington, 1953.

Walton, Sarah Georgia. "The Frelinghuysen-Zavala Treaty, 1884-1885." M.A. thesis, University of Virginia, 1953.

II. PUBLISHED SOURCES

1. Official Papers
   United States

   41st Congress, 2d Session. *Senate Executive Document 112*
                             House Executive Document 111
   44th Congress, 1st Session. *House Report 9*
   45th Congress, 3d Session. *House Report 8*
   46th Congress, 2d Session. *Senate Document 112*
                             House Reports 1120, 1121, 1127

46th Congress, 3d Session. *Senate Miscellaneous Document 42*
House Miscellaneous Document 13
House Reports 34, 224, 322
47th Congress, 1st Session. *Senate Executive Documents 21, 79, 155, 156, 181,*
194
Senate Miscellaneous Document 89
Senate Reports 120, 213, 368
House Executive Documents 1, 46, 68, 151, 209
House Miscellaneous Document 46
House Reports 67, 138, 1648, 1698
47th Congress, 2d Session. *Senate Report 1013*
House Executive Document 1
House Miscellaneous Document 6
House Reports 1827, 1860
48th Congress, 1st Session. *Senate Executive Documents 58, 62, 123*
Senate Miscellaneous Documents 12, 59
Senate Reports 76, 345, 393
House Executive Documents 1, 121, 154, 226
House Reports 281, 363, 750, 1445, 1568, 1848, 2149
48th Congress, 2d Session. *Senate Executive Documents 10, 26, 99, 120*
Senate Miscellaneous Document 45
House Executive Documents 1, 39, 156, 163, 226,
247
House Report 2655
49th Congress, 1st Session. *Senate Executive Document 196*
Senate Report 941
House Executive Document 50
House Reports 1645, 1647, 1648
49th Congress, 2d Session. *Senate Executive Documents 50, 77, 226*
50th Congress, 1st Session. *Senate Miscellaneous Document 64*
51st Congress, 1st Session. *House Report 3025*
53rd Congress, 2d Session. *Senate Executive Document 106*
53rd Congress, 3d Session. *House Executive Document 1*
56th Congress, 2d Session. *Senate Executive Document 231*

Congressional Record

Department of Commerce, Bureau of the Census, *Historical Statistics of
the United States, Colonial Times to 1957.* Washington, 1960.
Department of State. *Commercial Relations of the United States with Foreign
Countries.* Washington, 1856-1914.
———. *Papers Relating to the Foreign Relations of the United States.* Wash-
ington [1862——].
———. *Register of the Department of State.* Washington, 1869——.
———. *Reports from the Consuls of the United States on the Commerce,
Manufactures, etc. of their Consular Districts.* Washington, 1880——.
Tariff Commission, *Reciprocity and Commercial Treaties.* Washington, 1919.
Others
Chile, *Memoria que el Contra-almirante D. Patricio Lynch, jeneral en jefe
del ejército de operaciones en el Norte del Perú presenta al Supremo
Gobierno de Chile.* Lima, 1882.
Great Britain, House of Commons, *Sessional Papers, 1882,* LXXX. United
States, No. 2. "Correspondence Respecting the Imprisonment in Ireland
under the 'Protection of Person and Property (Ireland) Act, 1881' of Nat-
uralized Citizens of the United States."
———, *1882,* LXXX. United States, No. 3. "Correspondence Respecting the

Publication in the United States of Incitements to Outrages in England.
———, *1884*, LXXXIII. "Correspondence Respecting the Commercial Convention Concluded between Spain and the United States Relative to the West India Trade."
———, *1884-1885*, LXXXI. Commercial, No. 4. "Correspondence Respecting the Negotiation of a Treaty Regulating Trade between the British West India Colonies and the United States."
México, Ministerio de relaciones exteriores. *Correspondencia diplomática cambiada entre el gobierno de los Estados Unidos Mexicanos y los de varias potencias extranjeras.* 6 vols. México, 1882-1892.
———, Secretaría de fomento. *Reciprocidad comercial entre México y los Estados Unidos.* México, 1890.

2. Daily Newspapers
   Boston Evening Transcript
   Chicago Daily News
   Chicago Times
   Chicago Tribune
   Cincinnati Commercial Gazette
   Diario oficial (Mexico City)
   Louisville *Courier-Journal*
   El monitor republicano (Mexico City)
   National Republican (Washington)
   New Orleans *Times-Democrat*
   New York *Commercial Advertiser*
   New York *Daily Commercial Bulletin*
   New York *Evening Post*
   New York Herald
   New York Journal of Commerce
   New York *Sun*
   New York Times
   New York Tribune
   New York *World*
   Philadelphia Inquirer
   St. John's (New Brunswick) *Daily Telegraph*
   San Francisco Chronicle
   El siglo diez y nueve (Mexico City)
   Springfield (Massachusetts) *Daily Republican*
   Times (London)
   Toronto *Globe*
   Washington Post

3. Other Periodicals
   The American
   American Protectionist
   Atlantic Monthly
   Bay State Monthly
   Boston Sunday Herald
   Bradstreet's
   Bulletin du canal interocéanique
   Catholic World
   Commercial and Financial Chronicle
   Export and Finance
   Forum
   Harper's New Monthly Magazine

Harper's Weekly
Iron Age
Mexican Financier
Nation
North American Review
Saturday Review (London)
Westminster Review

The following dailies and weeklies were used through clippings enclosed with dispatches or private papers:

Daily News (London)
Daily Telegram (London)
Diario de Cundinamarca (Colombia)
Gaceta oficial (Havana)
El Guatemalteco (Guatemala City)
Havana *Weekly Report*
Japan Daily Herald
Japan Weekly Mail
El mensajero (San José de Costa Rica)
Morning Post (London)
La nación (Guayaquil)
Pall Mall Gazette (London)
Panama *Star and Herald*
Revista de las antillas (Havana)
Standard (London)

4. Books and Pamphlets

Adler, Cyrus and Aaron M. Margolith. *American Intercession on Behalf of Jews in the Diplomatic Correspondence of the United States, 1840-1938.* New York, 1943.

Alexander, W. D. *History of the Later Years of the Hawaiian Monarchy and the Revolution of 1893.* Honolulu, 1896.

American Iron and Steel Association. *Statistics of the American and Foreign Iron Trade in 1880-1885. Annual Report of the Secretary of the American Iron and Steel Association* [etc.]. Philadelphia, 1881-1885.

———. *Hold the Fort! A Collection of Fresh Facts and Arguments in Support of the Policy of Protection to Home Industry.* Philadelphia [1876].

Ammen, Daniel. *The Certainty of the Nicaragua Canal Contrasted with the Uncertainties of the Eads Ship-railway.* Washington [1886].

———. *The Errors and Fallacies of the Interoceanic Transit Question. To Whom Do They Belong?* New York, 1886.

———. *The Old Navy and the New.* Philadelphia, 1891.

Angell, James Burrell. *The Reminiscences of James Burrell Angell.* New York and London, 1912.

Armstrong, William M. *E. L. Godkin and American Foreign Policy, 1865-1900.* New York, 1957.

Armstrong, William N. *Around the World with a King.* New York, 1904.

Ashley, Percy. *Modern Tariff History: Germany, United States, France.* 3d ed., New York, 1920.

Atkins, Thomas B. *The Interoceanic Canal across Nicaragua and the Attitude toward It of the Government of the United States.* [New York, 1890.]

Aydelotte, William Osgood. *Bismarck and British Colonial Policy. The Problem of South West Africa, 1883-1885.* Philadelphia, 1937.

Badeau, Adam. *Grant in Peace: From Appomattox to Mount MacGregor.* Hartford, Connecticut, 1887.

Bagenal, Philip Henry. *The American Irish and their Influence on Irish Politics*
n.p., 1882.

Barnes, James A. *John G. Carlisle, Financial Statesman*. New York, 1931.

Barrows, Chester L. *William M. Evarts*. Chapel Hill, North Carolina, 1941.

Beale, Harriet S. Blaine (ed.). *The Letters of Mrs. James G. Blaine*. 2 vols
New York, 1908.

Belmont, Perry. *An American Democrat; the Recollections of Perry Belmont*.
New York, 1940.

Bemis, Samuel Flagg (ed.). *American Secretaries of State and their Diplomacy*.
Vol. VII: Claude G. Bowers and Helen Dwight Reid. *William M. Evarts;*
James B. Lockey. *James G. Blaine*. Vol. VIII: Philip Marshall Brown. *Frederick T. Frelinghuysen*. 10 vols. New York, 1927-1929.

Blaine, James G. *Political Discussions: Legislative, Diplomatic, and Popular,*
1856-1886. Norwich, Connecticut, 1887.

Brookes, Jean I. *International Rivalry in the Pacific Islands, 1800-1875*. Berkeley,
California, 1941.

Brown, Henry Alvin. *Analyses of the Sugar Question* [etc.]. Saxonville, Massachusetts, 1879.

———. *Hawaiian Sugar Bounties and Treaty Abuses which Defraud the U. S.*
Revenue, Oppress American Consumers and Tax-payers, Discriminate against
Other Sugar-producing Countries, and Endanger American Sugar Industries.
Washington, 1883.

[———]. *Revised Analysis of Hawaiian Treaty Blunders. And the Profound*
Foreign Policy Humbug. [Washington, 1887.]

Bulnes, Gonzalo. *Guerra del Pacífico*. 3 vols. Santiago de Chile, 1955.

Burgess, Paul. *Justo Rufino Barrios*. Philadelphia, 1926.

Burnham, W. Dean. *Presidential Ballots, 1836-1892*. Baltimore, 1955.

Caldwell, Robert G. *James A. Garfield, Party Chieftain*. New York, 1931.

Callahan, James M. *American Foreign Policy in Mexican Relations*. New York,
1932.

The Campaign Book of the Democratic Party. The Republican Party Reviewed.
Its Sins of Omission and Commission. Why a Change Is Demanded by the
People. Washington, 1882.

Carey, Henry Charles. *The British Treaties of 1871 and 1874. Letters to the*
President of the United States. Philadelphia, 1874.

Chapman, Sydney John. *The History of Trade between the United Kingdom*
and the United States, with Special Reference to the Effects of Tariffs. New
York, 1899.

Chotteau, Léon. *Mes campagnes aux États-Unis et en France, 1878-1885. Discours*
et lettres. Projet de traité franco-américain. Motion votée par la chambre
des représentants de Washington. Résolution conjointe déposée au Sénat des
États-Unis et ajournée indéfiniment. Paris, 1893.

Clancy, Herbert J. *The Presidential Election of 1880*. Chicago, 1958.

Clyde, Paul Hibbert. *United States Policy Toward China. Diplomatic and Public*
Documents, 1839-1939. Durham, North Carolina, 1940.

Conroy, Hilary. *The Japanese Frontier in Hawaii, 1868-1898*. Berkeley and Los
Angeles, 1953.

Convention of the Representatives of the Louisiana Protected Industries. New
Orleans, March 12, 1884. New Orleans, 1884.

Coolidge, Mary Roberts. *Chinese Immigration*. New York, 1909.

Cordier, Henri. *Histoire des rélations de la Chine avec les puissances occidentales,*
1860-1902. 3 vols. Paris, 1901-1902.

Corthell, Elmer L. *An Exposition of the Errors and Fallacies in Rear-admiral Ammen's Pamphlet Entitled, "The Certainty of the Nicaragua Canal Contrasted with the Uncertainties of the Eads Ship-Railway."* Washington, 1886.

Cortissoz, Royal. *The Life of Whitelaw Reid.* 2 vols. New York, 1921.

Cosío Villegas, Daniel. *Estados Unidos contra Porfirio Díaz.* México, 1956.

——. *Historia moderna de México.* México, 1955——. Vol. V (*El Porfiriato: La Vida política exterior, Parte primera.*)

Creighton, Donald. *John A. Macdonald, the Old Chieftain.* Boston, 1956.

Crone, John S. *A Concise Dictionary of Irish Biography.* Dublin, 1928.

Crook, W. H. *Through Five Administrations.* New York and London, 1910.

Crowe, S. E. *The Berlin West African Conference, 1884-1885.* London, 1942.

Dalzell, George Walton. *The Flight from the Flag; the Continuing Effect of the Civil War upon the American Carrying Trade.* Chapel Hill, 1940.

Damon, Ethel M. *Sanford Ballard Dole and his Hawaii.* Palo Alto, California, 1957.

D'Arcy, William. *The Fenian Movement in the United States, 1858-1886.* Washington, 1947.

[Darneille, Benjamin Johnson.] *Review of the Monroe Doctrine and the Panama Canal.* By Grotius. Washington, 1882.

Dennett, Tyler. *Americans in Eastern Asia. A Critical Study of the Policy of the United States with Reference to China, Japan and Korea in the 19th Century.* New York, 1922.

Dennis, William Jefferson. *Tacna and Arica, an Account of the Chile-Peru Boundary Dispute and of the Arbitrations by the United States.* New Haven, 1931.

Dorsey, Florence. *Road to the Sea: the Story of James B. Eads and the Mississippi River.* New York, 1947.

[Draper, George.] *Some Views on the Tariff Question, by an Old Business Man. The American Market for the American People.* New York [1886].

Dudley, Thomas Haines. *The Cobden Club of England and Protection in the United States* [n.p. 1884?].

Encina, Francisco A. *Historia de Chile desde la prehistoria hasta 1891.* Santiago de Chile, 1951.

Evans, H. C., Jr. *Chile and its Relations with the United States.* Durham, North Carolina, 1927.

Fernon, Thomas Sargent. *Free Trade Means Serf Pay and Famine Fare.* Philadelphia, 1880.

Fiske, Bradley A. *From Midshipman to Rear Admiral.* New York, 1919.

Fitzmaurice, Edmond. *The Life of Granville George Leveson Gower, Second Earl Granville, K.G., 1815-1891.* 2 vols. London, 1905.

Fletcher, Robert Samuel. *A History of Oberlin College from its Foundation through the Civil War.* 2 vols. Oberlin, Ohio, 1943.

Ford, Worthington C. (ed.). *Letters of Henry Adams, 1858-1891.* Boston, 1930.

Foster, John W. *Diplomatic Memoirs.* 2 vols. New York, 1909.

The Franco-American Treaty of Commerce. Reports and Resolutions Adopted in the United States and France. Paris, 1879.

Fuchs, Carl Johannes. *The Trade Policy of Great Britain and Her Colonies Since 1860.* London, 1905.

Fuess, Claude M. *Carl Schurz, Reformer (1829-1906).* New York, 1932.

[García Calderón, Francisco.] *Mediación de los Estados Unidos en la guerra del Pacífico. El Señor Doctor Don Cornelius A. Logan y el Dr. D. Francisco García Calderón.* Buenos Aires, 1884.

Gardiner, Alfred George. *The Life of Sir William Harcourt.* 2 vols. London, 1923.

Gibson, Florence E. *The Attitudes of the New York Irish toward State and National Affairs, 1848-1892.* New York, 1951.

Greenslet, Ferris. *James Russell Lowell.* Boston, 1905.

Gregg, Robert D. *The Influence of Border Troubles on Relations between the United States and Mexico, 1867-1910.* Baltimore, 1937.

Griffis, William Elliot. *Corea, Without and Within.* Philadelphia, 1885.

Gwynn, S. L. and Tuckwell, Gertrude. *Life of the Right Honourable Sir Charles Dilke, Bart., M.P.* 2 vols. London, 1917.

Haight, Frank A. *A History of French Commercial Policies.* New York, 1941.

Hall, Henry. *American Navigation, with Some Account of the Causes of its Recent Decay, and of the Means by which its Prosperity May Be Restored.* New York, 1880.

Hamilton, Gail [Mary Abigail Dodge]. *Life of Blaine.* Norwich, Connecticut, 1895.

Harrington, Fred Harvey. *God, Mammon, and the Japanese; Dr. Horace N. Allen and Korean-American Relations, 1884-1905.* Madison, Wisconsin, 1944.

Harris, Norman Dwight. *Europe and Africa.* Boston, 1927.

Hayes, Rutherford B. *Diary and Letters of Rutherford B. Hayes.* Edited by Charles R. Williams. 5 vols. Columbus, Ohio, 1922-1926.

Henderson, John B., Jr. *American Diplomatic Questions.* New York, 1900.

Hesseltine, William B. *Ulysses S. Grant, Politician.* New York, 1935.

Hird, Frank. *H. M. Stanley, the Authorized Life.* London, 1935.

Hirsch, Mark D. *William C. Whitney, Modern Warwick.* New York, 1948.

Howe, George Frederick. *Chester A. Arthur, a Quarter-Century of Machine Politics.* New York, 1934.

Hurlbert, William H. *Meddling and Muddling—Mr. Blaine's Foreign Policy.* New York, 1884.

Hutchins, John G. B. *The American Maritime Industries and Public Policy, 1789-1914, an Economic History.* Cambridge, Massachusetts, 1941.

Ireland, Gordon. *Boundaries, Possessions, and Conflicts in Central and North America and the Caribbean.* Cambridge, Massachusetts, 1941.

Johnson, Allen and Dumas Malone (eds.). *Dictionary of American Biography.* 22 vols. New York, 1928-1944.

Jones, Chester Lloyd. *Guatemala, Past and Present.* Minneapolis, 1940.

Jones, F. C. *Extraterritoriality in Japan, and the Diplomatic Relations Resulting in its Abolition, 1853-1899.* New Haven, 1931.

Josephson, Matthew. *The Politicos, 1865-1896.* New York, 1938.

Joyner, Fred Bunyan. *David Ames Wells, Champion of Free Trade.* Cedar Rapids, Iowa [1939].

Kasson, John Adam. *Information Respecting Reciprocity and the Existing Treaties.* Washington, 1901.

Keasbey, Lindley Miller. *The Nicaragua Canal and the Monroe Doctrine.* New York, 1896.

Keenleyside, Hugh L. *Canada and the United States; Some Analysis of the History of the Republic and the Dominion.* New York, 1929.

Keim, Jeannette. *Forty Years of German-American Political Relations.* Philadelphia, 1919.

Keith, Arthur Berriedale. *The Belgian Congo and the Berlin Act.* Oxford, 1919.

Kelley, William D. *The Proposed Reciprocity Treaty: an Address Delivered by Request of Representatives of the Leading Manufacturing Industries of the United States, at the Academy of Music, Philadelphia, October 28, 1874.* Philadelphia, 1874.

King, J. W. *The War-Ships and Navies of the World.* Boston, 1880.

Knaplund, Paul and Carolyn M. Clewes (eds.). "Private Letters from the British Embassy in Washington to the Foreign Secretary, Lord Granville, 1880-1885." Vol. I. *Annual Report of the American Historical Association for the year 1941.* 3 vols. Washington, 1942.

Langer, William L. *European Alliances and Alignments, 1871-1890.* New York, 1931.

Laughlin, James Laurence and H. Parker Willis. *Reciprocity.* New York [1903].

Lawrence, T. J. *Essays on Some Disputed Questions in Modern International Law.* 2d ed. Cambridge, 1885.

Le Caron, Henri [Thomas Miller Beach]. *Twenty-Five Years in the Secret Service; the Recollections of a Spy.* London, 1892.

Leff, D. W. *Uncle Sam's Pacific Islets.* Stanford, California, 1940.

Lightner, O. C. *The History of Business Depressions.* New York [1922].

Logan, Rayford W. *The Diplomatic Relations of the United States with Haiti, 1776-1891.* Chapel Hill, North Carolina, 1941.

McElroy, Robert. *Levi Parsons Morton.* New York, 1930.

McHenry, Estill (ed.). *Addresses and Papers of James B. Eads, Together with a Biographical Sketch.* St. Louis, 1884.

Mack, Gerstle. *The Land Divided. A History of the Panama Canal and Other Isthmian Canal Projects.* New York, 1944.

Malloy, William M. (ed.). *Treaties, Conventions, International Acts, Protocols and Agreements between the United States and Other Powers, 1776-1909.* 2 vols. Washington, 1910.

Masterman, Sylvia. *The Origins of International Rivalry in Samoa, 1845-1884.* Stanford, California, 1934.

Merritt, Edwin A. *Recollections, 1828-1911.* Albany, New York, 1911.

Miller, Clarence Lee. *The States of the Old Northwest and the Tariff, 1865-1888.* Emporia, Kansas, 1929.

Miller, John F. *Nicaragua Canal: Address Delivered before the Chamber of Commerce, Board of Trade, and Manufacturers' Association of San Francisco, June 17, 1885.* San Francisco, 1885.

Millington, Herbert. *American Diplomacy and the War of the Pacific.* New York, 1948.

Montague, L. L. *Haiti and the United States, 1714-1938.* Durham, North Carolina, 1940.

Morgan, James Morris. *America's Egypt. Mr. Blaine's Foreign Policy.* New York, 1884.

Morison, E. E. *et al.* (eds.). *The Letters of Theodore Roosevelt.* 8 vols. Cambridge, Massachusetts, 1951-1954.

Morse, H. B. *International Relations of the Chinese Empire.* 3 vols. London, 1910-1918.

——— and Harley Farnsworth MacNair. *Far Eastern International Relations.* Boston, 1931.

Muzzey, David Saville. *James G. Blaine, a Political Idol of Other Days.* New York, 1934.

Nelson, M. Frederick. *Korea and the Old Orders in Eastern Asia.* Baton Rouge, Louisiana, 1945.

Nevins, Allan. *Abram S. Hewitt, with Some Account of Peter Cooper.* New York, 1935.

———. *Grover Cleveland, a Study in Courage.* New York, 1933.

———. *Hamilton Fish; the Inner History of the Grant Administration.* New York, 1936.

———. *Study in Power: John D. Rockefeller, Industrialist and Philanthropist.* 2 vols. New York, 1953.

New York Chamber of Commerce. *Annual Report of the Chamber of Commerce of the State of New York. 1885.* New York, 1885.

———. *Proceedings of the Chamber of Commerce of the State of New York, Relative to the Free Navigation of the Congo. January 10, 1884.* New York, 1884.

New York Free Trade Club. *The Spanish Treaty Opposed to Tariff Reform. Report of a Committee of Inquiry Appointed by the New York Free Trade Club.* New York, 1885.

Noyes, Alexander Dana. *Forty Years of American Finance.* New York, 1909.

Oberholtzer, Ellis Paxson. *A History of the United States since the Civil War.* 5 vols. New York, 1917-1937.

O'Brien, Conor Cruise. *Parnell and his Party, 1880-1890.* Oxford, 1957.

O'Hegarty, P. S. *A History of Ireland under the Union, 1801 to 1922.* London, 1952.

Palmer, Norman Dunbar. *The Irish Land League Crisis.* New Haven, 1940.

Parks, E. Taylor. *Colombia and the United States, 1765-1934.* Durham, North Carolina, 1935.

Paullin, Charles Oscar. *Diplomatic Negotiations of American Naval Officers, 1778-1883.* Baltimore, 1912.

[Phelps, Seth L.] *Review of the Proposed Tehuantepec Ship-railway. June 1, 1881.* [Washington, 1881.]

Platt, Thomas C. *The Autobiography of Thomas Collier Platt.* New York, 1910.

Pletcher, David M. *Rails, Mines, and Progress: Seven American Promoters in Mexico, 1867-1911.* Ithaca, New York, 1958.

Poor, Henry Varnum. *Twenty-two Years of Protection.* New York [1888].

Porritt, Edward. *Sixty Years of Protection in Canada, 1846-1907; Where Industry Leans on the Politician.* London, 1908.

Powell, Fred W. *The Railroads of Mexico.* Boston, 1921.

Puleston, William Dilworth. *Mahan.* New Haven, 1939.

Reflections on the Nicaragua Treaty. Is It Constitutional? Is It Expedient? [No publisher, 1884?]

Report to the Provisional Interoceanic Canal Society by the Executive Committee. March 16th, 1883. [Washington, 1883.]

Richardson, David M. *Our Country; its Present and Future Prosperity.* Detroit, 1882.

Richardson, James D. *A Compilation of the Messages and Papers of the Presidents, 1789-1897.* 10 vols. Washington, 1898.

Richardson, Leon Burr. *William E. Chandler, Republican.* New York, 1940.

Rippy, J. Fred. *The United States and Mexico.* New York, 1926.

Robertson, James Barr. *Great Britain, the United States, and the Irish Question.* London, 1883.

Robinson, Chalfont. *A History of Two Reciprocity Treaties: the Treaty with Canada in 1854, the Treaty with the Hawaiian Islands in 1876, with a Chapter on the Treaty-making Power of the House of Representatives.* [New Haven, 1904.]

Rodrígues, José Carlos. *The Panama Canal; its History, its Political Aspects, and Financial Difficulties.* New York, 1885.

Romero, Emilio. *Historia económica del Perú.* Buenos Aires, 1950.

Russell, Charles Edward. *Blaine of Maine, his Life and Times.* New York, 1931.

Russell, H. B. *International Monetary Conferences; their Purposes, Character and Results.* New York, 1898.

Ryden, George Herbert. *The Foreign Policy of the United States in Relation to Samoa.* New Haven, 1933.

Sandmeyer, Elmer Clarence. *The Anti-Chinese Movement in California*. Urbana, Illinois, 1939.

San Francisco Board of Trade. *Report of a Special Committee on Inter-oceanic Canal. "The Key of the Pacific."* San Francisco, 1880.

San Francisco Chamber of Commerce. *Franco-American Commerce. Statements and Arguments in Behalf of American Industries against the Proposed Franco-American Commercial Treaty* [etc.]. San Francisco, 1879.

Schoenhof, Jacob. *The Destructive Effect of the Tariff upon Manufacture and Commerce and the Figures and Facts Relating Thereto*. 2d ed. New York, 1884.

Schuyler, Eugene. *American Diplomacy and the Furtherance of Commerce*. New York, 1886.

Searles, John Ennis, Jr. *A Few Facts Concerning the Hawaiian Reciprocity Treaty*. Washington [1886].

Sensabaugh, John Franklin. *American Interest in the Mexican-Guatemalan Boundary Dispute*. Birmingham, Alabama [1940].

Sherman, John. *Recollections of Forty Years*. 2 vols. New York, 1895.

Sherman, W. R. *The Diplomatic and Commerical Relations of the United States and Chile, 1820-1914*. Boston, 1926.

Shufeldt, Robert W. *Liberia. The U. S. Navy in Connection with the Foundation, Growth and Prosperity of the Republic of Liberia*. Washington, 1877.
———. *The Relation of the Navy to the Commerce of the United States*. Washington, 1878.

Silk Association of America. *Proposed Franco-American Treaty. Address of Léon Chotteau, and Reply of the Revenue Laws Committee, Silk Association of America*. [New York], 1879.

Smalley, George W. *Anglo-American Memories*. New York, 1910.

Smith, John Lawrence, *Interoceanic Canal: Practicability of the Different Routes, and Questionable Nature of the Interest of the United States in a Canal*. Louisville, 1880.

Smith, Theodore C. *The Life and Letters of James Abram Garfield*. 2 vols. New Haven, 1925.

Spalding, Rufus Paine. *A Bird's-Eye View of the Hawaiian Islands, with Some Reflections upon the Reciprocity Treaty with the United States*. Cleveland, 1882.

Spears, John R. *The History of Our Navy from its Origin to the End of the War with Spain, 1775-1898*. 5 vols. New York, 1899.

Sprout, Harold and Margaret. *The Rise of American Naval Power, 1776-1918*. Princeton, 1939.

Stanley, Henry Morton. *The Congo and the Founding of its Free State: a Story of Work and Exploration*. 2 vols. New York, 1885.

Stanwood, Edward. *American Tariff Controversies in the Nineteenth Century*. 2 vols. Boston, 1903.

Stead, Alfred (ed.). *Japan by the Japanese*. London, 1904.

Stevens, S. K. *American Expansion in Hawaii, 1842-1898*. Harrisburg, Pennsylvania, 1945.

Stolberg-Wernigerode, Otto zu. *Germany and the United States of America during the Era of Bismarck*. Reading, Pennsylvania, 1937.

Strauss, Eric. *Irish Nationalism and British Democracy*. New York, 1951.

[Strobel, Edward Harry.] *Mr. Blaine and his Foreign Policy*. Boston, 1884.

Talbot, Thomas H. *The Proudest Chapter in his Life. Mr. Blaine's Administration of the State Department. His Conduct of South American Affairs*. Boston, 1884.

Tansill, Charles Callan. *The Foreign Policy of Thomas F. Bayard, 1885-1897*. New York, 1940.

————. *Canadian American Relations, 1875-1911*. New Haven, Connecticut, 1943.

————. *The Canadian Reciprocity Treaty of 1854*. Baltimore, 1922.

————. *The Purchase of the Danish West Indies*. Baltimore, 1932.

Tarbell, Ida M. *The Tariff in Our Times*. New York, 1911.

Taussig, F. W. *Some Aspects of the Tariff Question*. Cambridge, 1915.

Taylor, A. J. P. *Germany's First Bid for Colonies*. New York, 1938.

Thomas, Harrison C. *The Return of the Democratic Party to Power*. New York, 1919.

Thompson, Richard W. *The Interoceanic Canal at Panama. Its Political Aspects. The "Monroe Doctrine"* [etc.]. Washington, 1881.

Thomson, Robert S. *Fondation de l'état indépendant du Congo; un chapitre de l'histoire du partage de l'Afrique*. Brussels, 1933.

Townsend, Mary Evelyn. *The Rise and Fall of Germany's Colonial Empire, 1884-1918*. New York, 1930.

Travis, Ira D. *The History of the Clayton-Bulwer Treaty*. Ann Arbor, Michigan, 1899.

Treat, Payson J. *Diplomatic Relations between the United States and Japan, 1853-1895*. 2 vols. Stanford, California, 1932.

Tyler, Alice Felt. *The Foreign Policy of James G. Blaine*. Minneapolis, 1927.

Vagts, Alfred. *Deutschland und die Vereinigten Staaten in der Weltpolitik*. 2 vols. New York, 1935.

Valadés, José C. *El porfirismo, historia de un régimen: El nacimiento (1876-1884)*. México, 1941.

Vogt, Paul L. *The Sugar Refining Industry in the United States—its Development and Present Condition*. Philadelphia, 1908.

Volwiler, A. T. *The Correspondence between Benjamin Harrison and James G. Blaine, 1882-1893*. Philadelphia, 1940.

Welles, Gideon. *The Diary of Gideon Welles*. 3 vols. Boston, 1911.

Wells, David A. *The Equities in the (Customs) Taxation of Sugar*. New York, 1894.

————. *Freer Trade Essential to Future National Prosperity and Development*. New York, 1882.

————. *How Congress and the Public Deal with a Great Revenue and Industrial Problem*. New York, 1880.

————. *Our Merchant Marine, How it Rose, Increased, Became Great, Declined and Decayed, with an Inquiry into the Conditions Essential to its Resuscitation and Future Prosperity*. New York, 1882.

————. *The Question of Ships* [etc.]. New York, 1890.

————. *Recent Economic Changes and their Effect on the Production and Distribution of Wealth and the Well-being of Society*. New York, 1889.

————. *The Sugar Industry of the United States and the Tariff*. New York, 1878.

[Williams, Alfred.] *The Interoceanic Canal and the Monroe Doctrine*. New York, 1880.

Williams, Charles R. (ed.). *Diary and Letters of Rutherford Birchard Hayes*. 5 vols. Columbus, Ohio, 1922-1926.

Williams, Mary W. *Anglo-American Isthmian Diplomacy, 1815-1915*. Baltimore, 1916.

Williamson, Harold Francis. *Edward Atkinson, the Biography of an American Liberal, 1827-1905*. Boston, 1934.

Willson, Beckles. *America's Ambassadors to England*. New York, 1929.

————. *America's Ambassadors to France*. New York, 1929.

Wilson, Alexander J. *Reciprocity, Bi-Metallism, and Land-Tenure Reform*. London, 1880.

Wittke, Carl Frederick. *The Irish in America*. Baton Rouge, Louisiana [1956].

Wriston, Henry M. *Executive Agents in American Foreign Relations*. Baltimore, 1929.

Wynne, William H. *State Insolvency and Foreign Bondholders*. Vol II. 2 vols. New Haven, 1951.

Wyse, L. N. B. *Le canal de Panama. L'Isthme américain. Explorations; comparaison des tracées étudiés. Négotiations; état des travaux*. Paris, 1886.

Yeselson, Abraham. *United States-Persian Diplomatic Relations, 1883-1921*. New Brunswick, New Jersey, 1956.

Young, John Russell. *Around the World with General Grant, ex-President of the United States, to Various Countries in Europe, Asia, and Africa in 1877, 1878, 1879* [etc.]. 2 vols. New York, 1899.

Younger, Edward L. *John A. Kasson; Politics and Diplomacy from Lincoln to McKinley*. Iowa City, Iowa, 1955.

5. Articles

Bastert, Russell H. "Diplomatic Reversal: Frelinghuysen's Opposition to Blaine's Pan-American Policy in 1882," *Mississippi Valley Historical Review*, XLII (March 1956), 653-71.

———. "A New Approach to the Origins of Blaine's Pan-American Policy," *Hispanic American Historical Review*, XXXIX (August 1959), 375-412.

De Leon, Daniel. "The Conference at Berlin on the West African Question," *Political Science Quarterly*, I (1886), 103-39.

Dennett, Tyler. "American Choices in the Far East in 1882," *American Historical Review*, XXX (October 1924), 84-108.

———. "American Good Offices in Eastern Asia," *American Journal of International Law*, XVI (1922), 1-25.

———. "Early American Policy in Korea, 1883-1887," *Political Science Quarterly*, XXXVIII (March 1923), 82-103.

Dozer, Donald M. "The Opposition to Hawaiian Reciprocity, 1876-1888," *Pacific Historical Review*, XIV (1945), 157-83.

Kaiser, Chester W. "J. W. Foster y el desarrollo económico de México," *Historia mexicana*, VII (July-September 1957), 60-79.

Kiernan, V. G. "Foreign Interests in the War of the Pacific," *Hispanic American Historical Review*, XXXV (February 1955), 14-36.

Ladenson, Alex. "The Background of the Hawaiian-Japanese Labor Convention of 1886," *Pacific Historical Review*, IX (December 1940), 389-400.

Morgan, John T. "The Future of the Negro," *North American Review*, CXXXIX (July 1884), 81-84.

Nichols, Jeannette P. "Silver Diplomacy," *Political Science Quarterly*, XLVIII (December 1933), 565-88.

Noble, H. J. "The Korean Mission to the United States in 1883," *Transactions of the Korea Branch of the Royal Asiatic Society*, XVIII (1929), 1-27.

———. "The United States and Sino-Korean Relations," *Pacific Historical Review*, II (1933), 292-304.

Owsley, Harriet Chappell. "Henry Shelton Sanford and Federal Surveillance Abroad, 1861-1865," *Mississippi Valley Historical Review*, XLVIII (September 1961), 211-28.

Paullin, Charles O. "A Half Century of Naval Administration," *Proceedings of the United States Naval Institute*, XXXIX (September 1915), 1217-67.

———. "The Opening of Korea by Commodore Shufeldt," *Political Science Quarterly*, XXV (September 1910), 470-99.

Pletcher, David M. "Inter-American Shipping in the 1880's: A Loosening Tie," *Inter-American Economic Affairs*, X (Winter 1956), 14-41.

———. "México, campo de inversiones norteamericanas, 1867-1880," *Historia mexicana*, II (April-June 1953), 564-74.

———. "Mexico Opens the Door to American Capital, 1877-1880," *The Americas*, XVI (July 1959), 1-14.

Rippy, J. Fred. "British Investments in the Chilean Nitrate Industry," *Inter-American Economic Affairs*, VIII (Autumn 1954), 3-11.

———. "Justo Rufino Barrios and the Nicaraguan Canal," *Hispanic American Historical Review*, XX (1940), 190-97.

———. "Relations of the United States and Guatemala during the Epoch of Justo Rufino Barrios," *Hispanic American Historical Review*, XXII (1942), 595-605.

Romero, Matías. "Mr. Blaine and the Boundary Question between Mexico and Guatemala," *Journal of the American Geographical Society*, XXIX (1897), 281-330.

———. "Settlement of the Mexico-Guatemala Boundary Question, 1882," *Journal of the American Geographical Society*, XXIX (1897), 123-59.

Russ, William A., Jr. "Hawaiian Labor and Immigration Problems before Annexation," *Journal of Modern History*, XV (1943), 204-23.

Seager, Robert, II. "Ten Years before Mahan: the Unofficial Case for the New Navy, 1880-1890," *Mississippi Valley Historical Review*, XL (1953), 491-512.

Snyder, L. L. "The American-German Pork Dispute, 1879-1891," *Journal of Modern History*, XVII (1945), 16-28.

Thomson, Robert S. "Léopold II et la Conférence de Berlin," *Le Congo, Revue générale de la Colonie belge*, XII (October 1931), 325-52.

———. "Léopold II et le Congo, révélés par les notes privées de Henry S. Sanford," *Le Congo, Revue générale de la Colonie belge*, XII (February 1931), 167-96.

———. "Léopold II et Henry S. Sanford," *Le Congo, Revue générale de la Colonie belge*, XI (October 1930), 295-331.

Venable, A. L. "John T. Morgan, Father of the Inter-Oceanic Canal," *Southwestern Social Science Quarterly*, XIX (1939), 376-87.

Weigle, R. D. "Sugar and the Hawaiian Revolution," *Pacific Historical Review*, XVI (1947), 41-58.

Wilgus, A. Curtis. "James G. Blaine and the Pan-American Movement," *Hispanic American Historical Review*, V (1922), 662-708.

Willis, Henry Parker. "Reciprocity with Cuba," *American Academy of Political and Social Science, Annals*, XXII (1903), 129-147.

Index